P9-DEH-163

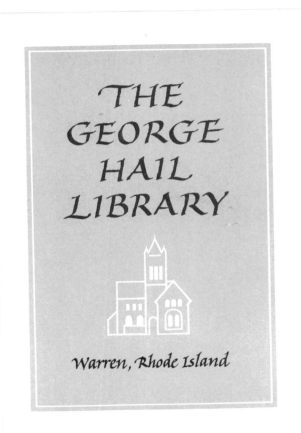

THE
GEORGE
HAIL
LIBRARY

Warren, Rhode Island

48-98

American Journalists

GETTING THE STORY

American Journalists

GETTING THE STORY

DONALD A. RITCHIE

OXFORD UNIVERSITY PRESS
NEW YORK · OXFORD

Oxford University Press
Oxford New York
Athens Auckland Bangkok Bogotá Bombay
Buenos Aires Calcutta Cape Town Dar es Salaam Delhi
Florence Hong Kong Istanbul Karachi
Kuala Lumpur Madras Madrid Melbourne
Mexico City Nairobi Paris Singapore
Taipei Tokyo Toronto Warsaw
and associated companies in
Berlin Ibadan

Copyright © 1997 by Donald A. Ritchie

Published by Oxford University Press, Inc.
198 Madison Avenue, New York, New York 10016

Oxford is a registered trademark of Oxford University Press

All rights reserved. No part of this publication may be reproduced, stored in a
retrieval system, or transmitted, in any form or by any means, electronic, mechanical,
photocopying, recording, or otherwise, without the prior permission of Oxford University Press.

Library of Congress Cataloging-in-Publication Data

Ritchie, Donald A.
American Journalists / Donald A. Ritchie.
p. cm. — (Oxford profiles)
Includes bibliographical references and index.
ISBN 0-19-509907-9
1. Journalists—United States—Biography—Juvenile literature.
[1. Journalists.] I. Title. II. Series.
PN4871.R58 1997
070.92'273—dc20
[B] 96-29208
CIP
AC

1 3 5 7 9 8 6 4 2
Printed in the United States of America
on acid-free paper

On the cover: (clockwise from top left) Horace Greeley, Walter Cronkite,
and Margaret Bourke-White

Frontispiece: Reporters call in a story.

Design: Sandy Kaufman
Layout: Loraine Machlin
Picture research: Marty
Baldessari, Laura Kreiss,
Andrea Lynch

Contents

Preface

Who decides what's news?

Reporters gather facts for news stories that are published or broadcast, but they get their assignments from editors. Editors choose what to print or how much time to give a story, but they must answer to their publishers and producers. Because news is a business seeking customers, you as the purchaser of newspapers and magazines or as a viewer of television news broadcasts also help determine the types of stories that get reported.

Technology further shapes the news: printing presses made newspapers possible, and improvements in the presses spurred the mass-circulation magazine. The telegraph and the telephone accelerated the speed at which news traveled. Radio and television added spoken words and pictures. Computers are further revolutionizing how news is gathered, written, and spread.

From colonial printers to modern reporters, men and women have been drawn into the journalism profession for various reasons. Most sought a stimulating and rewarding career and wanted to shape public policy. Most thrive on competition for "scoops" and the glory of a headline story. Some journalists have been crusaders driven by a sense of mission for which they have been willing to risk their lives. Some have been entrepreneurs and media empire builders, seeking to gain power and profits.

In a speech to *Newsweek* correspondents in 1963, publisher Philip L. Graham described journalism as a "first rough draft of a history." Historians, like the general public, rely on journalists to get the story first, track down the leads, frame the issues, and shape public opinion about people and events. But journalists can report on only a small fragment of what happens on any given day. They concentrate on what they consider the most meaningful, unusual, or entertaining information—stories that people want or ought to know about. Although the media seek to be a mirror on society, a mirror may distort according to the angle at which it is held.

Journalists strive to be objective, but their own backgrounds, experiences, and identities determine how they view the world, whom they chose to interview, what questions they ask (or do not ask), and how they interpret the facts they collect. In their quest for news, the media have often ignored or overlooked significant events, ideas, and whole groups of people. *Who* reports the news therefore makes a difference.

In this volume you will find profiles of 57 American journalists whose lives span the past 300 years. They are grouped into four time periods. These individuals were included because they achieved some fame, had a significant impact on their profession, or were in some way representative of the different kinds of reporters, editors, publishers, and broadcasters of their eras. Eighty other shorter biographies suggest the wide variety of American journalists who have shaped the news. If you want to know more about American journalists, a Further Reading list is provided with each profile, and a general reading list follows at the end of the book.

Donald A. Ritchie
U.S. Senate Historical Office

People gather at the village post office to hear the latest news in "War News from Mexico," painted by Richard Caton Woodville in 1848.

1 Freedom of the Press (1700–1860)

When Christopher Columbus returned from his first voyage across the Atlantic, news of his adventure spread quickly through Europe, aided by Johann Gutenberg's recent invention of a printing press that used movable type. Soon printing traveled to the Western Hemisphere, where the earliest known printed news was a report on an earthquake, published in Mexico City in 1541. A century later, in 1645, a report on Indian policy was printed in Boston. By 1690 Boston also saw the first newspaper in North America: *Publick Occurrences Both Forreign and Domestick*, although only a single edition of that paper appeared. In 1704 the *Boston News-Letter* began publication, lasting until the American Revolution.

From the start, colonial officials in America tried to control the pesky printers. They required printers to seek government licenses and to place "published by authority" on their mastheads. Printers were also regularly threatened with prosecution for libel (for printing stories that slandered or ridiculed public officials). Benjamin Franklin's older brother James served time in prison because his newspaper offended authorities in Boston. Yet juries could sympathize with the printer, as John Peter Zenger's trial in New York demonstrated in 1735. As Americans moved toward independence from Great Britain, colonial newspapers helped sway the "minds and hearts of the people," in John Adams's eloquent phrase. Most papers denounced British tyranny, although some journalists remained loyal to the Crown, an editorial decision that would eventually cost them their papers and their property. Following the Revolution, newspapers provided the forum to debate the new Constitution and to launch the first political parties. Partisan editors made no pretense at being objective. Their papers aimed to swing public opinion toward the party that supported them financially.

Although the framers of the Constitution believed in a free press, they omitted it from the original document. In *The Federalist Papers*, Alexander Hamilton reasoned that freedom of the press "must altogether depend on public opinion, and on the general spirit of the people and of the government." Opponents of the Constitution bitterly protested the lack of specific protections of citizens' rights. James Madison responded by proposing a series of amendments that became the Bill of Rights. The First Amendment guaranteed that Congress would make no law to abridge the freedom of the press. The First Amendment, did not, however, stop Congress only a few years later from enacting Alien and Sedition Acts that sent editors to prison for criticizing the government.

Initially, American newspapers were either "party papers" (underwritten by political parties to support their candidates) or dull business sheets that announced ship arrivals and commodity prices. That changed in 1833, with the publication of the *New York Sun,* which sold for just a penny. The "penny press" launched the independent newspaper that drew its revenue from subscriptions and advertisements rather than political patronage. Seeking to attract readers, these papers adopted breezy styles and lively features. James Gordon Bennett's *New York Herald,* founded in 1835, used sex and murder to sell papers, while Horace Greeley's *New York Tribune* engaged readers with a mix of ideas, literature, and politics.

For some, journalism was a business; for others it offered a means of promoting their ideals and ambitions. Abolitionists, women, Native Americans, and many others found their voice either as editors or correspondents. The free expression of ideas carried risks, however, from libel suits to physical attacks upon those who took unpopular stands. The abolitionist Elijah P. Lovejoy died trying to protect his printing press from a proslavery mob. The Cherokee editor Elias Boudinot lost his paper and his life when he tried to get his nation to abandon its ancestral lands and move west. Beyond the legal assurances of the First Amendment, it was the willingness of such journalists to face danger and hazard all that guaranteed a free press in America.

John Peter Zenger

IN DEFENSE OF FREEDOM OF THE PRESS

I n one of the most dramatic trials held in colonial America, the printer John Peter Zenger was charged with seditious libel. By seditious libel, his accusers meant that articles that had appeared in his paper, the *New-York Weekly Journal*, had defamed the government. The law was clear, said the prosecutors: the newspaper had brazenly criticized the governor, and its printer should be punished. But Zenger's attorney, Andrew Hamilton, appealed to the jury, arguing that if the stories were true, then the printer had committed no libel and should go free. The jury's decision would have profound consequences on the freedom of the press in America.

Born in Germany, John Peter Zenger had sailed for America in 1710, when he was just 13 years old. During the long ocean voyage, his father died on the ship. When they reached the colony of New York, his mother, Johanna, had to raise three children by herself. In 1711 she apprenticed her son to a printer, William Bradford. Bradford taught John Peter Zenger to set type and roll the hand presses. Eventually, the young man set out for his own career as a printer.

When John Peter Zenger was tried for libel in 1735, his lawyer, Andrew Hamilton, used freedom of the press as his defense. The jury agreed with Hamilton and acquitted Zenger.

"Gentlemen of the jury, were you to find a verdict against my client, you must take upon you to say the papers referred to in the information, and which we acknowledge we printed and published, are false, scandalous and seditious; but of this I can have no apprehension. You are citizens of New York; you are really what the law supposes you to be, honest and lawful men; and according to my brief, the facts which we offer to prove were not committed in a corner; they are notoriously known to be true; and therefore in your justice lies our safety."

—from *A Brief Narrative of the Trial of John Peter Zenger, Printer of The New-York Weekly Journal* (1736) by James Alexander

Zenger married Mary White of Philadelphia in 1719 and the couple settled in Chestertown, Maryland. The Maryland assembly made him the official printer of the colony. But tragedy struck in 1720 when Mary died. Zenger returned to New York with their infant son and married Anna Catherina Maulin. The following year he became a freeman, or naturalized citizen.

After working for a year as a partner with his old master, Bradford, Zenger set up his own print shop. There he printed many political and religious pamphlets, mostly in Dutch because his English was still poor. He also printed New York's first arithmetic textbook. He had a good business, but a political storm was approaching that would soon wash over him.

In 1732 the new royal governor arrived in New York. Governor William Cosby was arrogant, hot-tempered, and greedy, and it did not take long for him to alienate the colonists. Until Cosby appeared, the New York merchant Rip Van Dam had served as acting governor. Cosby demanded half of Van Dam's salary as acting governor. Van Dam countered by demanding half the benefits that Cosby had gotten since the king had appointed him (a shrewd move considering that Cosby's rewards had been three times higher than Van Dam's). Cosby sued Van Dam in the New York Supreme Court. When Van Dam's attorneys argued that this was the wrong court to hear the case, the court's chief justice, Lewis Morris, agreed with them. An angry Governor Cosby retaliated by dismissing Morris from the court. The governor appointed James De Lancey chief justice in Morris's place.

Morris, himself a wealthy merchant, sought revenge. At that time the only newspaper in the colony was William Bradford's *New York Gazette*. Since Bradford also collected a salary as the official printer, he could not publish anything critical of the governor. So, in 1734, Morris and his friends put up the money for a newspaper, the *New-York Weekly Journal*, that would be free to assail Cosby and his policies. For the paper's printer they hired Bradford's former apprentice, John Peter Zenger.

For the first time New York had an independent newspaper that dared to attack the government and ridicule the governor. One favorite device was to run mock advertisements for the return of lost animals—whose descriptions obviously resembled the governor and his circle of supporters. The paper also published rhymes and songs that taunted Cosby. The governor considered Zenger's *Journal* to be scandalous and believed it would turn the people against him. At first the governor used Bradford's *Gazette* to attack his critics. Then, in 1734, Chief Justice De Lancey called a grand jury to indict Zenger for libel. But the colonists on the grand jury refused to vote for an indictment. The governor then tried to have four issues of the *Journal* be "burnt by the hands of the Common

John Peter Zenger

BORN
1697
Germany

DIED
July 29, 1746
New York, New York

ACCOMPLISHMENTS
Printed *New-York Weekly Journal*
(1733–46)

THE
New-York Weekly JOURNAL.

Containing the freſheſt Advices, Foreign, and Domeſtick.

MUNDAY Auguſt 18th, 1735.

To my Subſcribers and Benefactors.

Gentlemen ;

I Think my ſelf in Duty bound to to make publick Acknowledgment for the many Favours received at your Hands, which I do in this Manner return you my hearty Thanks for. I very ſoon intend to print my Tryal at Length, that the World may ſee how unjuſt my Sufferings have been, ſo will only at this Time give this ſhort Account of it.

On *Munday* the 4*th* Inſtant my Tryal for Printing Parts of my Journal *No.* 13. and 23. came on, in the Supreme Court of this Province, before the moſt numerous Auditory of People, I may with Juſtice ſay, that ever were ſeen in that Place at once ; my Jury ſworn were,

1 *Harmanus Rutgers,*
2 *Stanley Holms,*
3 *Edward Man,*
4 *John Bell,*
5 *Samuel Weaver,*
6 *Andrew Marſchalk,*
7 *Egbert Van Borſen,*
8 *Thomas Hunt,*
9 *Benjamin Hildrith,*
10 *Abraham Kiteltaſs,*
11 *John Goelet,*
12 *Hercules Wendover,*

John Chambers, Eſq; had been appointed the Term before by the Court as my Council, in the Place of *James Alexander* and *William Smith,* who were then ſilenced on my Account, and to Mr. *Chambers*'s Aſſiſtance came *Andrew Hamilton,* Eſq; of *Philadelphia* Barreſter at Law ; when Mr Attorney offered the Information and the Proofs, Mr. *Hamilton* told him, he would acknowledge my Printing and Publiſhing the Papers in the Information, and ſave him the Trouble of that Proof, and offered to prove the Facts of thoſe Papers true, and had Witneſſes ready to prove every Fact ; he long inſiſted on the Liberty of Making Proof thereof, but was over-ruled therein. Mr. Attorney offered no Proofs of my Papers being *falſe, malicious* and *ſeditious,* as they were charged to be, but inſiſted that they were Lybels tho' true. There were many Arguments and Authorities on this point, and the Court were of Opinion with Mr. Attorney on that Head : But the Jury having taken the Information out with them, they returned in about Ten Minutes, and found me *Not Guilty* ; upon which there were immediately three Hurra's of many Hundreds of People in the preſence of the Court, before the Verdict was returned. The next Morning my Diſcharge was moved for and granted, and ſufficient was
ſub_

After his acquittal, Zenger thanked the jury and published the proceedings of his trial in his *New-York Weekly Journal.*

Hangman"—which was the way the government in England handled offensive publications. But the New York Assembly would not approve that order.

Failing at these efforts, the governor's council ordered the sheriff to arrest John Peter Zenger. The council set bail so high that he could not pay it. So Zenger remained in jail for months until his case was tried. Meanwhile, Anna Catherina published the newspaper—following the instructions that her husband had given her through a hole in the door of his prison cell. His imprisonment roused public sympathy for Zenger and his paper.

Zenger's lawyer was James Alexander. Ironically, Alexander was also editor of the *Journal* and had most likely written the articles that had gotten the printer arrested in the first place. But since these pieces were unsigned, the printer bore responsibility for them. In the preliminary hearings, Alexander and his partner, William Smith, attacked the governor and his judges for tyrannically disregarding the laws of England and New York by holding the printer as a prisoner. These charges outraged Chief Justice De Lancey. Accusing the lawyers of playing for "applause and popularity," the judge disbarred them. Alexander was the best lawyer in New York, but he knew where to recruit a skilled replacement.

When the trial opened on August 4, 1735, the prominent Philadelphia attorney Andrew Hamilton rose in Zenger's defense. An eloquent advocate, Hamilton had established his own record of opposition to Pennsylvania's governor, which made him sympathetic to Zenger's cause. The prosecutor told the jury that under New York's laws "seditious libel" meant any publication that reflected badly on the government or tended to breed people's contempt for the government. Chief Justice De Lancey agreed that under the law any criticism of the government, even if true, was libelous.

In his response Hamilton ignored both the law and the judge. He turned to the jury and asked: How could people stop oppressive governors if they could not publish truthful accusations against them? How could there be liberty without freedom of the press? Hamilton defined libel as something false and malicious. Since Zenger's newspaper had printed the truth, even though it was critical of the govern-

ment there had been no libel. Chief Justice De Lancey instructed the jury to ignore this defense and consider the law as it was written. In a very short while the jury returned its verdict: not guilty. The courtroom broke out in cheers.

Newspapers throughout the American colonies printed news of Zenger's acquittal. The case did not change the libel laws; that would take many more years to happen. But it did show the hostility that colonial juries felt toward this type of libel case, and it made governors more hesitant to act against critical printers. John Peter Zenger went free. Governor Cosby died in 1736, and soon afterward James Alexander and William Smith were permitted to practice law again. Alexander also compiled his notes on the trial, including Hamilton's brilliant speech to the jury, and published them as a book. That account helped make the Zenger case a step forward on the road to the 1st Amendment to the Constitution, in 1791, which guaranteed freedom of the press.

FURTHER READING

Alexander, James. *A Brief Narrative of the Trial of John Peter Zenger, Printer of The New York Weekly Journal*. Edited by Stanley Nider Katz. Cambridge, Mass.: Belknap Press of the Harvard University Press, 1972 [1736].

Leonard, Thomas C. *The Power of the Press: The Birth of American Political Reporting*. New York: Oxford University Press, 1986.

Levy, Leonard W. *Emergence of a Free Press*. New York: Oxford University Press, 1985.

Smith, Jeffrey A. *Printers and Press Freedom: The Ideology of Early American Journalism*. New York: Oxford University Press, 1988.

Benjamin Franklin

THE PRINTER WHO COULD ALSO HANDLE A PEN

The first newspapers in colonial America were published by printers eager to keep their print shops fully occupied. The most fortunate received contracts to publish the colony's laws and other official declarations. Generally, these printers were craftsmen and not writers by training or talent. For their news they reprinted items from British and European newspapers, shipping reports, verses, and religious sermons, or they collected items about local affairs submitted by various writers. One notable exception

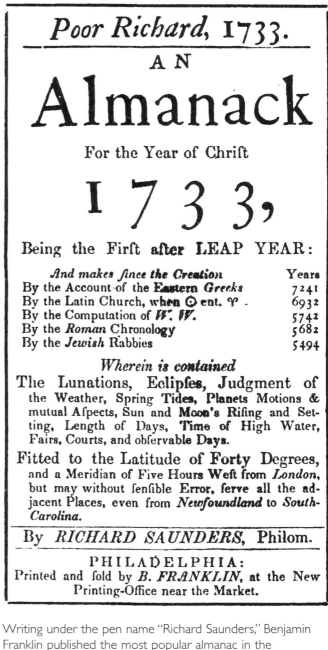

Writing under the pen name "Richard Saunders," Benjamin Franklin published the most popular almanac in the American colonies.

A printer, newspaper publisher, and postmaster, Benjamin Franklin became one of the most prosperous men in America.

was Benjamin Franklin. As a teenager working in his brother's print shop in Boston, and later in his own shop in Philadelphia, he not only printed newspapers but wrote for them. His humorous and pungent pieces attracted many subscribers. "This was one of the first good Effects of my having learnt a little to scribble," Franklin later recalled in his *Autobiography*. "The leading Men, seeing a News Paper now in the hands of one who could also handle a Pen, thought it convenient to oblige & encourage me."

In writing, as in everything else that he mastered during his long and remarkable life, Benjamin Franklin taught himself. His father, Josiah, had migrated from England to America in search of religious freedom. After settling in Boston, he earned a living making candles and soap. Ben was his 15th child from two marriages. Since there was not enough money to send Benjamin to college, Josiah took him out of school at age 10 to work in the candle- and soap-making shop. Ben hated this work and longed to run off to sea as a sailor, but his father was adamantly opposed. Instead, when Ben turned 12 he was apprenticed to work in his brother James's print shop. Under the terms of the apprenticeship, he was expected to remain in his brother's service until he reached 21.

A bright boy, Franklin became proficient in printing and made himself useful to his brother, setting type, working the press, delivering orders, and keeping the books. Although not an adventurous life like going to sea, working in the print shop offered him access to the many books in a bookstore attached to the shop. He spent many nights sitting up reading, returning the books to the store in the morning before they were missed. He read widely in literature, mathematics, science, and philosophy. Sundays he spent alone reading at the print shop, escaping the religious services that his

father had compelled him to attend. Franklin began writing some poetry, which his brother printed and sent him out to sell. One of these poems, the *Light House Tragedy*, is about the drowning of a captain and his two daughters. "They were wretched Stuff," Franklin later admitted. Although the poems were popular, his father discouraged him by warning that most poets became beggars. Franklin abandoned poetry but he honed his prose-writing skills, which over time became "a principal Means of my Advancement," as he wrote in his autobiography.

Ben's brother, having trained in London, aspired to publish a colonial paper that was outspoken and independent. In 1721 James Franklin founded the fourth newspaper ever to appear in the colonies, the *New-England Courant*. Other colonial papers were published "by authority" of the government and reflected the government's views. By sharp contrast, the *Courant* attacked the powerful ministers and others who ran the Massachusetts Colony, and it became a painful thorn in their side. As the apprentice in the shop, Ben watched how his brother's friends amused themselves by writing for the paper, and he grew anxious to write something himself. Disguising his handwriting, he produced a satirical article signed "Silence Dogood," supposedly written by a middle-aged widow. He slipped the piece under the shop door one night. James published it, and several more articles, before he discovered that the author was his young brother and halted the "Silence Dogood" series.

In 1722 the *Courant* published an essay criticizing the colonial government's meager efforts at chasing pirates. This so outraged Boston's authorities that they arrested James Franklin and imprisoned him in the jail across the street from his print shop. While James was confined, the teenage Ben ran the shop and put out the paper. When James was released from jail, the colony ordered that he no longer print the *New-England Courant* or any other paper without official permission. But James made sure that the paper continued to appear by listing the name of Benjamin Franklin as the new printer.

Although the young apprentice was an asset to the print shop, he admitted in his *Autobiography* that he could also be "saucy & provoking." Benjamin thought that James demanded too much of him and took their disputes to their father, who usually sided with his younger son. James, however, frequently lost his temper and beat his brother. For the rest of his life, Benjamin Franklin was convinced that his older brother's treatment had left him with an "Aversion to arbitrary Power." In order to name Ben as printer of the *Courant*, James freed him from his apprenticeship. He made Ben secretly sign new papers binding him to further service, but Ben knew that these papers could never be used against him in court. Tired of being beaten, Ben made up his mind to leave. Since James Franklin had already made sure that no other printing house in Boston would hire him, Ben Franklin ran away from his brother, his apprenticeship, and Boston. In 1823 he traveled to Philadelphia.

Just 17 and with little money in his pocket, Franklin was nevertheless confident that he had a trade and was "a pretty good Workman." In Philadelphia he took a job with the printer Samuel Keimer. According to Franklin, Keimer was "something of a Scholar" who loved discussions and arguments but knew very little about running a print shop. After a year with Keimer, Franklin sailed for England to improve his printing skills. He worked in a London printing house, went to plays, read many books, and published a pamphlet entitled *A Dissertation on Liberty & Necessity, Pleasure and Pain.*

In 1726, when Franklin returned to Philadelphia, Keimer invited him to take over the management of his printing house. Before long, however, the two got into a fight and Franklin quit. His friend Hugh Meredith suggested that they start their own printing business, with Meredith's wealthy father putting up the money for them to open their shop.

Benjamin Franklin wanted to start a newspaper. At the time the only paper in Philadelphia was Andrew Bradford's *American Weekly Mercury*. Franklin considered it to be "a paltry thing, wretchedly managed, no way entertaining"—yet it was making a profit. Franklin reasoned that a better written paper could not fail. But his former employer, Keimer, learned of his plans and announced that he was starting a new paper first. Franklin scuttled Keimer's scheme by writing eight amusing pieces under the name "Busy-Body," which were published in Bradford's *Mercury*. The "Busy-Body" articles attracted so much attention that they overshadowed Keimer's new paper. With only a few subscribers signed up, Keimer sold the paper to Franklin "for a Trifle," according to Franklin, who quickly turned the paper into a profitable venture.

Franklin's newspaper, *The Pennsylvania Gazette*, had a more attractive type and was better printed than its competitor. What is more, it had Franklin's sprightly style. He believed that newspapers could improve readers' minds, but he also believed that people were more likely to read and learn from lively and entertaining writing. His political commentaries were far less critical and controversial than his older brother's had been. And he took pains not to libel any government officials. His paper appealed to the political leaders of Pennsylvania, who talked so much about it that more and more people felt encouraged to subscribe. At the

Benjamin Franklin

BORN
January 17, 1706
Boston, Massachusetts

DIED
April 17, 1790
Philadelphia, Pennsylvania

EDUCATION
Boston Grammar School and George Brownell's School

ACCOMPLISHMENTS
Published *The Pennsylvania Gazette* (1729–66), *Poor Richard's Almanack* (1732–57), and *General Magazine* (1741); author of the "Silence Dogood" letters (1722) and *The Autobiography of Benjamin Franklin* (1790)

> *"In the Conduct of my Newspaper I carefully excluded all Libelling and personal Abuse, which is of late Years become so disgraceful to our Country."*
>
> —from *The Autobiography of Benjamin Franklin* (1790)

time, his rival, Bradford, printed the public laws and other official business. In his *Autobiography* Franklin describes how an address of the legislature to the governor appeared in such "a coarse blundering manner" that Franklin reprinted it, "elegantly & correctly," and sent copies to all the members of the legislature. After comparing the differences, the legislature voted Franklin and Meredith as their official printers.

While Franklin succeeded, his partner, Meredith, failed. Hugh Meredith was not much of a writer or pressman, and he was seldom sober. When Meredith's father fell into debt, he sued to recover his investment in their print shop. Fortunately, other friends came to Franklin's rescue and put up the money that helped him buy Meredith out of the partnership. For his part, Meredith realized that he was not cut out for either printing or city living, and he returned to farming.

An entrepreneur at heart, Ben Franklin set out to make his fortune. He opened a stationer's shop in addition to his print shop and began to make money and pay off his debts. His habits of vegetarianism and temperance helped him save his money. "In order to secure my Credit and Character as a Tradesman," he wrote, "I took care not only to be in *Reality* Industrious & frugal, but to avoid all *Appearances* of the Contrary. I dressed plainly; I was seen at no Places of idle Diversion; I never went out a-fishing or shooting." When he bought paper for his shop, he personally pushed the load on a wheelbarrow through the streets of Philadelphia. This gave him a good reputation with the city's business community, who saw him as industrious and increasingly sought his business. "I went on swimmingly," Franklin bragged. By contrast, Samuel Keimer's printing business declined until he was forced to sell his shop to

pay his debts. "He went to Barbados," noted Franklin in his autobiography, where he never missed an opportunity to make an object lesson, "& lived there some Years, in very poor Circumstances."

When Franklin first came to Philadelphia, he stayed at a boardinghouse run by the Read family. There he met their daughter, Deborah. In 1730, when they were both 24, he and Deborah Read married. As he later recorded in his *Autobiography*, "she proved a good and faithful Helpmate, assisted me much by attending the Shop, we throve together, and have ever mutually endeavored to make each other happy." They had two children, and Franklin, always a flirtatious "ladies' man," had two other children, both out of wedlock. In later years, Deborah took care of Franklin's Philadelphia business interests while he traveled widely on political and diplomatic missions.

Although the newspaper made him famous within the province, Franklin earned even wider fame from a series of 26 almanacs, which were annual books containing weather forecasts, tide charts, and other useful information. The almanacs began appearing in 1732. Written under the pseudonym of Richard Saunders, they were published as *Poor Richard's Almanack*. Franklin wanted them to be both entertaining and useful. Just as he looked upon his newspaper as a way of instructing the people, he saw the almanacs as a way of reaching people who rarely read any other books. Wherever there was an empty space in the almanac, Franklin filled it with proverbs and educational mottoes, such as "Early to Bed, and early to Rise, makes a Man healthy, wealthy, and wise." He encouraged people to work hard and be thrifty not only to acquire wealth, but as necessary virtues in their own right. Franklin argued that it was just as difficult for those in

As a young printer in London in 1726, Benjamin Franklin worked with this press. It is now on display in the Smithsonian Institution's National Museum of American History in Washington, D.C.

need to act honestly as it was "hard for an empty Sack to stand upright." His almanacs were filled with such pithy sayings. In 1757, while sailing to England, he compiled many of these sayings into a long preface for his last almanac. This essay, which became known as "The Way to Wealth," was reprinted widely in the colonies and in Europe.

The almanacs sold about 10,000 copies a year, an enormous circulation considering that the population of the 13 American colonies was only 3 million, and revenue from advertisements in his newspaper also brought him "a very considerable Income." In 1736 Franklin became clerk of the Pennsylvania General Assembly, a position he held until 1757. Being clerk gave him the lucrative business of printing the laws. He also became postmaster of Philadelphia. He noted with some satisfaction that when his old competitor, Bradford, had been postmaster, he had refused to allow postal riders to carry Franklin's papers. Once he held the post himself, however, Franklin was already wealthy enough that he did not feel it was necessary to retaliate against Bradford. In 1741 Bradford and Franklin started rival magazines, but Bradford's *American Magazine* and Franklin's *General Magazine* lasted no more than a few months.

By middle age Benjamin Franklin dominated the printing business in Philadelphia and had amassed enough wealth to free him to turn his attentions from business to inventions, scientific experiments, and public affairs. As a prosperous merchant, Franklin owned a number of household slaves, since slavery was still legal in colonial Philadelphia. As he grew older, however, he condemned slavery and became president of the Pennsylvania Society for Promoting the Abolition of Slavery (he eventually freed his own slaves). Concerned about the security of the colonies, in 1754 Franklin drafted the Albany Plan of Union, which, although it was not adopted, served as a forerunner of the union of the colonies when they declared their independence from Great Britain in 1776. Several of the colonies hired Franklin as their agent in Britain, and during the American Revolution he became the new republic's minister to France.

Aside from George Washington, Ben Franklin became the best known and most admired American of his era. Although young men had taken charge during the Revolution, Franklin was the old sage, giving advice freely as he had once loved to do in his newspapers and almanacs. At age 81 he served as a delegate to the Constitutional Convention in Philadelphia, never missing a day's session. In 1788 he started writing his autobiography, which was published shortly after his death in 1790. It quickly became a classic account of a self-made man who lifted himself from "Poverty & Obscurity" to wealth and recognition, and of the opportunities that America offered those who had self-motivation and discipline.

FURTHER READING

Conner, Paul W. *Poor Richard's Politicks, Benjamin Franklin and His New American Order*. New York: Oxford University Press, 1965.

Fay, Bernard. *The Two Franklins: Fathers of American Democracy*. 1933. Reprint, New York: AMS Press, 1969.

Franklin, Benjamin. *The Autobiography of Benjamin Franklin*. 1790. Reprint, Boston: Bedford Books of St. Martin's Press, 1993.

———. *The Papers of Benjamin Franklin*. Edited by Leonard W. Labaree. 30 vols. New Haven: Yale University Press, 1959–93.

———. *The Writings of Benjamin Franklin*. Edited by Albert Henry Smyth. 10 vols. New York: Macmillan, 1905–7.

Leonard, Thomas C. *The Power of the Press: The Birth of American Political Reporting*. New York: Oxford University Press, 1986.

Lopez, Claude-Anne, and Eugenia W. Herbert. *The Private Franklin, The Man and His Family*. New York: Norton, 1975.

Smith, Jeffery. *Franklin and Bache: Envisioning the Enlightened Republic*. New York: Oxford University Press, 1990.

———. *Printers and Press Freedom: The Ideology of Early American Journalism*. New York: Oxford University Press, 1988.

Wright, Esmond. *Franklin of Philadelphia*. Cambridge: Harvard University Press, 1986.

Thomas Paine

REVOLUTIONARY
PAMPHLETEER

I

n ill health from typhus fever, Tom Paine stepped off the boat in Philadelphia on November 30, 1774, after a long, queasy ocean voyage from England. Behind him lay years of failure in business, government service, and marriage. Armed only with a letter of introduction from Benjamin Franklin, whom he had met in London, Paine sought to build a new life in America. He arrived just as the colonies were moving toward declaring their independence from Great Britain, an event that finally gave Paine his mission in life. In January 1776 he published *Common Sense*, the most influential pamphlet of the American Revolution. "We have it in our power to begin the world over again," Paine assured his new countrymen, "...the birthday of a new world is at hand."

Thomas Paine hailed from the quiet English town of Thetford, where his Quaker father made corsets. He attended the local grammar school until he was 13, when he left school to apprentice with his father. Young Paine hated corset making and at 17 tried to run away to sea on the

After trying his hand at corset making, sailing, and tax collecting in England, Thomas Paine emigrated to America and found success as a political pamphleteer.

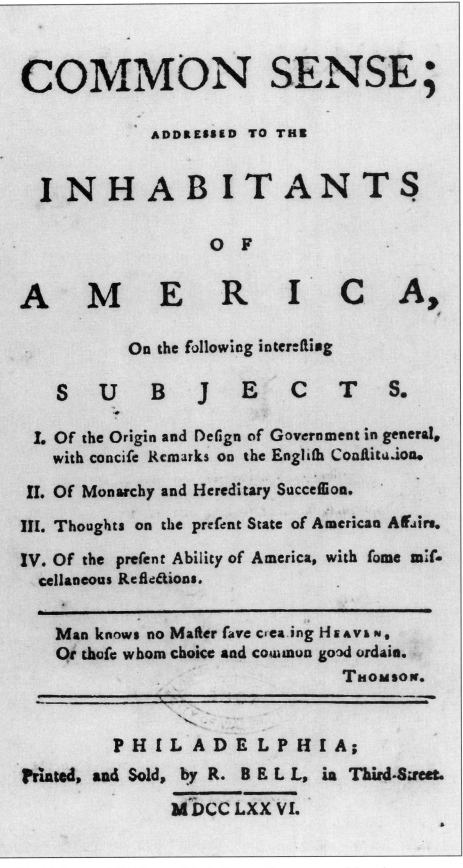

Published in January 1776, Thomas Paine's *Common Sense* prepared Americans for independence by arguing convincingly that the American colonies deserved to be free of English rule.

privateer *Terrible*. Fortunately, his father stopped him. Most of the ship's crew died in a sea battle soon afterward. In 1756 Paine signed on to another privateer, *King of Prussia*, and spent some time at sea. He eventually returned to corset making in London and then set up his own shop in Sandwich, England. There he met and married Mary Lambert. She died less than a year later, possibly in childbirth. Mary's father was a customs officer, which inspired Paine to change occupations. He passed the entrance examinations and became a tax collector. After three years, he was dismissed from the service for an infringement of the rules, and he went back to London, where he briefly taught English. The salary was so low that he could barely survive, so he apologized to the Excise Board and got his tax-collecting job back. Assigned to the town of Lewes, Paine lived in the home of Samuel Olliver, who ran a tobacco shop. After Olliver died, Paine married his daughter Elizabeth and assisted her in running the shop.

Collecting taxes put Paine in a position "to see into the numerous and various distresses" caused by the burden of taxation, as he wrote in a pamphlet. England at the time was suffering from rising prices, declining wages, poverty, and lawlessness. These conditions made Paine sympathetic toward the poor, especially since he had so often skirted poverty himself. In 1772 Paine wrote his first political pamphlet, *Case of the Officers of Excise*, as an appeal to Parliament for higher salaries. His fellow tax collectors sent him to London to lobby Parliament in their behalf, but the members of Parliament showed little concern for the unpopular tax collectors. Not only did they reject his appeal, but Paine was again dismissed as a tax collector. In Lewes his shop failed and he separated from his wife, making him more than ready to emigrate to America.

But Paine was not simply a failed corset maker and tax collector. His genuine intelligence spurred him to read extensively, especially in science, and to conduct his own scientific experiments. Over the years he had made many contacts with scientists and mathematicians in London, and through them met the American agent Benjamin Franklin. Franklin, himself an amateur scientist, liked Paine and encouraged him to go to America. Franklin helped by writing a letter of introduction addressed to his son-in-law, the Philadelphia merchant Richard Bache.

Paine arrived in Philadelphia during troubled times. The Boston Tea Party had taken place in December 1773, and the First Continental Congress opened in the fall of 1774. As America's financial and commercial capital, Philadelphia, like other colonial cities, had been hurt by British trade policies, and a spirit of liberty was spreading through all classes.

Seeking a living, Paine submitted some writing samples to the printer and bookseller Robert Aitken. Aitken was so impressed by what he read that he hired him as editor of the *Pennsylvania Magazine*. In September 1775, Paine wrote to Franklin that subscriptions had more than doubled since he had taken over the editorship in February.

Paine was more than an editor. He wrote poems, essays, and political pieces for the magazine under a variety of pseudonyms. Showing his disdain for pomp and power, he denounced all forms of aristocracy. "When I reflect on the pompous titles bestowed on unworthy men," he wrote, "I feel an indignity that instructs me to despise the absurdity." At the same time he leveled an attack on American slavery and defended the "natural rights" of the enslaved. Barely removed from Britain himself, Paine quickly became a convert to the American independence movement.

The battles of Lexington and Concord took place in April 1775, and the Second Continental Congress convened in Philadelphia in May. But Americans worried that they stood little chance against the powerful British army and navy, and many wanted to preserve the existing social and political systems. To counter these arguments, Paine wrote the essay *Common Sense*, which he published in January 1776. "My motive and object in all my political works, beginning with *Common Sense*," he later asserted, "...have been to rescue man from tyranny and false systems and false principles of government, and enable him to be free."

The British system was not the most perfect government in the world, Paine argued. Americans would not lose their constitutional rights by rebelling. There were no advantages left in remaining yoked to England. Nor was there any good reason to perpetuate the English monarchy and aristocracy in the new world. Americans deserved a republic—an elected government without a king.

Common Sense made Americans stop and reexamine themselves and their cause, and it helped prepare public opinion for the Declaration of Independence, which followed six months later. In a brief time the pamphlet sold 150,000 copies, owing its phenomenal success as much to its style as its message. Paine rejected a high literary style and wrote in a clear and direct manner that most readers could easily grasp. "As it is my design to make those that can scarcely read understand," he explained, "I shall therefore avoid every literary ornament and put it in language as plain as the alphabet." Paine mingled wit and rage in a way that appealed to average citizens who had grown angry over their treatment by the upper class. Paine's rhetoric was more radical and democratic than most other Revolutionary

Thomas Paine

BORN

January 29, 1737
Thetford, England

DIED

June 8, 1809
New Rochelle, New York

EDUCATION

Thetford Grammar School

ACCOMPLISHMENTS

Editor, *Pennsylvania Magazine* (1775); author of *Common Sense* (1776), *The Crisis* (1776–83), *Rights of Man* (1791–92), and *The Age of Reason* (1793–95)

"These are the times that try men's souls. The summer soldier and the sunshine patriot will in this crisis, shrink from the service of his country; but he that stands it now deserves the love and thanks of man and woman. Tyranny, like hell, is not easily conquered; yet we have this consolation with us, that the harder the conflict, the more glorious the triumph."

—From *The American Crisis*, No. 1 (December 1776)

leaders, who were often wealthy men with considerable property and even owned slaves.

"Have you seen the pamphlet *Common Sense?*" The British-born American General Charles Lee asked George Washington. "I never saw such a masterly, irresistible performance." Lee felt "convinced by the arguments, of the necessity of separation." Paine had originally planned to issue *Common Sense* as a series of letters to newspapers, but when no editor dared to publish the explosive essay, he took it to a print shop and had it printed as a pamphlet, anonymously.

Those loyal to the British Crown responded immediately. In April 1776 the *Pennsylvania Gazette* published an attack on *Common Sense*, signed "Cato," after the orator who had roused public attention in ancient Rome. Its author, the Anglican clergyman William Smith, wanted reconciliation with Great Britain and attacked Paine as a foreigner. Paine answered with letters printed in the *Pennsylvania Journal* in April and May, which he signed "The Forester," presumably to identify himself with the freedom of the American forest. He defended his original arguments and added that as for being a foreigner: "A freeman, Cato, is a stranger nowhere—a slave, everywhere."

In July 1776, when Congress declared the colonies independent,

Paine enlisted in the militia. He later served as aide-de-camp to General Nathaniel Greene. While in the army, he began writing *The Crisis*, a series of pamphlets designed to rally public opinion to support the war. "These are the times that try men's souls," began the first *Crisis*, published on December 19, 1776. His words so moved George Washington that he ordered the pamphlet read aloud to his troops, just before their first victory at the battle of Trenton.

Paine continued *The Crisis* in 13 parts through 1783, contributing its profits to the war effort. He also worked for a while as secretary to the Committee for Foreign Affairs of the Congress. But as magnificent as Paine was as a propagandist rallying the public in time of crisis, he was temperamentally unsuited for the day-to-day operations of government, and once again lost his job. Throughout the war, Congress conducted all of its business in secret session. When members of Congress discovered that Paine had leaked information from his committee to a newspaper, they fired him. After the war, he continued publishing essays in various newspapers, seeking to unify the new nation. Writing in the *Providence* (Rhode Island) *Gazette*, from December 1782 to February 1783, he called for a federal constitution to replace the inadequate Articles of Confederation, to make American independence more secure. He also published a pamphlet endorsing a sound national financial system, in advance of Alexander Hamilton's similar proposals.

Paine's own finances were as precarious as ever. In 1783 he appealed to Congress for help in recognition of his efforts on behalf of the Revolution. After much foot dragging, Congress awarded him $3,000 and a farm in New Rochelle, New York, that the government had confiscated from a Loyalist. Paine devoted himself to science and inventions, and designed a single-arch bridge. Feeling unappreciated in America, he took the model abroad to present to the French Academy of Sciences and the British Royal Academy. Paine was in Europe when the French Revolution took place in 1789, inspiring him to write *The Rights of Man*. He believed that the American and French revolutions would lead to a world revolution overthrowing all monarchies and aristocracies. This view proved to be so unpopular in England that he was indicted for seditious libel and found guilty—although by then he had fled the country for France.

Although he enthusiastically embraced the fervor of the French Revolution, Paine was out of step with its increasingly violent nature. He argued unsuccessfully against the execution of King Louis XVI. During the Reign of Terror in 1793, Paine was arrested and imprisoned for 10 months. He was finally released in the custody of the American minister to France, James Monroe. During his imprisonment, he had begun writing *The Age of Reason*, in which he declared his disbelief in all churches and organized religions. Although he believed in a God who governed the universe, his opponents denounced him as an atheist. Paine also published an angry open letter to George Washington, whom he had once venerated but had come to view as embodying the conservative nature of the new American government. His *Letter to George Washington* ruined what was left of his popularity in America.

A rootless citizen of the world, Tom Paine returned to the United States in 1802, at the age of 65. When President Thomas Jefferson invited Paine to the White House, one Federalist newspaper vilified him as "irreligious, depraved, [and] unworthy to associate with the President of the United States."

Other old friends from the Revolution were embarrassed to be associated with Paine and did their best to keep their distance. While riding back to New York, one stagecoach driver refused to allow him to board, saying that he was afraid God would strike them with a lightning bolt if Paine was a passenger. When Paine died in New Rochelle in 1809, the local Quakers refused his request for burial in their cemetery. Paine was buried at his farm, but later a friend had his bones removed to England; their location, however, remains unknown.

Never a modest man, Tom Paine boasted that he had "not only contributed to raise a new empire in the world, founded on a new system of government, but...[had] arrived at an eminence in political literature, the most difficult of all lines to succeed and excel in." He had indeed created a new style of political writing that appealed to a mass audience. Later generations have remembered him as bold, original, and courageous in his willingness to challenge all forms of tyranny in defense of human freedom and liberty.

FURTHER READING

Foner, Eric. *Tom Paine and Revolutionary America*. New York: Oxford University Press, 1976.

———, ed. *Thomas Paine: Collected Writings*. New York: Library of America, 1995.

Keane, John. *Tom Paine: A Political Life*. Boston: Little, Brown, 1995.

Middlekauff, Robert. *The Glorious Cause: The American Revolution, 1763–1789*. New York: Oxford University Press, 1982.

Vail, John J. *Thomas Paine*. New York: Chelsea House, 1990.

Wilson, Jerome D., and William F. Ricketson. *Thomas Paine*. Boston: Twayne, 1978.

Margaret Green Draper

LOYALIST PUBLISHER

Following the battle of Bunker Hill in June 1775, the American Continental Army led by General George Washington began a siege of Boston that lasted until March 1776, when British troops were forced to evacuate the city. During those months of siege, all but one of Boston's six newspapers closed down. The sole exception was the *Massachusetts Gazette*—at the time America's oldest continuously published newspaper. The paper's publisher, Margaret Green Draper, resolutely continued to bring out her paper until British navy transports loaded troops and supplies for departure. Finally, she closed her shop and on March 17 sailed with more than 1,000 other Loyalists who chose exile in Halifax, Nova Scotia, rather than join the American Revolution.

Margaret Green Draper inherited a long tradition of colonial printing. She was the great-granddaughter of Samuel Green, who ran the Cambridge (Massachusetts) Press (forerunner of the Harvard University Press), and the granddaughter of the Boston printer Bartholomew Green. Her parents were Thomas and Ann Green, and her father was most likely also a printer.

In the colonial era, postmasters originally transmitted the news. In 1704 Boston postmaster John Campbell brought out the first issue of the first newspaper in America, the *Boston News-Letter*. Bartholomew Green printed the paper and became its owner in 1721. Boston printers traditionally kept their businesses within their families, with one generation training the next as apprentices and successors. When Green died, the *News-Letter* passed to his son-in-law, John Draper, who published it until his death in 1762. His son, Richard Draper, then took over the paper and changed its name to *Massachusetts Gazette and Boston Weekly News-Letter*. Appointed official printer to the colonial government of Massachusetts, he proudly placed the king's coat of arms on the paper's masthead. A staunch Loyalist, Richard Draper opened his papers to many authors who defended the British Crown, the Parliament, and the royal governor.

On May 30, 1750, Richard Draper had married his cousin Margaret Green. They had no children of their own, but they adopted Margaret's niece. Draper worked hard as a printer and his print shop became one of the most successful in the colonies, producing many publications in addition to the newspaper. The profits from his business enabled him to build a handsome brick home near the print shop.

Many colonial newspapers felt threatened by the British Parliament's imposition of a Stamp Act in 1765. This tax required a one-cent stamp to be placed on all newspapers.

THE Massachusetts Gazette:
AND Boston Weekly News-Letter.

Number 3671.

Draper's — THURSDAY, February 10, 1774.

BOSTON, Feb. 10.

THURSDAY the third Inſtant, at a General Council, held at the Council Chamber in this Town, the following Gentlemen were nominated by his Excellency the Governor, to the reſpective Offices hereafter mentioned; to which Nominations his Majeſty's Council adviſed and conſented, viz.

George Wheaton, Eſq; to be a Juſtice of the Peace for the County of Briſtol.

Mr. James Williams, jun. to be a Coroner for the ſame County.

James M'Cobb, Eſq; to be a ſpecial Juſtice of the Inferior Court of Common Pleas for the County of Lincoln.

William Gardiner, Eſq; to be a Juſtice of the Peace for the ſame County.

Samuel Bancroft, Eſq; to be a Juſtice of the Peace for the County of Middleſex.

Ezra Houghton, Eſq; to be a Juſtice of the Peace for the County of Worceſter.

Mr. Gardner Chandler, jun. to be a Coroner for the ſame County.

Nathan Lord, Eſq; to be a Juſtice of the Peace for the County of York.

Meſſrs. Joſeph Hobbs, Benjamin Staple and Benjamin Maſſey, to be Coroners for the ſame County.

On Thurſday laſt the General Aſſembly made choice of the following Civil Officers for the Year enſuing, viz.

Hon. HARRISON GRAY, Eſq; Treaſurer.
Hon. THOMAS CUSHING, Eſq; Commiſſary General.
Hon. JAMES RUSSELL, Eſq; Impoſt-Officer.

Mr. JEDEDIAH PREBBLE, jun. } Truck Maſter at Fort Pownall.

NOTARIES PUBLIC,

Suffolk, Mr. Dudſon Kilcup, and Mr. Henry Alline, jun.
Eſſex, Mr. John Nutting, Mr. Thomas King, Mr. Samuel Sayer, William Atkins, Eſq; and Daniel Witham, Eſq;
Middleſex, Mr. Nathaniel Gorham.
Plymouth, Mr. Ephraim Spooner.
Barnſtable, Solomon Otis, Eſq; Mr. Joſeph Parker, Mr. Joſeph Doane, and Mr. Winſlow Lewis.
Briſtol, Jerathmeel Bowers, & Eliſha Toby, Eſqrs.
York, Daniel Moulton, Eſq; Charles Chauncy, Eſq; and Mr. Ebenezer Sayer.
Cumberland, Mr. Theophilus Parſons.
Lincoln, Mr. Thomas Moulton.
Dukes-County, Mr. John Peas.
Nantucket, Mr. Stephen Huſſey.

Laſt Friday the Honorable Houſe of Repreſentatives made Choice of the Rev. Mr. Gad Hitchcock, of Pembroke, to preach the Sermon at the anniverſary Election of Councellors the laſt Wedneſday in May next.

Briſtol, ſs. Province of the Maſſachuſets-Bay.

AT a legal Town-Meeting at Freetown, in ſaid County, on Monday the 17th Day of January, A. D. 1774, on purpoſe to know the Minds of the Inhabitants of ſaid Town reſpecting a Body of People aſſembled together at Boſton, on the Sixteenth Day of December laſt paſt, and then deſtroying 342 Cheſts of Tea.

Capt. George Chaſe was choſen Moderator of ſaid Meeting.—After ſome Debates and duly conſidering the bad Conſequences which probably may ariſe from the Proceedings of ſaid Body, the Queſtion was put, whether the Town would act on the Affair, and it paſſed in the affirmative. Then the Town made Choice of Thomas Gilbert, Abiel Terry, James Winſlow, Eſq'rs, Capt. Jael Hathway, and Dr. Bullock, a Committee to draw up ſome Votes and Reſolves, reſpecting the deſtroying ſaid Tea, and lay the ſame before this Meeting on Wedneſday the 26th Day of this Month, at Eleven o'Clock in the Forenoon. Then the Meeting was adjourn'd to that Time. When the Town met according to Adjournment, and the Committee reported the following Reſolves, viz.

1ſt, That it is the Duty of this Town, at this Time, to expreſs our Sentiments in Matters which ſo nearly concern us, more eſpecially as there ſeems to be Reaſon to fear there is a Spirit of Anarchy, Diſorder and Confuſion prevailing in ſome Parts of this Province.

2d, Reſolved, That the Body of People at Boſton, on the 16th Day of December taking upon themſelves the State and Appellation of a Body of People, who did not endeavour to prevent a Number of People (in Indian Dreſs or Diſguiſe) from acting their ſavage Nature in the Deſtruction of the Tea aforeſaid, as we apprehend, was not done their Duty, but was contrary to Law, and we fear will bring upon us the Vengeance of an affronted Majeſty, and alſo plunge us in Debt and Miſery, when the injured Owners of ſaid Tea ſhall make their Demand for the Value of the ſame.

3d, Reſolved, That this Town do hereby declare, that we abhor, deteſt, and forever bear our Teſtimony againſt the Proceedings of the Body and Indians aforeſaid, or any others who have or ſhall act in any riotous Manner, it being ſo very contrary to the Spirit of our Laws and the Liberty of the People.

4th, Reſolved, That Thomas Gilbert, Eſq; our preſent Repreſentative, do, and he is hereby inſtructed to uſe his utmoſt Endeavour as a Member of the Hon. Houſe of Repreſentatives, that ſome effectual Means, if poſſible, be taken to prevent for the future all ſuch riotous and mobiſh Proceedings, and if Demand ſhall be made by the Owners of ſaid Tea for the Damage done them by the Body or Indians aforeſaid, that he appear and uſe his Endeavour, and vote againſt any Part thereof being paid by us, who are ſo innocent of deſtroying the ſame.

5th, Voted, That theſe Votes and Reſolves be fairly recorded in the Town-Book and a Copy thereof tranſmitted to the Preſs, that the World may know our Minds reſpecting our Liberties and good Government, and the Reſolutions we have to obey the good Laws of our Land, which under God this Province for a long Time have been in the enjoyment of.

Thomas Gilbert,
Abiel Terry,
James Winſlow,
Jael Hathway,
Jeſſe Bullock.

This is a true Copy of Record, examined and compared by me,

Zebedee Tiſdy, Town-Clerk.

MR. DRAPER, pleaſe to inſert the following in your Gazette, and you'll oblige one of your readers, and a friend to the publick.

WHILE the good people of this Province are ſtruggling for their Rights and Privileges, and uſing their utmoſt efforts for the preſervation of their liberties and properties from the invaſion of foreign powers; is it not unaccountably ſtrange that they ſo tamely ſuffer themſelves to be robbed (not of their liberties) but of their lives and properties? and that by a ſet of men within their own bowels, I mean by thoſe vile impoſters with which our country towns eſpecially ſwarm in a ſurpriſing manner within theſe few years paſt, who call themſelves Doctors of Phyſick, but really deſerve no better title than that of Knaves and Quacks; the generality of them having but very few, and ſome none of the qualifications neceſſary for that noble and truly honorable profeſſion: one principal reaſon of this growing evil appears to be either through a miſtaken notion of the eaſineſs of obtaining this noble art, or for ſake of a little gain among the country phyſicians who thereby encouraged many idle perſons (who having but poor ſtomachs for labour) by offering to inſtruct them in ſo ſhort a time as about two years, and for the ſmall ſum of ninety or a hundred dollars. Thus we ſee many young men of very dull geniuſes who are bad readers of plain Engliſh and worſe ſpellers, who know not a word of Latin or Greek, and can ſcarcely write their names ſo as to be legible; yet away they go to a Phyſician, who takes them under his care to inſtruct them in phyſick and ſurgery, who perhaps has about half a dozen volumes for his pupils to tumble over, who not being verſed in grammar are ſorely nonpluſſed in finding the meaning, and it ſoon becomes a dry ſtudy to them, and being very idle they ſoon begin to rove abroad and divert themſelves among the female ſex, and it often happens by uſing too much freedom they are caught in a ſnare, and when little more than half the term of their apprenticeſhip is expired, they are obliged to enter into the State of matrimony, and ſo upon the practice of phyſick; others who ſerve their whole term are but little better, they all being ſhockingly ignorant of the fundimentals of that valuable art.—They have learnt to let blood, and draw teeth, and adminiſter a puke and a glyſter, they can tell you the human Body is compoſed of fleſh and bones and cover'd with ſkin; that there is a ſtomach to receive the food we eat to nouriſh us, and that there are outlets for the urine and excrements; but as to the different organs, &c. which conſtitute and keep in play the human machine, they can give you little better account than a common ruſtic can give of the fine ſprings and ballances which cauſes the vibrations of a watch, or of the revolutions of the planets around the ſun; away they run to the apothecary and furniſh themſelves with medicines which they are groſsly ignorant as to the nature and uſe of.

Thus they commence gentlemen-doctors and ride about with an air of importance, deceiving the credulous and honeſt people, quacking their naſty potions on their fellow-creatures: Among this herd you may obſerve the timid or fearful quack, and the bold and raſh quack, the firſt if he happens to uſe the proper medicine gives ſo ſmall doſes that they are not ſufficient to eradicate the diſeaſe, and ſo he kills his patient in a lingering manner, or lays a foundation for a train of chronic diſorders which makes his whole life miſerable; the laſt throws in at all adventures largely, ſo pops off his patient from the ſtage immediately; of the firſt of theſe you will hear ſome of the poor ignorant females ſay he is a careful doctor and won't do no hurt if he can't do any good, and I like ſuch an one beſt; and of the other when his patient dies ſuddenly, ſome will ſay their time was come and doctors can't ſave life.

After this manner theſe deceivers practice their butchery on their fellow-creatures, and when they have practiced ſix months or perhaps a year, you ſhall ſee them riding in ſtate with two or three apprentices attending them; after this manner is kept up and increaſed a race of caterpillers on the common-wealth; and ſo great is their increaſe that notwithſtanding the rapid increaſe of the people, and the extenſiveneſs of our new ſettlements, the poor creatures are ſorely cramped for want of room to work in, for in many country towns which are ſcarcely ſufficient to ſupport one accompliſhed practitioner you will find three or four of theſe deſpicable wretches ſtarving for employment, envying and ſlandering each other, uſing every baſe and low method to eſtabliſh his own reputation; one will tell you he has a ſecret remedy which is infallible in curing the rheumatiſm and gout, another has a ſecret remedy for curing the bilious cholic which never fails, another cures cancers though never ſo inveterate, another is a wonderful boneſetter, who ſets vaſt numbers of bones which were never out of place. Thus the honeſt and induſtrious people are impoſed on from day to day by theſe vile pretenders to phyſick, which is too ſhocking for any ſerious and conſiderate perſon to behold in this pleaſant land, where all other arts and ſciences flouriſh and are brought to ſo great perfection:—it is greatly to be wiſhed that ſome worthy gentlemen profeſſors of the medical art (as many there are in this province who really deſerve that character who are men of learning and candour) would form ſome honorable plan for eſtabliſhing the practice of phyſick and ſurgery on a firm and permanent Baſis, and that a petition may be laid before our General Aſſembly for their ſerious conſideration, that wholſome laws be made and put into practice to prevent for the future ſuch vile impoſitions on the publick. PHILO REI-PUBLICÆ.

BOSTON, February 10.

We learn from Portſmouth, that thro' the aſſiduity of Col. John Fenton, Juſtice of the Peace for the County of Grafton, the famous or rather infamous Glazier Wheeler of Cohoſs, who ſome time ſince eſcaped from Worceſter Goal, was apprehended in the Night of the 21ſt of laſt Month, for paſſing counterfeit Dollars; alſo one Peter Hobart, an Accomplice, who has turned King's Evidence and given ſuch a Clue to Wheeler's Plans, as cannot fail of the moſt ſalutary Effects.

On the 22d of December laſt was celebrated at Plimouth the anniverſary of their Anceſtors firſt landing in New England; On which Occaſion the Rev. Mr. Turner, of Scituate, deliver'd a Diſcourſe in the Rev. Mr. Robbins's Meeting-Houſe, from Zach. iv. part of the 9th and 10th verſes. After which a very ſuitable Dinner was prepar'd at Mr. Howland's, where a great Number of the People, with five of the Clergy, were genteely entertained; and the Day and Evening very agreeably ſpent, and to the honor of all preſent.—Every Countenance being expreſſive of gratitude and joy, and every Tongue exuberant in bleſſing the Memory of their pious Fore-Fathers.

We hear from Philadelphia, that an Expreſs was arrived there with an account that a Party, conſiſting of Perſons who had ſerved, during the late War, in the two Virginia Regiments raiſed for the defence of that Colony, had taken poſſeſſion of Pittſburg, with a deſign of ſurveying, dividing, and ſettling themſelves upon that Place, and the Lands adjacent to it.

A Correſpondent deſires us to mention, that there is now living at Wrentham, in the 83d Year of his Age, one Joſiah Cook, who has had 12 Children by one Wife, 9 of whom lived to be married, and have Children; ſo that this venerable old Gentleman hath had deſcended from him 79 Grand-Children, and 47 Great Grand-Children, in all 138.

PHILADELPHIA, January 19.

On Saturday the firſt Inſtant, were executed at Eaſton, Northampton-county, purſuant to their ſentence, Thomas Wilſon, alias John Hurrin, about 26 years of age, for the murder of William Hewit, in 1768: and Alexander Buchan, about 32 years old, for a burglary. By their confeſſion it appears they have been old offenders, though both young men, and came into Maryland under the benefit of the act of Parliament, " for the BETTER " peopling of America." At, and going to, the place of execution, they behaved in a moſt ſolemn and penitent manner; but eſpecially Buchan, who ſpoke at the tree a conſiderable time with the greateſt earneſtneſs, to a large number of ſpectators, who were, ſeemingly, very much affected by it. He in particular addreſſed himſelf to youth, exhorting them to take warning by his unhappy and ignominious death. Hurrin, though ſilent, was all the time drowned in tears; and by his truly great diſtreſs, affected the ſpectators very much.

THIS DAY PUBLISHED,
Adorn'd with an elegant Engraving of the Author,
[Price 3s. 4d. L. M. Bound.]

POEMS,
On various Subjects, Religious and Moral.
By PHILLIS WHEATLY,
A Negro Girl.

Sold by Meſſ'rs COX & BERRY,
At their Store in King-Street, Boſton.
N. B. The Subſcribers are requeſted to apply for their Copies.

All Perſons having Demands on the Eſtate of John MiddleWendell, late of Boſton, Merchant, deceaſ'd, are deſired to bring in their Accounts in order to ſettle, and thoſe Perſons indebted to ſaid Eſtate are deſired to pay the ſame to Katharine Wendell, Adminiſtratrix.

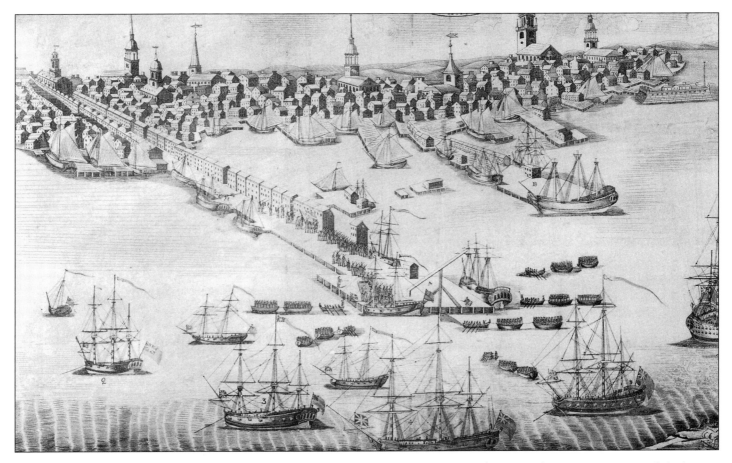

Paul Revere made this engraving of British troops landing in Boston in 1768 to enforce the unpopular new taxes. Even though revolutionary sentiment was growing in Boston, Margaret Draper continued to publish her husband's Loyalist newspaper after his death.

Considering their existence threatened, colonial newspapers took the lead against British policies. More and more colonial newspapers opposed British rule. In the battle for what John Adams called "the minds and hearts of the people," Patriots could voice their complaints in such papers as the *Massachusetts Spy* and the *Boston Gazette*. But printers whose newspapers were sympathetic to the British viewpoint, or even tried to remain neutral, were often threatened with boycotts and violence.

Draper persisted in his Loyalist views, but it took a toll on his health. He died on June 6, 1774, at the age of 47. With no sons or sons-in-law to succeed him, management of the print shop and paper went to his widow, Margaret. Her first issue of the *Gazette*

appeared on June 9. A month before Richard's death, he had gone into partnership with John Boyle. But Boyle's sympathies leaned toward the revolutionary cause and he wanted the paper to side with the Patriots. Margaret simply could not work with him, and they both agreed that he should quit the paper. She produced the *Massachusetts Gazette* on her own for several months before taking a new partner, John Howe, who shared her views.

It was a dangerous time to be a Loyalist publisher, especially one as outspoken as "Mother Draper" (as older women were then commonly called). In 1774, after the Boston Tea Party, the British government passed the "Intolerable Acts," which closed the port of Boston until the lost tea was paid for, and quartered British

Margaret Green Draper

"To the PUBLIC. . . .

Mrs. Draper being under the Necessity of procuring some reputable Means of Subsistence, proposes to continue publishing the paper herself; and hopes by the assistance of her Friends to give full Satisfaction to its former Customers, and the Public in general . . . and flatters herself that she shall meet with such assistance as may enable her to keep up the credit which the Paper had for a long Time sustained in the Days of her deceased husband."

—from the *Massachusetts Gazette and the Boston Weekly News-Letter* (August 11, 1774)

BORN

May 3, 1727
Boston, Massachusetts

DIED

1804
London, England

ACCOMPLISHMENTS

Publisher, *Massachusetts Gazette and the Boston Weekly News-Letter* (1774–76)

troops in Boston homes. Draper's *Gazette* defended the British "Intolerable Acts" and criticized the colonists' nonimportation agreements—boycotts of British goods. She reprinted articles from Loyalist newspapers in New York. She attacked the Continental Congress and predicted that the Patriot cause would end in defeat. Boston Patriots sought to censor her paper and voted that it be "burned by the common hangman." When an effort by British troops to seize American arms at Lexington and Concord led to a bloody clash with the local minutemen, Boston became the front line of the American Revolution. In this hazardous situation, all the other newspapers in the city suspended publication. Draper alone continued printing, protected by the military authorities.

Only when the British evacuated the city did Margaret Draper stop printing. After 72 years of continuous publication, Boston's first newspaper closed its doors. After she departed, her home and print shop were confiscated and sold by the new American government. Margaret Draper and John Howe sailed to Halifax. After a few months there, she traveled on to Great Britain. Deprived of all her property, she petitioned the British government for a pension. After lengthy deliberation, a British Commission on Enquiry awarded her a pension in recognition of her loyalty to the crown in perilous times. Margaret Draper died in England, never having returned to her native land.

FURTHER READING

Brown, Wallace. *The Good Americans: The Loyalists in the American Revolution.* New York: Morrow, 1969.

Hudak, Leona M. *Early American Women Printers and Publishers, 1639–1820.* Metuchen, N.J.: Scarecrow, 1978.

Stark, James H. *The Loyalists of Massachusetts, and the Other Side of the American Revolution.* 1910. Reprint, Clifton, N.J.: Augustus M. Kelley, 1972.

John Fenno

FEDERALIST PUBLISHER

Even before George Washington had left Mount Vernon to journey north to New York City for his inauguration as President of the United States in April 1789, a New York newspaper began publishing in support of his administration. The first issue of editor John Fenno's semiweekly *Gazette of the United States* appeared on April 11, promising to "hold up the people's own government in a favorable light," and to endear "the GENERAL GOVERNMENT to the PEOPLE." For Fenno, "the people" meant those wealthier merchants, shippers, and planters, who had endorsed the new Constitution and a stronger central government. Most of the other American newspapers at that time also represented mercantile interests and backed the new administration, but Fenno's paper, located at the very seat of government, endeavored to speak *for* the new administration.

John Fenno was a big, bulky, good-natured man with a large family to support. Having failed in the importing business, he came to New York from Massachusetts with a plan to publish a stately "court" paper for President Washington's administration. Fenno little suspected that the praise he heaped on Washington's receptions and on Secretary of the Treasury Alexander Hamilton's bold economic programs would trigger an angry opposition movement. The *Gazette* repulsed Secretary of State Thomas Jefferson, who saw it as a "Tory paper" that was undermining the ideals for which Americans had fought their revolution, and was aiming to create a monarchy and aristocracy. When Jefferson set out to establish an opposition press, Fenno soon found himself at the center of a bitter "newspaper war."

Born in Boston in 1751, John Fenno was the son of Mary Chaplan and Ephraim Fenno. His father was a leather dresser who also ran an ale house. Fenno attended the Old South Writing School near the Boston Common, and after graduation worked as an assistant teacher there. His penmanship earned him a post as secretary to General Artemas Ward during the Revolution. In 1777 he married Mary ("Polly") Curtis, who came from a wealthy family. One of her uncles lent Fenno money to enter the importing business after the war, but he proved to be a poor businessman. After importing more goods than he could sell, he fell deeply into debt.

Fenno had also gained some experience as an editorial assistant on Benjamin Russell's newspaper, the *Massachusetts Centinel*. Armed with letters of introduction and a loan from prominent Federalists in Massachusetts—some of whom were relatives of his wife—the 38-year-old Fenno traveled to

New York City and presented himself to Rufus King, a Federalist leader and U.S. senator from New York. Fenno reminded King of the intense battle to ratify the new Constitution, when newspapers had played a key role in winning public support for the Constitution. He proposed to publish a newspaper that would continue to support the Constitution and the Washington administration. The new government, he pointed out, would inevitably face many difficulties and would need support from a newspaper published by someone completely in sympathy with "the Federalist interest."

Fenno would publish the paper only if the Federalists could promise him government printing contracts to make the venture financially successful. When Senator King assured him of such support, Fenno launched the *Gazette of the United States*. It appeared in New York from April 1789 until October 1790, and then moved to Philadelphia along with the federal government.

Most previous newspaper publishers had been printers, for whom newspapers were but one of many jobs handled by their print shops; but John Fenno was primarily an editor. Fenno

John Fenno's *Gazette of the United States* promoted the administration of George Washington and the economic programs of Alexander Hamilton.

President Washington (right) consults with Secretary of State Thomas Jefferson (left) and Secretary of the Treasury Alexander Hamilton in this portrait in the U.S. Capitol, painted by Constantino Brumidi. As a Federalist publisher, John Fenno not only supported the government's policies but also printed articles written by prominent Federalists, such as Hamilton.

collected and spread news and opinion, mailing copies to postmasters and other newspaper editors throughout the country. He worked doggedly at the job, confessing to a friend that managing the paper "employs all my time—it absorbs my whole attention in such a manner that I have not known a pleasing moment of relaxation."

A small three-column paper, the dignified *Gazette* rarely adopted an insulting tone toward its opponents. It counted on prominent Federalists like Rufus King, John Adams, and Alexander Hamilton to contribute articles, which they published under

such pseudonyms as "Pacificus," "An American," and "Plain Facts." Hamilton, in particular, found the *Gazette* a handy means of spreading his ideas, and he made sure that the Treasury Department gave Fenno its printing jobs. For a while even Secretary of State Jefferson gave Fenno orders for printing the laws. With such support, Fenno added the words "By Authority" to his masthead. This was a British custom suggesting that a paper was officially approved and supported by the government.

The Federalists cheered Fenno's paper. Representative Fisher Ames of

Massachusetts, for instance, declared that "no printer was ever so *correct* in his politics." The *Gazette* defended the interests of "COMMERCE" and promoted establishment of "PUBLIC CREDIT," using capital letters to highlight these chief ingredients of Hamilton's programs. Hamilton's chief rival, Thomas Jefferson, bristled when he read what he called Fenno's "hymns and chants," which he suspected of promoting Hamilton for President.

By July 1789 the *Gazette* had 600 subscribers, which paid just enough to cover its printing. Lacking advertising, Fenno had to appeal to wealthier Federalists for financial support. By 1791 the paper's financial condition had improved. Fenno claimed 1,000 subscribers in different states. He was also sending out 120 copies to postmasters and other newspapers for exchange and reprinting. However, the *Gazette* could never have survived without political patronage. In 1793, when he needed money to continue publishing, Fenno went to Hamilton for a $2,000 loan. The Federalists considered it in their best interests to keep his paper in business.

Much against his nature, Fenno was doing editorial battle with such adversaries as Philip Freneau's *National Gazette* and Benjamin Bache's *Aurora*. Having always intended to publish a serious and tasteful paper, Fenno was offended when his critics called him "court printer" and a "vile sycophant." He responded poorly to such criticism and had little talent for tirades. At one point, Fenno declared that those newspaper publishers who were "abusers of government" were mostly people "from other countries who having lately escaped from bondage, know not how

to enjoy liberty." Freneau pounced on this statement and announced to his own readers that the *Gazette of the United States* had denigrated them as "foreigners" out "to overturn the government." At times the battle spread beyond the pages of the newspapers. During one encounter on a Philadelphia street, the young, hot-tempered Benjamin Bache beat the massive John Fenno with his cane.

During the summer of 1792, while Washington pondered whether to run for a second term as President, the emerging opposition party known as Republicans feared that Hamilton might succeed to the Presidency. Freneau's *National Gazette* launched a fierce attack on Hamilton and his economic programs. After taking the abuse quietly at first, Hamilton decided to retaliate. He called Fenno into his library to dictate a small piece questioning whether Freneau's employment as a State Department clerk was just a cover to underwrite his newspaper publishing. From August through December 1792, Hamilton published a steady stream of essays under many different names, aimed directly at Jefferson, while at the same time resolutely defending his own economic policies. Freneau's and Jefferson's allies responded furiously, and the newspaper war lasted for the rest of the year. The exchange contributed to the birth of formal political parties in America.

A devastating yellow fever epidemic hit Philadelphia during the summer of 1793. For three months, as many as 100 people a day died of the fever. Thousands evacuated the city, among them newspaper subscribers and advertisers. Falling revenues caused Philip Freneau to close the *National*

John Fenno

BORN

August 23, 1751
Boston, Massachusetts

DIED

September 14, 1798
Philadelphia, Pennsylvania

EDUCATION

Old South Writing School, Boston

ACCOMPLISHMENTS

Editorial assistant, *Massachusetts Centinel* (1780s); editor and publisher, *Gazette of the United States* (in New York, 1789–90; in Philadelphia, 1790–98)

> "At this important Crisis, the ideas that fill the mind, are pregnant with Events of the greatest magnitude—to strengthen and complete the UNION of the States—to extend and process their COMMERCE, under equal Treaties yet to be formed—to explore and arrange the NATIONAL FUNDS—to restore and establish the PUBLIC CREDIT—and ALL under the auspices of an untried System of Government, will require the ENERGIES of the Patriots and Sages of our Country—Hence the propriety of increasing the Medium of Knowledge and Information."

—from the *Gazette of the United States* (April 15, 1789)

Gazette. Always the optimist, Fenno remained in the city throughout the epidemic with his wife and 14 children. Fenno had to suspend the *Gazette of the United States* for three months, but with the aid of Federalist loans later reopened the paper, converting it from a semiweekly to a daily, the *Gazette of the United States and Daily Evening Advertiser.*

Government printing contracts made Fenno's *Gazette of the United States* essentially the "official organ" of the Washington and John Adams administration and set a model for other pro-administration papers to follow. Every President until Abraham Lincoln had a newspaper that served as his official forum and whose printing was subsidized by government contracts. John Fenno continued publishing until 1798, when another epidemic hit Philadelphia. Once again he declined to leave. "As it is my duty to continue here so long as other printers remain at their posts, I shall remain here also," he wrote, "trusting in that almighty power which has so graciously protected me and mine heretofore." But this time Fenno contracted the fever. He died on September 14, 1798.

His 19-year-old son, John Ward Fenno, took over the paper and ran it for two more years, until he sold it in 1800. Like the Federalist party that it so consistently supported, the *Gazette* lingered for a few more years before shutting down entirely in 1818.

FURTHER READING

Elkins, Stanley, and Eric McKitrick. *The Age of Federalism*. New York: Oxford University Press, 1993.

Hench, John B., ed. "Letters of John Fenno and John Ward Fenno, 1779–1800." *Proceedings of the American Antiquarian Society* 89 (1979): 299-368; 90 (1980), 163-234.

McDonald, Forrest. *Alexander Hamilton: A Biography*. New York: Norton, 1979.

Miller, John C. *The Federalist Era, 1789–1801*. New York: Harper & Row, 1960.

Smith, Culver H. *The Press, Politics, and Patronage: The American Government's Use of Newspapers, 1789–1875*. Athens: University of Georgia Press, 1977.

Philip Freneau

PATRIOT, POET, AND PROPAGANDIST

The United States was not yet divided between political parties when George Washington became the country's first President in 1789. Still, deep disagreements existed over how government should be conducted. Washington's cabinet contained both Secretary of State Thomas Jefferson and Secretary of the Treasury Alexander Hamilton, who held starkly opposite views on public policy. Soon a pro-administration Federalist party emerged in support of Hamilton's economic plans. The Federalists found support in John Fenno's newspaper, the *Gazette of the United States*, which was first published in New York City in 1789. The next year, when the government moved to Philadelphia, Fenno's paper moved with it. Jefferson and his close ally, James Madison, felt they needed a paper of their own to oppose Hamilton. They persuaded a sympathetic editor, Philip Freneau, to move to Philadelphia and start a new "Republican" newspaper, the *National Gazette*, that would promote their ideas and take the first steps toward an opposition political party.

A poet and sailor as well as a journalist, Philip Freneau believed that there was no virtue in an impartial press. His instinct was to attack his enemies.

Madison and Philip Freneau (originally spelled Fresneau until changed by Philip for simplicity) had been friends since they were college students together. Freneau's family were Huguenots (French Protestants) who fled persecution and sought religious freedom in the New World. Pierre Fresneau became a wine merchant in New York City and married Agnes Watson, the daughter of a wealthy landholding family in New Jersey. Their first child, Philip, was born on January 2, 1752. That same year the family bought a 1,000-acre estate near Monmouth, New Jersey, and built a summer home they named Mount Pleasant. Philip Freneau grew up surrounded by books and art and received first-rate schooling. But in the 1760s, changing British policy, including higher taxes under the Stamp Act, caused an economic crisis in the colonies. In 1767, when Philip was 13, his father died. He had been deeply in debt and hounded by creditors. His father's fate and his family's uncertain finances left the young Freneau suspicious of creditors and other "moneyed interests," attitudes that would strongly influence his later politics and editorial writing.

Despite his family's financial problems, Philip was able to attend the College of New Jersey (now known as Princeton), where he met and perhaps roomed with James Madison. Freneau studied philosophy, science, and classical literature in Latin and Greek, and he won recognition for his poetry. At his graduation in 1771 he and another classmate read their joint patriotic poem, "The Rising Glory of America," which they published the next year as a pamphlet.

As America moved steadily toward independence from Great Britain, Freneau lent his pen to the cause. His verses satirized the British military leaders in the colonies as cowardly and cruel, and denounced Tories and Loyalists (Americans who supported the British) as traitors. But rather than join the fight for liberty, Freneau left home to take work as secretary for a wealthy planter on the West Indian island of Santa Cruz. In that lovely tropical setting he wrote some of his best poems, "Santa Cruz," "The Jamaica Funeral," and "The House of Night." He also wrote love poetry to a young woman who rejected him, a disappointment that led him to seek his future elsewhere.

He returned to New Jersey in 1778, only to find that war and devastation had come shockingly close to Mount Pleasant. Freneau enlisted in a New Jersey regiment, engaged in skirmishes with the British, and was shot in the knee. These experiences caused his poetry to shift from satire to anger and realism, notably in "American Independence," published during the war. But the poet at heart was less of a soldier than a sailor. Having always loved the sea, he became captain of the *Indian Delaware*, a small supply ship that ran the British blockade and attacked British merchant ships. In 1780 he signed on to the crew of the *Aurora*, a larger privateer. When the British captured the *Aurora*, they took Freneau prisoner. He was confined to the *Scorpion*, a British prison ship anchored in New York harbor. The dirty and overcrowded conditions on the ship and the poor quality of the food caused Freneau's health to decline sharply. His six weeks' imprisonment left him emaciated and in pain, and produced his bitterest poem, "The British Prison Ship," which called for Americans to "Rouse from your sleep, and crush the thievish band,/Defeat, destroy, and sweep them from the land."

Since the British still controlled New York, Freneau traveled to Philadelphia. There an acquaintance, Francis Bailey, published a patriotic newspaper, the *Freeman's Journal*, supported by Bailey's position as official printer for the Continental Congress. In April 1781 Bailey announced that a "young philosopher" would be editing the paper. Freneau did copyediting and proofreading and wrote editorials, poetry, and prose pieces for about a year. The bantam-sized Freneau sharpened his skills at writing ferocious tirades against the British and their sympathizers in America. Victory at Yorktown in December 1781 ended the war. Although he continued to contribute to the *Freeman's Journal*, he earned his living more as a clerk in the Philadelphia post office. Feeling confined in this job, in 1784 he sailed for Jamaica. On that voyage his ship encountered a hurricane, the inspiration for his poem "Verses Made at Sea, in a Heavy Gale." This and other poems, which appeared over the byline "Captain Freneau," were published throughout the United States and won further fame for the "poet of the Revolution."

After several years at sea, Freneau returned to New Jersey and in 1790 married Eleanor Forman of Middletown Point, near Mount Pleasant. Needing a more secure source of income, Freneau took up journalism again. He accepted an offer from the owners of the *Daily Advertiser*, New York City's first daily paper, to be its editor. For months the *Advertiser* ran his poetry and unsigned articles, defending such republican heroes as Tom Paine and Thomas Jefferson. Freneau also ridiculed the political bargaining in Congress over the location of the new capital, but in 1790 the federal government moved to Philadelphia, where it would wait over the next decade while federal buildings were being constructed in the new capital city of Washington, D.C.

When the government moved, the pro-Federalist *Gazette of the United States* moved with it. Thomas Jefferson wanted a paper in Philadelphia to counteract editor John Fenno's aristocratic preferences, and his support for Secretary of the Treasury Alexander Hamilton's financial programs, which called for federal taxes, tariffs, and a central bank to promote an industrial economy. Jefferson had never met Freneau, but James Madison recommended him highly. At first Freneau turned down Jefferson's request and talked of starting a "country paper" in Monmouth, New Jersey. But Madison talked Freneau into reconsidering, especially by appealing to his hatred for anything British. Madison warned that pro-British forces were taking over the U.S. government through Hamilton's programs. Freneau agreed to go to Philadelphia to launch the *National Gazette*. To support this enterprise, Secretary of State Jefferson arranged for Freneau to earn additional funds as a translator in the State Department.

The first issue of the *National Gazette* appeared on October 31, 1791. It reprinted news from British, French, and Dutch newspapers, together with letters from various correspondents, government documents, court decisions, and the debates in Congress. Freneau invited "all decent productions of entertainment in prose or verse" and promised to base his paper on "the great principles upon which the American Revolution was founded." It was not to be just a Philadelphia paper, but a national paper. Freneau mailed copies—at reduced postage rates—to subscribers, postmasters, and

Philip Morin Freneau

BORN
January 2, 1752
New York, New York

DIED
December 19, 1832
Near Matawan, New Jersey

EDUCATION
B.A., College of New Jersey (later renamed Princeton), 1771

ACCOMPLISHMENTS
Contributor, *United States Magazine* (1779); editor and contributor, *Freeman's Journal* (1781–84); editor and contributor, *New York Daily Advertiser* (1790–91); editor, *National Gazette* (1792–93); editor, *Jersey Chronicle* (1795–96); editor, *New York Time Piece and Literary Companion* (1797–98); contributor, *True American* (1822)

Freneau's *National Gazette* published the official acts of the federal government while editorially attacking the Washington administration.

other newspapers throughout the states. Other newspapers clipped and reprinted its articles, spreading its message further.

At first the *National Gazette* adopted a politely restrained tone. Although clearly supportive of Jefferson and Madison, the paper did not criticize Hamilton. It printed Hamilton's Report on Manufacturers (in which Hamilton argued that the federal government should encourage industries in the United States) in full and without comment. This neutrality helped build the new paper's reputation as a reliable source of news. But having started in journalism by writing patriotic propaganda that mercilessly assailed the

Tories during the Revolution, Freneau saw no virtue in an impartial or objective press. His instinct was to attack his enemies.

As editor, Freneau campaigned for openness in government. He was outraged that the Senate met in secret, even though the House of Representatives conducted its business in full view of the public and press. Promising to publish accounts of the debates in Congress, Freneau conducted a crusade to shame the Senate into opening its doors. "It rests then with the people themselves, who are the fountain of government," he wrote, "to demand the free circulation of political information, and to open those avenues of intelligence which every government finds its account in obstructing." The Senate finally gave up in 1794 and ordered a public gallery constructed in its chamber.

A financial panic in March 1792 changed the tone of the *National Gazette*. On March 15 Freneau started publishing letters signed "Brutus." These letters attacked Hamilton's plan to refund Revolutionary war debts. The "Brutus" letters charged that the plan would benefit the wealthy few at the expense of the mass of people and "transfer the best resources of the country forever into the hands of the speculators." In April, Freneau published James Madison's anonymous letter, "The Union: Who Are Its Real Friends?" which warned against the rising business interests that threatened to overwhelm American farmers, and against the corrupting influence of aristocracy. The *National Gazette* accused Hamilton of trying to turn the American government into a monarchy, while it lavished praise on Jefferson as an "illustrious Patriot."

Such attacks eventually got under Hamilton's skin. He responded with anonymous articles in Fenno's *Gazette of the United States*. In July 1793, trying to disguise his identity by writing under the initials "T.L.," Hamilton wondered whether Freneau collected his government salary for his translations or for his publications. Observing that Freneau's paper published articles that vilified the Washington administration and opposed its policies, Hamilton commented: "In common life it is thought ungrateful for a man to bite the hand that puts bread in his mouth; but if the man is hired to do it, the case is altered." Freneau responded angrily, denying the accusations. In front of the mayor of Philadelphia, Freneau took an oath that he did not take orders from Jefferson but ran his paper "free—unfettered—and uninfluenced."

By now a "newspaper war" between the *Gazette of the United States* and the *National Gazette* was in full swing. Hamilton on one side and Jefferson and Madison on the other used "their" papers as weapons against each other. Hamilton turned his fire on Jefferson, identifying him as a "declared opponent" of almost everything the Washington administration stood for, and charging that Jefferson had been against ratification of the Constitution. Although Jefferson chose not to respond, James Madison and other friends employed their pens (and pen names) in his defense. Between August and December of 1792 the two sides assailed each other steadily. Much of the fury was due to their uncertainty about whether President Washington would accept a second term. If he declined, then Jefferson and Hamilton might be candidates to succeed him. Each side did everything possible to stop the other. That fall, however, Washington reluctantly agreed to run for a second term, and he easily won reelection. Still, by appealing to public opinion the newspaper war made it clear that political parties were a reality, and that the public must choose sides.

Freneau had once written with admiration for Washington. One of his poems, "To His Excellency General Washington," had praised Washington's "steadfastness in the face of defeat" and his military achievements during the Revolution. But Freneau despised the pomp and formality of Washington's administration as well as its support for Fenno's paper:

> The well-born sort alone, should
>   read the news,
> No common herds should get
>   behind the scene
> To view the movements of the
>   state machine:

"To the Freemen of America: A motion for opening the doors of the Senate chamber has again lost by a considerable majority—in defiance of instruction, in defiance of your opinion, in defiance of every principle which gives security to free men. What means this conduct? Which expression does it carry strongest with it, contempt for you or tyranny?"

—from the *National Gazette* (February 13, 1793)

One paper only, filled with courtly
    stuff,
One paper, for one country is
    enough.

As an avid supporter of the French Revolution of 1789, Freneau warmly applauded the new French minister to the United States, "Citizen" Edmond Genêt. He also attacked Washington's policy of neutrality in the war being waged between France and Great Britain. The *National Gazette* defended Genêt and insisted that the "hearts of *the people*" were with the French cause. Ultimately, however, the American public supported Washington and left Genêt discredited. During the controversy, President Washington was furious over the abuse he received from "that rascal Freneau" and asked Jefferson why the editor was on the State Department's payroll. Jefferson responded that he had no control over Freneau's paper, and argued that "no government ought to be without censors, & where the press is free, no one ever will."

When Jefferson resigned as Secretary of State in 1793, Freneau gave up his State Department clerkship. Freneau's attacks on the popular President of the United States also caused the *National Gazette* to lose subscribers. Rather than stay in Philadelphia during the yellow fever epidemic of 1793, Freneau shut down his financially failing newspaper. Federalists, who regarded the paper as "a public nuisance," celebrated. Republicans turned instead to newspapers published by Benjamin Franklin Bache as their official voice. With government printing contracts to subsidize him, John Fenno continued publishing the *Gazette of the United States* until 1798, when another yellow fever epidemic claimed his life. The election of 1800 saw Thomas Jefferson elected President. With that, the Federalist party went into decline and eventually disappeared. Assessing these events, Jefferson later gave much credit to Freneau for having "saved our Constitution, which was galloping fast into monarchy."

Philip Freneau took his type and other printing supplies back to New Jersey, where he published and edited the *Jersey Chronicle*. Unlike the aggressive *National Gazette*, the *Chronicle* was a small country paper based in Monmouth, New Jersey, that reprinted news from other Republican papers and no longer contributed original information to the national debate. Later, Freneau edited a New York literary journal, *Time Piece*, which offered assorted poetry, essays, and travel accounts. Pressed by creditors, the journal failed in December 1797. Freneau retired from editing and spent the rest of his life traveling and writing poetry and occasional essays for the press, during his voyages at sea or at his New Jersey farm. Many of his articles, as pungent as ever, were signed "An Old Soldier." In 1832 a poverty-stricken Freneau applied for a federal pension for his services in the American Revolution. In December of that year, at age 80, he died in a blizzard when he lost his way while walking home from a country store.

FURTHER READING

Axelrad, Jacob. *Philip Freneau: Champion of Democracy*. Austin: University of Texas Press, 1967.

Bowden, Mary Weatherspoon. *Philip Freneau*. Boston: Twayne, 1976.

Clark, Harry Hayden, ed. *Poems of Freneau*. New York: Hafner, 1960.

Elkins, Stanley, and Eric McKitrick. *The Age of Federalism*. New York: Oxford University Press, 1993.

Grotta, Gerald L. "Philip Freneau's Crusade for Open Sessions of the U.S. Senate." *Journalism Quarterly* 48 (Winter 1971): 667-671.

Koch, Adrienne. *Jefferson and Madison: The Great Collaboration*. New York: Oxford University Press, 1964.

Marsh, Philip M. *Philip Freneau: Poet and Journalist*. Minneapolis, Minn.: Dillon Press, 1967.

———, ed. *The Prose of Philip Freneau*. New Brunswick, N.J.: Scarecrow, 1955.

Smith, Culver H. *The Press, Politics, and Patronage: The American Government's Use of Newspapers, 1789-1875*. Athens: University of Georgia Press, 1977.

Benjamin Franklin Bache

THE OPPOSITION PRESS

Benjamin Franklin Bache inherited his famous grandfather's name and journalistic passions, but not his grandfather's appealing nature. In publishing his newspaper, the *Pennsylvania Gazette*, Benjamin Franklin had been careful to avoid libel and personal abuse. "Having contracted with my Subscribers to furnish them with what might be either useful or entertaining," Franklin explained, "I could not fill their Papers with private Altercation in which they had no Concern without doing them manifest Injustice." Franklin urged young printers to follow his example and not "pollute their Presses and disgrace their Profession by such infamous Practices." Yet his grandson, whose education Franklin had personally supervised, followed an entirely different course. During the Federalist era of the early American republic, Bache led the opposition press, angrily denouncing the administrations of George Washington and John Adams, and pushing public opinion toward the first change in party government in American history.

Benjamin Franklin had not approved of the marriage of his only daughter, Sarah, to Richard Bache, a jovial, pleasure-loving, and not particularly successful Philadelphia merchant. But Franklin was entirely devoted to their son, his namesake, Benjamin Franklin Bache, who was born in Franklin's house in 1769. When the colonies declared their independence from Great Britain in 1776, Franklin went to become America's agent in France during the Revolution. He took along his seven-year-old grandson, Benny Bache, planning to give him a superior education. Benny first attended school in Paris, where the lessons were in French. Before long, Franklin observed that his grandson spoke French better than English. Concerned that the French schools were too aristocratic, Franklin switched the boy to a more democratic school in Geneva, Switzerland.

Little Benjamin's grandfather never visited him in Geneva. Instead, he sent him practical advice of the sort he published in his *Poor Richard's Almanack* on hard work and developing good habits. Finally, in 1783, alarmed by reports that the boy was not eating well and living in poor conditions, Franklin moved the 14-year-old Benny back to Paris. He decided that his grandson needed a trade, and thought that his own trade of printing would enable the boy to "make his way good in the World."

Benny was sent to live and work with the printer François Ambroise Didot. He wrote in his diary, "My grandfather has induced Mr. Didot, the best printer of this Century, or that has ever been seen, to take me into his

Benjamin Franklin Bache's *Aurora,* originally known as the *General Advertiser,* drew notice for its coverage of congressional debates and for its publication of foreign news. As with most newspapers of the day, such news appeared on inside pages, while the first page was dedicated to advertisements and announcements.

house for a time to teach me his art." At last, in July 1785, Benjamin Franklin and his grandson returned to Philadelphia, where Benny had a joyful reunion with his parents and brothers and sisters. Bache enrolled in the University of Pennsylvania and graduated two years later. Still, his critics would later blame his radical politics on his "foreign" education.

Although Benjamin Franklin was now too old to return to printing, he still loved the business and proudly bought and furnished a printing house for his grandson to manage—under his supervision. The shop was located on Market Street, close to Franklin's

home. Bache began by publishing school textbooks, such as *Lessons for Children.* For more mature reading, he published the writings of the revolutionary pamphleteer Tom Paine, whose politics Bache greatly admired. He was devastated when his grandfather died in 1790. Benjamin Franklin left most of his estate to Bache's parents, but to Benny he left his printing supplies and equipment. Bache was determined to carry on his grandfather's views, opposing aristocracy and slavery and promoting democratic government. In 1791 he married Margaret Markoe, whom he had courted for several years. Struggling financially, he had to ask his parents for assistance to permit him to marry. Later, after he and Margaret married, he wrote to his parents, "I am no longer Little Benjamin, I am the large, bearded Benjamin, and what is worse—married. Yes at 22."

In 1790 the federal government moved from New York to Philadelphia, where it would remain over the next decade while the new capital was being built in the District of Columbia. With the government in his home city, Bache started a newspaper, which he dedicated to *"the public good,"* and which he promised would be strictly impartial. On October 1, 1790, the first issue of the *General Advertiser and Political, Commercial, Agricultural and Literary Journal* was published. In addition to political and economic issues, Bache planned to feature articles on the arts and sciences, to improve his readers' lives as well as their political awareness. The paper drew notice for its superior coverage of the debates in Congress and for its publication of foreign news. The *General Advertiser* appeared six days a week, and whenever Benjamin was away, Margaret brought the paper out.

In the first issue of the *General Advertiser,* Bache wrote: "If the PEOPLE are enlightened the Nation stands and flourishes, thro' ignorance it falls or degenerates." He did not intend to publish stories about "a horrid murder, shocking suicide, or...boxing battle," but planned to produce a positive paper that would help citizens build a new nation. Knowing that Secretary of State Thomas Jefferson would determine which newspapers would be paid to print the federal laws, Bache offered his services.

At that time about 100 newspapers operated in the new American nation, most of them favoring the Federalist party. Papers started in cities and were financially subsidized by commercial interests. These same commer-

cial interests supported Alexander Hamilton's economic plans—which Jefferson and his followers opposed. Jefferson was anxious to establish a newspaper in the new capital sympathetic to his Republican party (sometimes called the Democratic-Republican party—and not to be confused with the later Republican party that emerged over the slavery issue before the Civil War). Jefferson gave the government printing contracts to the printer of another Philadelphia newspaper. But he encouraged young Bache to make the *General Advertiser* a general distribution paper throughout the states, as the voice of the newly emerging Republican party. When Bache found that a daily newspaper was difficult to distribute outside of Philadelphia, Jefferson suggested that he publish a weekly edition that would summarize news from the daily paper. This effort also failed to take hold and Jefferson turned instead to Philip Freneau's *National Gazette,* which was founded in 1791.

At the time, Bache complained about the fatigue and anxiety of producing a daily paper. "I work hard, that's clear yet perhaps am not as economical as I ought to be, and want regularity in my business," he wrote to his father. But Bache persisted. Freneau's *National Gazette* lost money and closed by the end of 1793. That left Bache's paper the leading Republican newspaper for the rest of the decade.

The 1790s were turbulent times in both the United States and Europe. The French Revolution erupted in 1793, making news that attracted readers but that increasingly divided them into pro- and anti-French camps. Learning that the king and queen had been executed, and of others who perished in the Reign of Terror, the Federalists worried that the excesses of the French Revolution might spill over into America. By contrast, the Republicans saw the French as follow-

Benjamin Franklin Bache

BORN
August 12, 1769
Philadelphia, Pennsylvania

DIED
September 10, 1798
Philadelphia, Pennsylvania

EDUCATION
Private schools in France and Switzerland; B.A., University of Pennsylvania, 1787

ACCOMPLISHMENTS
Editor, *Philadelphia General Advertiser* (1790–94); editor, *Philadelphia Aurora* (1794–98)

"Profession costs nothing, and it will be remembered that the present [Washington] administration has been an administration of profession only; the profession of republicanism, but the practice of monarchy and aristocracy; the profession of sympathy and interest for a great nation and an ally struggling for liberty, but a real devotion to the cause of the combined despots; the profession of a neutral character, cold and indifferent to the warring power, but a warm and sincere attachment to Great Britain...in a word the profession of honor, justice, candor, dignity and good faith, when dishonor, injustice, treachery, meanness and perfidy have given a hue to our public proceedings. What an eight years glorious administration!"

—from the *Philadelphia Aurora* (December 17, 1796)

ing the example of the American Revolution. They worried that a conservative counterrevolution might suppress liberty in both France and the United States.

Devoutly pro-French, Bache's paper became increasingly strident in its attacks on anything that leaned toward the British or toward social or economic aristocracy. Since newspapers were then entitled to mail issues of their papers to other newspapers for free postage, many newspapers reprinted the articles that appeared in Bache's *General Advertiser*, which made itself heard throughout the states. He was outraged when President George Washington kept America neutral in the conflict between France and Great Britain. Bache saw Washington's followers—especially Secretary of the Treasury Alexander Hamilton—trying to remold the country after the British class system. He used his paper to defend the Jeffersonian ideal of an agrarian nation with a small central government against the Hamiltonian

plan for a stronger government that promoted banking and manufacturing.

Bache had originally praised President Washington for presiding with "dignity & wisdom," and he proclaimed widespread confidence in Washington's administration. But during Washington's second term, Bache concluded that the President was accepting too much advice from Hamilton. Bache was furious when Washington signed the Jay Treaty of 1795, settling American differences with Great Britain. He believed that the treaty sold out the general public in favor of the "privileged class" of merchants. From that point he set out to destroy Washington's public image. His newspaper, renamed the *Philadelphia Aurora* (and featuring a rising sun on its masthead), found nothing good to say about the President. At one point Bache even published some forged letters that made it seem as if Washington had been willing to give up the Revolution and make peace with Great Britain. Washington vehemently denied the charges. The President complained that Bache's papers were "outrages on common decency" and they had treated him like "a common pickpocket." The steady beat of criticism from the press made Washington happy to retire from the Presidency at the end of his second term in 1797.

Washington and other Federalists believed that papers like Bache's were stirring up the spirit of "faction," or party, and were inciting public opinion against the government. Bache, for his part, thought there was not enough democracy in America. Like Jefferson, Bache believed it essential to keep the people informed so that they would take charge of the government and not abandon their rights to wealthy elites. Although his language was exaggerated and extreme, his concern over the future of democratic government was real. His Federalist opponents were determined to go to great lengths to silence him and other opposition newspapers.

When the United States seemed on the brink of war with France, during the administration of John Adams, the Federalists accused Bache of being a "French hireling." Federalists in Congress steamed over their treatment in the *Aurora*. In 1798 House Speaker Jonathan Dayton barred Bache from taking notes on the proceedings from the floor of the House, where other journalists were allowed to operate. On July 14, 1798, President Adams signed the Alien and Sedition Act of 1798. This law made it a crime to publish "false, scandalous and malicious writing or writings against the government of the United States, or either house of the Congress of the United States, or the President of the United States." Bache protested that the law was a violation of the First Amendment to the Constitution, which protected the freedom of the press. Pretty soon, he warned, it would be treason simply "to laugh at the cut of a coat of a member of Congress."

That summer Bache was arrested for publishing information suggesting that the French were willing to make peace with the United States. He posted bail but did not live to stand trial. In August a yellow fever epidemic swept through Philadelphia. The safest thing would have been to leave the city and settle his family in the countryside for awhile. But Bache could not afford to suspend publication of the *Aurora*. There had been a price to pay for taking on so popular a figure as George Washington. Bache's attacks had driven away subscribers and advertisers and almost ruined his paper. Despite the danger, he labored away in Philadelphia. On September 3 his wife, Margaret, gave birth to their fourth child. Days later Bache contracted yellow fever and died. He was only 29 years old. His wife kept the *Aurora*

going, publishing an obituary that declared her husband "a man inflexible in virtue, unappalled by power or persecution." She hired his assistant, William Duane, to publish the *Aurora*, married him in 1800, and had five more children.

Benjamin Franklin Bache had always been sure he would triumph over his opponents, but he did not live to see the fruits of his labor. In 1800 Thomas Jefferson defeated John Adams for the Presidency. The Republican party took power and the Federalist party faded away. It was the nation's first peaceful transfer of power from one party to another, and a significant milestone in American democracy. Newspapers like Bache's *Aurora* had stirred and changed public opinion. Significantly, the new government allowed the Alien and Sedition Acts to expire, further assuring freedom of the press. As one Federalist congressman lamented, "The newspapers are an overmatch for any government."

FURTHER READING

Fay, Bernard. *The Two Franklins: Fathers of American Democracy*. 1933. Reprint, New York: AMS Press, 1969.

Rosenfeld, Richard N. *American Aurora: A Democratic-Republican Returns: The Suppressed History of Our Nation's Beginnings and the Heroic Newspaper that Tried to Report It*. New York: St. Martin's, 1997.

Smith, James Morton. *Freedom's Fetters: The Alien and Sedition Laws and American Civil Liberties*. Ithaca, N.Y.: Cornell University Press, 1956.

Smith, Jeffrey A. *Franklin and Bache: Envisioning the Enlightened Republic*. New York: Oxford University Press, 1990.

———. *Printers and Press Freedom, The Ideology of Early American Journalism*. New York: Oxford University Press, 1988.

Tagg, James. *Benjamin Franklin Bache and the Philadelphia Aurora*. Philadelphia, Pa.: University of Pennsylvania Press, 1991.

Elias Boudinot

JACKSONIAN ERA FOUNDER OF THE NATIVE AMERICAN PRESS

Aware that the white community outside the Cherokee Nation could communicate by writing on paper, the Cherokee Indian silver craftsman Sequoyah set out to empower his people with their own alphabet. Breaking up Cherokee words into syllables, he created symbols for each one. By 1821 Sequoyah had perfected his system, which Cherokees of all ages could learn in just a few days. Soon portions of the Bible were translated into the Cherokees' own language, and a movement started on behalf of printing the news in Cherokee as well. In May 1826 Elias Boudinot rose in the First Presbyterian Church in Philadelphia to appeal for funds to establish a Cherokee newspaper.

"You here behold an Indian," said the handsome young man, who dressed in white man's clothes and had taken a white man's name, "my kindred are Indians, and my fathers sleeping in the wilderness grave—they too were Indians." He stood before them, "delegated by my native country to seek her interest, to labor for her respectability, and by my public efforts to assist in raising her to an equal standing with other nations of the earth." Boudinot's eloquent and emotional appeal raised the money that purchased a printing press and had Sequoyah's symbols set into type. On February 21, 1828, at New Echota (now part of Georgia), the first issue of the *Cherokee Phoenix* was published, with columns printed alternately in English and Cherokee. The weekly paper was edited by Elias Boudinot.

He was born Galagina (which means "the Buck") Oowatie ("in a lonely cabin, overspread by the forest oak") in the mountains of the Cherokee Nation. The nation was then a vast territory covering portions of present-day Georgia, Alabama, North Carolina, and Tennessee. Of all the southeastern Indian tribes, the Cherokees had adjusted most to the white community's way of life. In addition to developing their own written language, the Cherokees adopted a constitution similar to the U.S. Constitution that established legislative, executive, and judicial branches. Many Cherokees farmed the land; some operated plantations and owned slaves. The fundamental difference between the two communities was that the Cherokees owned their land communally rather than individually.

As a young boy, Galagina began his education at a Christian mission school in Spring Place (in northwestern Georgia). He was a good student and at 15 was sent off by the missionaries to attend the Institute for Instructing and Educating the Heathen (also known as the Foreign Mission School) in Cornwall, Connecticut. While there, he took the

name of Elias Boudinot, after a statesman and philanthropist who had long been interested in helping Native Americans. Students at the school included his cousin John Ridge, other American Indians, Polynesians, and Chinese, as well as white Americans studying to be missionaries.

John Ridge was the son of Walking-on-the-Mountain-Tops, also known as The Ridge or Major Ridge because of his military service under General Andrew Jackson. A wealthy Cherokee planter, Major Ridge had adopted the white ways of life and wanted the best education for his son. When the younger Ridge fell in love with Sarah Bird Northrup, daughter of the steward of the school, and married her, a public furor erupted, since many white people objected to intermarriage between the races. Elias Boudinot also fell in love with a young townswoman, Harriet Gold. At first her father forbade the marriage, but when she fell

deathly ill, he relented. Harriet recovered and married Boudinot on March 28, 1826. As a result of the controversy over mixed marriages, the school closed.

Elias and Harriet Boudinot toured northeastern cities, lecturing and seeking funds to start a school and a newspaper in the Cherokee Nation. When their tour raised enough money, the General Council of the Cherokee Nation leased land in New Echota to build a print shop and newspaper office. A medical missionary serving among the Cherokee, Samuel Worcester, went to Boston to purchase the press and have the Cherokee type made. It was Worcester who named the weekly paper the Cherokee Phoenix—after the mythical bird consumed by fire but able to rise again from its own ashes. As editor, Boudinot printed the laws and public documents of the nation, Cherokee customs, and contemporary news, mostly reprinted

The *Cherokee Phoenix* was published in this building, now the New Echota State Historic Site in Georgia.

Under the editorship of Elias Boudinot, the *Cherokee Phoenix* appeared in both English and Cherokee. Boudinot wanted to debate the issues dividing the Cherokee Nation, but Chief John Ross wanted the paper to promote unity instead.

or rewritten from other newspapers, such as the *National Intelligencer*. "We do not wish to be thought as striving to rival other papers of the day, by exhibiting to the public learning, talents and information, for these we do not profess to possess," Boudinot wrote modestly in a letter soliciting subscriptions. His objective was to write for "the benefit of the Cherokees, who, as you know, are uninformed."

As editor, Boudinot wrote weekly editorials and translated them into Cherokee, a laborious task. "One cannot write fast in Cherokee," he commented. He was also proofreader and business manager for the paper.

Boudinot and Samuel Worcester further collaborated in producing the first Cherokee hymn book and Cherokee editions of the New Testament gospels. Boudinot devoted many of his editorials to the need for temperance. He saw liquor destroying Indians and causing violence in the community. "Among us, it has been a wide spreading evil," he wrote in the *Phoenix*. "It has cost us lives and a

train of troubles. It has been an enemy to our national prosperity, industry, and intellectual improvement."

The *Cherokee Phoenix* was not financially profitable. For all his work Boudinot earned only $300 a year as editor, less than what the printer received for printing the paper. In November 1828 Boudinot threatened to quit unless he got an assistant and a raise. Cherokee chief John Ross went before the General Council and insisted that the newspaper was so important for the Cherokee people that he would rather pay the money himself than see the paper fail. This plea convinced the General Council to raise Boudinot's salary and hire an assistant for the newspaper.

Like the newspaper, the Cherokee Council House and Court House were located in New Echota, a town with shops and homes much like those in any other southern town. The Cherokees hoped that by copying the white community they could live in peace with their white neighbors. But whites wanted their land, especially after gold was discovered in northeastern Georgia in 1829. White gangs, aided by a few Indian allies, raided the Cherokee lands, driving Cherokees from their homes. The state of Georgia refused to recognize the Cherokees as a sovereign nation and set up a lottery to distribute Indian lands among white settlers. Samuel Worcester and other missionaries were thrown into prison.

Chief John Ross went to Washington to plead his people's cause with President Andrew Jackson. Although Ross had once fought under Jackson's command, he could not convince him. While New England Whigs supported the Cherokees' claims in Congress, Jacksonian Democrats stood for states' rights. President Jackson argued that the Indians stood in the path of civilization, and he promoted passage of the Indian Removal Act, to move all tribes west of the Mississippi and away from white settlers. In March 1832 the Supreme Court ruled in favor of the missionaries and the Cherokees. Writing the majority opinion in *Cherokee Nation v. Georgia,* Chief Justice John Marshall asserted that the Indian tribes "had always been considered as distinct, independent, political communities, retaining their original natural rights." The laws of Georgia had no force in the Cherokee lands, Marshall declared, and white citizens of Georgia had no right to take Indian lands. When he heard this ruling, President Jackson reportedly said, "John Marshall has rendered his decision: now let him enforce it." Ignoring the Court, Georgia and the U.S. government continued policies aimed at removing the Cherokees.

The Cherokee Nation debated whether to stay on their ancestral homeland or go west. Boudinot's cousin John Ridge strongly doubted that the Cherokees could retain their native lands against Georgia and the federal government, and over time he persuaded his father and his cousin to

change their minds too. Boudinot wanted to make the newspaper a vehicle for conducting the debate. He believed that as public property the press should be as "free as the breeze that glides upon the surface." But Chief Ross completely disagreed. Ross warned that "the toleration of diversified views" in the newspaper would only stir commotion and confusion, which would prove disastrous to the nation. The chief insisted on *"unity of sentiment and action for the good of all,"* even if that meant stifling freedom of the press.

Rejecting such censorship, Boudinot resigned as editor in September 1832. The General Council appointed Ross's brother-in-law, Elijah Hicks, as editor. Hicks suppressed any differences of opinion and the paper noticeably declined in style and influence. In 1835 Boudinot's brother Stand Watie, who had helped him edit the *Cherokee Phoenix,* led a group that seized the press, type, and paper. Chief Ross protested this action to the U.S. Indian agent for the Cherokees, but the agent declined to intervene on the grounds that the press belonged to Boudinot because his fund-raising tours had financed its purchase. The Cherokee Nation never recovered the press.

Greater tragedy awaited the Cherokee Nation. Chief Ross returned to Washington to argue the Cherokees' case with the federal government. Taking advantage of divisions within the Cherokee Nation, the government instead negotiated with the rival faction led by John Ridge and Elias Boudinot, who sought the best possible terms if the Cherokees moved west. In December 1835 Ridge and Boudinot signed a treaty by which the federal government agreed to deposit $4.5 million in the U.S. Treasury to be held as credit for the Cherokee in return for their lands. The "Treaty Party," as those who signed it were called, left for the west, but the great majority of

Elias Boudinot

BORN
1803
Cherokee Nation, Georgia

DIED
June 22, 1839
Indian Territory, Oklahoma

EDUCATION
Foreign Mission School, Cornwall, Connecticut

ACCOMPLISHMENTS
Editor, *Cherokee Phoenix* (1828–32)

> "There is, in Indian history, something very melancholy, and which seems to establish a mournful precedent for the future events of the sons of the forest. We have seen everywhere the poor aborigines melt away before the white population.... Must they perish? Must they all...go down in sorrow to their grave?... Will you push them from you, or will you save them? Let humanity answer."
>
> —from *An Address to the Whites* (Philadelphia, 1826)

Cherokees opposed the treaty and refused to move. In 1838 U.S. army troops under General Winfield Scott forcibly evicted the Cherokees from their land and forced them on a "Trail of Tears" to the Indian Territory (in present-day Oklahoma). Of the 15,000 Cherokees who walked the trail, 4,000—many of them children or elderly—died of cold and exhaustion.

Tragedy also befell the Boudinot family. Harriet Boudinot died in 1836, soon after her seventh child was stillborn. With a large family to raise, Boudinot married Delight Sargeant, a white missionary who worked among the Cherokees. With his wife, Boudinot continued to travel through New England to seek financial and political help for the Cherokees.

In the Indian Territory the Boudinot family lived with the missionary Samuel Worcester while they built a house nearby. On June 22, 1839, several Cherokees called on Boudinot, asking for medicine. When he came out to help them, they stabbed and tomahawked him to death. On the same day other Cherokees dragged John Ridge from his home and murdered him, while another group ambushed Major Ridge and shot him dead. The conspirators had been part of a secret band, all of whom had lost family on the Trail of Tears. They had sworn revenge on those who had given away their ancestral lands without their consent. Boudinot fell victim to his zeal for preserving his people, his friend Worcester lamented. "In his own view he risked his life to save his people from ruin, and he realized his fears."

FURTHER READING

Collier, John. *The Indians of the Americas: The Long Hope*. New York: New American Library, 1947.

Debo, Angie. *A History of the Indians of the United States*. Norman: University of Oklahoma Press, 1970.

Ehle, John. *Trail of Tears: The Rise and Fall of the Cherokee Nation*. New York: Doubleday, 1988.

Moulton, Gary E. *John Ross: Cherokee Chief*. Athens: University of Georgia Press, 1978.

Perdue, Theda. *The Cherokee*. New York: Chelsea House, 1989.

Perdue, Theda, ed. *Cherokee Editor: The Writings of Elias Boudinot*. Athens: University of Georgia Press, 1996.

Elijah P. Lovejoy

MARTYRED
JOURNALIST

The movement to abolish slavery in the United States became entangled with freedom of the press when an abolitionist editor in Alton, Illinois, was killed by a mob trying to silence his newspaper. Elijah Pierce Lovejoy published a religious newspaper designed to save souls, and he had not intended to lead a crusade against slavery. But when his conscience led him into the antislavery movement, he increasingly devoted his paper to that unpopular cause, regardless of the danger to his life. A fighter for what he believed to be right, he knew that to surrender to threats and accept censorship would mean the end of a free press. Even more than his editorials, his death convinced countless other Americans to accept this view.

A fighter for what he believed to be right, Elijah P. Lovejoy would not accept censorship of his antislavery newspapers.

"Mr. Chairman, I do not admit that it is the business of this assembly to decide whether I shall or shall not publish a newspaper in this city. The gentlemen have, as the lawyers say, made a wrong issue. I have the right to do it. I know that I have the right freely to speak and publish my sentiments, subject only to the laws of the land for the abuse of that right. This right was given me by my Maker, and is solemnly guaranteed to me by the constitution of these United States and of this state."

—from an address Lovejoy made to an assembly in Alton, Illinois, four days before his death

Born in Maine, the oldest of nine children of the Reverend David Lovejoy and Elizabeth Patee Lovejoy, Elijah was raised in a stern religious household. He learned to read by using the Bible as his textbook, and grew up listening to his father's sermons on living a righteous life. Elijah was a physically well-built, athletic youth who won notice for his courage in sports, as he would in other endeavors throughout his life.

In 1823 Elijah Lovejoy entered the Baptist-sponsored Waterville College (now Colby College) in Maine. After graduating at the head of his class, he spent the next year teaching, but found the job unchallenging. He decided to try his luck out west in the new state of Illinois. Lovejoy had traveled only as far as Boston when he ran out of money. Unable to find a job there, he walked to New York City. On June 1, 1827, he recorded in his diary: "I am now 250 miles from home, in a land of strangers and but 80 cents in my pocket." In New York he found a temporary job selling newspaper subscriptions. Finally, a loan from a friend helped him to head west by boat and by wagon, with long stretches of walk-ing between rides. He eventually reached the Mississippi.

Since Missouri had no public schools at the time, Lovejoy went to St. Louis to open a school. The school was a financial success, and in 1830 he invested some of his profits in a half interest in the *St. Louis Times*, becoming the paper's editor. As a Whig, Lovejoy used the *Times* to support Henry Clay and criticize the Democrats, led by Andrew Jackson. Although his paper concentrated on Whig politics, it also opposed dueling and denounced the evils of alcoholic beverages. Rarely did his paper deal with slavery, except to carry advertisements for the sale of slaves or rewards for the return of those who had escaped.

While attending a revival meeting at the First Presbyterian Church in 1832, Lovejoy underwent a religious conversion. At that meeting he heard the fiery preacher declare that slavery was as great a sin as murder. Lovejoy made a profession of faith and joined the church. Feeling the need to follow his new religious zeal, he chose to sell the *Times* and become a minister. Returning East, Lovejoy enrolled in Princeton Theological Seminary, whose program he finished in a speedy 13 months. He could have spent his life safely as a minister in New England but felt drawn back to the West. When some prominent citizens in Missouri invited him to edit a religious newspaper in St. Louis, Elijah wrote his brother Owen: "They are impatiently calling me to the West, and to the West I must go."

That November the 31-year-old Lovejoy published the first issue of the *St. Louis Observer*, a Presbyterian newspaper. Lovejoy's paper was known for its extreme hostility to the Roman Catholic Church and its criticism of other Protestant churches that did not meet the editor's personal standards of theological purity. As before, his paper took positions against alcohol and tobacco, but now he also defended the rights of slaves. Although Lovejoy insisted he was not an abolitionist, he argued that slaves had souls and needed religious education just as white people did. Seeing the many instances of cruelty toward African Americans in Missouri, particularly the brutal murder of a black sailor by a mob in St. Louis, Lovejoy found his position steadily hardening. By 1834 he wrote an editorial calling for the end of slavery. These positions won little support in slaveholding Missouri, nor did they attract many advertisers to the *Observer*, which was always financially shaky.

In addition to his editorial duties, Elijah Lovejoy was an evangelist who traveled around the state. While preaching, he met Celia Ann French of St. Charles, Missouri. On March 4, 1835, they were married. Lovejoy described his wife as a tall, well-shaped woman with a fair complexion and large blue eyes, who was "intelligent, refined, and of agreeable manners." But as happy as they were, theirs would be a short and traumatic marriage.

Lovejoy's antislavery editorials and sermons angered slaveholders, who threatened to tar and feather him. In November 1835 a proslavery meeting in St. Louis passed a resolution declaring that freedom of the press did not include the right to discuss slavery, because that question too deeply affected "the vital interests of the slaveholding States" for them to tolerate any disagreement. Lovejoy responded by quoting the Missouri constitution, which promised everyone the right to speak and write freely on any subject. "The truth is, my fellow citizens, if you give ground a single inch, there is no stopping place," he warned.

Threats against the editor and the newspaper made the owners of the *Observer* nervously demand that he mute his rhetoric about slavery. When

Lovejoy refused, the owners asked for his resignation. But at the last minute they sold the *Observer,* and the new owner retained Lovejoy as editor.

After his editorial attacks against a lynch mob that burned a black man in 1836, mounting threats caused Lovejoy to leave St. Louis and move his family and his paper to the free state of Illinois. He headed 20 miles up the Mississippi River to Alton, then one of the largest and most prosperous cities in Illinois (Chicago, by contrast, was still a small town with a fraction of Alton's population). But Lovejoy's antislavery reputation preceded him, and even in the free state he encountered proslavery sentiment. When his printing press arrived by ship on a Sunday, the pious Lovejoy refused to move it to a more secure place on the Sabbath. A proslavery mob seized the press from the dock and threw it into the river.

Many of the townsfolk of Alton had emigrated from New England and were neither proslavery nor proabolitionist, but they were deeply troubled by the mob's action. A public meeting in Alton condemned the outrage and promised Lovejoy money to buy a new press. In return, the young editor assured them that he planned to publish a religious rather than an abolitionist paper. "When I was in St. Louis I felt myself called upon to treat at large upon the subject of slavery as I was in a state where the evil existed," he explained. "Now having come to a free state where the evil does not exist, I feel myself less called upon to discuss the subject than when I was in St. Louis. But, gentlemen, as long as I am an American citizen, and as long as American blood runs in these veins, I shall hold myself at liberty to speak, to write, and to publish whatever I please on any subject."

Of the four papers in Alton, the *Observer* quickly built the largest circulation, and Lovejoy appeared headed

Elijah P. Lovejoy

BORN
November 9, 1802
Albion, Maine

DIED
November 7, 1837
Alton, Illinois

EDUCATION
B.A., Waterville (now Colby) College, 1826; attended Princeton Theological Seminary, 1833

ACCOMPLISHMENTS
Editor, *St. Louis Times* (1830–32); editor, *St. Louis Observer* (1833–36); editor, *Alton Observer* (1836–37)

On November 7, 1837, a mob destroyed Elijah Lovejoy's printing press. He was shot and killed while trying to stop them.

for a prosperous future. But while the paper focused on religion, he continued to publish articles and editorials attacking slavery. The more people objected, the more militant he grew. On February 9, 1837, the *Observer* published an article entitled "What Is Slavery?" in which Lovejoy identified the economic recession that year as God's punishment for the sin of slavery. Citizens of Alton complained that the editor had broken his pledge not to publish an abolitionist paper.

Lovejoy felt certain that if he stood firm on his principles, others would change their minds and accept that he had been right. But the slavery issue proved to be too emotional for rational discussion. By July 1837 Lovejoy finally admitted to himself and his readers that he was an abolitionist.

Local anger rose against him and candidates ran for office promising to shut down his paper. Lovejoy was mobbed on the streets, and his home and the *Observer* office were ransacked. His printing presses were repeatedly dumped into the Mississippi. Proslavery newspapers cheered whenever the *Observer* was quieted, but antislavery papers in other cities helped raise the money for Lovejoy to buy new presses.

When a third printing press arrived from Cincinnati in September 1837, Lovejoy's friends gathered to protect it from a mob intent on destroying it. The mayor of Alton promised that the city would protect the press, so Lovejoy's supporters left. That night a mob forced its way into the storehouse, seized the press, and threw it into the river. Anticipating worse attacks, Lovejoy slept at night with a loaded weapon at his bedside.

Lovejoy had called for an Illinois antislavery convention to meet in Alton, in October, which further aroused his opponents. The popular Illinois state attorney general, Usher Linder, then called a public meeting in Alton to determine how to shut Lovejoy's newspaper down. "Why should I flee from Alton?" Lovejoy asked the audience. "Is this not a free state? When attacked by a mob at St. Louis, I came here to be at the home of freedom and of the law. The mob has pursued me here, and why should I retreat again? Where can I be safe if not here? Have I not a right to claim the protection of the laws?" Despite all the violence directed toward him, Lovejoy felt at peace because of his inner convictions. "Sir, I dare not flee away from Alton," he explained. "Should I attempt it, I should feel that the angel of the Lord with his flaming sword was pursuing me wherever I went." His remarks moved many in the audience to tears.

Early on the morning of November 7, a fourth press reached Alton's docks. Lovejoy's supporters quickly moved the press to a nearby warehouse. Facing no initial opposition, they believed they had won a bloodless battle for truth. But the rest of Alton feared the worst and merchants closed their shops to protect their goods. That night Lovejoy and his supporters—young abolitionists from nearby towns—stood guard at the warehouse. Before long a proslavery mob, fortified by liquor, marched on the warehouse and pelted it with stones and fired shots. With cries of "Burn them out!" the mob raised a ladder to the roof, aiming to set it on fire. Lovejoy and others rushed out and pushed the ladder over.

Meanwhile, a woman supporter went to the Presbyterian church to ring its bells. The bells drew a larger crowd, but none of the onlookers wanted to risk their lives stopping the mob. During a second attempt to set the building afire, Lovejoy again came out to push the ladder over. This time he was hit by five shots. "My God, I am shot!" he cried as he fell. He died instantly. Cheering when they learned he was dead, the mob demolished the press and tried to destroy the building. Most of Lovejoy's defenders retreated to save their lives, but one who remained pulled the handkerchief from the dead man's face and shouted, "See your work, brave men!" What was left of the mob dispersed. Two days later Elijah Lovejoy was buried—on his 35th birthday.

Illinois brought charges for inciting the riot not against the mob but against Lovejoy's defenders. In court Attorney General Linder said: "They talk of being friends to good order; lovers of law. Have they not taken the law into their own hands, and violated the law of man of God in depriving man of life? And for what? For a press! A printing press! A press brought here to teach the slave rebellion; to excite the slaves to law, to preach murder in the name of religion; to strike dismay in the hearts of the people, and spread desolation over the face of this land."

But the jury found Lovejoy's supporters innocent. Public opinion in Illinois and across the nation had been shocked by Lovejoy's murder. The case ruined Linder's political career and destroyed the reputation of Alton, which went into decline. Four months after her husband's death, Celia Ann Lovejoy gave birth to their second child, a daughter. Lovejoy's widow eventually married one of the men who had been in the warehouse that night

and who was wounded with him.

The mob had killed but not silenced the editor. Lovejoy's death shocked and shamed many others into carrying on his antislavery crusade. Newspapers condemned his murder, and ministers devoted sermons to "the martyr of Alton." Because Lovejoy died as much for freedom of the press as for freedom of the slaves, many Americans who had never seen or thought much about the slave system came to believe that either freedom would abolish slavery or slavery would abolish freedom.

New York Tribune editor Horace Greeley said of Lovejoy that "for the act of inflexibility maintaining the common rights of every citizen, he may well be deemed a martyr to public liberty." The rising young Illinois politician Abraham Lincoln denounced mob rule: "Let every man remember that to violate the law, is to trample on the blood of his father, and to tear the charter of his own, and his children's liberty." And at one meeting in Lovejoy's memory, a man named John Brown pledged himself to the destruction of slavery. The shots fired at Elijah Lovejoy had really been the first shots of the Civil War.

FURTHER READING

Dillon, Merton Lynn. *Elijah P. Lovejoy, Abolitionist Editor*. Urbana: University of Illinois Press, 1961.

Filler, Louis. *The Crusade Against Slavery, 1830-1860*. New York: Harper & Row, 1960.

Nye, Russell B. *Fettered Freedom: Civil Liberties and the Slavery Controversy, 1830-1860*. East Lansing: Michigan State University Press, 1963.

Simon, Paul. *Freedom's Champion: Elijah Lovejoy*. Carbondale: Southern Illinois University Press, 1994.

James Gordon Bennett

"THE NAPOLEON OF THE NEWSPAPER PRESS"

The distinguished journalist James Parton, writing in 1866, made a disdainful admission: the chief newspaper in the nation's greatest city was the *New York Herald*. Parton considered the *Herald* to be a "bad, good paper," for despite its gossip and scandal and mocking editorials, more people read it—and it put more correspondents in the field—than any other paper. "No matter how much we may regret this fact, or be ashamed of it," Parton wrote, "no journalist can deny it." What was worse, the entire American press seemed to be becoming "Heraldized," by which Parton meant more sensational. The man responsible for this happening was the *Herald*'s editor, James Gordon Bennett. Unlike other editors, Bennett had set out not to change society but to change the newspaper business. He thought newspapers too dull, and too tied to political parties and candidates. He wanted his paper to be exciting to read and unbound by any political strings, free to express any opinion that it wished.

James G. Bennett was born to a Roman Catholic family in predominantly Presbyterian Scotland. He was sent to a Catholic seminary, where he studied for the priesthood. Bennett was always a great reader, and the autobiography of Benjamin Franklin was one of his childhood favorites. His love of literature and history led him to leave the seminary for a career as a writer. His first published work, a tribute to the recently defeated French leader Napoléon Bonaparte, was published in a small Scottish journal. In 1819 Bennett emigrated to America. He landed first in Canada and later sailed for Boston. For a few years he worked as a clerk in a bookstore, then moved to New York City.

Bennett's first break in the newspaper business came when he met Aaron S. Willington, publisher of the *Charleston* (South Carolina) *Courier*. Willington, who happened to be in New York buying printing presses and supplies for his journal, hired Bennett as his editorial assistant. Bennett spent 10 months working for the *Courier*, learning the rudiments of newspaper work. Living in Charleston also made him sympathetic to the South and to its "peculiar institution" of slavery.

In 1823 Bennett left the *Courier* and returned to New York, where he lectured and wrote as a freelancer for several newspapers. He joined the staff of the *New York Enquirer* in 1827. The *Enquirer* was a Democratic paper, and Bennett was an avid supporter of the Democratic candidate for President, Andrew Jackson. Bennett started a series of humorous sketches that became very popular, but they seemed too irreverent for the paper and so they were canceled. Like most newspapers of the day, the *Enquirer* was gray and dull.

Tall, stoop-shouldered, and cross-eyed, young Bennett was assigned to cover sessions of the New York State legislature in Albany, and of the Congress in Washington. At the U.S. Capitol, he spent much of his time reading in the Library of Congress. One day he came across the letters of the British writer Horace Walpole about the king's court in England. These letters were so breezy and witty that he wondered why he should not try writing that way about the Washington of President John Quincy Adams. Modeling himself after Walpole, Bennett developed a style that mixed stories with analysis. His sketches were chatty, colorful, funny, and always very partisan. They were reprinted in other papers and drew attention to the young writer. In 1829, when his paper merged with another to become the *New York Courier and Enquirer*, Bennett was promoted to associate editor. However, in 1832, the paper switched from supporting Andrew Jackson to opposing him, causing Bennett to resign. During the Presidential campaign that year, he published a small Democratic paper, the *Globe*.

Bennett moved to Philadelphia to publish another Democratic newspaper, but encountered such intense fighting between factions within the local Democratic party that he gave up the paper. That experience convinced him that it was folly to try to edit party newspapers. Returning to New York, Bennett was impressed by the city's first "penny paper," the *New York Sun*, started in 1833 by Benjamin H. Day. The *Sun* was sold on street corners by vendors rather than by subscription, as the better papers were. These "better" papers, aimed at businesspeople, did not see the need to compete with the *Sun*. But when the *Sun* rejected Bennett for a job he decided to start

his own paper in competition, reasoning that the large middle- and working-class audience in the city would buy a newspaper that presented solid news in a spicy style. Among the partners he sought for this new venture was the young printer Horace Greeley, who turned him down.

In 1835, at the age of 40, Bennett launched his own penny newspaper, the *New York Herald*. With only $500 to invest in the business, Bennett operated out of the cellar of a building on Wall Street. His desk consisted of a plank across two flour barrels. He promised that the *Herald* would rely on common sense rather than any political party's doctrines. At first the paper focused on local news, police courts,

James Gordon Bennett set out not to change society but to change the newspaper business. He was a pioneer in the creation of mass-circulation newspapers.

During the Civil War, Bennett's *New York Herald* sent squads of correspondents out to cover the battlefields.

business activities, and theater reviews. Its style was short and snappy, emphasizing crime, accidents, and human-interest stories. In its early days Bennett handled practically every activity of the paper himself, writing editorials, reporting, and soliciting advertisements.

Bennett filled his paper with bits of gossip and scandal. "He laughed at everything and everybody," James Parton observed, and readers laughed with him. Bennett's hero, Andrew Jackson, aided the paper by warring against the Bank of the United States. This made Wall Street a focal point of the nation. Each afternoon, Bennett went out on Wall Street to pick up stock news, and he printed enough business information to give

respectable businessmen an excuse to purchase his paper—although they would blush when caught reading it. December 1835 saw a major fire on Wall Street, and Bennett with his notebook covered every aspect of it. The *Herald* published a picture of the Stock Exchange burning and a map of the burned-out district. "American journalism was born amid the roaring flames of the great fire of 1835," Parton observed. Bennett's paper became less notable for its editorial opinions (which blew every which way with public opinion) than for its colorful and concise news stories. No other paper at that time spent as much as Bennett did to get the news.

The circulation of the *Herald* rose steadily, particularly with its coverage of crime news and spectacular murder trials. The *Herald* won special notice for its reporting on the murder of Ellen Jewett, a beautiful young prostitute. Bennett himself visited the scene of the crime and interviewed the witnesses. He made the story not just a dull police report, but an examination of the morality of society. His coverage of the Jewett case made the *Herald* the best-known paper in New York.

A lapsed Catholic, Bennett married Henrietta Crean, a music teacher who had immigrated from Ireland. Though they were married in the Catholic Church, Bennet did not hesitate to attack Catholic policies in the *Herald*. In turn, the paper was denounced from church pulpits. But every controversy just made more people want to read the paper. By attacking his church, the editor had demonstrated that nothing was sacred to him, in religion as well as in politics. By promising to avoid "the dirt of party politics," as he put, it Bennett felt himself free to express his candid opinions on every public issue. Above all, he argued: "An editor must always be with the people, think with them, feel with them, and he need fear nothing. He will always be right, always strong, always popular, always free."

Although Bennett picked up ideas from many other journalists, he was never shy about taking credit for innovations in the press. He called himself "the Napoleon of the newspaper press." He claimed responsibility for starting the mass-circulation newspapers and for keeping them free from political control. He sent correspondents to London, Paris, and Washington to send back the news and to beat his competitors. He expanded his paper's coverage of the city's social elites. He began printing woodcut illustrations and maps, with pictures of murder victims, crime scenes, dancing girls, and Presidential inaugurations. The *Herald* covered prize fights and other sporting news, as well as train wrecks and steamboat sinkings. Bennett had a knack for knowing what readers wanted. He raised the price of the paper to two cents and enlarged the paper by a third and purchased new presses that could print more papers faster. He organized a fleet of newsboats to be the first to get the news from arriving ocean vessels. He was also quick to embrace the telegraph as a way of getting stories quickly, ahead of his competition. Above all, he hired the largest corps of reporters and correspondents of any newspaper in the country.

By the late 1830s Bennett's *Herald* carried more advertisements than any other paper. He let anyone advertise who could pay for it, even those who produced quack medicines and groups with which he disagreed, such as abolitionists who wanted to end slavery. His politics leaned toward the Democrats but were independent of the party. Bennett opposed Democratic candidates but usually supported the views in the Democratic party's platform. He strongly endorsed Manifest Destiny, the idea that the United States was destined to spread across the North American continent. He favored annexation of Texas and war with Mexico. He had contempt for American Indians and black slaves. Yet in 1856 Bennett supported the antislavery Republican candidate, John C. Frémont, for President. He switched back to the Democrats, and then in 1860 endorsed a moderate Unionist, John Bell, for President.

James Gordon Bennett

BORN

September 1, 1795
Keith, Banffshire, Scotland

DIED

June 1, 1872
New York, New York

EDUCATION

Public schools and Blair's College, a Catholic seminary (1810–14)

ACCOMPLISHMENTS

Editorial assistant, *Charleston Courier* (1822–23); reporter, *New York Courier* (1825); regular contributor to the *National Advocate* and the *Mercantile Advertiser* (1826); legislative correspondent, *New York Enquirer* (1827–29); associate editor, *New York Courier and Enquirer* (1829–32); editor and publisher, *New York Globe* (1832); editor and publisher, *Pennsylvanian* (1833); editor and publisher, *New York Herald* (1835–66)

> *"Our only guide shall be good, sound, practical common-sense, applicable to the business and bosoms of men engaged in every-day life. We shall support no party, be the organ of no faction or coterie, and care nothing for any election or any candidate, from President down to constable."*
>
> —from the *New York Herald* (May 6, 1835)

Since the *Herald* was the biggest paper in country and had the largest number of reporters covering the Civil War, President Abraham Lincoln did everything possible to win Bennett's support. Lincoln tried to appoint Bennett American minister to France, but the editor declined the offer. Bennett opposed Lincoln's Emancipation Proclamation as "unnecessary, unwise and ill-timed." He also opposed Lincoln's reelection, believing the President had become captive of the abolitionists. He referred to Lincoln as "the imbecile joker."

A very wealthy man, Bennett settled into retirement during the 1860s. He had his talented managing editor, Frederic Hudson, train his son, James Gordon Bennett, Jr., to run the paper. In 1866 the younger Bennett, then 25 years old, took over management of the *Herald*. Bennett, Sr., lived until 1872. When he died, his rival, the *New York Tribune*, credited him as an outstanding collector of news. "Editorially he was cynical, inconsistent, reckless, and easily influenced by others' opinions, and by his own prejudices," wrote Horace Greeley's *Tribune*, but "he knew how to pick out of the events of the day the subject which engrossed the interest of the great number of people, and to give them about that subject all they could read. The quality might be bad, and generally was; but it suited the multitude, and the quantity at any rate was abundant.... He made the newspaper powerful, but he made it odious."

FURTHER READING

Carlson, Oliver. *The Man Who Made the News*. New York: Duel, Sloan and Pearce, 1942.

Crouthamel, James L. *Bennett's New York Herald and the Rise of the Popular Press*. Syracuse, N.Y.: Syracuse University Press, 1989.

Fermer, Douglas. *James Gordon Bennett and the New York Herald: A Study of Editorial Opinion in the Civil War Era, 1854–1867*. New York: St. Martin's, 1986.

Pray, Isaac C. *Memoirs of James Gordon Bennett and His Times*. 1855. Reprint, New York: Arno, 1970.

Seitz, Don Carlos. *The James Gordon Bennetts: Father & Son Proprietors of the New York Herald*. 1928. Reprint, New York: Beekman, 1974.

Tucher, Andie. *Froth & Scum: Truth, Beauty, Goodness, and the Ax Murder in America's First Mass Medium*. Chapel Hill: University of North Carolina Press, 1994.

Horace Greeley

THE ECCENTRIC
EDITOR

Everyone recognized the *New York Tribune's* editor, Horace Greeley, by his habitual costume of oversized boots, rumpled trousers, a battered hat, and a white overcoat with pockets bulging with papers. His pink face fringed with white whiskers added to his curious appearance. Greeley's politics often matched his eccentric dress. He advocated such radical issues for his day as the antislavery movement, women's rights, temperance, pacifism, and vegetarian diets. One British visitor described Greeley as a "half-cracked" editor who pushed his causes to extravagance. Yet, unlike other editors who followed whatever direction the winds of public opinion happened to be blowing, Greeley defended his causes no matter how unpopular. A dedicated reformer who hated injustice, he used his newspaper to make his country a better place for everyone.

Growing up on his family's farm in New Hampshire, Horace Greeley had attended local schools irregularly. But

Editor Horace Greeley often personally covered the news for the *New York Tribune*. Here Greeley, standing at the right, makes a visit to the front lines during the Civil War.

With one of the largest daily and weekly circulations, the *New York Tribune* invested in the newest printing technology. This view of the *Tribune*'s press room appeared in *Frank Leslie's Illustrated News* on July 20, 1861.

he was always an avid reader. When his family lost the farm during a financial panic in 1819, the Greeleys moved first to Vermont and then to Pennsylvania. Fourteen-year-old Horace stayed behind in Vermont as an apprentice printer for a small weekly paper, the *Northern Spectator*. After learning the printing trade, he tied his belongings in a sack, slung it over his shoulder, and set out in 1831 to make his fortune in New York City.

Greeley set type at the *New-York Morning Post* and other papers until he and a friend saved enough money to open a printing shop. But Greeley also wanted to write and publish. In 1834 he invested his profits in a new weekly magazine called the *New-Yorker*. Under his editorship, the magazine mixed essays and reviews of literature and

politics, attacking the Democratic party and supporting the Whig party's reform programs. In 1836, at a boardinghouse that catered to vegetarians, Greeley met and married an equally strong-minded schoolteacher, Mary Cheney.

When the Panic of 1837 drove the *New-Yorker* near bankruptcy, financial rescue came from Thurlow Weed, editor of the *Albany Evening Journal* and boss of the New York State Whig party. Weed admired Greeley's politics and writing style, and hired him to edit a Whig newspaper in Albany, the *Jeffersonian*. In Albany, Greeley also reported on the state legislative debates for Weed's newspaper. In 1840 the Whigs hired him again to edit the *Log Cabin*, a paper that promoted the Presidential campaign of William

Henry Harrison. With Harrison's victory, Greeley expected a political job as his reward. But the more conservative Whigs considered Greeley to be too radical in his views, and offered him nothing. Vowing never to be dependent on any political party again, Greeley set out to start his own independent newspaper.

The first issue of the *New York Tribune* appeared on April 10, 1841. It was a "penny paper," costing just one cent and intended to reach a working-class audience. Although independent, Greeley did not think any paper could be politically neutral and still have anything worthwhile to say about the issues of the day. He wanted the *Tribune* to be loyal to its convictions rather than to its party. And those convictions, he announced, were: "Anti-Slavery, Anti-War, Anti-Rum, Anti-Tobacco, Anti-Seduction, Anti-Grogshops, Brothels, [and] Gambling Houses."

In addition to the daily *Tribune*, Greeley combined the *New-Yorker* and the *Log Cabin*, along with reprinted editorials and articles from the daily paper, to create the *Weekly Tribune*. At a time when there were few magazines, this weekly edition won enormous popularity in the rural areas of the Midwest, and it far outsold the daily edition. Rising circulation allowed Greeley to expand his newspaper from 20 columns to 24, then to 28. By 1850 it reached 58 columns, about the size of the best papers in London. Greeley also started a European edition of the *Tribune* (still published today as the *International Herald Tribune*).

Rising revenue enabled him to hire a talented staff. Greeley's managing editor, Charles Dana, later became a leader of public opinion as the vigorous editor of the *New York Sun*. His

assistant editor, Henry Raymond, later founded the *New York Times*. Greeley hired Margaret Fuller, feminist editor of *The Dial* literary magazine, to write social commentary, and Karl Marx, author of *The Communist Manifesto*, to write about British politics. His writers were—as one of them said—"resolute, brilliant, capable, irresponsible, intolerant [and] not above setting things on fire for the fun of seeing them burn." Greeley wanted his writers to sign their own work, at least with their initials or other distinctive mark so that they would become known to the public. He signed his own "H.G." at the bottom of his editorials and letters.

Greeley succeeded in spreading his reform ideas, turning his paper into a political bible for countless Americans. But Greeley was not content to be an editor and writer—he also hungered to run for office. In 1848 he won a seat in Congress to fill a few unexpired months of a term. There he used his privileges as a member to gain access to other representatives' travel vouchers and published an exposé accusing them of overcharging the government for travel to their home districts. Greeley left Congress satisfied that he had made himself its most hated member.

In 1854 Illinois senator Stephen Douglas rocked the nation by winning passage of the Kansas-Nebraska Act. This law repealed the Missouri Compromise and allowed settlers in western territories to decide for themselves whether they would permit slavery. Greeley branded the act a great fraud that would eventually allow slave labor to push free labor out of the territories. Abandoning the Whig party, Greeley threw his paper behind the creation of a new antislavery Republican party. He returned to

Horace Greeley

BORN

February 3, 1811
Near Amherst, New Hampshire

DIED

November 29, 1872
Pleasantville, New York

EDUCATION

Some public schools; largely self-taught

ACCOMPLISHMENTS

Editor, *New-Yorker* (1834–41); editor, *Jeffersonian* (1838–39); editor, *Log Cabin* (1840–41); reported legislative debates for *Albany Evening Journal* (1837–41); editor, *New York Tribune* (1841–72); author of several books, including *The American Laborer* (1843), *A History of the Struggle for Slavery Extension or Restriction in the United States from the Declaration of Independence to the Present Day* (1856), *An Overland Journey from New York to San Francisco in the Summer of 1859* (1860), *The American Conflict: A History of the Great Rebellion in the United States of America, 1860–'65* (1864–66), *Recollections of a Busy Life* (1868), *Essays Designed to Elucidate the Science of Political Economy* (1870), and *What I Know About Farming: A Series of Brief and Plain Expositions of Practical Agriculture as an Art Based upon Science* (1871)

"The marrow of the news-paper is not countained in its reports, Telegraphic or other, but in that broad generalization which condenses and distills the essence of those reports as they are and foreshadows them as they shall be."

—from the *New York Tribune* (April 10, 1850)

Washington to cover the arrival of Republicans in Congress. On one occasion the editor was beaten up on the Capitol grounds by an angry Democratic congressman who objected to his critical editorials. The furor that the *Tribune* raised over the Kansas-Nebraska Act not only contributed to the creation of the Republican party, but boosted circulation of the *Weekly Tribune,* which rose from 75,000 to 112,000 during the first six months of 1854.

Although the Republicans were a sectional party, Horace Greeley was at heart a nationalist. Famous for the advice "Go West, Young Man" (although he was actually quoting someone else), Greeley endorsed construction of a railroad to the Pacific. He also supported free land for those who wished to settle the West. In 1859 he went west to California, stopping along the way in Colorado (where the town of Greeley is named for him), and Utah (where he published one of the first newspaper interviews, with the Mormon leader Brigham Young).

Despite Greeley's continental vision, the nation was splitting apart over slavery. A pacifist, who believed there could be no good war or bad peace, Greeley at first was willing to see the South go their own separate way peacefully. But when the Confederates fired on Fort Sumter, in 1861, he reluctantly concluded there was no alternative but to fight to restore the Union. "On to Richmond!" read the banner headline in the *Tribune.*

Pushed on by public opinion, the Union army lost the first battle of the war at Bull Run. Taking much blame for the defeat, Greeley promised never again to criticize army tactics. Many

people never forgave Greeley and his paper for inciting the war. During the New York City draft riots of 1863, mobs tried to storm the *Tribune*'s offices singing "hang Horace Greeley from a sour apple tree" to the tune of "The Battle Hymn of the Republic." Yet during the war, sales of the daily Tribune shot to 65,000, and the *Weekly Tribune* to 250,000.

The *Tribune* considered President Abraham Lincoln to be too cautious and moderate. Greeley pressed Lincoln to sign the Emancipation Proclamation and was disappointed that it did not end slavery altogether. Lincoln tried his best to appease the cantankerous editor, dutifully responding to the editor's criticisms. In 1864 Greeley urged Lincoln to send a delegation to meet with Confederate peace emissaries in Canada. Lincoln shrewdly gave the job to Greeley, who bore the blame when the negotiations failed. In the Presidential elections that year, Greeley looked vainly to find a candidate to replace Lincoln. Not until after the President's assassination did Greeley concede that Abe Lincoln had been the "indispensable hero" of the Civil War.

After the war, Greeley followed an even more erratic course. A believer in racial justice, he supported the constitutional amendments ending slavery and granting black men the right to vote. Yet he was critical of legislation designed to help the freedmen. The *Tribune* regularly assailed the Reconstruction governments in the South. What he really wanted was a peaceful return of the Southern states to the Union. In 1867 Greeley triggered his greatest controversy by going to Richmond, Virginia, to post bond for former Confederate president

Jefferson Davis, a prisoner since the end of the war. Greeley hoped that this gesture would further reunite the sections. Instead, it stirred an angry reaction in the North and caused a decline in *Tribune* sales.

Appalled by the graft and corruption in the administration of President Ulysses S. Grant, Greeley bolted from the Republican party that he had once helped create. In 1872 the split-away Liberal Republican party nominated Greeley to run for president. The Democratic party, which he had spent a lifetime attacking, nominated him as well. Greeley made his campaign a crusade for reform and national reconciliation. He campaigned widely, giving numerous speeches. However, the Republicans had an easy time using Greeley's own words against him. He also offered a tempting target for such editorial cartoonists as Thomas Nast.

Days before the election, Mary Greeley died. "I am not dead but wish I were," Horace Greeley wrote. The election brought him defeat in a landslide that crushed his political ambitions. Greeley tried to resume his editorship of the *Tribune*, which he had given up during the campaign. But he found his old office occupied, and his control of the paper diminished.

His losing campaign had further hurt circulation of the *Tribune*. Worried over the paper's financial survival, Greeley suffered a mental collapse and died in a sanatorium on November 29, 1872. President Grant, members of the cabinet and Congress, governors, and other leaders joined the funeral procession for America's most influential and eccentric newspaper editor.

FURTHER READING

Baehr, Harry W., Jr. *The New York Tribune Since the Civil War*. New York: Dodd, Mead, 1936.

Fahrney, Ralph Ray. *Horace Greeley and the Tribune in the Civil War*. 1936. Reprint, New York: Da Capo Press, 1971.

Greeley, Horace. *The American Conflict: A History of the Great Rebellion in the United States of America, 1860–'65*. 2 vols. 1864–66. Reprint, New York: Negro Universities Press, 1969.

———. *The American Laborer*. 1843. Reprint, New York: Garland, 1974.

———. *Essays Designed to Elucidate the Science of Political Economy*. 1870. Reprint, New York: Garland, 1974.

———. *A History of the Struggle for Slavery Extension or Restriction in the United States from the Declaration of Independence to the Present Day*. Freeport, N.Y.: Books for Library Press, 1970.

———. *Recollections of a Busy Life*. 1868. Reprint, New York: Arno Press, 1970.

Isely, Jeter A. *Horace Greeley and the Republican Party, 1853–1861: A Study of the New York Tribune*. 1947. Reprint, New York: Octagon, 1965.

Kluger, Richard. *The Paper: The Life and Death of the New York Herald-Tribune*. New York: Knopf, 1986.

Lunde, Erik S. *Horace Greeley*. Boston: Twayne, 1981.

Schulze, Suzanne. *Horace Greeley: A Bio-Bibliography*. New York: Greenwood, 1992.

Stoddard, Henry Luther. *Horace Greeley: Printer, Editor, Crusader*. New York: Putnam, 1946.

Van Deusen, Glyndon G. *Horace Greeley: Nineteenth Century Crusader*. 1953. Reprint, New York: Hill & Wang, 1964.

Margaret Fuller Ossoli

FEMINIST FOREIGN CORRESPONDENT

Newspapers in the 19th century rarely hired writers of literary essays. They were not even likely to employ a woman. But in 1844 the innovative editor Horace Greeley invited Margaret Fuller to write literary criticism for the *New York Tribune*. An independent-minded feminist, Margaret Fuller first came to Greeley's attention when he read one of her essays, "The Great Lawsuit—Man versus Men, Woman versus Women," in *The Dial*, an intellectual literary magazine that she edited. Fuller's decision to leave the refined, philosophical circles of New England for the harsh realities of New York journalism changed her writings and her life.

As a child, the strong-willed Sarah Margaret Fuller renamed herself after her mother, Margaret. Her father was a congressman whose political career ended because he refused to compromise in any way in his opposition to slavery. He favored Margaret, the oldest of his seven children, and insisted that she get the same education as a boy. Young Margaret learned Latin, Greek, French, and Italian and read Shakespeare and the great epics of ancient Greece and Rome. Long hours of study gave her headaches and nightmares—and also an intellectual arrogance that made others feel uncomfortable around her. Unpopular with other children, she moved from school to school.

After her father's death, she cared for her invalid mother and worked to support her younger brothers and sisters. While teaching school in Boston, Massachusetts, Margaret Fuller made friends with many of the bright young men at Harvard, but the prejudices of her era barred her from either attending its classes or using its library. Fuller sought out her idol, the philosopher Ralph Waldo Emerson, but at first he was less than impressed with her. "Her extreme plainness," he wrote of their first meeting, "a trick of incessantly opening and shutting her eyelids,—the nasal tone of her voice,—all repelled; and I said to myself, we shall never get far." But their conversation changed his mind, and Emerson concluded that Margaret Fuller was "a very accomplished and very intelligent person," as he wrote in a memorial after her death. He invited her to attend meetings of the Transcendental Club.

The Transcendentalists were philosophers who believed that the spiritual quality of life was more important than the material things of everyday existence. They met regularly to talk over history, literature, and morality, and planned to start a magazine to spread their ideals. In 1840 they launched *The Dial*, but had no money to pay an editor. When Margaret Fuller took on the unpaid assignment, the men acknowledged that she was well read and a great talker, but they were skeptical of her literary abilities. Yet she skillfully edited the essays of Emerson, Henry David Thoreau, and other intellectuals of her era, and when their copy was not enough to fill the journal she wrote many items herself about poetry, literature, art, and society.

Margaret Fuller was a feminist who wanted to be economically self-reliant and independent of any man. She expressed her opinions in her essays, which came to the attention of Horace and Mary Greeley, who subscribed to *The Dial*. Horace Greeley invited Fuller to move to New York, live in his home, and write essays for his newspaper, the *New York Tribune*. A daily newspaper required a different kind of writing than Fuller had been accustomed to at a monthly literary magazine. She had difficulty learning to write faster and more concisely. But over time her style became less flowery and more factual, less straitlaced and more straightforward.

Although she continued to write about books, plays, and museums, Fuller's attention shifted to New York's many social problems. As a reporter for the *Tribune*, she visited women at Sing Sing prison and in the insane asylum on Blackwell's Island. Her articles about ethnic prejudices, capital punishment, poorhouses, and public health problems helped to raise public awareness. During her time in New York she published some 250 essays in the *Tribune*, most signed only by a star, since journalists at that time did not put their names on their newspaper articles.

In 1845 Fuller wrote a book, *Woman in the Nineteenth Century* (published by Greeley), which discussed the relations between women and men. She called for equal treatment of men and women and demanded that women have the same educational

opportunities. Her "radical" ideas inspired many women and shocked many men. "No unmarried woman has any right to say anything on the subject," one male reviewer complained. "Woman is nothing but as a wife." The book's controversial approach helped it to sell out its first edition in one week. In 1848, when feminist leaders held the Seneca Falls Convention to demand equal rights for women, particularly the right to vote, Fuller's book served as a central topic of conversation, and it helped to shape the women's movement in the 19th century.

While writing for the *New York Tribune*, Margaret Fuller shifted her attention from literary issues to social problems, at home and abroad.

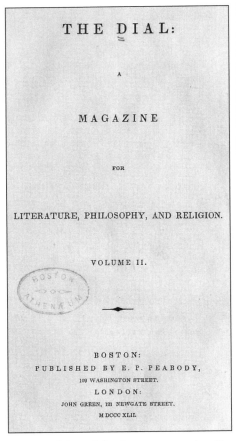

THE DIAL:

A

MAGAZINE

FOR

LITERATURE, PHILOSOPHY, AND RELIGION.

VOLUME II.

BOSTON:
PUBLISHED BY E. P. PEABODY,
109 WASHINGTON STREET.
LONDON:
JOHN GREEN, 121 NEWGATE STREET.
M DCCC XLII.

Fuller's editing of the literary magazine *The Dial* brought her to the attention of the *New York Tribune*'s editor, Horace Greeley.

For years Margaret Fuller had wanted to travel abroad, to study and to write books on history and philosophy. A lack of funds and a fear of the sea held her back. In 1846 Greeley offered her the chance to go to Europe and write dispatches for the *Tribune*. "I feel that, if I persevere, there is nothing to hinder my having an important career now," she wrote. "But it must be in the capacity as a journalist, and for that I need this new field of observation." She wanted to see how Europe was responding to industrialization, particularly the problems of working-class housing, sanitary conditions, poverty, and the status of working women. She was stunned by the human suffering that she confronted. "Poverty in England has terrors of which I never dreamed at home," she wrote back to the *Tribune* in her first dispatch as one of America's first foreign correspondents.

From England, Fuller traveled to France, where she examined the day-care centers for the children of working mothers, the spread of prostitution, and the "slavelike" conditions of some workers. From Italy she sent back dramatic dispatches on the Italian revolution for independence from France and Austria. "I am very tired of the battle with giant wrongs, and would like to have some one younger and stronger arise to say what ought to be said, still more to do what ought to be done," she wrote to the *Tribune* from Italy. "Enough! If I felt these things in privileged America, the cries of mothers and wives beaten at night by sons and husbands for their diversion after drinking, as I have repeatedly heard them these past months...have sharpened my perception as to the ills of woman's condition and the remedies that must be applied. Had I but genius, had I but energy, to tell what I know as it ought to be told!"

In Rome, Margaret Fuller fell in love with a young Italian nobleman,

Giovanni Angelo Ossoli della Torre. He was a man of action rather than an intellectual. Together they plunged into the revolution, and she became a participant in the events she covered. Her dispatches offered Americans dramatic first-person accounts of the revolution—her best writing ever. At the same time Fuller was also running a hospital for wounded Italian troops and soliciting financial support from her American readers. "Art is not important to me now," she explained. "I take interest in the state of the people...." Since it was difficult for a non-Catholic to marry a Catholic in Italy at that time, it was never clear whether she and Ossoli were legally married. However, she took Ossoli's name and bore his child.

Fuller's last dispatch appeared in the *Tribune* on February 13, 1850, after the revolution had been crushed. "At this moment all the worst men are in power," she concluded, "and the best betrayed and exiled." With the French conquest of Rome, Margaret, Giovanni, and their son left Italy. Returning to the United States, they were within sight of Long Island when their ship was wrecked in a storm. They were all lost at sea. A saddened editor Greeley paid tribute to Margaret Fuller as "the most remarkable and in some respects the greatest woman whom America has yet known."

FURTHER READING

Balducci, Carolyn Ferleppa. *Margaret Fuller: A Life of Passion and Defiance*. New York: Bantam Books, 1991.

Capper, Charles. *Margaret Fuller: An American Romantic Life, Volume I: The Private Years*. New York: Oxford University Press, 1992.

Chevigny, Bell Gale. *The Woman and the Myth: Margaret Fuller's Life and Writings*. Boston: Northeastern University Press, 1994.

"Italy, naturally so rich, but long racked and impoverished by her oppressors, greatly needs money to arm and clothe her troops. Some token of sympathy, too, from America would be so welcome to her now. If there were a circle of persons inclined to trust such to me, I might venture a promise the trust should be used to the advantage of Italy. It would make me proud to have my country show a religious faith in the progress of ideas, and make some small sacrifice of its own great resources in aid of a sister cause, now."

—from the *New York Tribune* (April 4, 1848)

Dickenson, Donna. *Margaret Fuller: Writing a Woman's Life*. New York: St. Martin's, 1993.

Fuller, Margaret. *At Home and Abroad, or Things and Thoughts in America and Europe*. Edited by Arthur B. Fuller. 1856. Reprint, Port Washington, N.Y.: Kennikat Press, 1971.

———. *Life Without and Life Within; or Reviews, Narratives, Essays, and Poems*. Edited by Arthur B. Fuller. 1860. Reprint, Upper Saddle River, N.J.: Literature House, 1970.

———. *Memoirs of Margaret Fuller Ossoli*. Edited by Ralph Waldo Emerson. 1852. Reprint, New York: B. Franklin, 1972, 2 volumes.

———. *Papers on Literature and Art*. 2 vols. Edited by Arthur B. Fuller. 1846. Reprint, New York: AMS Press, 1972.

———. *The Portable Margaret Fuller*. Edited by Mary Kelley. New York: Penguin Books, 1994.

———. *Summer on the Lakes*. 1843. Reprint, Urbana: University of Illinois Press, 1991.

———. *"These Sad But Glorious Days": Dispatches from Europe, 1846-1850*. Edited by Larry J. Reynolds and Susan Belasco Smith. New Haven: Yale University Press, 1991.

———. *Woman in the Nineteenth Century*. 1845. Reprint, New York: Oxford University Press, 1994.

Kornfeld, Eve. *Margaret Fuller: A Brief Biography with Documents*. Boston: Bedford Books, 1997.

Mills, Kay. *A Place in the News: From the Women's Pages to the Front Pages*. New York: Dodd, Mead, 1988.

Mitchell, Catherine, ed. *Margaret Fuller's New York Journalism: A Biographical Essay and Key Writings*. Knoxville: University of Tennessee Press, 1995.

Myerson, Joel. *The New England Transcendentalists and The Dial: A History of the Magazine and Its Contributors*. Rutherford, N.J.: Farleigh Dickinson University Press, 1980.

Stern, Madeline B. *The Life of Margaret Fuller*. New York: Greenwood Press, 1991.

Von Mehren, Joan. *Minerva and the Muse: A Life of Margaret Fuller*. Amherst: University of Massachusetts Press, 1994.

Wilson, Ellen. *Margaret Fuller: Bluestocking, Romantic, Revolutionary*. New York: Farrar, Straus & Giroux, 1997.

Margaret Fuller Ossoli

BORN

May 23, 1810
Cambridge, Massachusetts

DIED

June 19, 1850
At sea off Fire Island, New York

EDUCATION

private schools

ACCOMPLISHMENTS

Editor, *The Dial* (1840–42); literary critic and correspondent, *New York Tribune* (1845–46); foreign correspondent, *New York Tribune* (1846–50); author of *Summer on the Lakes* (1843), *Woman in the Nineteenth Century* (1845), *Papers on Literature and Art* (1846), *At Home and Abroad, or Things and Thoughts in America and Europe* (1856), and *Life Without and Life Within; or Reviews, Narratives, Essays, and Poems* (1860)

Jane Grey Swisshelm

FURIOUS EDITOR

In the 19th century "woman's sphere" meant keeping house for husband and children. Unmarried women might teach or even work in a factory, but ultimately they were expected to marry, raise families, and subordinate themselves to their husbands. Not all women accepted those boundaries, and some sought to find their own voice outside the home. A few broke through the barriers of prejudices to enter the field of journalism. Jane Grey Swisshelm resented her lack of legal rights as a married woman and rebelled against conventional restraints on women's freedom. Demanding her own rights, she also spoke for the poor and needy, and she vented her fury against slavery in newspapers that she edited in Pittsburgh and on the Minnesota frontier. Because she believed deeply in her positions, she showed no mercy toward her opponents. The sarcasm and scorn of Jane Swisshelm's editorials made all those who crossed her regret the experience.

Born into a family of devout Scottish Presbyterians, she was named Jane Grey Cannon after a distant ancestor, Lady Jane Grey (who had spent nine days as queen of England before she was executed in 1554). A rigidly religious upbringing made Jane intolerant of all sinful behavior and insistent on righteousness. While she was a child, her father, Thomas Cannon, died of tuberculosis, as did four of her brothers. Concern for Jane's health caused her mother, Mary, to remove her from boarding school. She helped her widowed mother support the family and at 15 began teaching school in Wilkinsburg, the town outside of Pittsburgh where they lived.

There she met James Swisshelm, a wealthy young man, tall, muscular, and handsome. With his black hair and whiskers, dressed in black and riding on a black horse, he was her "black knight." He was attracted to Jane, who was described as having a "slight figure, of less than medium height, with pleasant face, eyes beaming with kindliness, soft voice, and winning manners." He admired her intelligence, courage, and frankness. They were married in 1836.

James Swisshelm brought his bride to a home dominated by his mother. The two strong-willed women never got along. James and his mother, both devout Methodists, urged Jane to convert to their faith and become a preacher. Jane steadfastly refused, since in her church women never preached. She did make other changes in her life, which she always regretted. Although she had a talent for painting, after she married she felt it necessary to put away her brushes and devote herself to her duties as a wife. She also felt such a lack of privacy in married life that she destroyed all her diaries and letters. Finding it impossible to live under the same roof with her mother-in-law, Jane eventually moved to a small house behind the family home.

In an effort to restore peace to his household, James Swisshelm took his wife to Louisville, Kentucky, in 1838 and went into business with his older brother. Kentucky gave Jane her first direct views of slavery. She was horrified to see slave women beaten and children sold. Jane Swisshelm made no secret of her antislavery feelings. Other boarders in the house where they lived warned her: "You had better take care how you talk, or we will give you a coat of tar and feathers." Undaunted, she started a school for free black children, but after she received threatening letters that the school would be burned she was forced to close the school. Swisshelm then turned to profitable work as a seamstress. When her husband's business failed, he depended on her income.

In 1839, over her husband's protests, Jane Swisshelm returned home to care for her critically ill mother. She warned James that she would never again live in a slave state. After a while, he grew tired of waiting and followed her back to Pennsylvania. They settled on a farm that she called Swissvale, for which the town outside Pittsburgh was later named. Much to her shame, her husband filed a claim against her mother's estate, charging it for Jane's nursing services. Although James was acting within his legal rights, his action made Jane feel that she was just his servant. For the rest of her life she argued vehemently for the independent rights of married women.

Jane Swisshelm held strong views on many social issues. In the early 1840s she wrote a series of articles attacking capital punishment that were published anonymously in a Pittsburgh

newspaper. Adopting the pen name "Jennie Deans," she also published articles in defense of women's rights and against slavery. Her husband encouraged her to write and to sign her own name. "He had not given up the idea that I should preach," Jane recognized. "Indeed, he held me accountable for most of the evils in the world, on the ground that I could overthrow them if I would."

In 1844 the Liberty party ran an antislavery candidate for President of the United States. Swisshelm submitted articles supporting the party, signed with just her initials, "J.G.S.," for fear

Jane Grey Swisshelm held strong views on women's rights, abolition of slavery, and other social issues. She never hesitated to publish those views in her newspapers.

This 19th-century print suggests that women's only appropriate "spheres" were those involving housework or the social graces. Swisshelm, however, thought otherwise and used her writing to promote political causes.

slavery movement needed another paper. Investing her inheritance from her mother, she started her own newspaper, the *Pittsburgh Saturday Visiter*. Working out of another editor's office, Swisshelm wrote, edited, corrected proof, and sold advertisements and subscriptions for the *Visiter*. The paper's name came from a verse in the Old Testament Book of Jeremiah: "Shall I not visit for these things, saith the Lord, and shall not my soul be avenged on such a nation as this?" Swisshelm held slavery to be a sin, for which she blamed northerners as much as southerners. Complacent northerners were "poor, sniffling, whiffling, driveling, pitiful...'white slaves'" to southern ambition and power, she wrote. Like the prophet Jeremiah, whom she quoted, she was full of fury over such wickedness and could not hold it in.

The *Saturday Visiter* started with two subscribers and by its second year had reached 6,000. Copies went to every state and territory and to Canada and England. Its editorials were frequently republished in other papers, helping to fan the antislavery movement and the sectional tensions of the era. The *Visiter* attracted attention as much for the novelty of a woman editing a political paper as for her abolitionist views. Conscious of her role, Swisshelm dressed very plainly and never relied on "feminine attraction" to promote her journalism. "When a woman starts out in the world on a mission, secular or religious, she should leave her feminine charms at home," she reasoned. Most male editors scorned the idea of a woman editor, but Horace Greeley gave her paper respectful recognition and reprinted some of her editorials in his *New York Tribune*.

of embarrassing the party "with the sex question." Soon there was a regular demand for her writing. "My style I caught from my crude, rural surroundings," she commented, and so was familiar to her readers. "I was not surprised to find the letters eagerly read."

When the Liberty party paper, the *Albatross*, went out of business in 1847, Jane Swisshelm felt sure that the anti-

Jane Grey Swisshelm

In 1850 the U.S. Senate sought to reach a compromise over the issue of slavery in the territories. "The danger was imminent, the crisis, alarming, and the excitement very great," Swisshelm recalled. "I longed to be in Washington." Boldly, she wrote to Horace Greeley and offered herself as a Washington correspondent. A supporter of women's rights, Greeley decided to hire her at five dollars a letter. Her first Washington letter appeared on an inside page of the *Tribune* on April 12, 1850. Within three days "Mrs. Swisshelm's Letters," as they were titled to highlight the novelty of a woman correspondent, were appearing on the front page.

Swisshelm found the public gallery too noisy and distracting to hear the debates. She went to Vice President Millard Fillmore and petitioned to be admitted to the press gallery, the special section reserved for reporters. Since no woman had ever sat there before, Fillmore tried to discourage her. She would find the press gallery unpleasant, he argued; she would attract undue attention. But she held her ground and Fillmore gave in. Her appearance in the press gallery caused only a minor stir, since more dramatic events were happening on the Senate floor below. During the debate that day, Missouri senator Thomas Hart Benton physically threatened Mississippi senator Henry Foote, who drew a pistol for protection. "I sat in the reporters' gallery, directly opposite the gentlemen," Swisshelm told her readers, "and saw it all."

Her Washington reporting ended abruptly. Swisshelm hated the senator from Massachusetts, Daniel Webster, for breaking with the antislavery forces to support the Compromise of 1850, which traded restrictions on slavery in

the West for a law that would return fugitive slaves in the East—which abolitionists vigorously opposed. She had heard rumors about Webster's immoral private life and planned to publish them to prevent Webster from ever being elected President. Her friends warned her against publishing the story: "It would ruin you, ruin your influence, ruin your work. You would lose your *Tribune* engagement." But Swisshelm was determined to go ahead "and let God take care of the consequences." The blunt little article appeared in the *Visiter* and was "copied and copied" by other newspapers—but not by the *Tribune*, which supported Webster. An embarrassed Horace Greeley fired Jane Swisshelm.

In 1851 Swisshelm gave birth to a daughter, Henrietta, and divided her life between journalism and parental duties. The strain caused a breakdown in her health. Finally admitting that her marriage had been a mistake, Swisshelm decided to leave both her husband and her paper. "After fifteen years in his mother's house I must run away or die," she wrote. "So I ran away." In 1857 she and her daughter boarded a riverboat and sailed to Minnesota, where her sister lived. James Swisshelm eventually obtained a divorce on the grounds of desertion, and then remarried.

When Jane Swisshelm left the *Saturday Visiter*, she believed her public work had ended. By settling in the northwestern territory of Minnesota, where slavery was prohibited, she thought that she could distance herself from that "national curse." But she learned that federal troops had been withdrawn from Minnesota to maintain peace between pro- and antislavery factions in the Kansas territory. The departing troops left the

BORN

December 6, 1815
Pittsburgh, Pennsylvania

DIED

July 21, 1884
Swissvale, Pennsylvania

EDUCATION

Briefly attended Edgeworth, a girls' boarding school

ACCOMPLISHMENTS

Contributor, *Dollar Newspaper* and *Neal's Saturday Gazette* (Philadelphia) and *Spirit of Liberty, Commercial Journal,* and *Albatross* (Pittsburgh) (1842–47); editor, *Pittsburgh Saturday Visiter* (1847–52) and *Family Journal and Visiter,* (1852–57); Washington correspondent, *New York Tribune* (1851); editor, *St. Cloud Visiter* (1857–58); editor, *St. Cloud Democrat* (1858–63); contributor, *New York Tribune* and *Chicago Tribune* (1863–66); editor, *The Reconstructionist* (1865–66); author of *Letters to Country Girls* (1853), *True Stories About Pets* (1879), and *Half a Century* (1880)

"I have so set my heart upon talking to the people of Minnesota before the coming insanity of the next political campaign, that I cannot readily give it up. I want to see Minnesota free!—to see the day when a slave cannot breathe the air of the North Star State!... This Western vineyard has no laborer to spare; and little as I can do, it is all for which I am accountable."

—from the *St. Cloud Democrat* (March 15, 1860)

Minnesota settlers vulnerable to raids by Sioux Indians. She realized that she could never escape the consequences of slavery no matter where she went, and that she had not lost her fury over its injustice.

The owner of a defunct newspaper in St. Cloud, Minnesota, invited her to revive the paper. At that time Minnesota was a pro-Democratic territory whose government was dominated by southern sympathizers appointed by Democratic President James Buchanan. Swisshelm warned her publisher that she was an abolitionist, but he assured her that she could take any political position she pleased—so long as the paper attracted more settlers to St. Cloud. With just a small amount of type and a limited supply of paper, she began to publish the paper that she renamed the *St. Cloud Visiter*.

The local Democratic leader, Sylvanus (Sam) Lowry, advised Jane Swisshelm that he would help the paper financially if it backed the Democratic party. Surprisingly, she agreed and accepted his support. In February 1858 the *Visiter* announced that it would endorse James Buchanan's reelection on the grounds that "the Democratic party is likely to succeed in reducing all the poor and friendless of this country to a state of slavery." Although true to her promise, her endorsement actually condemned Buchanan and Lowry. Vowing to crush her paper, Lowry arranged for his ally James Shepley to make a public speech that portrayed Swisshelm as a meddlesome woman. She replied with an editorial that seemed to mock Shepley's wife. That night, men broke into the *Visiter*'s office, destroyed the press, scattered the type, and left a note warning that her next offense would incur a more serious penalty.

Instead of ruining Swisshelm, this act of vandalism encouraged the rest of the town's leaders to rally behind her. Business leaders put up money to buy a new press and type and to provide her with necessary operating funds. Republican newspapers throughout the territory published the story and defended freedom of the press. The notoriety put Swisshelm in demand as a popular lecturer around the territory. Outraged over this turn of events, James Shepley filed a $10,000 libel suit against the *Visiter* and the people who had put up money to help the paper. To protect her supporters, Swisshelm ran an editorial that absolved Lowry and Shepley and promised never to mention the controversy again in the *Visiter*. If her opponents thought they had won, they were wrong. Overnight a new newspaper appeared—the *St. Cloud Democrat*, edited by Jane

Swisshelm. Its first issue ran an obituary for the *Visiter* and went right back to blasting Sam Lowry. "We have pledged *our* honor that the paper we edit will discuss any subject we have [in] mind," she proclaimed. No one dared challenge her again. Despite the *Democrat*'s name, the paper strongly supported the new Republican party, and Swisshelm won recognition as "the mother of the Republican party" in Minnesota.

When the Civil War began, Jane Swisshelm grew impatient with President Abraham Lincoln's slowness in emancipating the slaves. She was also greatly alarmed over Indian raids that occurred in Minnesota during the war. In 1862 she went to Washington to dissuade Lincoln from showing any leniency toward those Indians involved in the raids. Despite her suspicions of Lincoln, when she first saw the President, "his sad, earnest, honest face was irresistible in its plea for confidence." Shaking his hand on a receiving line, Swisshelm said, "May the Lord have mercy on you, poor man, for the people have none." Lincoln laughed heartily. Jane Swisshelm also became a close personal friend of Mary Todd Lincoln.

Once in Washington, Jane Swisshelm decided to stay and help care for the many wounded soldiers in the capital. She sold her interest in the *St. Cloud Democrat* and supported herself by working as a clerk in the War Department. At the end of the war, she launched another newspaper in Washington, *The Reconstructionist.* Its editors defended the Radical Republican demands for strict Reconstruction of the South and protection of the freedmen. The Radicals wanted to readmit the Southern states only if they ensured the civil rights and liberties of the former slaves. President Andrew Johnson adopted a more lenient attitude and promised a speedy readmission of the South, leaving the freedman's fate to the Southern white governments. Since her paper fiercely criticized President Andrew Johnson's moderate policies, Johnson retaliated by firing her from the War Department.

In declining health and with no pension, Swisshelm worried about her future. She decided to return to Pittsburgh and bring suit to recover the property that had been held by her former husband. In court she won a small house at Swissvale and enough money to support her for the rest of her life. The case of *Swisshelm* v. *Swisshelm* became a landmark ruling in establishing married women's property rights. Jane Grey Swisshelm later wrote her memoirs, *Half a Century*, which offered her one last chance to fight old battles and settle old scores, and to show that events had proved her right. Her memoir amply demonstrated that, even in retirement, she had lost none of the fury that drove her editorial career.

FURTHER READING

Larsen, Arthur J., ed. *Crusader and Feminist: Letters of Jane Grey Swisshelm, 1858-1865.* St. Paul: Minnesota Historical Society, 1934.

Ross, Ishbel. *Ladies of the Press: The Story of Women in Journalism by an Insider.* 1936. Reprint, New York: Arno, 1974.

Swisshelm, Jane Grey. *Half a Century.* 1880. Reprint, New York: Source Book Press, 1970.

Walker, Peter F. *Moral Choices: Memory, Desire, and Imagination in Nineteenth-Century American Abolition.* Baton Rouge, La.: Louisiana State University Press, 1978.

More American Journalists to Remember

Andrew Bradford (1686–1742), was a pioneer printer and publisher. Although overshadowed by his fellow Philadelphian Benjamin Franklin, Bradford founded the first newspaper published outside of Boston, the *American Weekly Mercury* (1728–54), whose 26 years of continuous publication made it one of longest-lived papers in the American colonies. In 1741 Bradford also started the first American magazine, appropriately named the *American Magazine*. A successful printer and seller of stationery supplies, he also supported his publications by holding such official positions as Printer to the Commonwealth of Pennsylvania (1712–30) and postmaster (1728–37).

Concerned with establishing an independent American identity after the American Revolution, **Noah Webster** (1758–1843) wrote school textbooks and the first *American Dictionary of the English Language* (1828). He also left his mark in journalism. In New York, Webster founded a daily newspaper, the *American Minerva* (later renamed the *Commercial Advertiser*) in 1793 and a semiweekly, the *Herald, A Gazette for the Country* (later renamed the *Spectator*) the next year. In these papers he created the first regular editorial column—opinion pieces that supported the Federalist party—and used the publications to promote a distinctly American literary tradition. Finding the day-to-day pressures of journalism too taxing, the scholarly Webster gave up the editorship of his papers in 1798 and eventually sold them in 1803 in order to devote himself to his writing and to compiling the dictionary that continues to bear his name. Today, many dictionaries are still called "Webster's."

An Irish immigrant to America, **Matthew Lyon** (1749–1822) served in the American Revolution and engaged in a number of businesses, from tavern keeping to mill operating, before he founded the *Farmer's Library* newspaper in 1793. He moved it to Fair Haven, Vermont, in 1795.

When Vermont became a state, Lyon ran for the U.S. House of Representatives. After losing his first races, he was elected in 1797. His speeches and writings were bitterly opposed to the administration of John Adams and led to his arrest and conviction under the Alien and Sedition Acts. He ran for reelection from his jail cell and won, a significant victory for freedom of the press and freedom of expression in America.

After the death of Benjamin Franklin Bache in a yellow fever epidemic, **William Duane** (1760–1835) married his widow and took over as editor of the Philadelphia *Aurora* (1798–1822). He was arrested in 1799 for protesting the

Alien and Sedition Acts but was acquitted at trial. An avid Jeffersonian, in 1800 he published the text of a still-secret bill to alter the electoral college—a Federalist plan to prevent Jefferson's election as President. Jefferson's supporters in the Senate leaked the bill to Duane, triggering the first congressional investigation of the press. Duane refused to testify before the Senate, which voted the editor in contempt but was otherwise powerless to punish him.

The weekly news magazine owes its beginning to **Hezekiah Niles** (1777–1839). Having gotten his start as a printer on the Philadelphia *Aurora,* and later as editor of the *Baltimore Evening Post* (1805–11), Niles was an ardent Jeffersonian. Yet when he aimed for a national audience with his weekly magazine, *Niles' Weekly Register* (1811–35), he sought to be an "honest chronicler," presenting a balanced account of events. The 16-page weekly compiled speeches, documents, and national and international news but carried no advertising. Although not a partisan publication, *Niles' Weekly Register* enthusiastically promoted Henry Clay's "American System" of internal improvements, protective tariffs, and national banking.

Benjamin Henry Day (1810–89), the father of the "penny press," began his career as a printer's apprentice for Samuel Bowles II's *Springfield Republican* in Massachusetts. Day then moved to New York to be a printer for the *New York Evening Post* and the *Journal of Commerce.*

Seeking to publish his own paper for the "common man," in 1833 Day established the *New York Sun,* with the motto "It Shines for All." Selling for one cent, the paper aimed at a middle- and working-class audience. Declining profits and several libel suits persuaded Day to sell the *Sun* in 1838, an act he later described as "the silliest thing he ever did." He published other newspapers and magazines throughout his career, but the *Sun* remained his greatest achievement.

One of Benjamin Day's fellow printers in New York, **Arunah S. Abell** (1806–88) embraced the notion of the "penny press" and founded the *Philadelphia Public Ledger* in 1836 and the *Baltimore Sun* in 1837. Intensely competitive, Abell constantly strove to get the news fastest, using carrier pigeons, express trains, pony express, steamboats, stagecoaches, and the telegraph to build the *Sun* into Baltimore's leading newspaper.

William Cullen Bryant (1794–1878) spent more than 50 of his 83 years as editor of the *New York Evening Post.* Trained as a lawyer and gifted as a poet, Bryant disdained the flashiness of the "penny press" and instead published an eminently respectable if somewhat stuffy newspaper. Long a Democratic supporter, Bryant shifted the *Post's* editorial endorsement to the new Republican party in 1855 over the slavery issue.

Joseph Gales, Jr. (1786–1860) and **William W. Seaton** (1785–1866) published the leading newspaper in Washington, D.C., the *National Intelligencer* (1810–64). The two brothers-in-law, diminutive Gales and towering Seaton, worked together harmoniously, reporting the debates in the House and Senate, serving as official printers to Congress, operating the biggest printing shop in Washington, and producing the "official organ" for several Presidential administrations. Beginning as Jeffersonian Republicans, they shifted their allegiance to the Whig party, and eventually lost their influence as their party disintegrated.

Joseph Gales, Jr. (left) and William Seaton, both experts in using shorthand, covered the debates in the U.S. House of Representatives and the Senate for the *National Intelligencer,* their Washington newspaper.

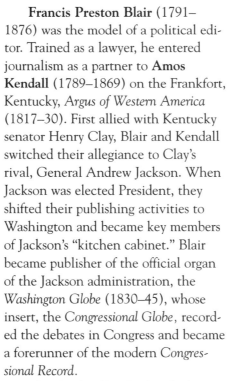

Francis Preston Blair (1791–1876) was the model of a political editor. Trained as a lawyer, he entered journalism as a partner to **Amos Kendall** (1789–1869) on the Frankfort, Kentucky, *Argus of Western America* (1817–30). First allied with Kentucky senator Henry Clay, Blair and Kendall switched their allegiance to Clay's rival, General Andrew Jackson. When Jackson was elected President, they shifted their publishing activities to Washington and became key members of Jackson's "kitchen cabinet." Blair became publisher of the official organ of the Jackson administration, the *Washington Globe* (1830–45), whose insert, the *Congressional Globe,* recorded the debates in Congress and became a forerunner of the modern *Congressional Record.*

The death of her husband when she was 34 caused **Sarah Josepha Hale** (1788–1879) to turn to a life of writing to support her children. After publishing a successful novel, she became editor of the *American Ladies' Magazine* in 1827. Ten years later she was invited to Boston to edit *Godey's Lady's Book* (1837–77), advertised as the first magazine edited by women for women. Reaching a circulation of 150,000, *Godey's Lady's Book* published works by Longfellow, Poe, Hawthorne, and other American literary figures. Hale generally accepted the traditional roles of women as wives and mothers, but her concern over health issues led her to support the admission of women into medical training. She also advocated college education for women and interspersed other serious issues with news of current fashions.

The social reformer **Frances (Fanny) Wright** (1795–1852) was born in Scotland and came to the

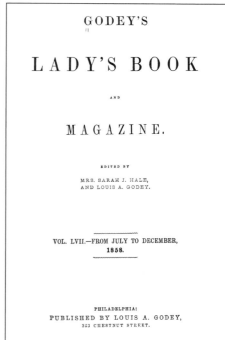

A typical illustration and cover of the popular *Godey's Lady's Book*. It was the first magazine edited by women for women.

United States at the age of 23. She wrote and acted in plays, but gained a wider reputation as the author of American travel literature which became extremely popular in Europe. Attracted to the egalitarian theories of Robert Owen, Wright ventured to his utopian community in New Harmony, Indiana. There she edited the *New Harmony Gazette* (later renamed the *Free Enquirer*) from 1828 to 1832. Wright's paper promoted equality for women, the end of capital punishment and imprisonment for debt, and other social reforms, although she could not bring herself to endorse the antislavery movement. She gave up both her editing and lecturing careers following the birth of her first child.

In 1827 *Freedom's Journal* became the first African-American newspaper. The Reverend **Samuel E. Cornish,** pastor of the African Presbyterian Church in New York, raised the money to hire as the paper's editor **John B. Russwurm** (1799–1851) a recent graduate of Bowdoin College in Maine. The two men quarreled over the issue of colonization of blacks in Africa, which Cornish opposed, causing him to disassociate himself from the paper. Russwurm edited the paper until 1829, when he left for the independent African nation of Liberia, where he published the *Liberia Herald*.

Cornish took control of *Freedom's Journal,* changing its name to *Rights of All* and publishing it for six more months.

William Lloyd Garrison started the *Liberator* in 1831 to protest against slavery. He closed the paper in 1865, when slavery was abolished.

The leading antislavery paper was the *Liberator*, published by a white abolitionist, **William Lloyd Garrison** (1805–79). Having started as a printer's apprentice at 13, Garrison's first editorial post was on the *Newburyport* (Massachusetts) *Free Press* in 1826. He later edited papers in Bennington, Vermont, and Baltimore, Maryland.

Having become convinced of the immorality of slavery, Garrison launched the *Liberator* in Boston, in 1831, with a credo that concluded: "I am in earnest—I will not equivocate—I will not excuse—I will not retreat a single inch—AND I WILL BE HEARD." His paper outraged the South, irritated much of the North, stimulated debate and sometimes riot, and eventually stirred the public conscience. As an editor and publisher, Garrison made his mark by advocating reasoned discussion and free inquiry, no matter how controversial the subject. When the Constitution was amended to abolish slavery in 1865, Garrison closed the *Liberator*, believing its work was done.

Anne Newport Royall (1769–1854), the widow of a veteran of the American Revolution, wrote travel literature before settling in Washington to publish two newspapers, *Paul Pry* (1831–36) and *The Huntress* (1836–54), whose names suggest their nature. Her papers were known for their satirical style, gossip, and polemics on corruption and reli-

gion. Her fiery temperament once caused her to be convicted as a "common scold" and sentenced to be dunked in the Potomac River. However, fellow journalists paid a fine to prevent the sentence from being carried out.

The English-born Henry Carter's (1821–80) father wanted him to join his glove making business, but the boy wanted to become an engraver. He secretly published his first engravings under the pseudonym **Frank Leslie** (Leslie was his father's middle name). Having perfected his skills on the *Illustrated London News*, he immigrated to the United States in 1848. In Boston he worked as an engraver for *Gleason's Pictorial* before moving to New York in 1854 to start *Frank Leslie's Illustrated News*. Rather than simply print attractive pictures, Leslie tied illustrations to the news of the week. In 1854 he also launched *Frank Leslie's Lady's Gazette of Fashion and Fancy Needlework*, employing many of the same writers, artists, and engravers to produce both popular mass-circulation publications.

In 1874 Leslie divorced his wife and married one of his writers, **Miriam Folline Squier** (1836–1914). When he died, she legally changed her name to Frank Leslie and continued to manage and edit his publications.

University of Vermont graduate **Henry J. Raymond** (1820–69) deeply impressed editor Horace Greeley, who made him his chief editorial assistant on the *New York Tribune* in 1841. Far more conservative than Greeley, and disturbed by his many causes, Raymond left to edit the *New York Courier and Enquirer* in 1843. In 1850 he became managing editor of *Harper's New Monthly Magazine*. Then, in 1851, Raymond and George Jones (one of Greeley's financial managers) founded the *New York Times*. They pledged that the new paper would "allay, rather than excite, agitation." They avoided sensationalism and declared the paper's political independence. Raymond, however, held political ambitions. He served in the New York state legislature and the U.S. House of Representatives, roles that distracted him from editorial duties. His paper survived his inattention to become the national newspaper of record.

Born in Canada, **Joseph Medill** (1823–99) moved to Ohio as a child and got his start in journalism editing the *Coshocton* (Ohio) *Republic* (1850–52) and the *Cleveland Leader* (1852–55). In 1855 he accepted an offer to come to the emerging city on Lake Michigan to edit the *Chicago Tribune*, a position he held for nearly half a century. Active in Whig and Republican politics, Medill became an ally of the Illinois politician Abraham Lincoln and was among the first to advocate Lincoln's candidacy for President in 1860. Always a booster of Chicago, after the disastrous fire of 1871 he was elected mayor on a "Fire-Proof" ticket. Medill became the patriarch of a powerful family in journalism. In later years his grandchildren would dominate newspapers in Chicago, New York City, and Washington, D.C. Northwestern University's Medill School of Journalism is named for him.

Samuel Bowles III (1826–78) joined his father's newspaper, the *Springfield* (Massachusetts) *Republican*, when he was 17 and inherited the paper after his father's death in 1851. Originally a Whig paper, the *Springfield Republican* took a strong antislavery position and played a leading role in the creation of the Republican party. Although he declined offers to write for the more prominent *New York Tribune*, Bowles wrote editorials that were reprinted nationally, and he made his paper the most notable "country journal" of its day.

Sarah Jane Clarke Lippincott (1823–1904) wrote under the pen name "Grace Greenwood." She served as an assistant editor of the abolitionist paper the *National Era* (1850–52) and was a correspondent for many newspapers, including the *New York Tribune* and *New York Times*. She moved from poetry and literary essays to character sketches of political personalities. She frequently wrote in a light and humorous vein but also dealt with serious issues, from slavery to women's rights.

The development of wireless telegraph technology led one cartoonist in 1899 to ask: "If we can send words through the air, why not everything else?"

2 Technology Transforms Journalism (1860–1900)

Competition among the press made speed an essential part of the news. "Recent" news once took weeks and months to arrive from Europe or even from other states. Some entrepreneurs used carrier pigeons to carry their dispatches and give their newspaper the advantage over the others. Railroads and other improvements in transportation hurried the collection of news. Then, in 1844, the telegraph annihilated space. By 1846 the Associated Press was established to pool telegraph news for New York newspapers. The telegraph not only promoted swiftness but objectivity as well. Since the AP's client papers had many different political leanings, its reporters kept to the facts and left opinions to the editors. The wire services developed the "inverted pyramid" style of reporting, placing the basic information of "who, what, when, where, why, and how" in the first few paragraphs and following with more specific information that editors might publish, condense, or discard.

Greater speed and efficiency and reductions in cost also came with the inventions of the telephone, the typewriter, and the Linotype machine. In 1886 the *New York Tribune* became the first newspaper set on Ottmar Mergenthaler's Linotype machines, which replaced slower hand-set printing with a keyboard. Since the new presses greatly speeded production times, deadlines could be pushed further back and newspapers could become even more current with their news. Improvements in the presses made it affordable to publish illustrations in newspapers—but they also made possible the mass-circulation magazines that provided new competition for the daily newspaper.

The growth of cities and industries in the years after the Civil War further changed American newspapers. Advertising revenues doubled every decade, enabling newspapers to free themselves from dependence on political parties. The printers, partisans, and propagandists of earlier generations made way for professional journalists. News reporters increasingly collected evidence on events as they happened and refrained from offering opinions. Most reporters continued to write anonymously. Briefly during the Civil War, the army had ordered war correspondents to sign their names to their dispatches to hold them accountable for what they wrote. After the war, most reporters gladly abandoned bylines for the security of writing under pen names.

Innovative publishers, such as Joseph Pulitzer and William Randolph Hearst, battled for readers and advertising revenues using everything from sensational news stories to cartoons. The first newspaper comic—the appropriately tinted "Yellow Kid"—gave their papers their identity as the "yellow press." When the real news was too dull, the "yellow press" made its own, concocting stunts and building some of their reporters into celebrities. Pulitzer's *New York World* sent Nellie Bly around the world, while Hearst's *New York Journal* dispatched Richard Harding Davis to cover the revolution in Cuba. The publishers' fevered competition raised suspicions that the "yellow press" was agitating for war with Spain simply to sell newspapers.

Daniel H. Craig

FIRST WITH THE NEWS

To attract readers and stay in business, newspapers have to get news as quickly and inexpensively as possible. Early in the 19th century, newspaper editors exchanged their papers with other newspapers through the mail. Exchange editors clipped out articles from out-of-town papers and reprinted them to supplement the local news that the paper had gathered itself. Readers always wanted to know what was happening elsewhere in America and around the world. Crop failures in Europe, for instance, would raise farm prices in the United States—and those who learned that news first would most profit by it. News from Europe came fastest on British ships of the Cunard line, which made their first stop in Halifax, Canada. There an enterprising news broker, Daniel H. Craig, devised ways of speeding the news from Halifax to newspapers in Boston and New York.

Craig had his roots firmly in New England. His grandfather had fought in the American Revolution, and his father had fought in the War of 1812. As a young man, Craig

An enterprising news broker always in search of the quickest way to transmit information, Daniel Craig moved from carrier pigeons to the telegraph to carry the news.

In the early 1800s flocks of carrier pigeons carried the news faster than any other means of land or sea transportation.

associated with Arunah S. Abell, a founder of the *Baltimore Sun*. Together they experimented with using carrier pigeons to carry the news from Washington to Baltimore. Craig later took this technique north to sell news from Europe to Boston newspapers.

The Cunard line's speedy ships stopped first in Canada before sailing to Boston. The next day, when the steamers left for Boston, Daniel Craig would be on board, carrying a basket of birds. During the two-day trip, he read all the European newspapers on board and printed the most important news on tiny pieces of tissue paper. He attached these reports to the legs of the carrier pigeons. When the Massachusetts coast came into view, he released his birds. They carried the news to Boston hours before the ship reached the city. When the birds returned home, Craig's wife, Helena, would distribute the news to their clients among the Boston papers and telegraph it to Wall Street brokers and to New York papers, such as James Gordon Bennett's *Herald*. The intensely competitive Bennett paid Craig a $500 bonus for every hour that he received European news ahead of other New York newspapers.

When the other papers complained to the Cunard line about Craig's unfair advantage, one ship captain seized Craig's basket of pigeons. Anticipating such trouble, Craig had hidden one of the birds in his pocket. "I went on the deck and flew the bird close to the captain's head," Craig later recalled. "He darted into his stateroom and caught his rifle, but before he got a chance to shoot, the bird was a mile above him, flying straight to his home in Boston, a hundred miles away."

Six competing New York newspapers formed the New York Associated Press (NYAP) in 1846 to pool their efforts and expenses to collect news over the new telegraph. The telegraph lines did not yet extend to Halifax,

apprenticed in a newspaper office. Rather than go to work as a reporter for any paper, however, he saw that there was value in news as a commodity. He could collect news from other sources and sell it to those who bought and sold stocks and bonds and who needed to anticipate how events might affect the markets. He also sold news to other newspapers for a profit.

In the late 1830s he went to Baltimore, Maryland, where he became

however, and news still had to be shipped to Boston. Since the British ships docked for a day in Halifax before sailing on to Boston, the NYAP chartered a steamer, the *Buena Vista*, to leave Halifax as soon as it collected the European newspapers, reducing the delivery time by a day. Once again Daniel Craig foiled the NYAP's plans by booking passage on the *Buena Vista*. Once again his birds beat the ship with the news. By then the New York newspapers concluded that they could not beat him. "Letting such a man as Mr. Craig, whose energy and activity we cannot destroy, or cripple, be let loose," one newspaperman commented, "...looks to us like utter madness." In 1850 the New York newspapers hired Craig as their European news agent in Halifax. The next year they brought him to New York as the general telegraph agent of the New York Associated Press. Craig accepted the offer because he recognized that the telegraph would soon make his pigeons obsolete. By 1858 the Atlantic cable had been laid, carrying the news instantly across the ocean.

As the new manager of the NYAP, Craig worked to expand its services beyond its six New York sponsors and "bring all the leading Presses of the country into one general telegraphic news scheme," Craig wrote to the managers of all telegraph companies in 1851. He created a national system of news collection and distribution over the telegraph wires. Under Craig's system, Associated Press reporters gathered news from local papers in their regions and telegraphed this news to the AP's headquarters in New York. Editors at headquarters condensed these reports into news dispatches and wired them to member papers across the nation. "All shall contribute, in proportion to means and relative advantages to be derived, to the expense and trouble of collecting and transmitting, from one end of the union to the other, all important news," Craig explained, "...the wish being to raise the standard of telegraphic reports, both as regards the *matter* and the *manner* of the same—to make them what they ought to be— *reliable for accuracy,* and the medium through which all *really important* or decidedly interesting news shall be placed before the public, with the utmost dispatch."

As a businessman, Craig always seemed cool and composed, but as one observer commented, "no man with a face so calm and a manner so suave ever stirred a pot so lively." He persuaded his competitors to merge with the NYAP and brought member newspaper editors and publishers into line. Craig established NYAP rules that prohibited member newspapers from publishing stories gotten from any other wire service. Nor could these newspapers have their own reporters use the telegraph to send them special reports. This policy helped standardize the news that papers published all over the country. Craig's competitors warned that he could "regulate the tone of the news dispatches; he is editor in chief of the Press of the whole country." But since the NYAP was under the control of the major New York newspapers— which took entirely different political and ideological stances from each other on the issues—the wire service offered an essentially neutral reporting of the news, without coloration by any single party line. NYAP reporters were told to send factual news without any personal interpretation.

During the Civil War, Craig's cooperative system broke down. Desperate for news from the battlefront, newspapers sent out their own special correspondents, who telegraphed them exclusive reports to beat their competitors. Unable to count on local papers to cover the many aspects of the war, the AP also had to send out its own reporters. The

Daniel H. Craig

BORN

November 3, 1811
Rumney, New Hampshire

DIED

January 5, 1895
Asbury Park, New Jersey

EDUCATION

Printer's apprentice, *Plymouth* (New Hampshire) *Gazette* and *Lancaster* (Massachusetts) *Gazette*

ACCOMPLISHMENTS

News broker for European news (1830s–50); Halifax agent, New York Associated Press (1850–51); general telegraph agent, New York Associated Press (1851–66)

> *"All shall contribute, in proportion to means and relative advantages to be derived, to the expense and trouble of collection and transmitting, from one end of the Union to the other, all important news—as well that relating to commerce as to general events—the wish being to raise the standard of telegraphic reports, both as regards the matter and the manner of the same—to make them what they ought to be—reliable for accuracy, and the medium through which all really important or decidedly interesting news shall be placed before the public, with the utmost despatch."*
>
> —from a circular sent by Craig to the managers of all telegraph companies (May 1851)

result was that newspapers were able to restore much of their individuality without losing the benefits of the wire service.

The success of Craig's system depended on the number of newspapers that participated. The more newspapers that were members of the NYAP, the more news that could be gathered, the lower the costs (especially of telegraph tolls), and the higher the revenue that would be collected. The goal of making his wire service bigger, better, and less expensive led Craig to do everything possible to drive competing news services out of business. Once he had prevailed over other local and regional wire services, Craig made a vigorous effort to persuade the NYAP to buy some of the telegraph lines itself. Owning key portions of the telegraph service, he believed, would make the telegraph company "a tail to the Associated Press kite."

At the same time, the telegraph industry itself was consolidating. In the early 1850s there had been some 50 competing telegraph companies that put up duplicate lines, many of them hastily built and unreliable. In 1856 the Western Union Telegraph Company was organized to replace this chaos with a consolidated telegraphic network. By 1866 Western Union was America's largest corporation and its first national industrial monopoly. Until then, the NYAP had relied on rivalries between telegraph companies to keep its rates low. Seeing this advantage disappear, Craig believed it necessary to arrange a merger between the NYAP and Western Union. Under his plan, the telegraph company's operators all over the country would help collect the news. The telegraph company would also deny its services to the NYAP's rivals. In return, Western Union wanted a majority of the NYAP's stock, meaning that the New York publishers would give up their control of the service. When the publishers found out about Craig's secret negotiations, they fired him. The always enterprising Craig set up a rival news service, the United States and European News Agency, but papers that published his reports were expelled from the NYAP. He also allied himself with the NYAP's major rival, Western Associated Press. In 1867 the New York Associated Press and Western Associated Press reached a news-sharing agreement, putting an end to Craig's influence. Craig settled into a comfortable retirement. The independent news broker was replaced by big-business consolidation of the field. But the wire service that Daniel Craig forged had integrated America's many local newspapers into a national news system.

FURTHER READING

Blondeheim, Menahem. *News Over the Wires: The Telegraph and the Flow of Public Information in America, 1844–1897.* Cambridge: Harvard University Press, 1994.

Czitrom, Daniel J. *Media and the American Mind: From Morse to McLuhan.* Chapel Hill: University of North Carolina Press, 1982.

Schwarzlose, Richard Allen. *The Nation's Newsbrokers.* 2 vols. Evanston, Ill.: Northwestern University Press, 1989–90.

Thompson, Robert Luther. *Wiring a Continent: The History of the Telegraph Industry in the United States, 1832–1866.* 1947. Reprint, New York: Arno, 1972.

Frederick Douglass

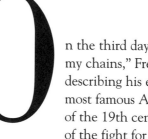

FOR FREEDOM AND EQUITY

"O n the third day of September, 1838, I left my chains," Frederick Douglass wrote, describing his escape from slavery. The most famous African-American journalist of the 19th century made himself a symbol of the fight for freedom and equality in America. Before the Civil War, his newspapers, *North Star* and *Frederick Douglass's Paper*, campaigned for emancipation. After the war, his *New National Era* crusaded for the freedmen's civil rights. Beyond the message that his papers printed, Douglass firmly believed that the very act of a former slave publishing a newspaper would prove the racial prejudices of his day to be wrong.

Frederick Douglass was born on Maryland's Eastern Shore to a slave woman and a white man whose identity he never learned. Raised by his grandparents, Betsy and Isaac Bailey, he was named Frederick Augustus Washington Bailey. When the children of the plantation were old enough, they were taken to live near their master at Wye House, and to Frederick's dismay, his grandmother left him there when he was six. Later, he was sent to Baltimore to work as a house servant. "I had been treated as a *pig* on the plantation," he later wrote; "in this new house, I was treated

Frederick Douglass's newspaper, *The North Star,* carried the banner: "Right is of no sex—truth is of no color—God is the Father of us all, and all we are brethren."

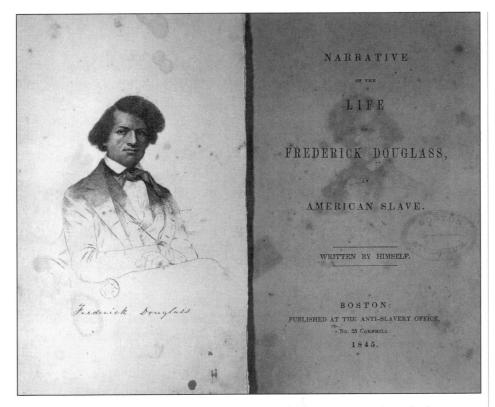

When some people doubted that Frederick Douglass had ever been a slave, he published his autobiography. It became a best-seller in the years before the Civil War.

as a *child*." Most significantly, his mistress, Sophia Keitley, taught him how to read and write. He learned quickly, and soon was reading the Bible and newspapers, where he first came across the word "abolition." In 1833 young Frederick was sent back to the Eastern Shore, where he was hired out as a laborer. When one of his masters attempted to beat him, he fought back and was not struck again. His self-confidence rose—he felt himself a man and wanted to become a free man.

Sent back to Baltimore, he was hired out as an apprentice caulker in the Baltimore shipyards. While in Baltimore, Frederick met Anna Murray, a free black woman. Together they planned his escape to freedom. She lent him the money he needed for a train ticket North. Dressed as a sailor, he boarded the train heading north to New York. Soon after, Anna joined him and they were married. Despite being in the North, he worried that he could be arrested and returned as a fugitive slave, so he changed his name to Douglass. Abolitionists arranged for him and Anna to sail for Rhode Island,

where he worked as a laborer at whatever jobs he could get, often finding doors closed to him because of his race. There, in New Bedford, the first of their five children was born in 1839.

That same year Douglass attended an antislavery meeting and spoke in public for the first time. The topic was the return of former slaves to Africa. Douglass strongly opposed such colonization and told the audience of the advantages of being free in America. His earnestness impressed his listeners, and a report of his speech later appeared in William Lloyd Garrison's abolitionist newspaper, *The Liberator*, leading to invitations to tell his story to other assemblies.

In 1841 the Massachusetts Anti-Slavery Society employed Douglass as an antislavery orator. Sent to speak in many states, he frequently traveled with William Lloyd Garrison. Not every audience was receptive, and at several stops the men were mobbed and jeered by those who considered abolitionists to be troublemakers. Douglass's powerful and persuasive antislavery speeches were also printed in the *New York Tribune* and as pamphlets, which abolitionists cited as proof of the abilities of a black man. So articulate was Douglass that some people doubted he had ever been a slave, which led him to write his first autobiography, *Narrative of the Life of Frederick Douglass*. Published in 1845, it gathered many favorable reviews, including one by Margaret Fuller in the *New York Tribune*. The book became a best-seller and was translated into several languages.

In his autobiography Douglass admitted his real name and fugitive status, making it dangerous for him to remain in the United States. And so in 1845 he went abroad to speak throughout England, Ireland, and Scotland, sending back articles to the *The Liberator* and other antislavery papers. The visit to Great Britain gave Douglass contacts with the leaders of the British antislavery movement. British friends raised money to buy his freedom officially, and they promised to support his plans to start a newspaper.

By contrast, William Lloyd Garrison opposed such competition to his own paper. "The land is full of the wreck of such experiments," he warned. Garrison argued that editing a newspaper would cut back Douglass's antislavery lecturing. But Douglass believed that his editing and publishing a paper "would be a *telling* fact" against the prejudice "which so universally prevails in this country against the colored race."

When he returned to the United States in 1847, Douglass settled in Rochester, New York, near the Canadian border, where he could help smuggle other fugitive slaves out of the country. On December 3, 1847, the first issue of Douglass's weekly paper, *The North Star*, appeared. Although not the first paper published by an African American, it drew the greatest attention. "In the publication of the paper," he wrote, "I shall be under no party or society, but shall advocate the slave's cause." Subscriptions came in slowly, however, and Douglass had to mortgage his home to keep the paper going. He was especially disappointed not to receive more support from black Americans, and his paper attracted only one black subscriber for every five white subscribers. To raise money for the paper, he continued making lecture tours and often had to write his articles "on the wing." Antislavery supporters came to his aid. The British abolitionist Julia Griffiths not only raised money for *The North Star* but came to Rochester to help put out the paper during Douglass's absences. By 1851 the paper had 4,000 subscribers and was self-sustaining.

The North Star published essays and poetry by black and white abolitionists, but the largest share of the paper was given over to Douglass's own speeches and editorials. He made it a point to sign his articles F. D. to prove that a self-taught fugitive slave could write correctly. He edited the paper carefully to avoid typographical and grammatical errors, to show that his paper could compete with any other newspaper.

In the summer of 1851 *The North Star* merged with the *Liberty Party Paper*, a much smaller weekly paper edited in Syracuse for the antislavery Liberty Party. The paper was renamed *Frederick Douglass's Paper*, and its motto, "All Rights for All," reflected Douglass's growing conviction that the abolition of slavery would not be enough in itself. He insisted that the freedmen must enjoy social, economic, and political equality, including the right to vote to protect their liberties. In that same philosophy, he endorsed equal rights for women in education and in voting. Douglass's paper often carried stories of his own refusal to be treated as a second-class citizen when traveling by train or dining and lodging in public places. He sought to inspire other free blacks to stand up for their rights, and promoted the ideal that the races could live together as equals.

Most abolitionists wanted to end slavery through legal and political means, but Douglass also encountered John Brown, who was not opposed to shedding blood. Brown wanted to recruit him for a guerrilla-style raid into the South to stir a rebellion of the slaves against their masters. Douglass admired Brown, but he thought his plans stood little chance of success and declined to join him. When Brown was captured raiding the federal arsenal at Harpers Ferry in western Virginia in 1859, the governor of Virginia identified Douglass as part of the conspiracy and demanded his arrest. Fearing that he might be sent to Virginia to be hanged along with Brown, Douglass fled to Canada and from there to Great

Frederick Douglass

BORN

Around February 14, 1817
Tuckahoe, Maryland

DIED

February 20, 1895
Washington, D.C.

EDUCATION

Taught to read while a houseboy in Baltimore, Maryland; otherwise self-educated

ACCOMPLISHMENTS

Editor, *The North Star* (Rochester, New York, 1848–51); editor, *Frederick Douglass's Paper* (1851–60); editor, *Douglass's Monthly* (1858–63); editor, *New National Era* (Washington, D.C., 1870–74); author of *Narrative of the Life of Frederick Douglass* (1845), *My Bondage and My Freedom* (1855), and *Life and Times of Frederick Douglass* (1881)

"What shall be done with the Negro? . . . This question met us during the war; and will certainly meet us after the war, unless we have the wisdom, the courage, and the nobleness of soul to settle the status of the Negro, on the solid and immovable basis of Eternal justice. I stand here tonight therefore, to advocate what I conceive to be a solid basis, one that shall fix our peace upon a rock. Putting aside all the hay, wood, and stubble of expedience, I shall advocate for the Negro, his most full and complete adoption into the great national family of America. I shall demand for him the most perfect civil and political equality, and that he shall enjoy all the rights, privileges and immunities enjoyed by all members of the body politic."

—from "The Present and Future of the Colored Race in America," *Douglass's Monthly* (November 1862)

Britain. His weekly newspaper shut down, although from abroad he continued publishing his magazine, *Douglass's Monthly*.

The election of 1860 brought the Republican party to power and triggered the secession of the Southern states and then the Civil War. Douglass returned to the United States to support the war effort and to lobby President Abraham Lincoln for emancipation of the slaves. Hoping to receive a military commission, Douglass terminated *Douglass's Monthly* in 1863, announcing his plans to go South to recruit black soldiers. (Two of his sons signed up to serve in the Union army.) He closed his publications in the same room where they had begun 16 years earlier. "It has been during these sixteen years," he reflected, "immovable in its principles as it has been permanent in its local habitation." Since his writings now appeared in many newspapers around the country, Douglass believed he could retire from publishing his own papers because the white press was now willing to publish any arguments or appeals he wished to make in behalf of his race.

Douglass rejoiced over the emancipation of the slaves but felt dismayed over the treatment of the freedmen after the war. He called for "liberty for all, chains for none; the black man a soldier in war, a laborer in peace; a voter at the South as well as at the North; America his permanent home, and all Americans his countrymen." In 1870 he joined a group of stockholders to found a new newspaper, the *New Era*, "in the interest of the colored people of America; not as a separate Class, but as a part of the WHOLE PEOPLE." At first Douglass served as corresponding editor, but after a few months he purchased the paper and moved to Washington to edit it personally, renaming it the *New National Era*. Although the paper appealed to an integrated audience, Douglass especially wanted it to serve as a standard "for my people which would cheer and strengthen them in the work of their own improvement and elevation." Later, when he became president of the Freedman's Bank in Washington, he turned management of the newspaper over to his sons.

In 1873 a severe financial panic rocked the nation. Among the victims of the depression that followed were the Freedman's Bank and the *New National Era*, which both shut down in 1874. Despite the end of his careers in journalism and banking, Douglass remained active in public life. In 1877 President Rutherford B. Hayes appointed Douglass marshal of the District of Columbia, making him the first black appointee confirmed to office by the U.S. Senate. And in 1889 President Benjamin Harrison appointed him minister to Haiti.

Anna Douglass died in 1882, and two years later Frederick Douglass married Helen Pitts, a white woman. When this action sparked criticism, he wryly observed that his first wife had been the color of his mother and his second the color of his father. The Douglasses resided at Cedar Hill, a large house overlooking Washington, D.C. There he continued his writing, surrounded by his extensive library. Although discouraged about the condition of African Americans after Reconstruction, Douglass was brought back to the lecture hall through his friendship with the African-American journalist Ida Wells-Barnett, who persuaded him to direct his oratory against the crime of lynching. Frederick Douglass delivered his last public address in 1894, when he was 77, denouncing corruption in politics and calling for equal rights for all. Politically active to the end, he had just returned from a women's rights rally in Washington when he collapsed and died at Cedar Hill.

Frederick Douglass is seated beside his wife, Helen, and her sister (standing) in this photograph taken toward the end of his long career as a journalist and public official.

FURTHER READING

Bontemps, Arna W. *Free At Last: The Life of Frederick Douglass*. New York: Dodd, Mead, 1971.

Bullock, Penelope L. *The Afro-American Periodical Press*. Baton Rouge: Louisiana State University Press, 1981.

Douglass, Frederick. *Frederick Douglass in His Own Words*. Edited by Milton Meltzer. San Diego: Harcourt Brace, 1995.

———. *The Frederick Douglass Papers*. Edited by John W. Blassingame. 5 vols. New Haven: Yale University Press, 1979–1992, 5 volumes.

———. *My Bondage and My Freedom*. 1855. Reprint, Urbana: University of Illinois Press, 1987.

———. *Narrative of the Life of Frederick Douglass*. 1845. Reprint, New York: Dover, 1995.

———. *The Oxford Frederick Douglass Reader*. Edited by William L. Andrews. New York: Oxford University Press, 1996.

Foner, Philip S. *Frederick Douglass*. New York: Citadel Press, 1964.

Huggins, Nathan I. *Slave and Citizen: The Life of Frederick Douglass*. Boston: Little, Brown, 1980.

McFeely, William S. *Frederick Douglass*. New York: Norton, 1991.

Senna, Carl. *The Black Press and the Struggle for Civil Rights*. New York: Franklin Watts, 1993.

Voss, Frederick. *Majestic in His Wrath: A Pictorial Life of Frederick Douglass*. Washington, D.C.: Smithsonian Institution Press, 1995.

Wolseley, Roland E. *The Black Press, U.S.A.* Ames: Iowa State University Press, 1980.

Lawrence A. Gobright

THE WIRE SERVICES AND "OBJECTIVE" REPORTING

On Sunday, July 20, 1861, a flock of reporters joined members of Congress and other dignitaries to journey to the Virginia countryside, where they witnessed the first battle of the Civil War. The civilians expected to view a splendid victory by the Union army and a swift military defeat of the rebellion. Late in the afternoon, however, the tide of this "picnic battle" turned when the Confederates unexpectedly brought in reserve troops. The Union army retreated the 30 miles toward Washington, forcing reporters, senators, and representatives to hurry alongside them or face capture.

At nine o'clock that night, the field correspondent for the New York Associated Press arrived at the AP's Washington headquarters. So agitated that he could not write his story, he paced up and down with an unlit cigar in his teeth and dictated what he had seen to the AP's regular Washington correspondent, Lawrence Gobright. Gobright then rushed to the telegraph office to send the dramatic story to the AP member papers all across the nation. But the next day when the trains to Washington brought the out-of-town newspapers, Gobright discovered that none of them carried the story of the defeat. Military censors had stopped his dispatch from getting through. A veteran Washington correspondent, Gobright learned then that the war was going to change how the news was reported.

Larry Gobright first came to Washington in 1834. In those days, before railroads reached the capital, it took an entire day's wagon ride for news to get from Washington to Baltimore. Boats took days to carry the news farther away. Gobright worked as a printer until 1839, when he became a reporter for the *Washington Globe*, covering the debates in the House of Representatives. The job of a reporter in Gobright's day, unlike that of a modern-day reporter, was really that of a stenographer recording the debates as precisely as possible.

The *Globe* was a private, not a government, enterprise. It reported the debates of the House and Senate in its pages, which other newspapers around the country clipped and reprinted. Eventually, its reports were compiled into volumes, the forerunner of today's *Congressional Record*. Yet, while the publishers of the *Globe* were not being paid to report the congressional debates, they received federal funding as official printers of the government. As a Democrat, Gobright sought support from his party to launch a pro-Democratic newspaper in Batavia, Ohio. In 1840 the paper endorsed the Democratic candidate for President, Martin Van Buren. When Van Buren lost, Gobright gave up and returned to the capital as Washington correspondent for newspapers in his native Baltimore and other cities.

Washington was a relatively small town in the 1840s. The federal government generated most of its news during the months when Congress was in session—about half of the year. When Congress adjourned, reporters for out-of-town papers left with it. Since Gobright lived in Washington, he reported from there all year. For one six-week period in the mid-1840s, he was the *only* reporter sending news out of Washington, D.C.

In May 1844 the inventor Samuel F. B. Morse invited members of Congress to witness the first long-distance testing of his invention, the telegraph. After setting up a telegraph key in the Capitol in Washington, and another in Baltimore, Morse sent the first message: "What hath God wrought?" Soon another message came from Baltimore: "What is the news in Washington?" That year the *Baltimore Patriot* became the first newspaper to publish a telegraphic news dispatch, about a vote in the House of Representatives. By 1846 the biggest New York newspapers pooled their resources to form the New York Associated Press, which hired reporters in Washington and elsewhere to send them telegraphic news. Gobright became one of the AP's Washington reporters, covering the House of Representatives and various executive branch departments. He would hold the job for 33 years until his death.

At that time reporters generally worked for newspapers that were clearly identified with a particular political party, and they slanted the news to fit their party's positions. Gobright started as a Democrat, and while his dispatches for the Associated Press appeared in many Democratic newspapers, they also appeared in Whig papers, Republican papers, and independent papers. He could not take sides on any

issue, but had to present the facts with as little interpretation as possible. Newspapers would get their straight news from the Associated Press wire dispatches, and their opinionated commentary from their own "special correspondents," who interpreted events.

Politicians of all parties appreciated Gobright's neutrality, although they did not like everything he reported. The reporter cultivated sources in high places. One of his closest friends was a member of President James Buchanan's cabinet, who "leaked" secrets from the cabinet meetings that Gobright published. The angry President sent for

President Abraham Lincoln trusted Lawrence Gobright as an honest and truthful reporter and used his Associated Press reports to reach the American people.

Lawrence Gobright's bulletin and follow-up stories in the *New York Herald* alerted the world to President Lincoln's assassination. At the bottom of the second column is Gobright's first bulletin: "The President was shot in a theatre to-night, and is perhaps mortally wounded."

Gobright and demanded that he tell who was the source of the leak. "I would as soon tell you, Mr. President, as I would any other man, but I do not reveal the sources of my news," Gobright declared.

"But you might tell *me*," Buchanan persisted. Gobright explained: "Suppose, Mr. President, you were now to give me an item, and I published it; and that in response to an inquiry of a third party, I were to inform him that I received it from you—how would you like to have your name mentioned in that connection?" The President nodded: "I see the point."

Many Democrats remained furious with Gobright for publishing leaks that embarrassed the Democratic Buchanan administration. "I was the subject of much abuse, and was accused in more than one Democratic newspaper with being a 'Black Republican,' and deserved to have my head broken," he recalled. The accusation of "Black Republican" meant that he sided with the new antislavery Republican party. Horace Greeley, editor of the Republican-leaning *New York Tribune*, came to his defense: Gobright was "a Southern man by birth and education, and never, so far as we know, suspected of 'Black Republicanism,'" Greeley wrote. "We have always understood him to be a Democrat in politics, though we cannot remember that we ever heard him express a political opinion."

When the Civil War began in 1861, a horde of eager young journalists made Washington their headquarters for war news. Although he was still a middle-aged man, his gray hair, side whiskers, and genial attitude won Gobright the nicknames "Pop" and "Father Gobright." His younger competitors scoffed at him for simply publishing news items as he collected them from federal offices, and they accused him of being nothing more

than a "government agent." In fact, President Abraham Lincoln trusted Gobright to be honest and truthful, and the Lincoln administration used the Associated Press as a way of reaching the American people. A fellow correspondent, George Alfred Townsend, described Gobright as "a painstaking, responsible" reporter who was "chiefly concerned with things already passed" rather than speculating on what might happen in the future. "The Associated Press had the respect and confidence of the highest officers of the Government, and it gave the people outline news so that they were kept tolerably well and promptly informed of the facts at the capital."

President Lincoln had a habit of walking over to the War Department the last thing each night to read the latest reports telegraphed from the battlefield. Sometimes Lincoln invited Gobright to accompany him, and provided him with news for his dispatches (although the reporter was never to attribute this news to the President). Once, Gobright saw Lincoln read a report that General Ulysses S. Grant's army had been defeated near Vicksburg, Mississippi. Lincoln's hands and legs shook and his face had a ghastly color. Turning to Gobright in a faltering voice, the President said, "Bad news, bad news. *Don't say anything about this—don't mention it.*" But Gobright pointed out that the wire was merely a report, not an official communication, and from his experience, "more than one half of war rumors are false." Lincoln looked visibly relieved, and they later learned that the report was erroneous. Grant's troops captured Vicksburg.

The rest of the government shared Lincoln's reluctance to release bad news, not wanting to demoralize the public in the North or give comfort to the South. Government censors controlled what newspaper correspondents could send and clipped out of their dis-

Lawrence A. Gobright

BORN
May 2, 1816
Baltimore, Maryland

DIED
May 22, 1879
Washington, D.C.

ACCOMPLISHMENTS
Reporter, *Washington Globe* (1839–40); editor, *Batavia* (Ohio) *Sun* (1840); Washington correspondent, *Baltimore Clipper* and other papers (1841–46); Washington correspondent, New York Associated Press (1846–79); part owner and editor, *Washington Evening Star*; editor, *Washington Bee*; author of *Recollections of Men and Things at Washington During the Third of a Century* (1869), *Jack and Jill, For Old and Young* (1873, nursery rhymes), and *Echoes of Childhood: Old Friends in New Costumes from the Risen and Rising Generation* (1879, nursery rhymes)

patches anything that might be considered too negative or might give away military secrets. Other reporters observed that Gobright got more news through the censors than anyone else. When the Congress investigated military censorship of telegraph communications, they called Gobright to testify about why he seemed to be receiving special favors.

"My business is merely to communicate facts," Gobright explained. "My instructions do not allow me to make any comment upon the facts which I communicate. My despatches are sent to papers of all manner of politics, and the editors say they are able to make their own comments upon the facts which are sent to them. I therefore confine myself to what I consider legitimate news." Gobright was defining what later generations of reporters would call "objective" reporting of the news—taking no sides on the issues that they reported. Yet rather than celebrating his impartial reporting, he apologized for it, saying: "My despatches are merely dry matters of fact and detail."

The younger Washington reporters may have considered "Pop" Gobright past his prime, but simply by being on the job and working long hours he scored one of the greatest scoops in journalism history. On the night of April 14, 1865, Gobright was alone in his office, having filed what he thought was his last dispatch for that day. Suddenly he heard footsteps and an excited voice outside his door. A friend had just come from Ford's Theater to report that President Lincoln had been shot. Although Gobright could barely believe the

news, he went straight to the telegraph office and sent a short "special," or bulletin: "The President was shot in a theatre to-night, and is perhaps mortally wounded."

As the telegraph was broadcasting his dispatch, Gobright headed for the theater, where he entered the Presidential box and found blood on the back of the President's chair and the assassin's pistol still lying on the floor. Although guards kept him from entering the house where the President lay dying, he was able to interview those who had seen Lincoln being carried in. During the evening, Gobright filed other dispatches with each of his observations, piecing together the story for the nation's press. Gobright's later pieces provided more detail, but it was his one-sentence AP bulletin that first alerted the world to the dreadful news of Lincoln's assassination.

FURTHER READING

Andrews, J. Cutler. The North Reports the Civil War. 1955. Reprint, Pittsburgh, PA: University of Pittsburgh Press, 1983.

Blondheim, Menahem. News Over the Wires: The Telegraph and the Flow of Public Information in America, 1844–1897. Cambridge: Harvard University Press, 1994.

Marbut, F.B. News from the Capital: The Story of Washington Reporting. Carbondale: Southern Illinois University Press, 1971.

Ritchie, Donald A. Press Gallery: Congress and the Washington Correspondents. Cambridge: Harvard University Press, 1991.

Joseph B. McCullagh

CIVIL WAR
CORRESPONDENT

J oseph McCullagh speculated that the secret to his success as a journalist was his ability to "guess where Hell will break loose next." He had a knack for determining where the action would be and putting himself in the middle of it, often risking his life to get his story. While still a teenager, McCullagh rose to national fame in the "Bohemian Brigade" of newspaper correspondents who reported from the battlefield during the Civil War. Other reporters noted that, although baby-faced and short in stature, McCullagh was hot-tempered and able to swear like "a seven-foot pirate." Balancing this temperament with fairness and impartiality as a reporter, McCullagh eventually came to the attention of the nation's most embattled President. Fighting for his political life, Andrew Johnson would give the young reporter the chance to conduct the first on-the-record newspaper interview with a President of the United States.

Joseph McCullagh was born in Dublin, the son of a shoemaker. After the great potato famine devastated Ireland, Joe chose to leave to ease the burden on his parents. In 1853, at the age of 11, he left his native Ireland and

Signing his columns "Mack," Joseph McCullagh rose to fame as a member of the "Bohemian Brigade" reporting from the battlefield during the Civil War.

"WASHINGTON, D.C., Feb. 10, 1868—I called on the President last evening and had an interview with him of about an hour's duration. From the revival of the impeachment project and the recent correspondence between him and Gen. Grant, which I had been informed, on the authority of several eminently loyal newspapers, was literally "crushing" to A.J., I expected to find His Excellency in a prostrate and enfeebled condition, or perhaps "writhing in the agonies of despair."

—from an excerpt in the *Cincinnati Commercial* (February 13, 1868)

emigrated to America by himself. Joining thousands of others who sailed for the New World, he was penniless when he arrived in New York City. He became an apprentice printer for a paper called the *Freeman's Journal*. By the age of 16 he had made his way west to St. Louis, where he found a job setting type for the St. Louis *Christian Advocate*. It was the *Advocate*'s policy that all its employees must attend church, and Joe began going to a Methodist Sunday school. Taking his religion seriously, he enrolled in a stenography class to be able to record sermons accurately. Years later, when he became editor of the St. Louis Globe-Democrat, the paper became known as the "Great Religious Daily" because of its extensive coverage of church sermons.

McCullagh rented a room in the home of the Reverend William E. Babcock, where he took the opportunity to read books in Babcock's extensive personal library. Since Babcock wrote a weekly column for the *Missouri Democrat*, McCullagh confided to him his ambition to become a reporter. Babcock put in a good word for McCullagh at the paper, assuring the editors that "the boy had brains and would make his mark if given a chance." The only job open was that of a proofreader, but the 17-year-old so impressed the print shop foreman with his proofreading ability that he was hired immediately. Soon after, when one of the reporters left on vacation McCullagh took over his assignments temporarily. To the foreman's astonishment, on Joe's first day on the job he uncovered enough news to fill the entire column and a half allocated to local news. "The second day we squeezed in two columns for him. The third day we had to cut down the size of the type to get in his copy. I never saw anyone go at it like that boy," recalled the foreman. Having impressed his employers, McCullagh became a regular member of their reporting staff.

Always in search of controversy, McCullagh published an exposé of coach operators who regularly overcharged passengers for carrying them to and from the riverboats. Late one night, one of the carriage men jumped the young reporter and beat him. McCullagh returned to his office with two black eyes and declared that he would run the man out of St. Louis. He wrote so many critical stories that the man eventually came to the paper to beg for mercy. McCullagh kept his word and did not stop until the crooked carriage operator had left St. Louis.

On the eve of the Civil War, McCullagh covered the Missouri legislature. He was such a strong Unionist that Southern sympathizers began making threats against his safety. Yet while politicians often disagreed with him, they admired his shorthand skills, which allowed him to produce accurate accounts of their speeches. Illinois senator Lyman Trumbull was so unhappy over the way one of his speeches appeared in the *Cincinnati Gazette* that he complained to his editor, pointing out what a better job Joe McCullagh had done in St. Louis. The *Gazette's* editor then hired McCullagh to report on the 1860 Presidential campaign.

When the Civil War started, McCullagh returned to Missouri and joined the Union army. As a second lieutenant, he was assigned to be a stenographer for the flamboyant General John Charles Frémont. Equipped with a wagon loaded with a printing press, cases of type, and four printers, McCullagh also published a daily newspaper, giving the latest orders for Frémont's troops. Those who encountered him described McCullagh as slender as a rail, with light blond hair and looking even younger than his age, but speaking quickly and intensely and uttering "colossal oaths." McCullagh concluded that Frémont was an inept general and considered his military moves to be nothing but a farce. After Frémont lost his command, McCullagh resigned his commission and returned to the *Cincinnati Gazette* as a war correspondent. Like other correspondents of the day, for self-protection he used a pen name, writing under the name "Mack." Other reporters sometimes referred to him as "Little Mack."

Only 19 when he began as a war correspondent, McCullagh traveled down to Cairo, Illinois, where General Ulysses S. Grant and Commodore Andrew H. Foote were planning an assault on Fort Donnelson, the Confederate fort that controlled the mouth of the Tennessee River. McCullagh offered his services as a private secretary to Commodore Foote, which got him passage on Foote's flagship, the *St. Louis*. Sailing straight toward the fort's big guns, the *St. Louis* took 65 hits and was the worst-damaged gunboat in the fleet. McCullagh was standing next to the ship's pilot, who was killed by shrapnel. Commodore Foote was badly injured, while McCullagh remained one of the few on board to escape injury.

Later he went on to cover the battle of Shiloh, in Tennessee, and wrote a dispatch highly critical of the Union officers. Other correspondents read his dispatch and predicted that the *Gazette* would never print it. McCullagh vowed that if the paper did not, he would resign. When the publisher of the rival *Cincinnati Commercial* learned of McCullagh's dispute with his editors, he hired him away at twice the salary.

While in Kentucky in August 1862, McCullagh was captured by Confederate guerrillas and forced to march with them as a prisoner. When he finally convinced them that he was not a soldier, they set him free. He had to walk 80 miles back to Cincinnati. McCullagh described these exploits in his newspaper dispatches. But he drew even more attention for his astute analyses of military tactics. The *Chicago Tribune* later ranked "Little Mack" as one of the best war correspondents because "He was alert, active, and had a marvelously thorough knowledge of military maneuvers." Few correspondents could grasp a military situation so quickly. "He had the whole thing in his head all the time and could draw a diagram of the situation at any time." While reporting for the *Commercial*, McCullagh also began sending articles to the *New York Tribune* until soon the byline "Mack" became nationally known.

Americans formed their opinions about the war and the capabilities of various generals through what they read in the papers. At Vicksburg, McCullagh drew memorable images of General Grant slouched on his horse, whittling pieces of wood. When one attack failed, he reported that he overheard Grant say, "We'll have to dig our way in," in the tone of a man announcing that he was going to bed. Some Union generals were less impressed with the publicity they received. They complained that McCullagh's reporting

Joseph B. McCullagh

BORN

November, 1842
Dublin, Ireland

DIED

December 31, 1896
St. Louis, Missouri

EDUCATION

Left school at age 10

ACCOMPLISHMENTS

Reporter, *Missouri Democrat* (1859–61); war correspondent, *Cincinnati Gazette* (1861–62); war correspondent, *Cincinnati Commercial* (1862–63); Washington correspondent, *Cincinnati Commercial* and Associated Press (1863–68); managing editor, *Cincinnati Enquirer* (1868–70); managing editor, *Chicago Republican* (1870–71); managing editor, *St. Louis Globe-Democrat* (1871–96)

Faced with impeachment, President Andrew Johnson (left) granted interviews to McCullagh as a way of making his case to the public.

was so accurate that rebel armies were reading Northern newspapers to gain military intelligence. They were also unhappy that McCullagh's reporting was critical. By 1863 he was barred from entering Union army camps, which ended his career as a war correspondent.

The *Cincinnati Commercial* then sent its star reporter to Washington to cover Congress and the President. There he also wrote dispatches for the Associated Press that went to newspapers all across the nation. "Mack's" letters from Washington were rated by other journalists as "terse, incisive and sparse of adjectives," but showing the same ability to grasp political situations that he had demonstrated on the battlefields.

The Civil War ended in 1865, followed by a tumultuous era of Reconstruction. Recalling the epic struggle between Congress and President Andrew Johnson over Reconstruction policy, one Washington corespondent later reminisced that he would "rather run all the risks of the Gettysburg campaign again than go through the stormy times of Reconstruction." Other reporters described it as a "rough-and-tumble, hurley-burly time" that produced an endless supply of news stories. Although many reporters sided either with the President or the Congress, McCullagh's reporting of these events always demonstrated notable fairness and impartiality. These reports came to the attention of President Johnson at a time when Radical Republicans in Congress were determined to impeach Johnson and remove him from office. McCullagh was sitting in the Senate press gallery one day when he received a message that the President wanted to see him in the White House. Not only was Johnson willing to grant an interview, but he told McCullagh that he could report their conversation. This was unprecedented. Earlier Presidents had talked to reporters on the understanding that they were never to be quoted directly. All Andrew Johnson asked was that the reporter "put me down right." The President complained that "the d—n newspapers are as bad as the politicians in misrepresenting me. I don't want you to take my side, I can right these fellows singlehanded; but put me down correctly."

McCullagh did, and Johnson was so pleased with the results that he sent for him again. "I want to give these fellows hell," said the President, pointing toward Capitol Hill, "and I think I can do it better through your paper than through a message because the people read the papers more than they do messages."

During his Presidential interviews, McCullagh never carried a pen or paper. Despite his stenographic skills, he feared that Johnson would have grown more formal and less relaxed if he saw him taking notes. "He would have hesitated, stopped, asked the reporter to read his notes to him, and otherwise shown signs of concern which would have hindered the flow of his conversation and abated his interest," McCullagh later explained. "The only way was to get him started, and let him alone until he had run down, then wind him up with a new question." After the interview, McCullagh raced back to his rooms to reconstruct the conversation from memory. McCullagh was pleased that President Johnson narrowly escaped conviction and removal from office, and that his interviews may have helped influence public opinion and senators' votes.

After four tempestuous years reporting on events in Washington, McCullagh returned to Cincinnati to become managing editor of the *Cincinnati Enquirer*. Then he accepted a more lucrative offer to go to Chicago as editor of the *Chicago Republican*. But the great Chicago fire of October 1871 destroyed the newspaper's offices and printing plant and with it burned all of McCullagh's investments. "Little Mack" returned to St. Louis, where he had started, and eventually became

managing editor of the *St. Louis Globe-Democrat*, a post he held for the rest of his life. He made his fortune and expanded his reputation as a creative and demanding editor with high standards, who made the *Globe-Democrat* one of the most successful newspapers of its time.

Ahead of Joseph Pulitzer and William Randolph Hearst, McCullagh pioneered many of the characteristics that made modern newspapers. In gathering news the *Globe-Democrat* was aggressive—even sensationalist. It sponsored crusades for clean government and against gambling, drinking, and other social ills, had a biting editorial page, and filled its pages with illustrations. It conducted constant self-promotion to attract readers. McCullagh instructed his reporters to get exclusive news, but only if they stuck strictly to the facts. He wanted impartial, not partisan, stories, and he wanted to expose political scandal and corruption. Following those dictates, the *Globe-Democrat* became the dominant paper in booming St. Louis, standing up against Pulitzer's *St. Louis Post Dispatch*.

Journalism was Joe McCullagh's entire life. He never married, worked 12-hour days (from 12:30 in the afternoon until 12:30 at night), and rarely took a vacation. An associate described him as being "engrossed in the newspaper as some men are engrossed in their families. He felt it was his creation and its glory was his glory." The novelist Theodore Dreiser, who worked as a reporter for McCullagh from 1892 to 1893, said, "I often think of him in that small office, sitting waist-deep among his papers...his whole air one of complete mental and physical absorption in his work."

Over time, however, overwork caused nervous collapse. McCullagh's health declined and one night, dressed only in his nightshirt, he fell or jumped from his bedroom window. Although his doctor assumed that he had taken his own life, McCullagh's loyal staff believed that "the Chief" had fallen accidentally. Among the many tributes that were paid to "Little Mack" was one from a fellow Civil War correspondent, Henry Boynton, who recalled that McCullagh had always been a tough, unrelenting but unprejudiced journalist. "If his caustic paragraphs fell like blows, it was because of the truth they contained."

FURTHER READING

Andrews, J. Cutler. *The North Reports the Civil War*. 1955. Reprint, Pittsburgh: University of Pittsburgh Press, 1985.

Clayton, Charles C. *Little Mack: Joseph B. McCullagh of the St. Louis Globe-Democrat*. Carbondale: Southern Illinois University Press, 1969.

Ritchie, Donald A. *Press Gallery: Congress and the Washington Correspondents*. Cambridge: Harvard University Press, 1991.

Starr, Louis M. *Bohemian Brigade: Civil War Newsmen in Action*. 1954. Reprint, Madison: University of Wisconsin Press, 1987.

Taft, William H. *Missouri Newspapers*. Columbia: University of Missouri Press, 1964.

Weisberger, Bernard A. *Reporters for the Union*. 1953. Reprint, Westport, Conn.: Greenwood, 1977.

Mark Twain (Samuel Langhorne Clemens)

THE JOURNALIST
AS HUMORIST

A good many journalists in the mid-1800s adopted a "Bohemian" life-style. They took their name from the Czech region of Bohemia in Central Europe, famed for its vagabond ways. Free-spirited young men without family obligations, these reporters slept late in the morning and worked late into the evening. They patrolled jails, morgues, red-light districts, and taverns for news. They enjoyed good food and strong drink when they could afford it, and they cultivated a cynical view of society, government, and human nature. Many of these reporters harbored literary ambitions, and anticipated using their daily experiences to provide the material with which they would write the "great American novel." Many tried and failed, but one of them—Samuel Langhorne Clemens—emerged from the Bohemian life of a journalist in the 1860s to become the renowned author Mark Twain.

Sam Clemens was born in Missouri, the son of John Marshall Clemens, a lawyer, farmer, storekeeper, and land speculator—a dreamer who failed at one occupation after another. He died when Sam was just 12, leaving his wife and three children not much more than a parcel of land in Tennessee that they always hoped would bring their fortune—but never did. Sam's mother, Jane Lampton Clemens, believed that she was the descendant of English nobility. Their stories and others from the Mississippi River town of Hannibal, Missouri, where Sam spent much of his childhood, fed his fertile imagination.

Forced to leave school when his father died, Clemens became an apprentice printer. His work in print shops encouraged him to read and write, and he was always "scribbling" in his free time. He published his first newspaper article in a Hannibal paper that his older brother, Orion, edited. Then Sam hit the road, using his skills as a printer to find work all around the country, from St. Louis to New York, from Philadelphia to Iowa. Fascinated by the Mississippi River, he signed on as an apprentice pilot for the steamboats that traveled up and down the river to New Orleans. There he met colorful river men and women, ship captains, gamblers, and other travelers who would become characters in his later writing. He called the Mississippi his university.

In 1861 the Civil War shut off river traffic and ended his career as a pilot. Clemens joined an irregular Confederate military group, but after a couple of weeks decided that he was not the type to choose sides in any civil war. He quit to head west with his brother, Orion, who had gotten a job as secretary to the territorial governor of Nevada. For a while, Clemens tried prospecting. Although

Mark Twain (Samuel Langhorne Clemens)

Mark Twain (center) with fellow Washington correspondents George Alfred Townsend (left) and James A. Riley (right).

BORN

November 30, 1835
Florida, Missouri

DIED

April 21, 1910
Redding, Connecticut

EDUCATION

Public schools in Hannibal, Missouri

ACCOMPLISHMENTS

Contributor, *Hannibal Journal* (around 1849); reporter and San Francisco correspondent, *Territorial Enterprise* (Virginia City, Nevada, 1863–66); reporter, *San Francisco Call* (1864–66); traveling correspondent, *Sacramento Union* (1866); correspondent, *Alta California* (San Francisco, 1866–68); Washington correspondent, *New York Tribune* (1867–68); contributor, *New York Herald* and other papers (1867–68); author of numerous books, including *The Innocents Abroad* (1869), *The Gilded Age: A Tale of Today* (with Charles Dudley Warner, 1873), *Life on the Mississippi* (1883), and *Roughing It* (1886)

he discovered little gold or silver, he mined the wonderful characters of the other miners for his scribbling. He began writing colorful sketches signed "Josh"—a name suggesting a prankster, ready with a joke or witty remark.

In an article in the Virginia City, Nevada, *Territorial Enterprise* that appeared on February 2, 1863, Sam Clemens adopted the pen name "Mark Twain." The name came from a Mississippi River expression, "by the mark, twain," called out when a line sunk off the boat reached its two-fathom knot—indicating a safe depth of 12 feet. Clemens said he took the name from a steamboat captain who used to use that pen name when he wrote river news for the *New Orleans Picayune*. "He died in 1863," Clemens explained, "and as he could no longer need that signature, I laid violent hands upon it without asking permission of the proprietor's remains." That first piece mocked the exaggerated Fourth of July oratory of a Western politician. Other sketches captured the drama and absurdity of the rough, boisterous, good-humored, hot-tempered men of the frontier, mixing truth and fable into social satire. His articles were reprinted widely in the West, and in 1865 his

"I came across one of the lions of the country today at the Senate—General Sherman. The conversation I had with this gentleman therefore ought to be reported, I suppose. I said the weather was very fine, and he said he had seen finer. Not liking to commit myself further, in the present unsettled conditions of politics, I said good morning. Understanding my little game, he said good morning also. This was all that passed, but it was very significant. It reveals clearly what he thinks of impeachment. I regard this manner of getting a great man's opinion a little underhanded, but then everybody does it."

—from "Mark Twain in Washington," *Alta California* (January 15, 1868), at the time of the impeachment of President Andrew Johnson

piece on "The Notorious Jumping Frog of Calaveras County" carried his fame to many papers back East. Astonished at its popularity, Clemens wrote to his mother: "To think that, after writing many an article a man might be excused for thinking tolerably good, those New York people should single out a villainous backwoods sketch to compliment me on!"

Meanwhile, Twain had left Nevada and moved to San Francisco as a reporter for the *San Francisco Call*. Enjoying that city's Bohemian atmosphere, he described himself as "a man of convivial ways and not averse to social drinking." In 1866 the *Sacramento Union* sent him as a roving correspondent to visit the Sandwich Islands (also known as Hawaii) and write travel letters for the paper. Writing travel pieces suited Twain's restless, wandering nature. He next arranged for the San Francisco *Alta California* to send him on a tour of

Europe and the Holy Lands of the Middle East, where he sent articles from each stop.

Twain's voyage on the ship *Quaker City* to Europe and the Middle East in 1866 sealed Twain's national reputation as a humorist. Following immediately after the Civil War, his self-deprecating essays on how he and other adventurers from the New World encountered the Old World helped the war-weary American people to laugh a little at themselves. (As an example, of his exhausting tour of a European art gallery Twain wrote: "I am glad that the old masters are dead, and I only wish they had died sooner.")

After returning to the United States in November 1866, Twain planned to expand and edit his correspondence into a book, *The Innocents Abroad*. Although there was some demand for him as a public lecturer, he was not yet certain that his popular appeal would provide enough income to support him while he worked on the book. Instead, he persuaded Horace Greeley's *New York Tribune* to send him to Washington as a correspondent, to write humorous sketches of the Congress and the political scene. Paid by the article, rather than by salary by the *Tribune* and other papers, he supplemented his income by working as secretary to Nevada senator William Stewart. This kind of "moonlighting" was common among Washington journalists of the era. Underpaid by their newspapers, they worked part-time as clerks of congressional committees and secretaries to members of Congress, handling bills and constituent mail. While these jobs gained them valuable inside information and sources, they obviously could not write anything critical about their congressional employers.

Senator Stewart later described Twain as a "disreputable-looking person" who helped himself to the senator's cigars and whiskey and terrorized his landlady by smoking in bed. But Emily Briggs, a woman reporter in Washington, saw him instead as "quite a lion." "Mark is a bachelor, faultless in tastes," she wrote, who stood out from the crowd with his snowy white vests and lavender gloves. Others noted his drawling speech and "general air of being half asleep." His lectures in Washington were a great success.

As a writer, Twain found plenty of material in the capital. He hobnobbed with "these old Generals and Senators and other humbugs," as he described them. "Congress is the most interesting body I have found yet," he wrote in one of his newspaper columns. "It does more crazy things, and does them with a graver earnestness, than any State Legislature that exists, perhaps." Twain wrote many humorous accounts, but he also became increasingly outraged at the behavior he witnessed: the pious hypocrisy and arrogance that covered a corrupt scrambling for dollars in post-Civil War Washington. "This is the place to get a poor opinion of everybody," he wrote. Disgusted with the efforts of Congress to impeach President Andrew Johnson—which he called "simply boy's play"—Twain abruptly left Washington in March 1868 and returned to California.

He left, however, with many notes on the people and events he observed, and on his experiences as a newspaper correspondent and congressional staff member. He drew upon some of these notes for his short stories, most notably "My Late Senatorial Secretaryship." Other notes he saved for his first novel, a broad political satire called *The Gilded Age, A Tale of Today*, which

This illustration, entitled "The Pilgrim's Vision," is from Twain's first book, *The Innocents Abroad, or The New Pilgrim's Progress*, whose lengthy subtitle called the work an "account of the steamship *Quaker City*'s pleasure excursion to Europe and the Holy Land; with descriptions of countries, nations, incidents and adventures." The book's success ended Twain's career as a newspaper correspondent.

After leaving journalism, Twain became an enormously popular novelist. His accomplishments inspired other journalists to try to write the "great American novel."

painted a seedy portrait of lobbyists, politicians, and journalists that helped shape the nation's image of national politics and highlighted the need for reform.

By then, however, the bachelor Mark Twain had settled down, married, and given up his Bohemian vagabond existence. Leaving journalism behind, he was on his way to becoming the author of *Tom Sawyer, Huckleberry Finn, The Prince and the Pauper,* and *A Connecticut Yankee in King Arthur's Court,* some of America's most popular literature.

FURTHER READING

DeVoto, Bernard A. *Mark Twain's America*. 1932. Reprint, Cambridge: Houghton Mifflin, 1967.

Fatout, Paul. *Mark Twain in Virginia City*. Bloomington, Ind.: Indiana University Press, 1964.

French, Bryant Morley. *Mark Twain and the Gilded Age*. Dallas: Southern Methodist University Press, 1965.

Kaplan, Justin. *Mr. Clemens and Mark Twain: A Biography*. New York: Simon & Schuster, 1974.

Lynn, Kenneth S. *Mark Twain and Southwestern Humor*. Westport, Conn.: Greenwood, 1976.

Paine, Albert Bigelow. *Mark Twain, A Biography: The Personal and Literary Life of Samuel Langhorne Clemens*. 4 vols. New York: Harper, 1935.

Ritchie, Donald A. *Press Gallery: Congress and Washington Correspondents*. Cambridge: Harvard University Press, 1991.

Twain, Mark. *The Complete Short Stories of Mark Twain*. Edited by Charles Neider. New York: Bantam, 1957.

———. *The Innocents Abroad*. 1869. Reprint, New York: Oxford University Press, 1996.

———. *Life on the Mississippi*. 1883. Reprint, New York: Oxford University Press, 1996.

———. *Mark Twain's Letters from Hawaii*. Edited by A. Grove Day. London: Chatto & Windus, 1967.

———. *Mark Twain's San Francisco*. New York: McGraw-Hill, 1963.

———. *Roughing It*. 1886. Reprint, New York: Oxford University Press, 1996.

——— and Charles Dudley Warner. *The Gilded Age: A Tale of Today*. 1873. Reprint, New York: Oxford University Press, 1996.

Edwin L. Godkin

LEADER OF ELITE OPINION

hen E. L. Godkin surveyed the American scene during the late 19th century, he saw little to like. He believed American democracy had degenerated into mobs of uneducated voters who were electing political bosses and fostering corruption. From the Tweed Ring in New York City to the White House of Ulysses S. Grant, Godkin had no shortage of examples to demonstrate his point. His editorials sought to return America to its original ideals. Godkin's highly critical views never attracted large numbers of subscribers to his weekly journal, *The Nation*, or his daily newspaper, the *New York Evening World*. Yet those who did subscribe counted themselves the "best men" of their day—educated, genteel, and reform-minded. *The Nation*'s elite readers could rarely win an election against the political bosses, who were supported by the masses of voters, but Godkin's editorials explained their feelings of alienation from American life and identified the issues that might help them regain national leadership.

Born in Ireland, Edwin Lawrence Godkin later described himself as "an Irishman of English ancestry, bred in strong attachment to the English government, educated at an English school and Queen's College Belfast." His father, James Godkin, was a Congregational minister and also a journalist who edited a weekly paper, the *Christian Patriot*, and later the *Dublin Daily Express*. His son Edwin absorbed his admiration for the American Revolution. "American ideals were the intellectual food of my youth," he wrote years later.

At Queens College in Belfast, Edwin Godkin studied the British liberalism of John Stuart Mill and Jeremy Bentham. Liberalism, as they defined it, meant smaller government and free trade among nations. Godkin became a lifelong libertarian who opposed government programs to help the poor and unemployed and believed that every person was fully equipped to stand on his own without outside help.

After college Godkin felt undecided between law or journalism. He went to London to study law, but met his father's friend, the publisher John Cassell, who hired him to work on a new magazine, *The Workingmen's Friend*. At that time Godkin became fascinated with Hungarian efforts to win independence from Austria. Sketches about Hungary that he wrote for *The Workingmen's Friend* became his first book, which was a popular success.

The book appeared just as England became drawn into a war between Turkey and Russia in the Crimea, and the

Described as a "habitual critic," E. L. Godkin wrote editorials that shaped the thinking of a generation of reformers, most memorably the Mugwump faction of Republicans in 1884.

London Daily News hired Godkin to cover the war. As an inexperienced reporter, Godkin had little knowledge of military tactics and got some of his facts wrong, but his letters helped alert the British public to the terrible mismanagement of the British military. He made it clear that British officers had better family connections than military judgment. His reporting of British disasters in the Crimean War led to military reforms.

Godkin returned to Ireland to lecture about the war and became an editor of the *Belfast Northern Whig*. An ambitious young man, he did not want to be tied down to a small paper. In 1856 he resigned from the paper and left for the United States, where he planned to write articles for British papers about conditions in the American South. After landing in New York City, Godkin made friends with the writer Frederick Law Olmstead, who had recently traveled through the South for the *New York Times*, and who introduced him to New York journalism. In New York, Godkin resumed the study of law, while writing occasional pieces for the *New York Times* and *London Daily News*. He also fell in love with an American woman he described as "tall, brown-haired singularly elegant and beautiful": Elizabeth "Fanny" Foote. They married in July 1859 and soon after left to travel in Europe.

In 1861 the United States plunged into Civil War and Godkin wrote articles for the *London Daily News*, defending the Union side in the conflict. He also contributed pieces to the *New York Evening Post*, explaining European public opinion about the war. The Godkins sailed back to the United States in 1862, and he became editor of the *Sanitary Commission Bulletin*, publishing reports on wartime health conditions. The job paid well but bored him. He aspired to edit his own journal.

In June 1863 a group of young reformers met in the New York Union League (formed during the Civil War to support the Union effort) to discuss starting "an honest weekly paper." Within two years they had obtained sufficient funds to start a magazine called *The Nation*, with Godkin as its editor. Many of the original supporters were abolitionists who wanted to create a paper dedicated to the interests of the freedmen. Godkin, however, opposed giving African Americans the right to vote. Rather than spread democracy any further, he wanted to limit democracy to the educated elite.

This stance offended many of his abolitionist backers, who tried to remove him as editor. Instead, Godkin, Olmsted, and other allies bought control of *The Nation,* which Godkin continued to edit for the rest of the 19th century.

"We have no party backing as we aim to be an independent paper," Godkin asserted, noting that "radicals, conservatives, free traders, protectionists, infidels and evangelicals have all some reason for finding fault with us." Godkin's highly critical and often sarcastic attitude toward American society offended some readers, but it attracted college-educated men from older established families who felt uncomfortable with both the teeming masses of the poor and the newly rich industrialists. *The Nation* identified national goals and programs for them to support, and shaped their opinions. Godkin's magazine gave up any concern over freed blacks in the South and worried more about organized labor and high tariffs in the North. It trained its fire on political corruption in city, state, and national governments. It called for fewer elections and fewer political appointments, and advocated civil-service reform through which government jobs would be awarded according to merit rather than political patronage.

Political bosses denounced "snivel service" reform and dismissed Godkin and his followers as effete and unmanly "man-milliners" and "miss Nancys." But the educated elite embraced Godkin as society's "moral policeman." The distinguished Boston author James Russell Lowell observed that "every Friday morning, when *The Nation* comes, I fill my pipe and read it from beginning to end." The historian James Ford Rhodes testified that without *The Nation* his "mind was in chaos and I didn't feel that I had a safe opinion to swear by." Since none of the editorials or essays in *The Nation* were signed,

many people thought Godkin wrote them all. Although he actually contributed only a few pages to each issue, the magazine as a whole reflected his skeptical attitude toward the direction in which American society was moving.

When a group of Godkin's wealthy friends bought the *New York Evening Post,* they installed him as editor in chief of that daily paper in 1883. *The Nation* then became the weekly edition of the *Evening Post,* reprinting the best material from the newspaper for national distribution. Godkin relished the shift from weekly to daily journalism. *The Nation's* circulation had never risen high enough to employ a large enough staff, requiring him to write much of its material. Although a daily newspaper would require more work, it also had a bigger staff. He could go on long annual trips to Europe and the staff would publish the paper in his absence.

A greater editorial writer than editor, E. L. Godkin possessed a prose style that was clear, straightforward, and powerful, always tinged with irony and sarcasm. "Never write without conveying information or expressing an opinion with reasons," he admonished his staff. Yet he lacked—and even shunned—the creative spark of Horace Greeley or Joseph Pulitzer. Godkin's notion was to make the *Evening Post* "the paper to which sober-minded people would look at during crises...instead of hollering and bellering and shouting platitudes," as other papers often did. The *Evening Post's* circulation never passed 25,000 (in contrast, the more sensational papers published by Joseph Pulitzer and William Randolph Hearst were selling 400,000 copies of their daily papers and 600,000 of their Sunday editions in the 1890s). But as one local politician complained: "The trouble with the damned sheet is that every editor in New York State reads it."

Edwin L. Godkin

BORN
October 2, 1831
Moyne, Ireland

DIED
May 21, 1902
Brixham, England

EDUCATION
Graduated in 1851 from Queens College, Belfast, Ireland

ACCOMPLISHMENTS
Subeditor, *The Workingmen's Friend* (1851–52); correspondent, *London Daily News* (1853–55, 1858–65); editorial writer, *Belfast Northern Whig* (1855–56); editor, *Sanitary Commission Bulletin* (1862–63); editor, *The Nation* (1865–1900); editor in chief, *New York Evening Post* (1883–1900); contributor, *North American Review, Atlantic, Century, Scribner,* and other journals; author of *The History of Hungary and the Magyars* (1853), *Problems of Modern Democracy: Political and Economic Essays* (1896), and *Unforseen Tendencies of Democracy* (1898)

The Nation.

VOL. I.—NO. 1.   THURSDAY, JULY 6, 1865. $3 PER ANNUM.

CONTENTS.

JOSEPH H. RICHARDS, PUBLISHER, 130 NASSAU STREET, N. Y.

The Week.

THE WEEK has been singularly barren of exciting events. It is curious to see, however, what a stimulus the return of peace has given to political agitation. As nothing is now dependent on the fortune of war, orators and writers are entering the arena with a confidence which they never displayed as long as their arguments and predictions were liable to reversion or falsification at the hands of Lee or Grant.

On the cover of the first issue of *The Nation,* the journal notes that "the week has been singularly barren of exciting events." Godkin's magazine, however, went on to attack political corruption and advocate civil service reform. Through it, Godkin served as society's "moral policeman."

Although he published a pro-Republican paper, Godkin stunned party regulars in 1884 by declining to endorse the Republican candidate for President, James G. Blaine, and formally supporting the Democratic candidate, Grover Cleveland. Godkin dismissed Blaine as corrupt and described his supporters as driven by a hunger for government jobs. Cleveland, he reasoned, would support civil-service reform and lower the tariff. *The Nation* and the *Evening Post* led the "Mugwump" movement of Republican reformers who bolted their party and helped elect Cleveland the first Democratic President since the Civil War. (The *New York Sun* coined "mugwump," which was an Algonquin Indian word for a chief. The *Sun* contemptuously referred to the bolters as "little mugwumps" or little men who wanted to be big chiefs. The reformers then adopted the term as a badge of their independence.) Godkin advocated nonpolitical reforms as well, leading a campaign against spitting in public. At first many dismissed his editorials on spitting as "Godkin's crankiness," but his efforts culminated in antispitting signs being posted in public places to prevent the spread of disease.

Godkin's foreign birth and frequent criticism of American life led his opponents to accuse him of being unAmerican. Yet he felt thoroughly a part of his adopted country, even as he scorned its more outlandish fads and crudeness. Despite his gruff exterior, those closest to him insisted that he was no sour scold. He took great joy in living, was cheerful, and had a sense of humor. When he lectured at Radcliffe College in 1895, one of the students, Josephine Peabody, recorded his contradictory nature: "The dear old man looks so mildly happy and benignant while he regrets everything in the age and the country—so contented, while he gently tells us it were better for us had we never been born in this degenerate and unlovely age."

One of Godkin's young reporters on the *Evening Post* was Lincoln Steffens, who admired Godkin's "clever, forceful, [and] ripping" editorials. In their journalistic careers, both Godkin and Steffens sought to expose corruption in society. But unlike the muckraking Steffens, who uncovered the role of big business in political corruption, Godkin never saw any such connection. As he grew older and more conservative, Godkin built close friendships with Andrew Carnegie, J. P. Morgan, and other leading bankers and business leaders, and moved away from the reformers who were the friends of his youth. His publications denounced labor unions, strikes, and any government programs designed to help the needy and unemployed.

In the 1890s Godkin grew dismayed over the sensationalism of the "yellow press," which took its name from the yellow-colored cartoon character the Yellow Kid in "Hogan's Alley," which appeared in the *World*. Papers such as Pulitzer's *New York World* and William Randolph Hearst's *New York Journal* overwhelmed the *Evening Post* in circulation and made their impact felt on public opinion. Godkin saw imperialism as an Old

World practice that had no place in the New World. He blamed the "yellow press" for pushing U.S. politicians into the Spanish-American War of 1898. "Nothing so disgraceful as the behavior of these newspapers in the past week has ever been known in the history of American journalism," Godkin grumbled. "It is a crying shame that men should work such mischief simply in order to sell more papers." He grew increasingly despondent and pessimistic about the future of American democracy. "I came here fifty years ago with high and fond ideas about America," he commented. "They are now all shattered, and I have apparently to look elsewhere to keep even moderate hopes about the human race alive."

Godkin's personal life suffered similar depression. In 1873 his favorite daughter, Lizzy, died, and his wife never recovered from the shock. She became an invalid and died two years later. The grief-stricken Godkin fled from New York to Cambridge, Massachusetts. There he continued editing *The Nation*, which was said to be the best New York journal edited in Cambridge. In 1884 Godkin married the wealthy and socially prominent Katherine Sands. They lived in handsome style, entertaining and traveling widely. As his health deteriorated with age, Godkin spent longer periods of time recuperating in England. In 1889 he returned from one of his annual European trips to find that his son Lawrence, an attorney, had worked out an arrangement with the trustees of the *Evening Post* for Godkin to relinquish all his duties but retain his title as editor in chief until January 1, 1890. Soon afterward he suffered a stroke and sailed back to England. He continued

to write from abroad for the *Evening Post* until he died in 1902—just as the mood of the time was shifting to a more optimistic Progressive reform movement. The Harvard University president Charles Eliot Norton noted that, unlike the Progressives, Godkin never had the chance to work to find a remedy for the evils he exposed in his editorials. "The habitual critic," Norton concluded, "gets a darker or less cheerful view of the social and political state than one does who is actively engaged in efforts to improve that state."

FURTHER READING

Armstrong, William M. *E. L. Godkin and American Foreign Policy, 1865-1900*. New York: Bookman Associates, 1957.

———. *E. L. Godkin: A Biography*. Albany: State University of New York Press, 1978.

Beisner, Robert L. *Twelve Against Empire: The Anti-Imperialists, 1898-1900*. New York: McGraw-Hill, 1968.

Blodgett, Geoffrey. "Civil Service Reform and Public Morality." In *The Gilded Age*, edited by H. Wayne Morgan. Syracuse, N.Y.: Syracuse University Press, 1970.

Godkin, Edwin L. *Problems of Modern Democracy: Political and Economic Essays*. 1896. Reprint, Cambridge: Belknap Press of Harvard University Press, 1966.

———. *Unforseen Tendencies of Democracy*. 1898. Reprint, Freeport, N.Y.: Books for Libraries Press, 1971.

Sproat, John G. *"The Best Men": Liberal Reformers in the Gilded Age*. New York: Oxford University Press, 1968.

Summers, Mark Wahlgren. *The Era of Good Stealings*. New York: Oxford University Press, 1993.

Thomas Nast

REPORTING WITH PICTURES

Week after week during 1870, *Harper's Weekly* kept up an attack on Democratic party political machine Tammany Hall's domination of New York City, accompanied by scorching cartoons by Thomas Nast. William M. Tweed, the boss of Tammany Hall, complained, "I don't care a straw for your newspaper articles; my constituents don't know how to read, but they can't help seeing those damn pictures."

It was the *New York Times* that eventually uncovered the hard evidence of corruption that convicted Tweed and sent him to prison. But then Tweed escaped and fled to first Cuba, and then Spain. Spanish authorities distributed copies of Nast's cartoons that led to Tweed's capture and return to prison. America's first major political cartoonist had scored a

Political cartoonist Thomas Nast did his best work when an issue made him angry and raised his righteous indignation.

stunning triumph, one that dramatically demonstrated the power of pictures in journalism.

Thomas Nast was born in a military barracks in Germany, where his father played the trombone for a military band. An outspoken liberal at a time of political upheaval in the German states, the elder Nast sent his wife and six-year-old son to New York City in 1846 before joining them four years later after the liberal cause had failed in Germany. There, Tommy Nast attended public schools. When the Hungarian revolutionary leader Louis Kossuth visited New York in 1851, young Nast sketched a picture that was hung by the principal's desk. It was Nast's first publicly displayed artwork. Although his family hoped that he would follow his father's career in music, his talents clearly lay in drawing, and he was admitted to the Academy of Design.

In 1855 the English engraver Henry Carter, who had taken the name Frank Leslie, started *Frank Leslie's Illustrated Newspaper,* America's first fully illustrated journal. The 16-page weekly featured many illustrations of the events of the day, from politics to prizefights. The short, pudgy 15-year-old Nast approached Leslie and asked to draw for his paper. As a test, Leslie sent the boy down to the ferry docks and asked him to draw a picture of the Sunday morning crowd just at the last call of "All aboard!" Leslie doubted that the boy would succeed. What he asked for was not a sketch, but something that told a story with much commotion and action. On Monday morning Nast appeared with his picture. "Did you do that alone?" Leslie pressed. "Yes, sir," Nast responded, whereupon Leslie hired the boy as an illustrator for four dollars a week.

Drawing for *Frank Leslie's Illustrated Newspaper* proved to be an important part of Nast's education as an illustrator. He received technical training

from experienced engravers and learned to work under the pressures of weekly deadlines. American papers had lagged far behind English newspapers in their use of illustrations.

Photographs and other pictures could not yet be mechanically reproduced for newspapers and had to be engraved by hand. Editors and publishers considered this process to be too costly and time-consuming, and reporters sneered that pictures made "our eyes do the work of our brains." But readers were attracted to publications with pictures, and soon *Harper's Weekly* and the *New York Illustrated News* appeared as competition to *Frank Leslie's*. Artists like Nast used pen or pencil to draw their sketches, which engravers then copied onto blocks of wood. These woodcuts would then be inked to produce the printed engravings. To speed up the process for weekly deadlines, larger pictures were divided into sections, with different engravers copying each section.

Finding his talents in demand, Nast switched to the better-paying *New York Illustrated News*. That paper gave him a variety of assignments, from covering the trial of the abolitionist John Brown to going to England to sketch the boxing match between American champion John C. Heenan and English champion Thomas Sayers. After recording Heenan's victory, Nast headed to Italy to sketch scenes of Giuseppe Garibaldi's struggle for Italian independence. After these exhilarating experiences, Nast returned to New York to find his newspaper in such bad financial shape that it could pay him only a modest salary. Undeterred, on the day before his 21st birthday, Nast married Sarah Edwards, a cultured young woman who would make important contributions to his career as an illustrator.

The Civil War created a greater demand for pictures with news. The *News* sent Nast to Washington to

Thomas Nast

BORN
September 27, 1840
Landau, Germany

DIED
December 7, 1902
Guayaquil, Ecuador

EDUCATION
Entered the New York Academy of Design in 1854

ACCOMPLISHMENTS
Illustrator, *Frank Leslie's Illustrated Newspaper* (1855–57, 1862); illustrator, *New York Illustrated News* (1859–62); illustrator, *Harper's Weekly* (1862–86); freelance illustrator (1887-1902); managing editor, *Nast's Weekly* (1892–93); author of *Thomas Nast's Illustrated Almanac* (1871) and *Thomas Nast's Christmas Drawings for the Human Race* (1890)

> *"From a roving lad with a swift pencil for sale, he had become a patriot artist, burning with the enthusiasm of the time."*
>
> —journalist James Parton's description of Thomas Nast in 1877

sketch Abraham Lincoln's inauguration. Meanwhile, Nast sent some of his drawings to the more financially stable *Harper's Weekly*, which in 1862 put him on its regular staff at double his old salary. Publisher Fletcher Harper recognized Nast's artistic genius as well as his ability to work quickly. Harper encouraged Nast not simply to illustrate scenes but to draw from his imagination to make pictures that would tell a story. Nast used his pen to attack Southern guerrilla raiders, to commemorate fallen heroes, and to arouse Northern patriotism. Paying tribute to these impassioned pictures, President Lincoln later observed that "Thomas Nast has been our best recruiting sergeant."

Nast supported Lincoln but was contemptuous of Lincoln's successor, Andrew Johnson, because of Johnson's leniency toward the defeated South. During the many political battles of the Reconstruction era that followed the war, Nast sided with the Radical Republicans against President Johnson. Increasingly, he used caricature as a political weapon against "King Andy." Nast's pictures also defended the freedmen in the South, attacked the Ku Klux Klan, and supported the efforts of Congress to pass civil rights legislation. His greatest hero was General Ulysses S. Grant, who attributed his election as President in 1868 in large part to "the pencil of Nast."

Nast loyally defended President Grant, but *Harper's Weekly*, edited by the reform-minded George W. Curtis, lost faith in the scandal-ridden Grant administration. In 1872 Curtis supported the Liberal Republicans, who bolted from the party to support Horace Greeley for president. To the contrary, Nast's cartoons pictured Greeley as a fool and a traitor. Curtis objected to these attacks on his friends, and Nast confided to his wife that pressure was mounting to stop him from making fun of the Liberal Republicans, "but I hear

that Harper's will stick by me, no matter what will happen." Comparing himself to his editor, Nast said that when Curtis attacked someone with his pen he seemed to be apologizing for the act. "I try to hit the enemy between the eyes and knock them down."

In 1870 Nast began a series of cartoons that portrayed New York City as under Boss Tweed's thumb, accusing the Tweed Ring of looting the city's treasury. The rotund Tweed made a perfect symbol, and Nast drew him repeatedly, making him the embodiment of political corruption. One cartoon of the Tammany tiger mauling the republic before a satisfied Tweed carried the caption: "What are you going to do about it?" Nast's cartoons helped rouse the public from indifference and raise the cry for reform. Tweed's allies complained about the "Nast-y" pictures. The New York City school board responded by rejecting all of Harper Brothers' textbooks and buying new books from a corporation owned by the Tweed ring. Harper Brothers' board of directors almost gave in, until Fletcher Harper announced in disgust: "Gentlemen, you know where I live. When you are ready to continue the fight against these scoundrels, send for me." The company stood behind Nast and continued the fight.

The anti-Tweed campaign succeeded. Tweed went to prison, while the circulation of *Harper's Weekly* tripled. The Tweed cartoons made Nast internationally famous. E. L. Godkin's *Nation* commended: "Mr. Nast has carried political illustrations during the last six months to a pitch of excellence never before attained in this country, and has secured for them an influence on opinion such as they never came near having in any country."

Nast drew inspiration for his cartoons from diverse sources. His best work reflected issues that made him mad and raised his righteous indignation. From time to time he poked fun at himself in his cartoons as angry, impatient, and disgruntled with events. His wife, Sarah, a cultured woman who often read to him, suggested other themes from Shakespeare and often contributed literary quotations as captions. Nast also had a knack for finding the right symbols for his subjects. He was the first cartoonist to use the elephant to represent the Republican party and the donkey for the Democrats. Each Christmas he also drew his version of St. Nicholas, creating the popular image of Santa Claus.

In 1877 Nast's strong supporter Fletcher Harper died. At the same time the new Republican President Rutherford B. Hayes was pulling federal troops out of the South, signaling that Reconstruction had ended. Without Harper to intervene, editor George W. Curtis pressured Nast to hold his fire on the new President. Nast agreed, but he drew a cartoon of Uncle Sam pushing the cartoonist into a chair and admonishing, "Our Artist must keep cool, and sit down, and see how it works." When Curtis asked if Uncle Sam represented him, Nast replied that it represented Policy—adding that "Policy always strangles individuals."

Joseph W. Harper, Jr., succeeded his uncle as publisher of *Harper's Weekly*. The younger Harper shifted the magazine away from politics to seek a family audience. Nast complained that his cartoons were not being used as often as before, but Harper replied that he "ought to remember that we have to consider these matters from a business standpoint, as well as from their artistic matters." That same year, 1877, new competition arose when Joseph Keppler started *Puck* magazine. Printed in color, Keppler's political cartoons treated politics less passionately and more humorously than did Nast, who began to grow out of fashion. Political and economic issues of the

December 27, 1879

Stranger Things Have Happened.
Hold on, and you may walk over the sluggish animal up there yet.

day grew more complex and less clear-cut, further dampening Nast's slashing style.

The Presidential election of 1884 revived Nast's passions—and his reputation. Nast dismissed the Republican candidate, James G. Blaine, as unfit for the Presidency, blaming him for the moral decline of the Grand Old Party. After years of loyalty to the Republicans, both Nast and *Harper's Weekly* bolted and supported the

Nast popularized the images of the Republican elephant and the Democratic donkey. Here Senator Thomas Bayard tries to keep the Democratic party from leaping into "financial chaos," while the Republicans doze.

THE GREELEY TRIUMPH POSTPONED FOR THE PRESENT THE H.G. MOVEMENT SEEMS CRUSHED
TRIBUNE

THE SENATORIAL CABAL DESTROYED. NO HANKERING AFTER BOILED CROW

SHAM REFORM EXPOSED H.G. GONE WEST

NEW YORK TIMES

GRANT'S VICTORY OVERWHELMING MAJORITIES FOR GRANT DIX AND HAVEMEYER

HARPER'S WEEKLY SKETCHES

Th. Nast

TAMMANY RING BROKEN

REFORM TAMMANY DEAD.
K.K.K DEAD.
THE GREELEY PILL NO GO

November 23, 1872

Our Artist's Occupation Gone.

TH. NAST. "It's all very funny to you; but what am I to do now?"

Although Nast supported Ulysses S. Grant for President, after Grant's victory Nast drew himself as a dismayed man who would no longer have Grant's opponent—Horace Greeley—as a target for his cartoons.

Democratic candidate, Grover Cleveland. When the votes were counted, Blaine had lost the election. But the magazine had lost many of its subscribers and advertisers. Needing to restore its profits, the magazine felt even less tolerant of its temperamental artist. After submitting his annual Christmas picture in 1886, Nast quit *Harper's Weekly*.

He lectured, did freelance drawing, and briefly published his own magazine, yet Thomas Nast could never regain his former influence. He seemed to be a creature of a distant past. People wrote to *Harper's Weekly* referring to "the late Thomas Nast." He replied with a sketch of himself, proclaiming: "I still live." Having loyally supported Ulysses S. Grant for years,

Nast also lost all his savings when the former President's stock brokerage house failed. Ironically, Nast found himself down and out of favor just as the political cartooning he had pioneered was taking a firm hold in the daily newspaper. In the 1890s it became commonplace for newspapers to run editorial cartoons, but by then Nast's style had grown out of step with the times.

Deeply in debt, Nast turned to political patronage for his salvation. He sought a diplomatic appointment, preferably in Europe. Instead, in 1902 President Theodore Roosevelt—who said he learned his politics from Nast's cartoons—named the cartoonist American counsel in Guayaquil, Ecuador. It was not a prestigious post, but Nast could not afford to decline it. After only six months on the job in Ecuador, the "Father of the American Cartoon" died there of yellow fever.

FURTHER READING

Hess, Stephen, and Milton Kaplan, eds. *The Ungentlemanly Art: A History of American Political Cartoons*. New York: Macmillan, 1975.

Keller, Morton. *The Art and Politics of Thomas Nast*. New York: Oxford University Press, 1968.

Leonard, Thomas C. *The Power of the Press: The Birth of American Political Reporting*. New York: Oxford University Press, 1986.

Nast, Thomas. *Thomas Nast's Christmas Drawings for the Human Race*. 1890. Reprint, New York: Harper & Row, 1971.

Paine, Albert B. *Thomas Nast: His Period and His Pictures*. 1904. Reprint, New York; Chelsea House, 1980.

Vinson, J. Chal. *Thomas Nast: Political Cartoonist*. Athens: University of Georgia Press, 1967.

Henry Watterson

EDITORIAL FIREWORKS

ineteenth-century newspapers often spoke with the sole voice of their editor. An entire paper would reflect the views and personalities of a Horace Greeley or James G. Bennett, a practice known as "personal journalism." Since these editors also owned their newspapers, they had the freedom to take whatever stands they wished. By the 20th century, newspapers had become large corporations, and editors were employees without the power of ownership. News articles appeared under bylines and signed syndicated columns ran beside unsigned editorials. The exchange of one voice for many enabled newspapers to disavow anything they printed that might have offended their readers or advertisers. Bridging the two eras was Henry Watterson, who for 50 years edited the *Louisville* (Kentucky) *Courier-Journal*. "Marse Henry" ("Marse" was the old Southern expression for "Master") Watterson made his newspaper nationally famous with his vivid and distinctive

Editor Henry Watterson's appearance and his vivid and dramatic editorials personified the Old South, though he was opposed to the institution of slavery.

February 3, 1877

Fire and Water Make Vapor.
What a cooling off will be there, my countrymen!

Cartoonist Thomas Nast drew Henry Watterson as a wild Southern radical during the Hayes-Tilden Presidential campaign. A Tilden supporter, Watterson was outraged when the disputed election went to Rutherford B. Hayes.

editorials, his passion for politics, and his colorful personality. This "last of the personal journalists" personified the Southern newspaperman and spoke to the nation for his region.

Watterson's powerful and bombastic editorial style delighted readers from the Civil War through World War I. In the 20th century, when editorials diminished to just a few paragraphs,

Watterson continued to produce many columns and pages of editorial text. One of his correspondents described Watterson's editorials as "almost reckless, designed rather as fireworks thrown up to dazzle and bewilder than the steady light of his serious and resolute purpose." The *New York Times* commended the "Wattersonian style, pungent, vivid, superlatively personal, those adhesive epithets, that storm of arrows . . . the swift sarcasm, the free frolic of irresistible humor—it was as if the page was not written but spoken and acted before you."

Politics and journalism became part of Watterson's life from its very beginning. His father, Harvey Watterson, was elected to the U.S. House of Representatives as a Jacksonian Democrat from Tennessee. Harvey and his wife, Tilitha, arrived in Washington by stagecoach late in 1839, and their son, Henry, was born a few months later in a house they rented on Pennsylvania Avenue. As a child, Henry Watterson contracted scarlet fever, which weakened his eyes and made reading difficult. He learned to scan pages quickly to preserve his eyesight. Ill health kept him out of school, and he received his earliest education at home from his mother and from tutors. While the Wattersons lived in Washington, Henry spent his childhood roaming the corridors of the Capitol, listening to the debates in Congress.

In 1849 Harvey Watterson purchased the *Nashville Union*, and it was in this newspaper office that his son got his first lessons in journalism. The *Union* was a Jacksonian paper that strongly defended the union of the states against fire-eating pro-Southern newspapers. Harvey Watterson had grown up on a plantation but disapproved of slavery. His son, Henry, inherited this attitude. As a child, Henry once objected when a slave, Isaac, was beaten by an overseer. His grandfather gave Isaac to Henry, who set him free. "I cannot recall a time when I was not passionately opposed to slavery," Henry later asserted, "[I am] a crank on the subject of personal liberty, if I am a crank about anything."

Harvey Watterson returned to Washington in 1851 as assistant editor of the official Democratic party newspaper, the *Washington Union*, but when the paper endorsed the Kansas-Nebraska Act of 1854, permitting slavery in the territories, Harvey resigned in protest and took his family back to Tennessee. Young Henry remained in the North to attend the Academy of the Protestant Episcopal Church in Philadelphia. There he edited the school newspaper, the *Ciceronian*.

Upon his graduation in 1856, Henry rejoined his family in McMinnville, Tennessee. His father made him a present of a printing press. The 16-year-old Watterson published a two-page paper, the *New Era*, which covered local weddings, funerals, and farm prices. His fiery editorials denouncing the Republican candidate for President in 1856 were reprinted in the *Nashville American* and the *Washington Union*. Such favorable notice led Henry to believe he had a future in journalism. He went to New York City, where he wrote occasional articles for Horace Greeley's *New York Tribune* and served as a music critic for the *New York Times*.

Drawn back to Washington in 1858, Watterson took a job writing for the *Washington States*, a pro-Union paper. While in Washington, he met the writer Jane Casneau, who taught him the merits of short descriptive phrases such as nicknames to capture public attention and deflate pompous politicians. Watterson also became Washington correspondent for John Forney's *Philadelphia Press*, for which he covered John Brown's raid on Harpers Ferry. In March 1861 the manager of the Associated Press in Washington,

Lawrence Gobright, asked Watterson to help cover Abraham Lincoln's inauguration. Although he later counted Lincoln as the greatest hero of his life, Watterson felt only gloom and foreboding at the inaugural ceremony. He was a Unionist but also a Tennessean. That June, when Tennessee seceded from the Union, Watterson returned home and enlisted in the Confederate army.

Throughout the Civil War, Henry Watterson alternated between fighting the war and writing about it. Illness forced him to leave the army and return to Nashville in September 1861. There he became associate editor of the *Nashville Banner*, until the Union army occupied Nashville a few months later, closing the paper and forcing its editors to flee. Watterson briefly joined Colonel Nathan B. Forrest's Confederate cavalry in its guerrilla raids on the Union forces. After six hectic months with Forrest, Watterson accepted an invitation to edit a new newspaper, the *Chattanooga Rebel*. This little, four-page paper was aimed at the Confederate army rather than at the people of Chattanooga, Tennessee. Watterson obtained copies of Northern papers and summarized their accounts for Southern readers. His florid editorials helped make the *Rebel* the most widely read newspaper in the Confederate army. It was unabashedly propagandist in its criticism of the North and especially of President Lincoln, describing him as a "rude, vulgar, obscure, backwoods pettifogger." But Watterson also wrote about the creation of a new Southern nation based not on slavery and plantations but on factories and diversified farming.

The *Rebel* sought to boost Southern morale, but Watterson never hesitated to criticize Southern politicians and generals. His portrayals of Confederate general Braxton Bragg as inept caused Bragg to ban the paper from Confederate troops. Since this

Henry Watterson

BORN

February 16, 1840
Washington, D.C.

DIED

December 22, 1921
Jacksonville, Florida

EDUCATION

Private tutors; graduated from Academy of the Protestant Episcopal Church, Philadelphia (1856)

ACCOMPLISHMENTS

Editor, *New Era* (McMinnville Tennessee, 1856–58); occasional writer, *New York Tribune* (1858); music critic, *New York Times* (1858); editorial writer, *Washington States* (1858–61); Washington correspondent, *Philadelphia Press* (1858–61); editor, *Democratic Review* (1860–61); associate editor, *Nashville Banner* (1861–62); editor, *Chattanooga Rebel* (1862–63); assistant editor, *Atlanta Southern Confederacy* (1863); editor, *Cincinnati Evening Times* (1865); editor, *Nashville Republican Banner* (1865–68); editor, *Louisville Courier-Journal* (1868–1919); author of *Oddities in Southern Life and Culture* (1883), *History of the Spanish-American War* (1899), *The Compromises of Life, And Other Lectures and Addresses* (1903), and *"Marse Henry"; An Autobiography* (1919)

move cut off most of the paper's business, the other editors asked for Watterson's resignation. He then joined the staff of the *Atlanta Southern Confederacy*, but found the work depressing because the paper was so heavily censored. He rejoined the Confederate army and served as chief of scouts, keeping a nervous eye on General William T. Sherman's Union army, which was marching on Atlanta, and sending occasional battlefield dispatches to the *Confederacy*.

When Atlanta fell, Watterson knew the Confederacy could not survive much longer. Managing to get through Union lines, he returned to Tennessee. In search of work, he traveled north to Cincinnati, Ohio, where he was offered a job on the *Evening Times*. Soon after, when the editor was killed in a ferry accident, Watterson was promoted to editor in chief, despite having been a Confederate soldier. The publisher of the *Times* believed that Watterson would attract readers among Ohio's Peace Democrats. That April, Watterson was shocked by President Lincoln's assassination, which he counted as the most important news story of his career. In a reversal of his earlier writing, his editorial praised Lincoln's Presidency and blamed his assassination on Confederate president Jefferson Davis and "the Rebel camp." The South, he believed, had lost its greatest Northern champion. Although the *Times* was a good job, Watterson missed the South and soon returned to Tennessee to edit the *Nashville Republican Banner*—and reunite with the woman he had left behind.

In Chattanooga during the war, Watterson had fallen in love with Rebecca Ewing, the loveliest girl he had ever seen. She sang in the Presbyterian church choir, and for the first time he became a churchgoer. They were married on December 20, 1865, when Henry was 25 and Rebecca 21. In the Southern tradition, he thereafter called her "Miss Rebecca" until they were both in their 80s.

Watterson's editorial message at the *Banner* was that the South should forget and the North should forgive. He wanted to build sectional harmony and national unity, arguing that "rest and time to recover the waste of war, and a fair chance for the blessings of free men will satisfy the craving of most of us." His editorials took a moderate line, particularly toward the freedmen. Watterson considered that the abolition of slavery had been the best thing that could have happened to the South. He urged white Southerners to give blacks a helping hand, especially in creating schools. Northern newspapers reprinted his editorials as the words of a reasonable and reconstructed South. But Watterson believed that economic progress should precede political equality, and he was dismayed over the increasingly radical nature of Reconstruction.

In 1868, during the excitement over President Andrew Johnson's impeachment, Watterson received an unexpected offer to become editor of the *Louisville Journal*. Unlike Nashville, which felt like a depressed and defeated city after the war, Louisville prospered. Sitting on the major North-South railroad route, Louisville advertised itself as the "gateway to the South." A once powerful paper, the *Journal* had fallen behind two other papers in the city: the *Democrat* and the *Morning Courier*. Accepting the new post, Watterson went to the *Courier*'s owner, Walter Haldeman, and proposed a merger. "You need an editor. I need a publisher," Watterson contended. "Let us put these two papers together, buy the *Democrat*, and instead of cutting one another's throats, go after Cincinnati and St. Louis." When Haldeman agreed, the *Courier-Journal* was founded. "It is our aim to be just, to be liberal, to be conscientious," Watterson proclaimed. "It is our interest to be active, to be spirited, to be enterprising. We shall permit no paper in the West or South to surpass the *Courier-Journal* in all the essentials we have named." Watterson at 28 became editor, while Haldeman served as business manager.

As editor, Watterson quickly drew attention by his enthusiastic and often slashing editorials, and for his joyous personality. With his long hair and goatee, flashy clothes, fondness for poker and bourbon, he seemed the image of a Kentucky colonel. He also liked to dabble in politics. In 1872 Watterson joined the Liberal Republican movement opposed to President Ulysses S. Grant—for which Watterson coined the phrase: "Throw the Rascals Out." Watterson supported their candidate, Horace Greeley, for President. Despite Greeley's landslide defeat, Watterson believed his candidacy had helped shorten "the distance across the bloody chasm" of the war.

In 1876 Watterson worked even harder for the election of Samuel J. Tilden, the Democratic candidate for President. Tilden won the popular vote, but Republicans claimed the electoral votes of several states still under Reconstruction rule. In 1872 Watterson himself had won election to Congress in a special election. During the debates over the disputed election, he grew so outraged over Republican efforts to deny Tilden his victory that he called for 100,000 men to converge on Washington when the electoral votes were counted to make sure that the majority won. Although he insisted that he meant this to be a peaceful gathering, many people interpreted his call as advocating armed rebellion. A Thomas Nast cartoon portrayed Watterson as a wild Southern rebel. Tilden shrank from the proposal and the Republican Rutherford B. Hayes became President. Watterson later concluded that the missing ingredient in Tilden's character was "the touch of the dramatic"—a quality that he himself possessed in great measure.

Returning to Louisville after his only term in elected office, Watterson devoted himself to his paper, whose circulation rose dramatically along with the "New South." Watterson and Haldeman paid off the mortgage on their offices, raised salaries, and reaped the benefits of rising stock prices. Now a wealthy man, Watterson traveled widely in the United States and Europe. He became a popular lecturer on the colorful traits of the South. He hoped that by appealing to Northern audiences he would further bind the wounds of the war. During his absences, his strong editorial staff ran the paper for him, causing a trade paper, the *Journalist,* to sniff: "The paper is a good deal better run when Mr. Watterson is away from home than it is when he is in Louisville."

Unable to resist the attraction of Presidential politics, Watterson alternately promoted candidates for President and quarreled with them after they were elected. A conservative by disposition, he stood firm against Populism in the 1890s and disapproved of all schemes that would increase inflation in order to reduce debts. He especially opposed William Jennings Bryan's campaign for free silver, that is, a currency based on silver instead of gold. His opposition to Bryan's nomination—under the editorial slogan "No compromise with dishonor"—almost bankrupt the *Courier-Journal,* which angry Kentucky Democrats boycotted and burned. Watterson helped build back the paper's circulation by his strong support of the Spanish-American War. He viewed the war as another opportunity to bring the sections together, with Northerners and Southerners wearing the same uniform to fight a foreign enemy.

Watterson saw the editorial page as the place to help readers digest the news. After all the distractions and

excitement of the news pages, editorials, he said, should be "a raised dais in the center of a great hall, a seat of power and charm; an elevation from which to survey the passing show." As he aged, his editorials and his public image grew richer with his lively reminiscences of the Old South, the Civil War, and Reconstruction. He had lived some of the great moments of American history, and had known the players in the events. Styling himself "Marse Henry," in the old Southern tradition, his individuality transferred to his newspaper. He believed that when he wrote an editorial or delivered a public lecture his audience would identify him with the romantic "Lost Cause" of the South. He used

Although a Democrat, Henry Watterson broke with his party and opposed the nomination of William Jennings Bryan in 1896. This editorial cartoon depicts Watterson as a traveler in the Alps, where the high altitude is giving him nightmarish visions of Bryan, Populists, anarchists, and other radicals taking over his party.

"You ask me how do I feel? I can only tell you that I feel too much respect for myself, too much respect for my people and my Country, to fall into passionate, unmanly, imbecile oratory. The inauguration of Hayes, under these circumstances, is something of a calamity. But the world will not stop on its axis; the people will live, move and have their being; parties will continue to exist; politicians will plan and plot. I hope that I shall never be so weak, that our Southern men and women, who have borne so much will never be so weak, as to hang all earthly hope on any public or political event."

—from the *Louisville Courier-Journal* (February 20, 1877), following the electoral defeat of Samuel J. Tilden by Rutherford B. Hayes

that image to reunite America and to help Southern blacks. The African-American educator Booker T. Washington wrote of Watterson: "If there is anywhere a man who has broader or more liberal ideas concerning the Negro . . . I have not met him."

When Walter Haldeman died in 1901, his son Bruce Haldeman succeeded him as business manager of the *Courier-Journal*, but the younger man saw things differently than Watterson did. In 1915, before the United States had entered World War I, Watterson became enraged over German naval attacks on American merchant ships. His editorial denounced Germany and questioned the patriotism of pro-German Americans. Since Louisville had a large and wealthy German-American community, the *Courier-Journal*'s business manager, Bruce Haldeman, feared these editorials were costing the paper readers and advertisers. Watterson refused to tone down his rhetoric. He reminded Haldeman that newspapers do not edit themselves, and that editorials had given the paper "character, distinction and influence, and, I think also, prosperity." The feud only intensified, and Haldeman locked the connecting door between their offices. Finally, Watterson realized the time had come to retire. In 1919 both he and Haldeman sold their shares of the *Courier-Journal* to Robert Worth Bingham. Henry Watterson became editor emeritus, wrote occasional editorials, and worked on his memoirs. He died at age 80 while vacationing in Florida. Although very much a relic of another era, he was sorely missed by those who valued editorial courage and originality.

FURTHER READING

Andrews, J. Cutler. *The South Reports the Civil War*. 1970. Reprint, Pittsburgh: University of Pittsburgh Press, 1985.

Foner, Eric. *Reconstruction: America's Unfinished Revolution, 1863–1877*. New York: Harper & Row, 1988.

Marcosson, Isaac F. *"Marse Henry": A Biography of Henry Watterson*. New York: Dodd, Mead, 1951.

Wall, Joseph Frazier. *Henry Watterson, Reconstructed Rebel*. New York: Oxford University Press, 1956.

Watterson, Henry. *The Editorials of Henry Watterson*. Edited by Arthur Krock. New York: George H. Doran, 1923.

———. *"Marse Henry"; An Autobiography*. 2 vols. 1919. Reprint, New York: Beekman, 1974.

Julian Ralph

ANYTHING TO GET A STORY

As a reporter in New York City from the 1870s to the 1890s, Julian Ralph covered crime, scandals, fires, and other disasters. He believed that a reporter needed a "news instinct." Reporters had to get out of bed "new-born every morning" so they could approach all that they had to write about "with new eyes and fresh interest." They needed "a made-to-order sort of soul" to enable them to suffer whatever assignments came their way, and to be as "willing as a race-horse." They needed vigor and persistence. That credo described Ralph's own career. Tall and sturdy, he would go anywhere and do anything necessary to get his story.

Once he paid a miner to guide him down into a mine that had collapsed, ignoring warnings about the danger of explosion. Another time, while investigating the murder of a young girl, he became a suspect himself in the eyes of the girl's brothers. When they threatened him, he made that the lead in his front-page account. "If I have done anything uncommon in newspaper work," Ralph believed, "it has been in the way of covering . . . important events completely, and at great lengths, unaided and alone."

Ralph was the child of a stormy marriage. His parents had immigrated to New York from England. His father was a doctor in New York City. After the parents separated and divorced, the children went to live with their mother in Red Bank, New Jersey. Julian dropped out of school as a teenager to take a job as a "printer's devil," or apprentice, with the *New Jersey Standard*. Especially on smaller papers, printers often had the opportunity to write news as well as set type, and the composing room was a traditional training ground for future reporters. Julian Ralph's first chance came the day he wrote a piece describing the antics of a mad bull in the streets of a village. Reflecting on his own limited schooling, he later insisted that "newspapermen are born and not made," and was scornful of college-trained journalists.

Starting his own short-lived paper, and then serving as "acting editor" of a small paper in Massachusetts, Ralph decided to try the "big time" journalism of New York City. He was still only 19 years old. Most likely he got his first job by hanging around the offices of the *New York World* until something happened and there was no one else around to cover the incident. Ralph joined the staff of the *World* in the days before Joseph Pulitzer had bought the paper. The *World* was still an old-fashioned, prim and proper paper, edited by the scholarly Manton Marble. Its circulation was falling steadily, and his headquarters were in shabby condition. Yet, unlike many other papers of that era, whose reporters sent

"Lizzie Andrew Borden," said the Clerk of the court, "stand up." She rose unsteadily, with a face as white as marble.

"Gentlemen, have you agreed upon a verdict?" said the clerk to the jury.

It was so still in court that the flutter of two fans made a great noise.

"We have," said Foreman Richards boldly.

The prisoner was gripping the rail in front of the dock as if her standing up depended upon its keeping its place. . . .

"Jurors, look upon the prisoner. Prisoner, look upon the foreman."

Every juryman stood at right about-face, staring at the woman. There was such a gentle, kindly light beaming in every eye that no one questioned the verdict that was to be uttered. But God save every woman from the feelings that Lizzie Borden showed in the return look she cast upon that jury. It was what is pictured as the rolling gaze of a dying woman. She seemed not to have the power to move her eyes directly where she was told to, and they swung all around in her head. They looked at the ceiling; they looked at everything but they saw nothing. It was a horrible, a pitiful sight to see her then.

"What say you, Mr. Foreman?" said the gentle old clerk.

"Not guilty," shouted Mr. Richards.

At the words the wretched woman fell quicker than ever an ox fell in the stock yards of Chicago. Her forehead crashed against the heavy walnut rail of the dock so as to shake the reporter of the *Sun* who sat next to her, twelve feet away, leaning on the rail. It seemed that she must be stunned, but she was not. Quickly, with an unconscious movement, she flung up both arms and threw them over the rail and pressed them under her face so that it rested on them. . . . The verdict left the people where they began—asking one another who killed Mr. and Mrs. Borden.

—from the *New York Sun* (June 21, 1893)

their stories directly to the composing room, the *World* had a copydesk. Copydesk editors worked on reporters' prose and structure, took editorializing opinions out of the stories, and added to the journalistic education of a young reporter.

Among his assignments, Ralph was sent to cover a public flogging in Delaware, the last state to permit whipping of criminals. Horrified by what he saw, he wrote an article denouncing the practice. However, his editors stripped out all his indignation and published the barest facts. Ralph protested, and the *World* relented. His original story, "The Whipping-Post—Scenes and Incidents at a Delaware Flogging," appeared on his 20th birthday.

The ambitious young reporter switched to a new newspaper, the *New York Daily Graphic*, whose articles were accompanied by many engravings and cartoons. The *Daily Graphic* sent Ralph to Brooklyn to cover the sensational trial of the Reverend Henry Ward Beecher, who was accused of committing adultery with a member of his congregation. For six months, Ralph described the participants in the trial and the day-to-day events of the trial, all in great detail. The *Daily Graphic* installed a three-mile wire from the courtroom to its offices to get the news first. Ralph had an ability to write quickly, clearly, and at length. Other reporters swore that he "could write five thousand words about a cobblestone." A fellow journalist said that when Ralph wrote a column about a horse eating a woman's hat, "the reader became well acquainted with the horse, the woman, and the crowd that looked on."

His reporting of the Beecher trial was so good that it came to the attention of Charles A. Dana, editor of the *New York Sun*. The veteran Dana, who had once been managing editor of Horace Greeley's *New York Tribune*, was always looking out for new talent. Julian Ralph proved to be one of his greatest finds. Even though the *Sun* did not have the largest circulation in New York, it was one of the most prestigious newspapers of its time. In 1871 Joseph Pulitzer called the *Sun* the most "entertaining, and, without exception, the best newspaper in the world." The paper won fame for its unconventional treatment of the news and for Dana's merciless, slashing editorials.

Wages were higher on the *Sun* than on other papers. Reporters started on a salary until they had learned their craft. Then they were paid by the number of columns they wrote. For a prolific writer like Ralph, this was an opportunity to earn considerably more than he would on a flat salary. In 1875, the year he joined the *Sun*, Ralph returned to Red Bank to marry his childhood sweetheart, Isabella Mount. Life for them was a series of boardinghouses in Brooklyn, Greenwich Village, and elsewhere in New York, where they raised their five children. As a husband and father, Ralph was often absent. His workdays began at noon and lasted late into the night. He was often sent out of town on assignments.

Reporting was a demanding job, especially in the days before telephones. Reporters had to go out to get the news and rush back to their offices to write it up by deadline. Ralph developed a reputation as a sturdy "leg man," with the stamina to spend the day covering the news and the night turning out columns, which he wrote in pencil. Editor Dana wanted writing that was clear and to the point. His reporters learned by observation and by their sense of self-preservation what to write and what to avoid. It was Dana's city editor, John B. Bogart, who coined the classic definition of news: "When a dog bites a man, that is not news, because it happens so often. But if a man bites a dog, that is news."

In the 1880s the *Sun* sent Ralph to Albany to cover the state legisla-

Ralph joined the staff of the *New York Sun* in 1875, when the paper occupied this building near New York's City Hall.

ture, and in the 1890s made him their Washington correspondent. But he was never happy as a legislative reporter. He found debates in the state legislature and the Congress to be tedious and exasperating, and he hated posturing politicians. "The Senate was stu-

Reporter Julian Ralph (right) rides through Washington, D.C., while covering the inauguration of President Grover Cleveland in March 1893, for the *New York Sun*. This illustration appeared with an article Ralph wrote for the August 1893 issue of *Scribner's Magazine*.

pider than ever" began one of his accounts in 1885. His articles targeted bribery and corruption in government. Once when a state legislator tried to bribe him, Ralph declined because "I couldn't live to let an infernal rascal like you point me out as one of your kind."

In 1889 Ralph became convinced that the police were trying to pin a murder on an innocent boy. Ralph investigated and published evidence that the police had concealed some facts and distorted others. The case was already at trial, but after Ralph's

articles appeared the prosecution rested and the jury found the boy not guilty. Ralph proudly cited the case as evidence of "the power of a journalist," claiming that his articles had saved the boy from becoming the first to die in New York State's new electric chair. He was also a dogged competitor. Once an arson suspect confessed to Ralph. Not wanting to share the story with the rest of the press, the reporter convinced the police that he could make the man confess, but only if they withheld the news until after he had published his story. He was also known to wear disguises to collect his facts, and he rarely took notes during interviews for fear of putting his subjects on guard.

After 20 years with the *Sun*, Ralph began to feel restless. Having demonstrated ability early in his career, the daily demands of the paper seemed to be dull and routine. Like most newspapers of the era, the *Sun* did not give its reporters bylines. Although Ralph was well known among reporters, he was anonymous to the general public. In the 1880s he began writing magazine articles and books to which his name appeared next to the title, and he began to develop more of a public identity.

Then, in 1895, the wealthy publisher William Randolph Hearst set out to buy the best reporters for the *New York Journal*. Hearst not only paid top prices, but allowed his reporters to sign their names to their dispatches. Ralph accepted Hearst's offer and went to

Julian Ralph

BORN

May 27, 1853
New York, New York

DIED

January 20, 1903
New York, New York

EDUCATION

Public schools

ACHIEVEMENTS

Printer and reporter, *New Jersey Standard* (1868–70, 1872–73); managing editor, *Red Bank* (New Jersey) *Leader* (1871); acting editor, *Webster* (Massachusetts) *Times* (1871–72); reporter, *New York World* (1873–74); reporter, *New York Daily Graphic* (1874–75); reporter, *New York Sun* (1875–95); foreign correspondent, *New York Journal* (1895–97); freelance magazine writer (1890–1903); war correspondent, *London Daily Mail* and *New York Herald* (1899–1900); columnist, *Brooklyn Eagle* (1901–03); author of numerous books, including *The Sun's German Barber* (1883), *Our Great West: A Story of the Present Conditions and Future Possibilities of the New Commonwealths and Capitals of the U.S.* (1893), *Harper's Chicago and the World's Fair* (1893), *Alone in China, and Other Stories* (1897), *An American With Lord Roberts* (1901), *War's Brighter Side: The Story of the Friend Newspaper* (1901), and *The Making of a Journalist* (1903)

London as a foreign correspondent for the *Journal*. Although he enjoyed living in London, he soon realized he had made a mistake working for Hearst. Insisting that he had never stooped to "mere sensationalism or any sort of untruth," Ralph held Hearst's sensational style in contempt. He also found himself constantly undercut by Hearst, who sent famous novelists to cover stories that Ralph was also reporting. Ralph was furious when the *Journal* devoted so much space to Stephen Crane's accounts of the Greek-Turkish war and cut his own stories down. When the paper sent Mark Twain to cover Queen Victoria's Diamond Jubilee—a story that belonged to the London correspondent—Ralph decided to quit.

Ralph remained in London as a freelance writer, and in 1898 became a war correspondent for the *London Daily Mail* and the *New York Herald*. Covering the Boer War in South Africa was a dangerous assignment, especially for a man who had spent most of his life in the comforts of cities. Conditions in South Africa were rugged, and he suffered many injuries and illnesses. All his life, Ralph had hated and feared horses, and while covering the war his horse bolted and threw him into a wire fence, cutting him badly. Yet he continued reporting the battle. Worn out, Julian Ralph went back to New York, where he wrote weekly columns for the

Brooklyn Eagle, and continued publishing articles and books. Ill with cancer, he went to cover the Louisiana Purchase Exposition in St. Louis in 1904. It was his last story. Shortly after his return, the "prince of reporters" (as his admiring colleagues called him) died in a New York City boardinghouse.

FURTHER READING

Knightley, Philip. *The First Casualty: From the Crimea to Vietnam: The War Correspondent as Hero, Propagandist, and Myth Maker.* New York: Harcourt Brace Jovanovich, 1975.

Lancaster, Paul. *Gentlemen of the Press: The Life and Times of an Early Reporter: Julian Ralph of the Sun.* Syracuse: Syracuse University Press, 1992.

Leonard, Thomas C. *The Power of the Press: The Birth of American Political Reporting.* New York: Oxford University Press, 1986.

Ralph, Julian. *Our Great West: A Story of the Present Conditions and Future Possibilities of the New Commonwealths and Capitals of the U.S.* 1893. Reprint, Freeport, N.Y.: Books for Libraries Press, 1970.

———. *A Prince of Georgia, and Other Stories.* 1899. Reprint, Freeport, N.Y.: Books for Libraries Press, 1969.

Schudson, Michael. *Discovering the News: A Social History of American Newspapers.* New York: Basic Books, 1978.

Smythe, Ted Curtis. "The Reporter, 1880–1900: Working Conditions and Their Influence on the News." *Journalism History* 6 (Spring 1980).

Kate Field

A FAIR FIELD
FOR A WOMAN

Kate Field wished to make a name for herself, but early in life she realized that she lacked the talents that allowed women in the 19th century to rise to fame. As a schoolgirl, she ranked music as her first love and wanted to sing like Jenny Lind, the most popular vocalist of her day. But she lacked a powerful or expressive voice. "It is so very galling to see aimless, stupid, brainless girls get up and sing in a manner so far superior to my own," she lamented.

After music, literature most captured her interest. "I am passionately fond of reading," she wrote, "not trash, but literature of a high order." Although she dreamed of becoming a great writer, she conceded that "nature has not thus endowed me." She wanted to act, but her first major stage appearance was a critical disappointment. "Have I any talent?" she wondered. "I fear not." All the while, Kate Field avidly read newspapers, and there at last she found an outlet for her diverse interests.

Kate was born into a theatrical family. Her mother, Eliza Riddle Field, was a popular actress, and her father, Joseph M.

Finding many doors closed to her as a woman, Kate Field turned to journalism, becoming a correspondent and an editor as well as a noted lecturer. She eventually founded her own weekly, *Kate Field's Washington.*

Field, was an actor and playwright who operated theater companies in St. Louis and Mobile, Alabama. He also published a literary and theatrical review, the *Reveille*, in St. Louis with his partner, Charles Keemle. When their daughter was born in 1838, they named her Mary Katherine Keemle Field, but everyone called her Kate. Although the family traveled extensively with theater companies, Kate spent most of her childhood in St. Louis. When she was 16 she went to Boston to study at the Lasell Seminary for Girls. On the night that Kate made her singing debut in a school performance, word came that her father had died unexpectedly in Mobile. Not until after the performance was she told the news, and a local newspaper reported: "As the sad tidings were whispered about after the close of the entertainment, each heart seemed touched with melting sympathy for the unfortunate young lady whose evening's transition from delight to sadness was so sudden." Joseph Field had left nothing but a small life insurance policy for his family. Reduced finances made it necessary for Kate to leave school.

"Oh, if I were a man!" she wrote in her journal at the age of 17. "I pity myself, indeed, I do. There is not an ambition, a desire, a feeling, a thought, an impulse, an instinct that I am not obliged to crush. And why? because I am a woman, and a woman must content herself with indoor life, with sewing and babies." As a woman, many forms of employment were closed to her as she looked for ways to work to support herself and her mother. Fortunately, Kate's wealthy and childless aunt and uncle, Cordelia and Milton Sanford, practically adopted her. She accompanied the Sanfords on a tour of the major American cities, and then went abroad with them to live in Florence, Italy, then a center for American and British writers.

Before leaving for Europe, Field arranged to send occasional correspondence to the *Boston Courier*. She would be paid five dollars for each column about her travel experiences. The *Courier*'s editor also gave her letters of introduction to such eminent writers as Nathaniel Hawthorne, who was then living abroad. If Kate Field lacked the talent to become a great writer herself, she was always attracted to literary people. They, in turn, found her intelligent and charming. The British author Anthony Trollope was smitten with her long chestnut curls, fair complexion, and large blue eyes. She became close friends with Elizabeth Barrett and Robert Browning, and met George Eliot and other distinguished poets and novelists.

"Without an object in life, no one can be happy," Field wrote in 1861. "It is my only salvation that I can find food in the politics of the world; they fill up the vacuum that otherwise would yawn for want of friends and activity." That year, Civil War divided America, and she became absorbed with the news. Field avidly committed herself to the Union cause, arguing that "the Union has been betrayed, government property stolen, and the flag disgraced." It was a costly stand that alienated her pro-Southern uncle. Threatened with the loss of the allowance she received from him, she began writing for other newspapers.

Kate Field returned to America to live with her mother in Boston. The *Springfield* (Massachusetts) *Republican* hired her as one of its Boston correspondents, and she also wrote for the *Atlantic Monthly* and other magazines. The use of pseudonyms was then common in the press, and since her father had signed his articles as "Straws," she frequently signed her pieces "Straws, Jr." She wrote music, art, and drama criticism and commented on the great events of the day, such as President Lincoln's assassination. In the 1870s Field became a frequent contributor to

Kate Field

BORN

October 1, 1838
St. Louis, Missouri

DIED

May 19, 1896
On a steamer bound for Honolulu, Hawaii

EDUCATION

Mrs. Smith's Seminary, St. Louis, Missouri (1851–53); Lasell Seminary for Girls, Auburndale, Massachusetts (1854–56)

ACCOMPLISHMENTS

Correspondent, *Boston Courier*, *Springfield Republican*, *New York Tribune*, and other papers (1859–96); editor, *Kate Field's Washington* (1890–95); author of *Planchette's Diary* (1868), *Pen Photographs of Charles Dickens's Readings* (1868), *Hap-Hazard* (1873), *Ten Days in Spain* (1875), *History of Bell's Telephone* (1878), and *Charles Albert Fechter* (1882)

> *"The great comfort of America is that a woman is not always made to feel her sex. She really is allowed to exist as a human being, not, unfortunately, with all the liberty of a man, but still with so much more than elsewhere as by comparison to be free. In Europe, I never lose the sense of sex."*
>
> —from "European *versus* American Women," letter from London to the *New York Tribune* (August 5, 1873)

the *New York Tribune*, and her name grew increasingly familiar to newspaper readers. She also began delivering public lectures on her favorite subjects. A particularly popular lecture dealt with the British novelist Charles Dickens, whom she had met and heard read from his celebrated works. Another of her lectures, in sharp contrast, dealt with the fiery abolitionist John Brown. The *Boston Advertiser* noted that "Miss Field's voice is exceptionally musical, sweet, and agreeable; and it is but the simple truth to say she manages it admirably."

Field's myriad of enthusiasms made and lost her a fortune. In 1877 she became fascinated with the potentials of Alexander Graham Bell's new invention, the telephone. In return for the publicity she generated for Bell, she received stock in the Bell Telephone Company. The stock quickly multiplied in value and she invested most of the money in a project that aimed at simplifying the style of women's dresses and making them available at lower prices. Field served as president of the Cooperative Dress Association. Within a year's time, however, the cooperative failed and she lost her investment. She traveled widely, published books, acted in plays, all in search of fame and fulfillment, while turning down two offers of marriage. "I need a clear head to accomplish the work I must do in this world," she confided to a friend, "and nothing so unfit a sensitive

nature for mental exertion as emotional intensities."

The *New York Sun* in 1886 described Field as a remarkably self-possessed woman. "Newspaper correspondent, European tourist, monologue performer, lecturer, and woman of business, Kate Field has been before the public; and it is to her credit that in her various roles she has had always something to offer which the public has found it worth while to listen to." She lectured on any number of topics, ranging from temperance to opposition to the Mormon practice of polygamy. Many of these issues brought her into contact with the nation's political leaders and eventually drew her to Washington. The capital was the political hub of the nation, and she believed it would also become a social, literary, and artistic center as well.

On January 1, 1890, she published the first issue of her own "national newspaper," *Kate Field's Washington*. "I believe that 'men and women are eternally equal and eternally different'; hence I believe there is a fair field in Washington for a national weekly edited by a woman." Field's admirers from many areas invested in the weekly paper. The sprightly journal mingled fiction, philosophy, theater, art, society news, and politics, demonstrating her own wide range of interests—although, like Field herself, it lacked a central focus. She boosted Washington as a city, promoting education and writing

favorably about its expanding neighborhoods. At the same time she never hesitated to lecture and lobby the national lawmakers located there. "I fail to see why a Congress that is equal to regulating the army, navy, foreign affairs, the treasury, and agriculture," she wrote during the economic depression of 1893, "should not concern itself with the welfare of the masses upon whom depends the very existence of the republic."

Its editor's declining health caused *Kate Field's Washington* to discontinue publication in April 1895. The publication was such an example of personal journalism—she wrote most of its articles—that it could not continue without her. Field left for Hawaii to recuperate, planning to write travel pieces from the Pacific for the *Chicago Times-Herald*. Her last cause was to argue in favor of American annexation of the Hawaiian islands. Critically ill with pneumonia, she was sailing between the islands when someone asked if the native ukulele music outside her cabin was disturbing her. "Oh, no," she replied, "music is Paradise to me." She died later that night at sea.

FURTHER READING

Beasley, Maurine. "Kate Field and 'Kate Field's Washington': 1890-1895." *Records of the Columbia Historical Society of Washington, D.C., 1973–1974.* Charlottesville: University Press of Virginia, 1976.

Field, Kate. *Charles Albert Fechter.* 1882. Reprint, New York: B. Blom, 1969.

Ross, Ishbel. *Ladies of the Press: The Story of Women in Journalism by an Insider.* 1936. Reprint, New York: Arno, 1974.

Whiting, Lilian. *Kate Field: A Record.* Boston: Little, Brown, 1899.

Woodward, Helen Beal. "Kate Field: The Woman in the Footnote," in *The Bold Woman.* 1953. Reprint, New York: Books for Libraries Press, 1971.

Joseph Pulitzer

"ACCURACY, ACCURACY, ACCURACY!"

It seems ironic that Joseph Pulitzer, known during his lifetime as a sensationalist newspaper publisher, should be remembered through the awarding of Pulitzer prizes for excellence in journalism. But there is less contradiction than might be imagined. Pulitzer had a knack for salvaging failing newspapers. At just 31, he took over the ailing *St. Louis Post* and the *Dispatch* and turned them into the vibrant *St. Louis Post-Dispatch,* a crusader against corruption in the city. At 36 he moved into the cutthroat competitive world of New York journalism by purchasing the *New York World*. Within three years he had increased the *World*'s circulation 10 times over and made it one of the most influential papers in the nation.

He attracted readers by devising new journalistic techniques, including banner headlines, editorial cartoons, sports news, and women's news pages. He expanded local, national, and international coverage and drove his staff of reporters mercilessly, demanding exclusive news, colorful stories, and better writing. Above all else he demanded: "Accuracy, accuracy, accuracy!"

Joseph Pulitzer wanted to produce newspapers that people paid attention to, and he insisted on style and accuracy in his reporters' writing. John Singer Sargent painted this portrait of the publisher in 1905.

"God grant that The World *may forever strive toward the highest ideal—be both a daily school-house and a daily forum—both a daily teacher and a daily tribune—an instrument of Justice, a terror to crime, an aid to education, an exponent of true Americanism."*

—from the *New York World* (October 11, 1889)

Born in Hungary in 1847 to a Jewish father and Catholic mother, Pulitzer was just a boy when his father died. His mother's remarriage made him unhappy and he struck out for independence. He applied for a commission in the Austrian army, but his young age, poor eyesight, and scrawny build caused the army to reject him. He was similarly turned down by the French Foreign Legion and the British army in India. Finally, in Hamburg, Germany, he met agents recruiting for the Union army in the American Civil War. In 1864 the 17-year-old Pulitzer sailed to fight with the New York First Lincoln Cavalry.

Arriving in the United States able to speak German and Hungarian but almost no English, the lanky Pulitzer served for less than a year in the Union army, fighting in a few skirmishes. After the war he looked for work in New York City. Finding nothing, he headed west for St. Louis, Missouri, which had a large German-speaking community. He had so little money that he had to stoke a ferryboat's boiler just to pay his passage across the Mississippi. He became a U.S. citizen in 1867 and studied law, but his poor English and odd appearance worked against him in pursuing a career as an attorney. Instead, he took a job reporting for a German-language newspaper, the *Westliche Post.*

Always as excited by politics as he was by journalism, Pulitzer won an election to the Missouri state legislature in 1869 as a Republican. One newspaper endorsement described him as "a thoroughly upright young man with spirit, education, and definite talent." He served in the legislature while reporting for his paper as a legislative correspondent—an arrangement not yet seen as a conflict of interest. Over time, disillusionment with corruption in the administration of President Ulysses S. Grant caused Pulitzer to break with the Republicans and

become a Democrat. In 1878 he married Kate Davis, a cousin of Jefferson Davis, the former president of the Confederacy.

That same year, a bankruptcy sale was held for the *St. Louis Dispatch.* Pulitzer, now 31, put in a bid and bought the paper. It was not much of a prize, with its dilapidated office, broken-down printing presses, and declining circulation. What it had was an Associated Press franchise. This meant that it could get wire stories from around the nation and the world, giving it an advantage over papers without an AP franchise. Pulitzer merged it with another sickly paper that he bought out to form the *St. Louis Post-Dispatch.*

As a publisher, Pulitzer continued to write stories for his paper—having by then mastered English—and worked long hours along with his staff. From his corner office he would shout out suggestions and criticisms "in a high, harsh voice," according to his staff. He wanted to make the *St. Louis Post-Dispatch* the kind of paper that people paid attention to, for its style and for the issues it reported. He demanded vivid writing and shocking stories. When the *Post-Dispatch* investigated prostitution in St. Louis, for instance, it published a list of the seemingly respectable citizens who owned the buildings used as bordellos. (The headline read: "THE SOCIAL EVIL: SOME OF THOSE WHO RENT THEIR PROPERTY FOR IMMORAL PURPOSES.")

Pulitzer's paper crusaded against a lottery racket, a street-car monopoly, and an insurance fraud. Its headlines would often offer a "SHOCKING DISCLOSURE" or "GREAT SCOOP." As a result, its circulation rose—from 4,000 to 23,000 in three years—as did its advertising. In 1879 the paper could afford to expand from four pages to eight.

St. Louis was not a big enough market for Pulitzer's talents. The major center of journalism in the United States was New York City, but that metropolis was already so crowded with papers that it seemed doubtful that another could succeed. Pulitzer reasoned that most New York papers aimed at prosperous and educated readers, leaving room for a paper that sought to reach the masses. "There is room in this great and growing city," he declared, "for a journal that is not only cheap, but bright; not only bright, but large; not only large, but truly democratic . . . that will expose all fraud and shams, fight all public evils and abuses—that will serve and battle for the people with earnest sincerity."

Pulitzer purchased a run-down paper, the *New York World*, which he renamed the *World*. Founded as a Democratic paper in 1860, the *World* had long been snubbed by respectable people in New York. They remembered it as an organ for Copperheads (antiwar Democrats) during the Civil War, and for the corrupt municipal regime of Boss William Tweed in the 1870s. Pulitzer turned this decaying, despised little sheet into one of the richest and most powerful papers of the era. Between 1883, when he took it over, and 1885, its circulation increased 10 times over.

"I had a small paper which had been dead for years, and I was trying in every way I could think of to build up its circulation," Pulitzer later explained. "I wanted to put into each issue something that would arouse curiosity and make people want to buy the paper." When readers picked up Pulitzer's *World*, they noticed right away that it was different from other newspapers of the day. The *World* put editorial cartoons on the front page and sprinkled illustrations throughout the paper (technology at that time permitted the use of line drawings and engravings made from photographs, rather than photographs themselves). The *World* announced the news in banner head-lines, and in a slangy, personal style. It published poetry and short stories, featured women's news and sports news in order to be entertaining as well as informative. It crusaded for the interests of immigrants and poor people living in tenement houses. It rooted out vice and corruption and attacked the people responsible, whether politicians, business executives, or even the clergy. This style, so out of character with other papers, was seen as sensationalist.

When Pulitzer was asked why he did not make the *World* into a more respectable paper like the *New York Evening Post*, a serious paper read by more refined folks, he replied: "I want to talk to a nation, not to a select committee." Pulitzer sought a large audience because greater circulation meant more advertising, and more advertising meant more money, and more money meant more independence. Although always a partisan in his politics, Pulitzer's papers were never under the control of political parties or bosses. He felt free to say what needed to be said, regardless of which party it helped or hurt.

Pulitzer hired away the best reporters from other newspapers and paid them high salaries, but he also demanded much from them. A paper could never become great simply by reprinting the handouts it got from businesses and political figures and by summarizing what had happened each day. Its reporters had to go out and launch a crusade, start a fight, or dig up an exclusive. The novelist Theodore Dreiser, who once reported for the *World*, described its newsroom atmosphere as "every man for himself." Pulitzer pitted reporters against each other and promoted suspicion and antagonism among the staff to make them competitive and work harder. His reporters had a "kind of nervous, resentful terror in their eyes." Dreiser blamed Pulitzer's "aggressive, restless, working mood, and his vaulting ambi-

Joseph Pulitzer

BORN
April 10, 1847
Makó, Hungary

DIED
October 29, 1911
On his yacht near Charleston, South Carolina

EDUCATION
Privately tutored

ACCOMPLISHMENTS
Reporter, *Westliche Post* (St. Louis, Missouri, 1868–78); publisher, *St. Louis Post-Dispatch* (1878–1907); publisher, *New York World* (1881–1907)

THE SUNDAY WORLD
SEPT. 13.

8 FUNNY PAGES

THE SUNDAY WORLD

$500 GIVEN IN PRIZES TO MEN OF POLITICAL JUDGMENT.

| A Secret Society Initiation in Hogan's Alley | Queer Human Beings to be Seen at Newport |
| COLORED CARTOON | COLORED CARTOON |

An Eight Page Comic Weekly Printed in Colors, A Magazine and the Best Newspaper Published.

Introducing color comics helped to double the circulation of the *World*'s Sunday edition.

tion to be all that there was to be of journalist force in America . . . [for] making a veritable hell of his paper and the lives of those who worked for him." In the *World*'s pressroom, Pulitzer had cards pasted on the wall, reminding his staff: "Who? What? Where? When? How?" "The Facts—the Color—the Facts!" and "Accuracy! Terseness! Accuracy!"

In the Presidential campaign of 1884, the Republicans nominated James G. Blaine to head their ticket. Since Blaine's name had been linked to several major financial scandals, Pulitzer considered him to be a prime example of corruption in public life, and he set out to defeat him. Throughout the campaign, the *World* dug up whatever dirt it could find about Blaine, and it ran daily articles and editorial cartoons against him. In late October, just before the election, Blaine attended a lavish dinner in New York City. One of the speakers at the dinner, a Protestant minister, denounced the Democratic party as the party of "Rum, Romanism, and Corruption."

Although Blaine had sought to appeal to Catholic voters, he ignored the minister's slur. So did most of the newspaper reporters covering the dinner. Not the *World*—it plastered the quote across the front page of its paper and printed extra editions to reach the city's most heavily Catholic wards. Blaine lost New York by just 1,149 votes. Had he won the state's electoral votes, he would have won the election. The *World*'s relentless attacks cost him the White House.

In 1885 Pulitzer himself won a seat in the U.S. House of Representatives as a Democrat. He served only four months, however, finding that as a freshman member of the House he had less influence than he did as publisher of his newspaper. And service in Washington distracted him from his editorial duties in New York. He resigned his seat and returned to journalism, never to run for office again.

As the preeminent newspaper publisher of his day, Pulitzer in 1890 constructed for the *World* the tallest building in New York City. Its 10-story tower, capped with a gold dome, loomed over all its newspaper rivals. Pulitzer also dreamed up elaborate stunts, like sending Elizabeth Cochrane, who wrote as Nellie Bly, to beat the record of Jules Verne's fictional Phileas Fogg by going around the world in less than 80 days. In this way he invented news that would not otherwise have existed.

Pulitzer's critics accused him of "yellow journalism." This term for gaudy, unconventional, sensational journalism arose from a yellow-colored cartoon in his Sunday paper. One of Pulitzer's inventions was the Sunday comic strip, R. F. Outcault's "The Yellow Kid," which first appeared in 1894. Its popularity nearly doubled the circulation of the Sunday *World*. So much advertising poured in that Pulitzer increased the bulk of the Sunday paper and added more new features. But in 1896 a rich young upstart from California, William Randolph Hearst, hired away Pulitzer's entire Sunday staff, including the cartoonist Richard F. Outcault, for his rival *New York Morning Journal*. Hearst was not original. He shamelessly copied Pulitzer's style, but he had plenty of money and nerve. To compete with Hearst, Pulitzer cut the cost of his paper to one cent and raised advertising rates to make up the difference. Financially, it was a disastrous move that forced the *World* to cut back its number of pages and some of its reporting staff.

Pulitzer and Hearst competed for the same working-class readers, and the same advertisers, to dominate the New York newspaper field. Just as Pulitzer had bought his best reporters away from other papers, Hearst bought his reporters from the *World*. Hearst let most of his reporters sign their articles, while Pulitzer still resisted bylines—which caused some of Pulitzer's best staff members to desert him. Competition between the two newspaper giants reached its apex between 1896 and 1898 as both papers aroused public opinion against Spanish rule of Cuba, reporting on atrocities there—real or imagined—and demanding American intervention. Pulitzer's paper was never as crude and boasting about the war as Hearst's was, but both were influential in pushing the nation into war. Sensing that they had gone too far, Pulitzer took steps to tone down the *World*'s sensationalism and lift its standards.

As he grew older, Pulitzer suffered from insomnia, asthma, rheumatism, diabetes, and nervous conditions. His eyesight failed, leaving him blind and extremely sensitive to sound. He abandoned the city to spend months on his ocean-going yacht, and when he was back in Manhattan he lived in a soundproof vault within his mansion. He communicated with his editors by messenger, telegraph, and cablegram.

Concerned about the quality of journalism in America, in 1892 Pulitzer offered money to Columbia University to establish the nation's first school of journalism. The trustees, however, did not see journalism as a profession like law or medicine, and they rejected the offer. Many newspaper editors and reporters also scoffed at the idea. They had learned their trade by personal experience rather than from books and classrooms. Old-time reporters considered college training to be a waste of time. But in 1903 Pulitzer made a second, more successful effort to persuade Columbia to take his money and set up a journalism school. "My idea," he said, "is to raise the character of the profession to a higher level." The Columbia School of Journalism became a model for many others around the country.

Joseph Pulitzer retired from journalism in 1907 and died in 1911. The *World* gradually declined without his driving force. Despite a provision in his will that called on his sons to conduct the paper "as a public institution, from motives higher than mere gain," they found a loophole that enabled them to sell it. In 1931 the morning edition of the *World* was ended and the evening edition merged into the *World-Telegram*. In 1964 that paper further merged into the *World-Journal-Tribune*, and by 1966 the last remnants of the *World* disappeared. Pulitzer's name has lived on, however, in the annual prizes that he established in his will to recognize outstanding work in reporting, literature, drama, and history. On its editorial pages the *St. Louis Post-Dispatch* continues to print Pulitzer's promise:

> I know that my retirement will make no difference in its cardinal principles, that it will always fight for progress and reform, never tolerate injustice or corruption, always fight demagogues of all parties, never belong to any party, always oppose privileged classes and public plunderers, never lack sympathy with the poor, always remain devoted to the public welfare, never be satisfied with merely printing news, always be drastically independent, never be afraid to attack wrong, ether by predatory plutocracy or predatory poverty.

FURTHER READING

Juergens, George. *Joseph Pulitzer and the New York World*. Princeton, N.J.: Princeton University Press, 1966.

Leonard, Thomas C. *The Power of the Press: The Birth of American Political Reporting*. New York: Oxford University Press, 1986.

Seitz, Don C. *Joseph Pulitzer: His Life and Letters*. New York: Simon & Schuster, 1924.

Swanberg, W. A. *Pulitzer*. New York: Scribners, 1967.

Nellie Bly (Elizabeth Cochrane Seaman)

STUNT JOURNALIST

One day in 1885, Elizabeth Cochrane read a column in the *Pittsburgh Dispatch* that made her furious. Under the title "Women's Sphere," the writer denounced "those restless dissatisfied females" who want to go to work rather than stay home to make "a little paradise" for their husbands and children. "Women's Sphere," he insisted, was "defined and located by a single word—home." Elizabeth wrote an angry letter to the paper in response, signing it "Lonely Orphan Girl." Editor George A. Madden was so impressed with the letter's fire and earnest reasoning that he ran an ad asking for the "Lonely

Dressed in her distinctive traveling clothes, Nellie Bly set out to travel around the world in less than 80 days. She accomplished her goal.

> *"I succeeded in getting committed to the insane ward at Blackwell's Island, where I spent ten days and nights and had an experience I shall never forget. I took upon myself to enact the part of a poor unfortunate crazy girl, and felt it my duty not to shirk any of the disagreeable results that should follow."*

—from the *New York World* (October 9, 1887)

Nellie Bly (Elizabeth Cochrane Seaman)

BORN
May 5, 1864
Cochran's Mills, Pennsylvania

DIED
January 27, 1922
New York, New York

EDUCATION
Indiana State Normal School, Indiana, Pennsylvania (one term, 1879)

ACCOMPLISHMENTS
Reporter, *Pittsburgh Dispatch* (1884–87); reporter and columnist, *New York World* (1887–96); reporter and columnist, *New York Journal* (1912–16, 1919–22); author of *Six Months in Mexico* (1886), *Ten Days in a Mad-House* (1887), *The Mystery of Central Park* (1889), and *Nellie Bly's Book: Around the World in Seventy-Two Days* (1890)

Orphan Girl's" name and address, suggesting that she might publish a rebuttal. The next day Elizabeth Cochrane came to the newsroom, and within a few days her article "The Girl Puzzle" appeared in the *Dispatch*. Soon she was hired as a regular reporter for the paper.

Elizabeth had been born at Cochran's Mills, a small town near Pittsburgh, Pennsylvania. The town was named for her father, Michael Cochran (to be fancier, Elizabeth added an *e* to her last name). Cochran was a mill owner, lawyer, and judge. Her mother was his second wife, the former Mary Jane Kennedy. There were 15 children in the Cochran household, including five older brothers. In such surroundings she grew up hardy, resourceful, and self-reliant. Her father died and her mother remarried, but that unhappy marriage ended in divorce. Her mother moved the family to Pittsburgh. There, in the working-class boardinghouses where they lived, Elizabeth met many hardworking, underpaid women. She grew sympathetic to the conditions of the poor and became outraged over the smug male attitudes of papers like the *Pittsburgh Dispatch*.

Elizabeth Cochrane agreed to write for the *Dispatch* so long as she could cover stories that she considered to be important—stories about divorce, working conditions for "workshop girls," and the city's worst slum housing. As was customary for that time,

she did not write under her own name. Her editor suggested the pen name "Nellie Bly," a misspelling of the popular song by Stephen Foster:

> *Nelly Bly, Nelly Bly,*
> *Bring the broom along,*
> *We'll sweep the kitchen clean, my dear,*
> *And have a little song.*

As a measure of the attention that Bly's writing attracted, the *Dispatch* began printing her byline in bigger and bolder letters. Looking for new subjects to write about, in 1886 she went to Mexico to report on the sharp contrast between the lives of the Mexican rich and poor, and the need for reform. Elizabeth and her mother spent several months in Mexico sending articles to the *Dispatch*. After she filed a story on political corruption, the Mexican government strongly encouraged Nellie Bly to leave. Her more than 30 newspaper dispatches from Mexico were collected and published as her first book, *Six Months in Mexico*.

On her return from Mexico, she found that she had outgrown Pittsburgh, and she headed to New York City. After finding the doors shut to women reporters at many papers, she marched into the office of Joseph Pulitzer and asked to join his *New York World*. Impressed by her spunk, Pulitzer hired her. For her first story, she had herself committed to the insane asylum on Blackwell's Island, to investigate inhumane living conditions there. She

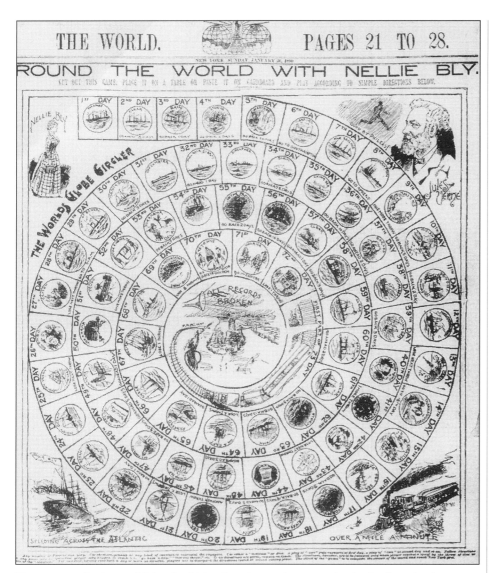

ROUND THE WORLD WITH NELLIE BLY.

To generate further publicity for Bly's trip, the *World* created a board game called "Round the World with Nellie Bly."

stole money from a woman's purse so that she could get herself thrown into jail and report on conditions there. She pretended to be the wife of a patent-medicine manufacturer who wanted to prevent government regulation, to get a lobbyist to show her how he bribed members of the state legislature. After collecting her information in each case, Bly discarded her disguises and published her findings in the *World*. She wrote in great detail and from a highly personal point of view. Women wrote to the paper about their problems, begging for help: "For God's sake, send Nellie Bly. She can do anything."

But the story that made Nellie Bly an international celebrity had nothing to do with social reform. In 1889 the *World* assigned her to travel around the world in less time than it took Phileas Fogg, the hero of Jules Verne's novel *Around the World in Eighty Days* (published in 1872). Dressed in a distinctive checked coat and peaked hat, and carrying one small bag, she sailed from New York City on November 14, 1889. Reaching Europe, she stopped in France to interview Jules Verne himself. Then she sailed the Mediterranean to the Middle East, went on to Singapore, Tokyo, and San Francisco, and took the train to New York.

Bly arrived back on January 25, 1890, after a record-setting trip that lasted 72 days, 6 hours, and 11 minutes. The *World* had published progress reports on her every stop. The newspaper generated further publicity by offering a free trip to Europe to the person who guessed the exact time her tour would take, and turning the event into a board game: "Round the World with Nellie Bly." Songwriters composed "Globe Trotting Nellie Bly" and "Nellie Blue Eyes." Manufacturers used her likeness to sell their products.

acted so convincingly that six doctors declared her insane. Ten days later the *World* arranged for her release. She immediately began writing stories about the wretched food, unsanitary conditions, and treatment of the inmates. "INSIDE THE MAD-HOUSE" read the headline. The articles led to a grand jury investigation and to another book, *Ten Days in a Mad-House*.

Disguising herself had worked so well that Nellie Bly tried it again and again. She posed as a recent immigrant looking for work to expose the practices of employment agencies. She took jobs in sweatshops to show how they exploited women workers. She

The trip made Nellie Bly larger than life and put her in demand as a lecturer. But it also made it impossible for her to find anything to report on that could rival her round-the-world stunt. She wrote a regular Sunday column in the *World*, covered labor troubles during the depression of 1893–94, and published exposés of corruption in Tammany Hall, the Democratic political machine that ran New York City. In 1895 she traveled west to investigate the condition of ranchers hit hard by summer droughts and severe winter weather. On the train back to New York she met Robert Livingston Seaman, a wealthy manufacturer and a regular reader of her articles in the *World*. At 70, he was 40 years older than she, but just days later, on April 5, 1895, they were married. Tired of assignments, deadlines, and constant traveling, Nellie Bly retired from newspaper reporting.

After her husband died in 1904, she managed his iron manufacturing company and won notice for considerate treatment of her employees. But the business failed and left her bankrupt. In 1912 Nellie Bly returned to journalism on the staff of William Randolph Hearst's *New York Journal*. Two years later, still in financial difficulty, she sailed for Europe to escape her creditors. When World War I trapped her in Austria, she sent back war correspondence under the headline "Nellie Bly on the Firing Zone." She returned to the *Journal* after the war, but the newspaper business had changed in her absence. Women reporters were not unusual anymore, and the younger women on the paper considered her to be less a role model than a curiosity from the past. She wrote an advice-to-the-lovelorn column, devoting much of it to stories about abused and abandoned children. "I have never written a word that did

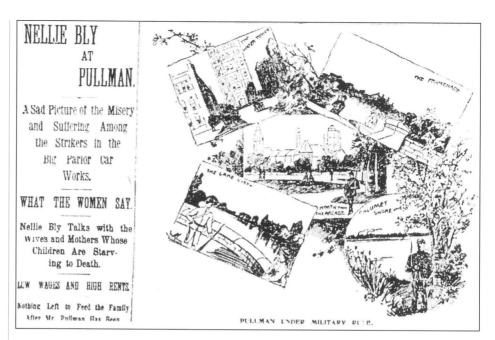

not come from my heart," she explained, "I never shall." When she died of pneumonia in 1922, she was remembered mostly for her earlier stunts. Yet Arthur Brisbane, her editor at the *Journal*, recalled that in her prime Nellie Bly "was the best reporter in America, and that is saying a good deal."

Having achieved celebrity status, Nellie Bly was featured in the headline of her story covering the 1894 Pullman strike.

FURTHER READING

Davidson, Sue. *Getting the Real Story: Nellie Bly and Ida B. Wells.* Seattle: Seal Press, 1992.

Ehrlich, Elizabeth. *Nellie Bly.* New York: Chelsea House, 1989.

Kroeger, Brooke. *Nellie Bly: Daredevil, Reporter, Feminist.* New York: Times Books, 1994.

Mills, Kay. *A Place in the News: From the Women's Pages to the Front Page.* New York: Dodd Mead, 1988.

Rittenhouse, Mignon. *The Amazing Nellie Bly.* 1956. Reprint, Freeport, N.Y.: Books for Libraries Press, 1971.

William Randolph Hearst

YELLOW JOURNALIST

Whenever William Randolph Hearst's *New York Journal* had trouble getting news, it cooked up stories itself. In 1897 the 34-year-old publisher sympathized strongly with the Cuban struggle for independence from Spain. Perhaps even more, he was driven by his own struggle to boost circulation against his rival, Joseph Pulitzer's *New York World*. Hearst's paper printed lurid stories about Spanish mistreatment of Cubans and sent the famed illustrator Frederick Remington to Havana to provide visual images for the paper. After a while, Remington telegraphed back to New York: "Everything is quiet. There is no trouble here. There will be no war. I wish to return." Hearst replied: "Please remain. You furnish the pictures and I'll furnish the war."

Hearst manipulated the news to goad the United States into war with Spain. When the Spanish forces arrested a young Cuban woman named Evangelina Cosio y Cisneros for plotting with the rebels, Hearst turned her into "the Cuban Joan of Arc." The *Journal* called on the women of America to petition their government on her behalf. Thousands responded, including President William McKinley's elderly mother. Then Hearst dispatched one of his reporters to Cuba to bribe the jailers and release the young woman, all the action trumpeted in banner headlines in his paper. Despite this publicity, a skeptical President McKinley resisted the urge for war. Then, on February 15, 1898, the U.S. battleship *Maine* exploded in Havana harbor. Although later evidence revealed that an internal explosion accidentally sank the *Maine*, the Hearst papers confidently spread the story that the Spanish had destroyed the ship with a mine. The sinking of the *Maine* proved too much for McKinley, who finally asked Congress for a declaration of war. Hearst's paper jubilantly ran a blurb on its masthead: "HOW DO YOU LIKE THE JOURNAL'S WAR?"

More seasoned newspapermen condemned such outlandish behavior as the efforts of an egotistical upstart with unlimited family money. They doubted that Hearst was ever as powerful as he liked to claim. The *Baltimore Sun*'s acerbic columnist H. L. Mencken agreed that Hearst had whooped up war in 1898 "simply because he was full of malicious animal magnetism, and eager for a bawdy show." But Mencken also conceded that Hearst shook the newspaper profession to its foundations. "American journalism before his time was extremely ponderous and platitudinous," Mencken wrote, but Hearst changed it by proving that the public really wanted a show, which he gave them with unparalleled daring and resourcefulness. "It was quite impossible for the old-fashioned papers to stand up to him; they had to follow him or perish."

William Randolph Hearst was born in a San Francisco hotel in 1863, four years after his father, George Hearst, paid $450 for a half-interest in a Nevada mine that turned out to be part of the Comstock Lode, one of the richest of all silver mines. This and several other mining ventures made Hearst fabulously wealthy. He married Phoebe Apperson, and William was their only child, whom they pampered and indulged. As a boy, he avidly collected stamps, coins, and porcelain, and loved visiting European art galleries, pursuits that in later life led to his compulsive buying of great art and other treasures. Sent to Harvard University, Hearst became the business manager for the *Harvard Lampoon*, a humor magazine. He also became a regular reader and admirer of Joseph Pulitzer's lively *New York World*. But as a student, Hearst was most noted for his pranks, which led Harvard first to temporarily suspend him and then expel him (after he delivered chamber pots to the faculty with the names of his instructors inside).

Hearst's father owned the *San Francisco Examiner*, a small, unprofitable paper that William proposed to take over and improve. He planned to model the paper after the *World*, which, he observed, "depends for its success upon enterprise, energy and a certain startling originality and not upon the wisdom of its political opinions or the lofty style of its editorials." Lacking any journalism experience, Hearst first took a job as a reporter for the *World*. Then, in 1887, after George Hearst had been elected to the United States Senate, he turned the *Examiner* over to William. The overjoyed young Hearst wrote to his father: "We must be alarmingly enterprising, and we must be startlingly original. We must be honest and fearless. We must have greater variety than we have ever had.

We must print more matter than we have printed. We must increase our force, and enlarge our editorial building." He pledged to spark "a revolution in the sleepy journalism" of California.

Twenty-three years old, tall, slender, shy, and speaking with a high-pitched voice, Hearst devoted his energy and his father's fortune to rebuilding the *Examiner*. He enlarged the paper and hired an energetic staff who treated news as a spectacle. They invited celebrities to the city and toured with them, jumped off ferryboats to test their crews, and rescued fishermen

The ambitious young William Randolph Hearst bought the *New York Journal* with the intention of beating all the rest of the New York press.

NAVAL OFFICERS THINK THE MAINE WAS DESTROYED BY A SPANISH MINE.

Mine or a Sunken Torpedo Believed to Have Been the Weapon Used Against the American Man-of-War---Officers and Men Tell Thrilling Stories of Being Blown Into the Air Amid a Mass of Shattered Steel and Exploding Shells---Survivors Brought to Key West Scout the Idea of Accident---Spanish Officials Protest Too Much---Our Cabinet Orders a Searching Inquiry---Journal Sends Divers to Havana to Report Upon the Condition of the Wreck. Was the Vessel Anchored Over a Mine?

Without evidence, Hearst's *New York Journal* blamed Spain for sinking the U.S. battleship *Maine*. Such sensationalist reporting provoked the outbreak of the Spanish-American War in 1898.

rose, although the paper continued to lose money. What they were after, one of his editorial writers explained, was "the gee-whiz emotion." They ran the paper so that when readers opened it, they would say, "Gee-whiz!"

At his death in 1891, George Hearst left his entire estate to his wife, Phoebe, fearing that William could not handle money. His son was greatly distressed because he had plans to expand into the New York markets, which would require a lot of money. Finally, in 1895, his mother sold her Anaconda Copper Company stock for $7.5 million and gave the money to William. He used it to purchase a New York newspaper, the *Journal*, which had morning and evening editions, slumped circulation and advertising, and a rundown building surrounded by more prosperous newspapers. Hearst intended to beat all the rest of the New York papers and to surpass even Pulitzer's *World*. His formula for success was based on his conviction that "the public is even more fond of entertainment than it is of information."

Hearst cut the price of the *Journal* to a penny, while he expanded its size to 16 pages. This caused him to lose money, but he had plenty to spend. Pulitzer ignored the competition at first, but within a year, the *Journal's* circulation had risen sharply and Hearst had lured away key members of Pulitzer's staff. Hearst hired the entire staff of the *Sunday World*, including the cartoonist R. F. Outcault, who drew the first newspaper comic, "The Yellow Kid." When the *World* hired another cartoonist to draw a yellow cartoon, the move spawned the term "yellow journalism" and made it a synonym for sensationalism. Pulitzer belatedly dropped the price of the *World* to one cent, but to compensate for the lost revenue he had to raise advertising

marooned on the rocks. "If news is wanted," Hearst once commented, "it often has to be sent for." Hearst also hired the first "sob sisters"—women reporters who wrote human interest stories and advice columns. Although wealthy himself, Hearst used the *Examiner* to fight the rich and champion the poor. He attacked powerful corporations, supported labor unions, and endorsed the income tax, causing his opponents to label him a radical. Meanwhile, the *Examiner's* circulation

William Randolph Hearst

rates. This sent many of his advertisers over to the *Journal.*

Both the *Journal* and the *World* were Democratic newspapers aimed at working-class readers—immigrants, the poor, and the underprivileged. In 1896 the *World* refused to support the Democratic Presidential candidate, William Jennings Bryan, because of his support for silver currency (instead of gold) to cause inflation that would help reduce farmers' debts. Hearst also disagreed with free silver, as the currency plan was called, but he threw his support behind Bryan largely to perplex Pulitzer. On the day after the election the *Journal* printed a record 1.5 million copies.

Many newspaper publishers disdained Hearst's "yellow journalism." One of Hearst's reporters, James Creelman, responded that his critics ignored the contributions that his papers made: "How swift they are to condemn its shrieking headlines, its exaggerated pictures, its coarse buffoonery, its intrusions upon private life, and its occasional inaccuracies! But how slow they are to see the steadfast guardianship of public interest which it maintains! How blind to its unfearing warfare against rascality, its detection and persecution of crime, its costly searchings for knowledge through the earth, its exposures of humbug, its endless funds for quick relief of distress."

Hearst understood the power of the press to shape public opinion, promote legislation, agitate for war, raise alarm about crime, and make and break political reputations. Despite his acute shyness, he determined to push himself into the public arena. Over his desk he hung a portrait of the emperor Napoléon, a sign of his own self-image.

After the notoriety he earned during the Spanish-American War, Hearst began to ready himself for elected office, aiming as high as the White House. Since 1897 he had been dating a showgirl, Millicent Willson, whom he finally married in 1903, convinced that a political career required a stable family life. They later had five sons.

Although William Randolph Hearst's name appeared on the masthead of a growing number of newspapers, the same urges that sold newspapers did not sell political leaders. The Hearst press aimed to startle its readers with bold headlines, stories about crime and scandals, and even doctored photographs. Conservatives shuddered at the "radical" Hearst in public office, and progressives like Theodore Roosevelt considered him a sheer demagogue. Nevertheless, in 1902 Hearst won election to Congress as a Democratic representative from New York. In 1904 he came close to winning the Democratic nomination for President. Reelected to Congress that year, he narrowly lost a race for mayor of New York in 1905. He chose not to run again for Congress in 1906 but instead campaigned for governor of New York. In another close race, Hearst lost to Republican Charles Evans Hughes. He tried once more for mayor before abandoning his political dreams. "I will never again be a candidate," Hearst pledged in 1909.

Returning to publishing, Hearst expanded his newspapers into a powerful national chain, and added a fleet of magazines. By his 60th birthday, in 1923, Hearst owned 22 daily newspapers, 15 Sunday papers, and 7 magazines, among them the *Boston American,* the *Chicago Herald-Examiner,* the *Los Angeles Herald-Express, Cosmopolitan,* and *Good Housekeeping.* One American family out of every four read a Hearst publication. As Hearst grew older, both his politics and his papers grew increasingly less reform-oriented and more conservative. His papers attacked political

BORN
April 29, 1863
San Francisco, California

DIED
August 14, 1951
Los Angeles, California

EDUCATION
Expelled from Harvard University, 1885

ACCOMPLISHMENTS
Business manager, *Harvard Lampoon* (1882–84); reporter, *New York World* (1886–87); publisher of numerous newspapers, including *Baltimore American, Boston American, Chicago Herald-American, Detroit Times, Los Angeles Herald-Express, Milwaukee Sentinel, New York American, New York Journal, New York Mirror, Omaha News-Bee, Pittsburgh Post-Gazette, San Francisco Examiner, Seattle Post-Intelligencer,* and *Washington Herald*; magazine publisher, *Cosmopolitan, Good Housekeeping, Harper's Bazaar, House Beautiful, Town & Country*; owner, International News Service, International News Reel Corporation, King Features, and radio stations in Baltimore, Milwaukee, and Pittsburgh

> "Action—that is the distinguishing mark of the new journalism. It represents the final stage in the evolution of the modern newspaper of a century ago—the 'new journals' of their day told the news and some of them made great efforts to get it first. The new journalism of today prints the news too, but it does more. It does not wait for things to turn up. It turns them up."
>
> —from an editorial in the *New York Journal* (October 17, 1897)

opponents of all stripes—from Theodore Roosevelt and Woodrow Wilson to Al Smith and Franklin D. Roosevelt. Hearst instructed his papers to call the New Deal the "Raw Deal." He condemned FDR's tax-the-rich schemes, and denounced taxes of all kinds. Having promoted war in 1898, he opposed American entry into World War I and became a leading isolationist in the 1920s and 1930s. To counteract criticism of some of these stands, Hearst's papers adopted an increasingly patriotic look, emblazoning their front pages with a flurry of American flags. Examining this curious record, the critic H. L. Mencken concluded that Hearst simply remained an aging college boy, "eager only to have a hell of a time." Trying to read any rationality into Hearst's theories of journalism left Mencken only "with a dizzy ringing in the ears."

By the 1920s Hearst had also lost much of his energy and creativity. He misjudged the popularity of the new "tabloids"—newspapers half the size of regular papers and easier to read in subways and trolleys, with even bigger headlines and trashier stories than Hearst's papers. Hoarding authority, "the Chief" (as Hearst preferred to be called) could not bring himself to delegate real power to his younger editors, and revenues from his papers began to slip. But the journalism critic A. J. Liebling concluded that Hearst's papers declined financially not so much because he was a bad manager but because they were bad papers.

Pursuits outside of journalism preoccupied Hearst in his later years. On a 375-square-mile ranch high above the Pacific Ocean on the California coast, he constructed a grandiose castle, San Simeon. He stocked the estate with the European art treasures he collected and turned its hills into the world's largest private zoo. Guests at San Simeon ranged from silent movie star Charlie Chaplin to President Calvin Coolidge. Despite amassing other castles, estates, ranches, and beach houses, Hearst never found sufficient room to unpack and display all the artwork he accumulated. He had also separated from his wife (although they never divorced) and had begun a lasting affair with the actress Marion Davies, whose movie career he bankrolled lavishly. Hearst's newspaper chain supported his extravagant lifestyle, but he spent money faster than his papers made it. "Pleasure is worth what you can afford to pay for it," he once said.

The Great Depression of the 1930s strained Hearst's resources, but he simply borrowed money rather than limit his extravagant purchases. Hearst always lacked self-discipline when it came to money, and he plunged into real estate, building theaters and hotels, all heavily mortgaged. In 1933 he even put up San Simeon as collateral for a loan. By 1937 his empire was near bankruptcy. To satisfy his creditors, Hearst turned financial control of his publications over to a financial manager, who shut down, merged, and sold the more unprofitable papers. Hearst's employees were laid off and salaries were cut—even Hearst's, from $500,000 a year to $100,000. Hearst had to sell some of his art treasures and stop making movies starring Marion Davies. He had to borrow $1 million from Davies, who had invested her money more wisely. Hearst's publishing empire was saved only by World War II, which caused circulation and advertising to rise again. It was a strange twist of fate for the isolationist Hearst, who had so strongly opposed American entry into the war.

Poor health forced Hearst to abandon San Simeon in 1947. He moved to Beverly Hills to be under the care of heart specialists, and he died there in 1951 at the of 88. Today William Randolph Hearst is perhaps better known through the image of Charles Foster Kane, the main character of the motion picture *Citizen Kane*, a caricature of Hearst's life, which chronicles a newspaper publisher's rise and fall. The film biography pictured his death amid the treasures he had obsessively collected during his lifetime and made the point that he could not buy political power as easily as he could buy art.

FURTHER READING

Carlisle, Rodney P. *Hearst and the New Deal: The Progressive as Reactionary.* New York: Garland, 1979.

Chaney, Lindsay, and Michael Cieply. *The Hearsts: Family and Empire—the Later Years.* New York: Simon & Schuster, 1981.

Hearst, William Randolph. *Selections from the Writings and Speeches of William Randolph Hearst.* Edited by Elon Farnsworth Tompkins. San Francisco: privately published, 1948.

Hearst, William Randolph, Jr. *The Hearsts: Father and Son.* Niwot, Colo.: Roberts Rinehart, 1991.

Littlefield, Roy Everett. *William Randolph Hearst: His Role in American Progressivism.* Lanham, Md.: University Press of America, 1980.

Proctor, Ben. *William Randolph Hearst: The Early Years, 1863–1910.* New York: Oxford University Press, 1998.

Swanburg, W. A. *Citizen Hearst: A Biography of William Randolph Hearst.* New York: Scribners, 1961.

Tebble, John. *The Life and Good Times of William Randolph Hearst.* New York: Dutton, 1952.

Winkler, John K. *William Randolph Hearst: A New Appraisal.* New York: Hastings House, 1955.

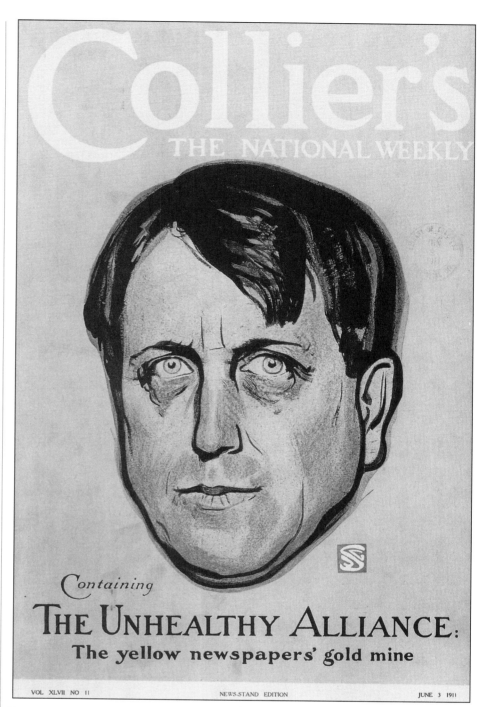

When Hearst ran for public office, his opponents labeled him a dangerous radical and demagogue.

Richard Harding Davis

THE ROMANCE AND ADVENTURE OF JOURNALISM

Newspaper reporters in the 1880s and 1890s cultivated a "Bohemian" image as rumpled, hard-drinking, free-spirited, quick-witted, cynical observers of their times. Breaking this mold, Richard Harding Davis fashioned himself into an impeccably dressed, sober, clean-living, action-loving journalist. The prolific Davis covered everything from crime to college athletics, published short stories, novels, and plays, and reported from the front lines in wartime. His travel writing and war correspondence introduced Americans to a world far beyond their own horizons, in an age of imperialism when the United States was first emerging as a world power. He came to personify the romance and adventure of journalism and attracted to the profession countless young men who hoped to imitate his dashing style.

Richard Harding Davis was born into a writing family. His mother, Rebecca Harding, was a popular writer whose first novel, *Margaret Howth*, appeared in installments in the *Atlantic Monthly* at the beginning of the Civil War. Written in a gritty, realistic manner, her story about the strenuous life of iron workers impressed many of America's leading literary figures. The story also attracted L. Clarke Davis, a Philadelphia lawyer, who traveled to her home in Wheeling, West Virginia, to meet the author. They later married and moved to Philadelphia, where their first child, Richard, was born in 1864. Rebecca Davis became a member of the editorial staff of the *New York Tribune* and continued to write novels and short stories. L. Clarke Davis later gave up the law to become editor of the *Philadelphia Public Ledger*.

Their eldest son was not a good student. "Nature put too much vitality into my limbs and too much imaginative ideas in my head to allow me to sit still for eight hours a day and think of serious things in books," he later rationalized. He had a difficult time in preparatory school and earned poor grades. When he attended Lehigh University, which was primarily an engineering school, he showed more interest in sports, dramatics, and editing the school paper than in attending classes. When he finished his third year, the faculty advised him to withdraw from the school. Furiously, he vowed to go further in life than any of his professors. He did achieve great fame, but his journalism career would show many of the same preoccupations and weaknesses of his college years: more fond of show than of study.

Hired as a cub reporter for the *Philadelphia Record*, he continued to act like a college boy. It irritated his editor that Davis dressed like an English dandy, with cane, gloves, and long yellow coat. One day the editor found Davis lolling around the sports desk and ordered him to take off his coat and gloves and finish a much-delayed story. When Davis persisted in wearing his gloves while writing the piece, he was fired. The incident sobered Davis, who ditched the gloves and cane and got down to work. He started reporting for the *Philadelphia Press*, covering routine stories around the city but giving each one an interesting or dramatic twist. His first major story was the terrible Johnstown Flood, where more than 2,000 people lost their lives after a dam broke. His colorful writing on the aftermath of the flood helped him gain a job as a reporter for the *New York Sun*.

Walking to work on his first day on the job, Davis was hustled by a notorious con artist. Playing along with the con man's scheme, Davis finally tackled him like a football player and held him until the police arrived. He wrote up the incident as his first story for the *Sun*, under the title "Our Green Reporter." By making himself the subject of the story, he instantly acquainted New Yorkers with the name Richard Harding Davis. Assigned to cover routine police stories, Davis reported with an attention to detail and an ability to spot just the right human-interest angle. Reporting on a man who perished in a fire, Davis noted that the man's alarm clock had been set to go off shortly after the fire. By writing that if the man had set the alarm a half hour earlier he would have been saved, Davis transformed a minor piece into a front-page story. Fond of stories that offered a thrill, Davis also wrote colorful accounts of college football games, helping to popularize his favorite sport.

Aside from journalism, Davis wrote popular short stories. One series of stories featured "Cortlandt Van Bibber," a swaggering, daring, aristocratic young man about town. Another, "Gallegher," involved a young messenger for a newspaper who solved a crime and got the scoop for his paper. In each case, Davis

With revolution brewing in Cuba, publisher William Randolph Hearst sent Richard Harding Davis to the island as his special correspondent—with notable publicity.

seemed to be the model for his own fiction. Further fixing his image in the public's imagination, the popular artist Charles Dana Gibson used sketches of Davis as a handsome and vigorous ideal of young manhood in his magazine illustrations. Davis received so many offers to write that his mother grew alarmed that he would be tempted to "do hack work for money."

Success came swiftly for Richard Harding Davis. In 1890, while still in

The action-loving Davis considered war correspondence the highest form of journalism and rarely missed a conflict around the globe.

his 20s, he was offered the job of managing editor on one of the nation's most prestigious magazines, *Harper's Weekly*. He took the post, promising to wake up readers "with a great big bang." Although the editorship offered an opportunity to shape American literature, Davis found that he was not temperamentally suited to edit other people's work. He wanted the glory of his own byline. Influenced by the writings of the British authors Rudyard Kipling and Robert Louis Stevenson, with their interest in exotic travel, Davis arranged to take time off from *Harper's* to tour the American West and then to visit England, sending back accounts of his adventures. These stimulating experiences caused him to vacate the editor's chair and spend the rest of his life as a roving correspondent. He wrote for whatever publications would pay him the highest fees—especially since he enjoyed the good life and spent money as fast as he earned it.

Davis's colorful, personal, and descriptive writing appealed to American readers who wanted to know more about the world. Yet he traveled so extensively and stayed so briefly in any one place that his material was often hastily written and ill-informed. He seemed more interested in entertaining his audiences than in educating them. A reviewer of one of his travel books sneered: "If Mr. Davis continues traveling and observing, he may at some time in the future acquire quite a fair amount of knowledge concerning the things of which he writes."

His fame and flair for writing caught the attention of the young publisher William Randolph Hearst, whose *New York Journal* was then engaged in a circulation war with Joseph Pulitzer's *New York World*. Hearst hired Davis for

what was then the staggering sum of $500 to cover the Yale-Princeton football game in 1895. The next year, with revolution brewing in Cuba, Hearst dispatched Davis and the artist Frederick Remington to Havana to get the news as colorfully as possible for the *Journal*. Like Hearst, Davis believed that the United States should enter the conflict and help Cuban rebels win their independence from Spain. His articles aimed at provoking American public opinion. In "The Death of Rodriguez," Davis described the execution of a rebel by a firing squad, ending with a description of Rodriguez's body "asleep in the wet grass, with his motionless arms still tightly bound behind him . . . and the blood from his breast sinking into the soil he had tried to free."

A story that drew even more attention was Davis's account of how Spanish authorities had strip-searched a young woman suspected of being a rebel. In his article, Davis neglected to mention who had conducted the search, and back in New York Remington drew a lurid picture of Spanish military officers ogling the naked woman. Always concerned about the illustrations for his writing, Davis was appalled. "I never wrote that she was searched by men," he protested. "Mr. Frederick Remington, who was not present, and who drew an imaginary picture of the scene, is responsible for the idea that the search was conducted by men. Had I seen the picture before it appeared, I should never have allowed it to accompany my article." Davis felt so shaken by Hearst's anything-goes tactics that he never wrote for his publications again.

Davis's war correspondence from Cuba appeared in newspapers in the United States and Great Britain, making him an international celebrity and also helping to publicize the exploits of Theodore Roosevelt and his Rough Riders. The two men became close friends, and later, as President, Roosevelt would offer Davis several diplomatic appointments that he declined. Both Davis and Roosevelt cherished the glory and challenge of warfare. As a war correspondent, Davis compared armies to football teams. He loved adventure, admired military officers, and demonstrated his own physical bravery by writing about his own narrow escapes. He considered war correspondence to be the highest form of journalism, and for the rest of his life he rarely missed a conflict around the globe.

In 1898 Richard Harding Davis went to South Africa to cover the Boer War. Although he greatly admired the British, even dressing and acting like a British officer, he became critical of British arrogance and grew sympathetic to the Dutch-speaking Boers he saw fighting for their independence. When the British army exerted censorship on his reporting, Davis crossed the lines to report from the Boers' side. "As I see it," he wrote "it has been a Holy War, this Burgher [a German term for the middle class, reflecting the Boers' Dutch ancestry] Crusade, and their motives are as fine as any that called a 'minute man' from his farm [the Minutemen were American farmers ready to respond in a minute to threats to their community, and who stood against the British during the American Revolution]." These sentiments outraged the British and cost Davis his membership in several fashionable London clubs. Later, Davis raised a similar furor in Europe by exposing Belgian colonial atrocities in the Congo.

When war in Europe erupted in 1914, Davis booked passage in a $1,000-a-day suite on the *Lusitania*, demonstrating his status as America's best-known war correspondent. He headed to Belgium and reported from Brussels when the German army marched into that city. A few days later, German troops captured him and found a photograph of him wearing a British uniform during the Boer War. Since none of the Germans had ever heard of him—something that wounded his pride deeply—they were convinced they had captured a British officer out of uniform as a spy and prepared to hold a court-martial. Then the British attacked, causing Davis's captors to retreat. He escaped and admitted that in all the previous wars he had covered he had never felt so frightened. The capture stripped away what was left of Davis's objectivity, and afterward he wrote of the Germans as "mad dogs" engaged in a "hellish war." He remained in Europe for another year but was disgusted that the British and French would not allow him to visit the front lines. "I'm not about to write sidelights," he declared, and returned to the United States.

In 1899 Davis had married Cecil Clark, an attractive and athletic young woman from a wealthy and socially prominent family. It was a progressively unhappy marriage and they divorced in 1912. By then, he had fallen in love with the chorus girl and vaudeville actress Bessie McCoy. They married in 1912, and two years later they had a daughter, Hope. Having long lived in hotels and apartments, Davis built a large house on a 200-acre estate he called Crossroads Farm, in Mt. Kisco, New York. Returning to Crossroads Farm from covering the war in Europe, he became ill and died there of heart disease in 1916, at the age of 52. The enormous fame of his lifetime evaporated soon after his premature death.

Richard Harding Davis

BORN

April 18, 1864
Philadelphia, Pennsylvania

DIED

April 11, 1916
Mt. Kisco, New York

EDUCATION

Enrolled in Lehigh University, 1882, but dropped out after three years

ACCOMPLISHMENTS

Editor of the *Lehigh Burr* (1885); reporter, *Philadelphia Record* (1886); reporter, *Philadelphia Press* (1886–89); reporter, *New York Evening Sun* (1889–91); managing editor, *Harper's Weekly* (1891–93); traveling correspondent (1892–1916); author of various books, including *Dr. Jameson's Raiders vs. the Johannesburg Reformers* (1897), *Cuba in War Time* (1897), *The Cuban and Porto Rican Campaigns* (1898), *A Year from a Reporter's Note-Book* (1898), *With Both Armies in South Africa* (1900), *Real Soldiers of Fortune* (1906), *The Congo and Coasts of Africa* (1907), *Notes of a War Correspondent* (1910), *With the Allies* (1914), *With the French in France and Salonika* (1916), and *The Novels and Stories of Richard Harding Davis* (1916, 12 volumes)

Adolfo Rodriguez was the only son of a Cuban farmer, who lives nine miles outside of Santa Clara, beyond the hills that surround that city to the north.

When the revolution broke out young Rodriguez joined the insurgents, leaving his father and mother and two sisters at the farm. He was taken, in December of 1896, by a force of Guardia Civile, the corps d'elite of the Spanish army, and defended himself when they tried to capture him, wounding three of them with his machete.

He was tried by a military court for bearing arms against the government, and sentenced to be shot by a fusillade some morning, before sunrise. . . .

His execution took place on the morning of the 19th of January, at a place a half-mile from the city, on the great plain that stretches from the forts out to the hills, beyond which Rodriguez had lived for nineteen years. At the time of his death he was twenty years old.

I witnessed his execution, and what follows is an account of the way he went to his death. The young man's friends could not be present, for it was impossible for them to show themselves in that crowd and that place with wisdom or without distress, and I like to think that, although Rodriguez could not know it, there was one person present when he died who felt keenly for him, and who was a sympathetic though unwilling spectator. . . .

The officer of the firing squad . . . hastily whipped up his sword, the men . . . leveled their rifles, the sword rose, dropped, and the men fired. At the report the Cuban's head snapped back almost between his shoulders, but his body fell slowly, as though some one had pushed him gently forward from behind and he had stumbled.

He sank on his side in the wet grass without a struggle or sound, and did not move again.

It was difficult to believe that he meant to lie there, that it could be ended without a word, that the man in the linen suit could not get up on his feet and continue to walk on over the hills, as he apparently had started to do, to his home; that there was not a mistake somewhere, or that at least some one would be sorry or say something or run to pick him up.

But, fortunately, he did not need help, and the priests returned—the younger one, with the tears running down his face—and donned their vestments and read a brief requiem for his soul, while the squad stood uncovered, and the men in hollow square shook their accoutrements into place, and shifted their places and got ready for the order to march, and the band began again with the same quickstep which the fusillade had interrupted . . . .

But as I fell in at the rear of the procession and looked back the figure of the young Cuban, who was no longer a part of the world of Santa Clara, was asleep in the wet grass, with his motionless arms still tightly bound behind him, with the scapula twisted awry across his face and the blood from his breast sinking into the soil he had tried to free.

—from "The Death of Rodriguez," the *New York Journal* (February 2, 1897)

His dashing example had drawn many into journalism—the young reporter H. L. Mencken of the *Baltimore Sun* called him the "hero of our dreams." But the generation of the 1920s, disillusioned by the World War, dismissed as hopelessly antiquated everything that Richard Harding Davis exemplified. The romantic image of war correspondence died with the advent of the horrors of modern warfare.

FURTHER READING

Knightly, Phillip. *The First Casualty: From Crimea to Vietnam: The War Correspondent as Hero, Propagandist, and Myth Maker.* New York: Harcourt Brace Jovanovich, 1976.

Lubow, Arthur. *The Reporter Who Would Be King: A Biography of Richard Harding Davis.* New York: Scribners, 1992.

Miner, Lewis S. *Front Lines and Headlines: The Story of Richard Harding Davis.* New York: Julian Messner, 1959.

Osborn, Scott Compton, and Robert L. Phillips, Jr. *Richard Harding Davis.* Boston: Twayne, 1978.

More American Journalists to Remember

George William Curtis (1824–92) long occupied "The Easy Chair," a social and literary column in *Harper's Monthly,* and simultaneously served as political editor of *Harper's Weekly* (1863–92). A leader in the reform movements of the Gilded Age, Curtis promoted the Liberal Republicans in 1872, an issue over which he clashed with his magazine's famous cartoonist, Thomas Nast.

During the Civil War, the American Painter **Winslow Homer** (1836-1910) came to public attention for his sketches, ranging from Lincoln's inauguration to military campaigns and scenes of camp life, that appeared regularly in *Harper's Weekly Magazine.* Homer continued to publish illustrations in *Harper's* until 1875, and also contributed to the Boston magazine *Every Sunday.* Magazine illustrating honed his skill at telling stories through pictures. His postwar paintings often featured images of everyday life, and one of his most popular pictures depicted children on recess from a one-room schoolhouse playing a game of "Snap the Whip." The magazines brought Homer's talent into countless homes

Winslow Homer sketched this Civil War scene of Union troops on a reconnaissance effort near Yorktown, Virginia, in 1862. Rebel forces are close by, in the woods in the background.

Under editor Charles A. Dana, the *New York Sun* adopted a concise, bright, and witty style that generally emphasized the human-interest side of the news.

and made him one of the most successful and popular artists of the late 19th century. His paintings now hang in the world's leading museums.

Writing under the pen name "Perley," **Benjamin Perley Poore** (1820–87) kept Americans informed and entertained on the politics and foibles of Washington, D.C., for 40 years. The *Boston Atlas* made him its Washington correspondent in 1847, but it was as correspondent for the *Boston Journal* (1854–83) that Poore established his reputation. His reporting included both daily dispatches on late-breaking news and weekly "Waifs"—which he defined as "things found and not claimed"—of gossip and other social news from the capital. A master of political patronage, Poore supplemented his newspaper income by serving as printing clerk of the U.S. Senate and producing numerous government documents, most notably the *Congressional Directory*.

A youthful, idealistic member of the Brook Farm commune, **Charles A. Dana** (1819–97) grew increasingly cynical about human nature as an editor of Horace Greeley's *New York Tribune* (1847–61) and as owner and editor of the *New York Sun* (1867–97). His editorials in the *Sun* were often brutal and merciless, carrying on personal and political grudges, but he also published the famous editorial, in reply to a little girl who had written to the paper: "Yes, Virginia, there is a Santa Claus." Under his editorship, the *Sun* hired a staff of highly talented reporters and adopted a style that was concise, bright, and witty—a style that generally emphasized the human interest side of the news.

Mary Clemmer Ames (1831–84) made a career in journalism after separating from her husband, a minor federal official, in 1865. An occasional correspondent to newspapers in the past, Ames began a "Woman's Letter from Washington" for the *New York Independent* the following year. She continued the column for the next 20 years, covering a range of subjects from women's rights to political corruption. She was the highest-paid woman journalist of her time. Ames wrote in "stately, solemn prose," said fellow correspondent Emily Briggs. "Sometimes it is bitter and pungent, as many of our public men know."

Drawn into journalism by his abolitionist sentiments which led him to cover the fight over slavery in Kansas, **Horace White** (1834–1916) joined the *Chicago Tribune* staff in 1857. He covered the debates between Abraham Lincoln and Stephen A. Douglas during their 1858 race for the Senate and served as Washington correspondent during the Civil War. Wartime speculation in stocks and bonds made him a fortune and enabled him to purchase a large share in the paper and return as its editor in chief (1865–74). Like the *Tribune*'s headquarters, much of White's fortune was consumed in the great Chicago fire of 1871. In later years he regained his wealth in railroad building and also gained his editorial voice when he succeeded E. L. Godkin as editor of the *New York Evening Post*. As editor of the *Post* (1897–1903), he became a leading critic of American imperialism and a spokesman for other liberal causes.

James Gordon Bennett, Jr. (1841–1918), often referred to as "The

Younger," inherited the *New York Herald* from his father. Taking over as editor in 1869, at age 25, he informed the staff, "I want you fellows to remember that I am the only one to be pleased." Bennett's most memorable triumph as editor was sending the reporter Henry Morton Stanley to find Dr. David Livingstone, a missionary missing in the African jungle. Stanley's success in 1872 drew worldwide attention to the *Herald*'s coverage. After taking over as publisher that year, following his father's death, Bennett lived a high life, spending much of it in Europe and aboard his yacht. In 1887 he created a Paris edition of the paper, known first as the *Paris Herald*, which in 1924 became the *International Herald-Tribune*.

Ambrose Bierce (1842–1914) won fame as a sarcastic and cynical columnist. Following his service in the Civil War, Bierce went west with the army, eventually settling in San Francisco. He published his first poem in 1867 and the next year was invited to join the staff of the *News Letter*, quickly becoming its editor. In 1875, as editor of the *Argonaut*, he began a column called "Prattle," which contained his increasingly cynical observations on human behavior and society. Over the years he wrote for other publications, ruminating on life and compiling his "Devil's Dictionary" (typical of its many witty saying—which are still quoted today— was his definition of *peace* as "a period of cheating between two periods of war"). William Randolph Hearst hired Bierce to write for his *San Francisco Examiner, New York Journal*, and *Cosmopolitan* magazine, giving his abusive humor and scathing commentary a national audience.

The first woman to write daily for a newspaper was **Jane Cunningham Croly** (1829–1901). Her columns of advice, fashion, and etiquette, written under the pen name "Jennie June," were the forerunner of women's pages in newspapers. First hired by Charles Dana to write for the *New York Tribune*, Croly served as fashion editor and women's editor for such papers as the *New York World* (1862–72), the *New York Times* (1864–72), and the *New York Daily Graphic* (1872–78). In later years her columns were printed in many newspapers across the country, predating the modern syndicated column. In 1889 she founded the Woman's Press Club of New York. Her son, Herbert Croly, founded the *New Republic* magazine.

As a boy, the Dutch immigrant **Edward Bok** (1863–1930) got his start reporting on children's parties for the *Brooklyn Daily Eagle*. He then became editor of a church publication, which in 1884 grew into the *Brooklyn Magazine*. In 1886 he founded the Bok Syndicated Press, which included material written specifically for women readers. Newspapers that subscribed to his service began publishing a "Bok page," which other papers copied as a "woman's page." Bok became editor of the *Ladies' Home Journal* (1889–1919). By using polls of his readers, he revised the format of the publication, increased readership, and influenced other journals directed at women readers. His autobiography, *The Americanization of Edward Bok*, which expressed his philosophy of publishing, won a Pulitzer Prize in 1921.

Jacob Riis photographed this tenement alley to illustrate his stories on New York City's slums.

Out of the ashes of Atlanta, burned by the Union army during the Civil War, journalist **Henry W. Grady** (1850–89) worked tirelessly to build and promote a "New South." A student during the war, Grady entered journalism during the Reconstruction era on the staff of the *Rome* (Georgia) *Courier* (1869–70). In 1872 he moved to Atlanta as editor of the *Atlanta Herald*, and as correspondent for numerous papers, North and South, eventually became managing editor of the *Atlanta Constitution* (1880–89). Through his editorials and public speaking, Grady urged reconciliation between the regions after the war and an economic rebuilding of the South, with more emphasis on industry and diversified farming. He supported civil rights for African Americans but also accepted segregation and opposed social equality of the races.

Second only to Frederick Douglass, the most successful and distinguished African-American journalist of the 19th century was **T. Thomas Fortune** (1856–1928). Born of slave parents in Florida, Fortune became a printer's apprentice on the *Jacksonville Daily Union*. After moving to Washington to attend Howard University, he met Douglass and worked on the black weekly, *People's Advocate*. Fortune then moved to New York, where he edited the *New York Globe* (1881–84) and the *New York Age* (1889–1907). He also wrote for such white mainstream papers as the *New York Sun* and the *Boston Transcript*. Beginning as a radical agitator on racial issues, Fortune shifted his position to become an ally of Booker T. Washington and racial accommodation. His service as a ghostwriter and publicist for Washington raised much criticism, but by the end of a long career he was hailed as the "dean of Negro journalism."

The reporter and editor **Finley Peter Dunne** (1867–1936) was best known for his creation of "Mr. Dooley," a fictional Irish saloonkeeper in Chicago. The character of Mr. Dooley commented humorously on the news of the day in a thick Irish brogue.

"I see be th' pa-apers," Dooley would begin his observations. The son of Irish immigrants, Dunne held a variety of reporting and editorial posts for Chicago papers, including the *Chicago Times* (1888–89), the *Chicago Tribune* (1890–91) and the *Chicago Journal* (1897–1900), before moving to New York to become editor of the *New York Morning Telegraph*. He edited the *American Magazine* (1906–13) before joining the staff of *Collier's* magazine, and eventually serving as its editor from 1917 to 1919.

As a police reporter, **Jacob Riis** (1849–1914) investigated urban poverty and helped spur the Progressive Era. A Danish immigrant who arrived in New York City in 1870, Riis reported for the *New York Tribune* (1877–88) and the *New York Sun* (1888–99). Riis explored the city's worst tenement houses and slums, photographing and writing articles for newspapers and magazines that highlighted the crime, unsanitary conditions, fire hazards, neglect of children, and other horrors that the public and public officials were ignoring. Riis also published several books, most notably, *How the Other Half Lives* (1892). He took New York police commissioner Theodore Roosevelt on personal inspection tours that influenced Roosevelt's concern for social welfare.

Whitelaw Reid (1837–1912), a small-town editor of the *Xenia* (Ohio) *News*, rose to national fame as a Civil War correspondent for the *Cincinnati Gazette* (writing under the pen name "Agate," which he took from the name for a printers' type size). In 1868 he joined the editorial staff of the *New York Tribune*, becoming managing editor the next year. Following Horace

POOR WHITELAW!

Greeley's death in 1872, Reid became the chief editor of the nation's most influential newspaper. From that post (which he held until 1905) he played a key role in state and national Republican politics. In 1892 Reid ran

Whitelaw Reid's editorials for the influential *New York Tribune* did not please everyone.

for Vice President on the Republican ticket—and lost. He served as U.S. ambassador to Great Britain in the administrations of Presidents William McKinley and Theodore Roosevelt.

Charles Nordhoff (1830–1901), who immigrated to the United States from Germany as a child, started as a printer's apprentice before joining the navy. His experiences provided abundant material for a series of books on life at sea, which, in turn, brought him back into journalism, first as an editor for the book publisher Harper & Row and then as managing editor of the *New York Evening Post* (1861–71). After a period of writing travel literature, he became Washington correspondent for the *New York Herald* (1874–90). A prolific writer, Nordhoff wrote a wide range of books on his travels and observations, including *Communistic Societies in the United States* and early studies of the West Coast (reprinted in 1987 as *Nordhoff's West Coast: California, Oregon, and Hawaii*). These books remain in print a century after their publication.

Seldom has an editor dominated a paper and a city as completely as did **William Rockhill Nelson** (1841–1915), who owned and edited the *Kansas City Star* from 1880 to 1915. Although trained as a lawyer, Nelson learned his journalism from his father, who published the weekly *Fort Wayne* (Indiana) *Sentinel*. For a while, Rockhill edited the *Sentinel*, but he sought a larger audience. He moved to Kansas City and founded the *Star*, which he made an aggressive advocate of civic improvement, championing such causes as better schools, better streets, and honesty in government. A large, rumpled man, Nelson was admired by his staff and by other journalists for his energetic and uncompromising crusades to better his city.

The public knew **George Alfred Townsend** (1841–1914) as GATH, a pen name he adopted from his initials and from a place mentioned in the Bible: "Tell it not in Gath, publish it not in the streets of Askelon." Joining the *Philadelphia Inquirer* in 1860, he became a Civil War correspondent for the *New York Herald* and the *New York World*. After the war, he served both as foreign correspondent and Washington correspondent for various newspapers, and his GATH columns were printed in nearly 100 papers. In 1872 his investigative reporting helped expose the Credit Mobilier scandal involving key members of Congress and the Ulysses S. Grant administration. He spent his later years writing history and fiction and building a large arch at "Gathland," his country home in western Maryland, to memorialize the work of Civil War correspondents.

Born in Maine, **Noah Brooks** (1830–1903) wrote first for newspapers in Boston. He moved west on various business ventures that finally took him to California, where he edited the *Marysville Daily Appeal*. In 1862 the *Sacramento Union* sent him to cover politics and the Civil War from Washington. His friendship with Abraham Lincoln led to an invitation to become the President's private secretary. After Lincoln's assassination, President Andrew Johnson appointed Brooks as a customs official in San Francisco, but eventually fired him over political differences. Brooks became managing editor of the San Francisco *Alta California* (1866–71). He returned east to work for the *New York Tribune* and *New York Times*, and finally retired in 1892 as editor of the *Newark Daily Advertiser,* after 30 years of coast-to-coast journalism.

Physical stamina seemed a necessity for the "legwork" of 19th-century journalism, but **Frank Carpenter** (1855–1924) was so frail that he spent much of his time in bed, dictating to his wife. "Retiring and seemingly slightly embarrassed," wrote a fellow reporter, "you would never take him for the brilliant journalist he is." Writing under the pen name "Carp," he had the reputation of a human dragnet. "Everything is fish that comes in his direction, to be written of now or stored away for use later on." Carp reported for the *Cleveland Leader* on politics in Ohio and Washington, D.C. In 1888 he began traveling around the world, having arranged for 15 newspapers to pay his expenses and publish his travel letters. His collected travel correspondence filled many volumes and also produced a popular series of readers that educated a generation of schoolchildren on world geography.

In the heyday of sensationalist journalism, as the papers of William Randolph Hearst and Joseph Pulitzer were battling for attention and circulation, **Adolph S. Ochs** (1858–1935) purchased the *New York Times* and made it a dignified newspaper of record. The son of Jewish immigrants from Germany, Ochs grew up in Knoxville, Tennessee, where at age 11

he started work on the *Knoxville Chronicle*. In 1878, at the age of 20, he bought controlling interest in the *Chattanooga Times*. In 1896 he jumped at the chance to purchase the nearly bankrupt *New York Times*. Emphasizing reliable, objective news rather than editorials, Ochs took as his paper's motto: "All the News That's Fit to Print." Under his leadership, the *New York Times* established itself as the nation's leading newspaper, long after the "yellow press" had faded.

Adolph S. Ochs, shown here making the first transatlantic radiophone call in 1927, made the *New York Times* the national newspaper of record.

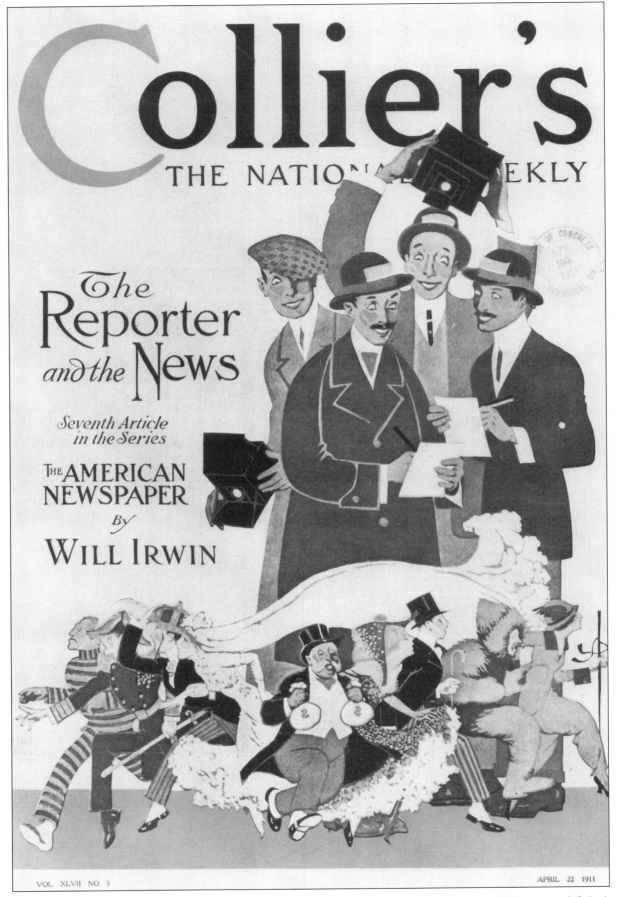

Collier's
THE NATIONAL WEEKLY

The Reporter and the News

Seventh Article in the Series

THE AMERICAN NEWSPAPER

By WILL IRWIN

VOL XLVII NO 5

APRIL 22 1911

Reporters loom over the stories they covered—and the scandals they uncovered—on this 1911 cover of *Collier's*.

3 Society's Critics (1900–1945)

The influence and power of the press rose to new heights during the Progressive Era at the beginning of the 20th century, when muckraking journalists exposed society's ills. The movement took its name from one of its critics, President Theodore Roosevelt, who used the image of "The Man with the Muckrake" from the 17th century religious tract *Pilgrim's Progress* to warn that anyone "who never thinks or speaks save of his feats with a muckrake, speedily becomes not a help to society, not an incitement to good, but one of the most potent forces for evil." Spurred by the desires of the new popular magazines to expand circulation, magazine writers traveled the nation rooting out corruption in city governments, unfair business practices, tainted foods, the use of child labor, and any number of other socially harmful conditions. Believing sunlight to be the best disinfectant, the muckrakers cast the light of publicity on what they saw wrong, and they expected their readers to respond. Public outrage did promote reform until readers grew tired of a steady diet of muckraking and became distracted.

By the 1920s "ballyhoo" had replaced muckraking. Tabloid newspapers emerged, relying on photographs, short, snappy text, and bold headlines. Sports and crime became staples of the news. The brash style of Walter Winchell helped turn gossip into news by focusing attention on personalities in the news, thus invading their privacy. The Baltimore journalist H. L. Mencken protested that the average American newspaper had "the intelligence of a Baptist evangelist, the courage of a rat, the fairness of a Prohibition boob-bumper, the information of a high-school janitor, the taste of a designer of celluloid valentines, and the honor of a police-station lawyer." A generation of young journalists would copy Mencken's cynical style.

The years immediately before World War I saw the largest number of newspapers in American history. Between 1910 and 1914 there were 2,600 daily papers, 400 of them in languages other than English. In later years the U.S. population increased, as did the number of copies of papers sold. Yet the number of newspapers steadily diminished. Newsprint shortages during the war caused problems for smaller publishers, and so did the increasing cost of new machinery. Newspapers began drawing their news not only from the wire services but from syndicates that produced features. Newspaper chains, the earliest founded by E. W. Scripps and William Randolph Hearst, began taking over the ownership of papers across the country.

Scoffing at the idea that journalists were born, not made, Joseph Pulitzer had long promoted the establishment of colleges of journalism to raise the standards of the next generation of reporters and editors. The University of Missouri started the first such program in 1908; Columbia University launched its school of journalism in 1912. Yet the paths to the mainstream press generally excluded women, African Americans, and recent immigrants, who had to fight to be heard. As a result, many started their own newspapers and press services.

A new medium—radio—offered new competition. In 1920 the Pittsburgh radio station KDKA carried Presidential election results on the air for the first time. The station got its news by telephone from the *Pittsburgh Post*. Newspaper reporters at first failed to take radio seriously. When a Washington correspondent made a mistake in his commentary on the air, he shrugged: "What does it matter, it's only radio." But during the Great Depression, radio carried the comforting voice of President Franklin D. Roosevelt into people's homes for fireside chats. Radio brought the drama of an eyewitness to the explosion of the great blimp *Hindenberg* in 1937, and Edward R. Murrow's live broadcasts from London during the German Blitz. Americans as a nation were drawn to their radios on December 7, 1941, to learn more about the Japanese attack on Pearl Harbor. That day the CBS television network broadcast the news over its experimental station WXBW. But it would be another decade before substantial numbers of Americans owned television sets.

As bylines became more common and journalists became better known, they and their profession became the subject of scrutiny. Upton Sinclair's bestselling novel *The Brass Check* (1919) portrayed a spineless press dominated by media barons and corrupted by its advertisers. The image of hard-bitten, wisecracking reporters was imbedded in the public's mind by Charles MacArthur and Ben Hecht's popular stage play *The Front Page* (1928), which later reached the screen in several movie versions. A more positive image of a small-town editor standing against homegrown fascism appeared in Sinclair Lewis's novel *It Can't Happen Here* (1935), and Lewis himself played the leading role in stage productions of the book. A far darker image of the press emerged in the classic film *Citizen Kane* (1940), based on the life of William Randolph Hearst. In reality, journalism had grown even more diverse, complex, and dramatic than portrayed in film and fiction.

Ida B. Wells-Barnett

CRUSADER FOR JUSTICE

Slavery still existed when Ida B. Wells was born in 1862, during the Civil War. Her mother, Lizzie Bell, was a cook who had been sold several times before being purchased by a carpenter in Holly Springs, Mississippi. The carpenter had taken in the slave Jim Wells as an apprentice, and permitted his cook and apprentice to marry. They had eight children, Ida being the first. After freedom, the strong-minded Wells quit his job and moved his family after his employer tried to make him vote for the Democratic ticket.

Ida was visiting her grandmother in 1878 when both her parents and three of her brothers and sisters died in a yellow

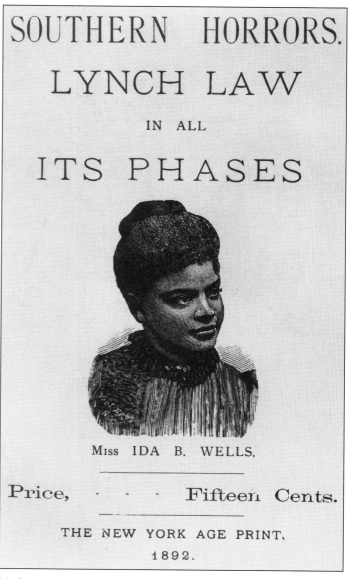

Ida B. Wells published in pamphlet form the shocking information about lynchings that she had first printed in the *New York Age* on June 25, 1892.

Ida B. Wells, standing on the left, posed with the widow and children of Thomas Moss, a lynching victim, in 1893.

city. One day while she rode the train to her teaching job, a conductor asked her to give up her seat in the "ladies' car" and move to a smoking car. Wells refused, arguing that she had purchased a first-class ticket. Several white men bodily removed her from the car while other passengers applauded. At the next stop she got off, returned to Memphis, and sued the railroad for unfair practices. A local court awarded her $500 in damages, but the railroad appealed and the Tennessee circuit court reversed the decision. She described the case in an article for a religious newspaper, the *Living Way*, which paid her court costs.

Wells had discovered her talents in journalism by editing a weekly newsletter, the *Evening Star*, for a black literary society in Memphis. She then began to write for a church paper, and in 1885 submitted a newspaper essay to the *New York Freedman*. For the next few years she combined teaching with newspaper writing. Using the pen name "Iola," she submitted articles about racial issues to newspapers in Detroit, Indianapolis, Little Rock, and New York City. She was the only woman to attend a conference of African-American editors. There she met T. Thomas Fortune, editor of the *New York Age*, who commented that she handled a pen "as handy as any of us men in newspaper work."

Wells purchased a one-third ownership of a Baptist newspaper, the *Memphis Free Speech and Headlight*, in 1889. Her partners were the business and sales managers, and she became the editor. Her ardent and militant editorials helped make the paper financially profitable. She denounced the federal government for not intervening

fever epidemic. Risking her own life, she went back home to care for the other children. Determined to keep the family together, at age 16 she supported her brothers and sisters by teaching in a rural school for a salary of $25 a month.

In 1883 she moved to Memphis, Tennessee, where there would be greater opportunities to work and to take classes at Fisk University. She taught in a black school outside the

against mob violence against blacks in the South. "Where are our 'leaders' when the race is being burnt, shot and hanged?" she demanded. When she criticized the inequality among blacks and whites in Memphis schools, the city did not renew her contract as a teacher and she supported herself fully by her newspaper work.

She was in Natchez, Mississippi, building circulation for the paper on March 9, 1892, when a lynch mob killed three young black men who ran a grocery store in Memphis. They died because a white grocer had been angered by their successful competition. Wells counted all three as good friends. Deeply outraged over the incident, she published editorials calling for blacks to leave Memphis because they could not expect justice there. Some 2,000 African Americans abandoned the city, causing some white business leaders to ask Wells to stop the exodus, but she refused.

Ida B. Wells used her newspaper to investigate lynchings in Memphis and throughout the South. Often white society had portrayed lynchings as its means of protecting the honor of white women. Wells, however, denounced lynching as really an effort to intimidate all blacks in the South. "Nobody in this section of the country believes the old thread-bare lie that Negro men rape white women," she wrote. This editorial sparked retaliation, and a mob sacked and destroyed her newspaper office. Wells was traveling in the North at the time and visited the prominent black publisher T. Thomas Fortune. "I am afraid you will have to stay," Fortune greeted her. When Wells did not understand, he asked: "Haven't you seen the morning paper?" He then handed her a new account of the attack on her paper. Admiring her courage, Fortune hired her as a staff writer for the *New York Age*.

Wells's first effort for the New York paper listed the names, dates, and places of the many lynchings that had taken place in recent years, to make the offenses fully known to people outside the South. She also published these findings in a booklet, *Southern Horrors: Lynch Law in All Its Phases*. Wells repeated her charges in public lectures in northern cities in the United States, becoming a leader in the crusade against lynching. Traveling to England to speak, she sent back dispatches to a Chicago newspaper under the heading "Ida B. Wells Abroad."

Not all African Americans shared Wells's militancy. Some urged her to soften her rhetoric and pursue a more gradual course of racial accommodation, as advocated by Booker T. Washington, rather than complete equality. She refused to bend, arguing that "the more the Afro-American yields and cringes and begs, the more he has to do so, the more he is insulted, outraged and lynched."

Breaking with T. Thomas Fortune—who considered her to be "a sort of bull in a china shop"—Wells moved to Chicago, where she published a booklet denouncing Chicago's Columbian Exposition of 1893 for ignoring black Americans. She also submitted articles to a black newspaper, the *Chicago Conservator*. Its editor, Ferdinand Lee Barnett, was also a lawyer and later an assistant state's attorney. They were married in 1895, and thereafter she used the name Ida B. Wells-Barnett. She served as editor of the *Conservator* until she began rais-

Ida B. Wells-Barnett

BORN

July 16, 1862
Holly Springs, Mississippi

DIED

March 25, 1931
Chicago, Illinois

EDUCATION

Rust University (high school) (1878); briefly attended Fisk University

ACCOMPLISHMENTS

Contributor to African-American newspapers (1887–1931); editor and part owner of the *Memphis Free Speech and Headlight* (1891–92); staff writer for *New York Age* (1892–93); correspondent, *Chicago Inter-Ocean* (1894); editor, *Chicago Conservator* (1895–97); author of *On Lynching: Southern Horrors, A Red Record, Mob Rule in New Orleans* (1895), and *Crusade for Justice: The Autobiography of Ida B. Wells* (1970)

"It is with no pleasure I have dipped my hands in the corruption here exposed. Somebody must show that the Afro-American race is more sinned against than sinned, and it seems to have fallen upon me to do so. The awful death-roll that Judge Lynch is calling every week is appalling, not only because of the lives it takes, the rank cruelty and outrage to the victims, but because of the prejudice it fosters and the stain it places against the good name of a weak race."

—from *Southern Horrors* (1892)

ing her four children. "I had already found that motherhood was a profession by itself," she explained, "just like schoolteaching and lecturing, and that once one was launched on such a career, she owed it to herself to become as expert as possible in the practice of her profession." Though she withdrew from active newspaper work, she never stopped crusading.

Uncompromising in her principles, Wells-Barnett continued to speak out against lynching, and she helped provide legal aid for blacks in the South. In 1898 she joined a delegation that called on President William McKinley to investigate the lynching of an African-American postmaster in South Carolina. She founded the Ida B. Wells Club to organize black women for social reform in Chicago, and also the first black woman suffrage organization, the Alpha Suffrage Club of Chicago.

In 1909 she participated in the Niagara meeting that started the National Association for the Advancement of Colored People. She fought against efforts to set up separate schools for black and white children in Chicago. She campaigned for candidates sympathetic to racial equality and in 1930 ran unsuccessfully for the Illinois state senate. When Wells-Barnett died the following year, the prominent black leader W. E. B. Du Bois paid tribute to her as the woman who "began the awakening of the conscience of the nation" against the atrocity of lynching.

FURTHER READING

Davidson, Sue. *Getting the Real Story: Nellie Bly and Ida B. Wells*. Seattle: Seal Press, 1992.

Holt, Thomas C. "The Lonely Warrior: Ida B. Wells-Barnett and the Struggle for Black Leadership." In *Black Leaders of the Twentieth Century*, edited by John Hope Franklin and August Meier. Urbana: University of Illinois Press, 1982.

Senna, Carl. *The Black Press and the Struggle for Civil Rights*. New York: Franklin Watts, 1993.

Streitmatter, Rodger. *Raising Her Voice: African-American Women Journalists Who Changed History*. Lexington: University Press of Kentucky, 1994.

Thompson, Mildred I. *Ida B. Wells-Barnett: An Exploratory Study of an American Black Woman, 1893–1930*. Brooklyn, N.Y.: Carlson, 1990.

Thornbrough, Emma Lou. *T. Thomas Fortune: Militant Journalist*. Chicago: University of Chicago Press, 1972.

Wells-Barnett, Ida B. *Selected Works of Ida B. Wells-Barnett*. Edited by Trudier Harris. New York: Oxford University Press, 1991.

———. *Southern Horrors and Other Writings: The Anti-Lynching Campaign of Ida B. Wells, 1892–1900*. Edited by Jacqueline Jones Royster. Boston: Bedford Books, 1996.

Lincoln Steffens

MUCKRAKER

rogressives at the beginning of the 20th century regarded the sunlight of publicity as the best medicine for curing society's ills. Ignorance promoted corruption, they believed, while exposure encouraged reform. Once the people learned the truth about dishonest politicians and ruthless business leaders, they would vote the crooks out of office and force both government and business to mend their ways. This faith in the educational power of the press drove the "muckraking" magazine writers to uncover and report on the social evils in cities, states, and the national government, in business monopolies, patent medicines, and the quality of the food that people ate. The most famous of all the muckrakers, Lincoln Steffens, felt certain that when people were fully informed they would demand progress and reform.

Joseph Lincoln Steffens—who always went by his middle name—spent an idyllic childhood in California. His

Lincoln Steffens believed that journalists should not just report on crime but should investigate the conditions that caused it.

"Every time I attempted to trace to its sources the political corruption of a city ring, the stream of corruption branched off in the most unexpected directions, and spread out in a network of veins and arteries so complex that hardly any part of the body politic seemed clear. It flowed out of politics into vice and crime, out of politics into business, and back again into politics. . . . Big, throbbing arteries ran out through the country over the State to the nation and back. The corruption of our American cities is political . . . but financial and industrial too."

—from *The Autobiography of Lincoln Steffens* (1931)

father, Joseph Steffens, had reached the Pacific coast in a wagon train in 1862. His mother, Elizabeth Symes, sailed to San Francisco from New York in search of a husband. His father became a prosperous merchant, and moved the family to Sacramento, where they lived in a large white house that later became the governor's mansion. As a child, Lincoln Steffens had the freedom to explore on horseback much of the surrounding California countryside. He described those years as "free, independent, full of romance, adventure, and learning, of a sort." Perhaps too independent and rebellious, his father thought as he sent the 15-year-old to a military boarding school to instill some discipline in him. Steffens later attended the University of California at Berkeley. An avid reader in English and history but an indifferent student in other classes, he graduated near the bottom of his class.

Joseph Steffens dreamed that Lincoln would follow him into the family business. The son had no interest in business, however, and insisted upon going abroad to study philosophy. Appreciating his son's talent for writing, the father offered to buy an interest in a San Francisco newspaper to keep him closer to home. But Steffens persisted until his father agreed to pay his way to the German universities at Heidelberg and Leipzig. In his studies there he sought a "scientific basis" for ethics, which he never found. But he did fall in love with one of his fellow students, Josephine Bontecou, who was 10 years older than he. They married in 1891 but hid the news from his parents. Steffens continued his studies in Paris until they returned to the United States in 1892.

A message from his father was waiting when he landed in New York: "By now you must know about all there is to know of the theory of life, but there's a practical side as well. It's

worth knowing. I suggest that you learn it, and the way to study it, I think, is to stay in New York and hustle." Enclosed was $100 to support him until he found work.

With a letter of introduction from his father, Steffens got a job as a reporter for the *New York Evening Post*. It was a highly respectable, old-fashioned, and conservative newspaper that avoided the type of crime and scandal stories that filled the Pulitzer and Hearst papers. The college-educated Steffens fit into its staff well as a "gentleman reporter," covering financial news on Wall Street. While on that assignment, he became fascinated with the Wall Street bankers like J. P. Morgan, and stockbrokers and speculators, inquiring into how they made the nation's financial systems work. "Having no prejudice for or against finance, I had no judgment, no point of view," he later wrote. "It was as it was, neither good nor evil. . . . I was only a reporter reporting."

From reporting on the rich and powerful, Steffens was shifted to the police beat, covering the poorest neighborhoods of Manhattan's Lower East Side. There he encountered newly arrived immigrants, slum dwellings, sweatshops, and crime. Patterning himself after the *Post*'s veteran crime reporter, Jacob Riis, Steffens trained himself to look behind the crime for the human-interest story at its root. Reporters should not be satisfied with just reporting an incident, he believed, but needed to investigate the conditions that caused crime and other social ills. The police beat gave Steffens a fascinating view of what he called the "complex, crude, significant but mixed facts of hard practical life." As a police reporter, he also came to admire the dynamic young police commissioner of New York, Theodore Roosevelt. Roosevelt made official information available to Steffens, while Steffens helped educate

Roosevelt about corruption within the police department.

In 1897 Steffens gave up reporting to become city editor of the New York *Commercial Advertiser*. He worked hard to enliven that paper by hiring fresh young reporters from the best universities. They made the paper lively, but its owners preferred it to remain safe and conventional. Steffens decided to leave newspaper work to try his hand at writing fiction. But fiction was not his talent. When that effort failed, he joined the staff of *McClure's Magazine*, first as an editor and then as a writer. Previously, the few national magazines in existence aimed at an elite or a scholarly readership. Now new printing technology made possible more inexpensively priced mass-circulation magazines. These magazines sought vast new national audiences. *McClure's* identified topics that the people wanted to read. It investigated the deteriorating conditions of cities and the hazards of work in large factories. For newspaper reporters like Steffens, the mass magazines also gave them more room to write, less stringent deadlines, and bylines—their names on their stories.

As an editor at *McClure's*, Steffens had hired a local journalist to write about corruption in government in St. Louis, Missouri, but he was unhappy with the result. Certain that there was more to the story, Steffens left the editorial desk to become a roving correspondent for the magazine. Steffens's training as a police reporter carried over well into his magazine writing. He wrote stories that were exciting and at the same time realistic. Some observers compared his articles for *McClure's* to detective stories, since they employed methodical research and deduction to expose the unlawful activities of politicians, business leaders, and other supposedly upright people. Steffens the reporter provided factual details, names, places, and the amount of bribes, to prove his arguments. He showed his readers how things really were, to shame them into taking action to reform the system.

Moving from city to city, Steffens uncovered and exposed similar incidents of corruption at each place. He found the source of this criminal behavior among the seemingly best elements in a community: "In all cities, the better class—the business men—are the sources of corruption," he later wrote in his autobiography. He accused business leaders of bribing and influencing government to promote their corporate needs, or indirectly of overlooking and ignoring such improper behavior. In every city his best sources of information were newspaper reporters. These reporters knew what was going on, but they could not report the truth in their local newspapers, for fear of losing their jobs or their papers' advertisers. Steffens's exposés were immensely popular. He collected and published them in a book called *The Shame of the Cities*.

In January 1903 *McClure's* published Steffens's article on "The Shame of Minneapolis." The same issue also carried an installment of Ida Tarbell's exposé on the Standard Oil Company, and Ray Stannard Baker's investigation of labor practices, "The Right to Work." Publisher S. S. McClure contributed an editorial that drew readers' attention to these articles not as isolated cases, but as part of a pattern. They revealed how political machine bosses, corporate leaders, and labor unions all showed contempt for the law. McClure challenged Americans to reclaim their liberty against such assaults. The issue caught public attention and helped launch modern investigative journalism—to which President Theodore Roosevelt gave the name "muckraking."

Although journalists like Steffens and Tarbell helped Roosevelt by rousing popular support for reform politics,

Lincoln Steffens

BORN
April 6, 1866
San Francisco, California

DIED
August 9, 1936
Carmel, California

EDUCATION
Ph.B., University of California at Berkeley (1889); attended the Sorbonne in Paris and the universities of Heidelberg and Leipzig

ACCOMPLISHMENTS
Reporter, *New York Evening Post* (1893–97); city editor, *New York Commercial Advertiser* (1897–1901); managing editor, *McClure's Magazine* (1901–06); part owner, *American Magazine* (1906–07); columnist, the *Carmelite*, *Controversy*, *Pacific Weekly* (1928–36); author of *The Shame of the Cities* (1904), *Struggle for Self-Government: Being an Attempt to Trace American Political Corruption to Its Source in Six States* (1906), *Upbuilders* (1909), and *The Autobiography of Lincoln Steffens* (1931)

the President felt troubled by their steady stream of negative articles. Roosevelt believed that some journalists were simply "lurid sensationalists" and worried that their writing would produce political demagogues who would whip up public outrage. (Roosevelt had the publisher and would-be politician William Randolph Hearst specifically in mind.) A steady drumbeat of exposés might make people feel that the political system was so rotten that reform was useless and that revolution was the only answer. Roosevelt decided to combat the "great amount of evil" which he saw mixed in with the truths told by the crusading journalists. In 1906 the President delivered a speech he called the "Man with the Muck-Rake." Taking his theme from a character in John Bunyan's classic 17th-century book, *Pilgrim's Progress*, Roosevelt described the man so intent on raking the muck (or filth) that he failed to see or appreciate the blue sky above. Similarly, reporters who concentrated only on what was "vile and debasing" never saw what was good about the world.

Roosevelt's attack took the steam out of the muckraking movement. While muckraking journalism continued, some of the most prominent writers tried to distance themselves from the charge. They denied that they were only interested in corruption, and insisted that they also appreciated the more positive aspects of American life. Steffens, Tarbell, Baker, and others left *McClure's* in 1906 to publish their own *American Magazine*, which would emphasize stories about "good people . . . coming out on top." Out of his contributions to the magazine came his book *Upbuilders*, inspiring profiles of business and civic leaders who were joining forces to build a better world.

While working with *American Magazine*, his reporting on turmoil around the world took Steffens out of the United States and further changed his attitudes. In 1914 he covered the revolution in Mexico, where he saw foreign investors (including Americans) exploiting a poor nation. His admiration of the Mexican revolutionaries led him to move away from liberalism and progressivism to look favorably at radical revolutionaries around the world. He concluded that revolutions were necessary to help backward countries advance economically and become more modern. He believed such revolutions necessary, even if they suppressed democracy.

Steffens's solution to political and moral problems was to find good, strong leaders to take charge. When he investigated American government, he had admired the take-charge leadership qualities of local politicians such as Missouri governor Joseph Folk and strong Presidents such as Theodore Roosevelt. In the 1920s, as he traveled the world, Steffens came to admire Vladimir Lenin, the communist leader of the Soviet Union, and Benito

Mussolini, the fascist dictator of Italy. Searching for signs of progress, he was blind to their tyrannies over political rights and civil liberties. Visiting the Soviet Union after the Russian Revolution, Steffens proclaimed that he had seen the future "and it works."

Josephine Steffens died in 1911, and in 1919 Lincoln Steffens met Ella Winter, a student at the London School of Economics. They were married in 1924, and Steffens's first child was born later that year. Returning to California, Steffens and his wife and son settled in Carmel. There he wrote articles for the local papers and devoted himself to his autobiography. The two-volume work turned out to be his most popular and lasting piece of writing. The *Autobiography* chronicled his life from boy on horseback to police reporter and muckraker. The theme of the books was his disenchantment with reform and his turn toward radicalism. His muckraking had taken place in "innocent days," he wrote; "we were all innocent folk."

Published during the Great Depression of the 1930s, when despairing Americans looked toward radical solutions to their economic problems, the *Autobiography* became a best-seller. Beyond its politics, the *Autobiography* also attracted an audience because of its lack of bitterness and its promise of moral regeneration through constant self-education and self-improvement. Lincoln Steffens offered his readers his own rule of journalism: "To look at facts, let them destroy an illusion, and not to be cast down, but go on studying the facts, sure that in those very same facts would be found constructive material with which to build up another illusion, no better perhaps, but other than the old one."

FURTHER READING

Filler, Louis. *Muckrakers: Crusaders for American Liberalism*. Chicago: Henry Regnery, 1968.

Horton, Russell. *Lincoln Steffens*. New York: Twayne, 1974.

Kaplan, Justin. *Lincoln Steffens: A Biography*. New York: Simon & Schuster, 1974.

Lyon, Peter. *Success Story: The Life and Times of S. S. McClure*. New York: Scribners, 1963.

Palermo, Patrick F. *Lincoln Steffens*. Boston: Twayne, 1978.

Steffens, Lincoln. *The World of Lincoln Steffens*. Edited by Ella Winter and Herbert Shapiro. New York: Hill & Wang, 1962.

Wilson, Harold. *McClure's Magazine and the Muckrakers*. Princeton, N.J.: Princeton University Press, 1970.

Winter, Ella. *And Not to Yield: An Autobiography*. New York: Harcourt, Brace & World, 1963.

Ida M. Tarbell

A JOURNALIST,
NOT AN ADVOCATE

Around 1900 the dynamic publisher S. S. McClure and the staff of *McClure's Magazine* debated among themselves how they could best explain to their readers the enormous growth in their time of business monopolies and trusts—companies that tried to control all of the production and sales of their product and to drive the competition out of business. The best idea seemed to be to focus on a single trust and show how it had grown. They tossed about various suggestions, but somehow felt dissatisfied.

Then one of the staff writers, Ida Tarbell, recalled her childhood in the oil fields of Pennsylvania. She told about

Ida Tarbell, whose first ambition was to be a biologist, brought to her journalism a scientist's insistence on factual accuracy.

how her father and others had been ruined when the Standard Oil Company had conspired with the railroads to drive smaller competitors out of business. With McClure's encouragement, she set out to research and write the story, but many of the people she sought to interview feared that if they cooperated with her, the giant oil company might seek revenge. Even her own father begged, "Don't do it Ida—they will ruin the magazine." Ida Tarbell pressed ahead, and her "History of the Standard Oil Company" became one of the great journalistic exposés of the muckraking era.

Ida Minerva Tarbell grew up near Titusville, Pennsylvania, where the first oil boom in the United States took place. Although a prosperous boom town, Titusville depended entirely on the railroads to ship its crude oil to refining points. But a few large refiners from outside the area pooled their resources and forced the railroads to give them rebates—or discounts—so they could ship crude oil and refine it more cheaply than anyone else. "I remember a night," Tarbell later said, "when my father came home with a grim look on his face and told how he with scores of other producers had signed a pledge not to sell to the Cleveland ogre that alone had profited from the scheme . . . the Standard Oil Company."

Science, not journalism, first inspired Tarbell. She was fascinated by nature and aspired to become a biologist. At that time the chief occupation for women was teaching, so she set out to get a college education and teach science. She determined that she would never marry. "It would interfere with my plan; it would fetter my freedom," she later wrote. "When I was fourteen I was praying God on my knees to keep me from marriage." After college she taught and worked as assistant to the president at Poland Union Seminary in Poland, Ohio. But

classes and administrative duties wore her down and left her no time for her microscope. She left the school to become an editorial assistant on the *Chautauquan* magazine. In 1874 the Chautauqua Movement was founded along the shores of Lake Chautauqua in upstate New York, where people gathered in the summers to hear speakers on religion and all areas of intellectual life. The magazine reflected these wide-ranging issues. Tarbell edited articles by others and began to write some herself about famous women in history.

After a while she decided that she needed more out of life, and she determined to go back to school. She had long since stopped looking for truth through a microscope and had shifted her interest from rocks and plants to human beings. When she told her editor in chief that she was going to study in Paris and would support herself by writing, he protested: "You're not a writer. You'll starve." Tarbell agreed that she lacked literary style, but felt that she made up for it by her confidence in her own sense of what really mattered in a subject, rather than relying on other people's opinions.

While studying history at the Sorbonne, Ida Tarbell sent articles to newspapers and magazines in the United States. A few of her pieces were published by the McClure Syndicate (which supplied news and features to many publications) and came to the attention of the publisher, S. S. McClure. When he visited Paris in 1892, he made it a point to meet her. Tarbell later described McClure as a vibrant personality whose enthusiasm and vision entirely captivated her. She accepted his invitation to write articles for his new magazine (immodestly named *McClure's*) and contributed a series on the life of Napoléon Bonaparte. The series ran from November 1894 to April 1895, spurring the magazine's circulation and helping it to survive the economic depression of the

Ida M. Tarbell

BORN
November 5, 1857
Near Erie, Pennsylvania

DIED
January 6, 1944
Bridgeport, Connecticut

EDUCATION
B.S. in biology, Allegheny College, Meadville, Pennsylvania (1880); M.A., Allegheny College (1883); graduate work at the Sorbonne, Paris

ACCOMPLISHMENTS
Editor and writer for the *Chautauquan* magazine (1883–90); contributing editor, *McClure's Magazine* (1893–1906); co-owner, *American Magazine* (1906–15); staff of *Red Cross Magazine* (1919); consulting editor, *Letter* magazine (1943–44); author of *A Short Life of Napoleon Bonaparte* (1895), *The Life of Abraham Lincoln* (1900), *History of the Standard Oil Company* (1904), *The Business of Being a Woman* (1912), *Ways of a Woman* (1915), *New Ideals in Business: An Account of Their Practice and Their Effects Upon Men and Profits* (1916), *Peacemakers—Blessed and Otherwise: Observations, Reflections and Irritations at the International Conference* (1922), *Life of Elbert H. Gary: The Story of Steel* (1925), *Owen D. Young: A New Type of Industrial Leader* (1932), and *The Nationalizing of Business, 1878–1898* (1936)

THE HISTORY OF
THE STANDARD
OIL COMPANY

BY

IDA M. TARBELL

AUTHOR OF
THE LIFE OF ABRAHAM LINCOLN, THE LIFE OF NAPOLEON BONAPARTE,
AND MADAME ROLAND: A BIOGRAPHICAL STUDY

ILLUSTRATED WITH PORTRAITS
PICTURES AND DIAGRAMS

VOLUME TWO

NEW YORK
McCLURE, PHILLIPS & CO.
MCMIV

JOHN D. ROCKEFELLER
A sketch from life by George Varian, made in Cleveland, October, 1903

In magazine form and later as a book, Ida Tarbell's *The History of the Standard Oil Company* riveted national attention and led to greater government regulation of business.

1890s. The popularity of the series prompted her to write a similar biography of Abraham Lincoln. Both series were later published as books, but the royalties from their sales were too meager for her to live on. Realizing that magazine writing could provide a reliable wage, Tarbell joined *McClure's Magazine* as a regular contributor.

The staff of the new magazine included such brilliant writers as Lincoln Steffens, David Graham Phillips, and Ray Stannard Baker. The "Chief," as they called McClure, urged them to be bold and take risks in generating new stories. He wanted current issues rather than history, and he was

impatient when writers took too long to research and write their pieces. When arguments broke out among the staff, Tarbell played peacemaker. Lincoln Steffens described her as "sensible, capable, and very affectionate, she knew each one of us and all our idiosyncracies and troubles. She had none of her own, so far as we ever heard." When the staff became deadlocked over an idea, Tarbell would go from office to office, mediating between the publisher, editors, and writers and settling their disputes.

Tarbell brought to her journalism a scientist's insistence upon factual accuracy and a historian's ability to sift through past evidence. When she began researching the history of the Standard Oil Company, she knew that Congress had investigated the oil industry and that many lawsuits had been filed against it. The mountains of evidence that the congressional committees and the courts had collected provided testimony taken under oath and other hard facts she needed to write the story. Some documents had been deliberately destroyed, but by hunting she turned up extra copies. Slowly she documented Standard Oil president John D. Rockefeller's obsession with driving all competitors out of business, no matter how small they were, in order to control the industry completely. Surprisingly, officials from Standard Oil not only agreed to talk with her, but were fairly candid. Perhaps they did not take a woman reporter all that seriously, and thought they could persuade her to write a sympathetic piece about their corporation. When the articles began to appear, others in the oil industry began sending her additional incriminating evidence.

In serial form, "The History of the Standard Oil Company" riveted the nation for months, boosting the circulation of *McClure's Magazine* and filling mailbags with letters of congratulations. Tarbell accused Rockefeller of having become fabulously wealthy by using rebates and other tactics that were contrary to the public good. The evidence that Standard Oil had used unfair tactics to drive smaller competitors out of business spurred progressive reformers to seek to break up the powerful trusts and establish government regulation of business practices. In 1911 the Supreme Court dissolved the giant Standard Oil Company into several companies (today Exxon, Mobil,

Chevron, and Amoco). Tarbell herself insisted that she had never been prejudiced against big business. "I was willing that they should combine and grow as big and rich as they could," she said, "but only by legitimate means." For its part, Standard Oil tried to discredit the series by portraying it as an angry woman's vendetta. One company executive called Tarbell "an honest, bitter, talented, prejudiced and disappointed woman who writes from her own point of view. And that view is from the ditch, where her father's wheelbarrow was landed by a Standard Oil tankwagon."

These charges stung her, as did President Theodore Roosevelt's attack on magazine writers, in which he accused them of looking only at what was wrong with America. Other critics assumed that Tarbell and other muckrakers were socialists who were bent on destroying capitalism. But Ida Tarbell considered herself to be "a journalist after the fact," not an advocate for any cause or ideology. She felt uncomfortable being identified with the muckrakers and felt that the muckraking magazines too often put their passion for subscriptions ahead of their passion for facts. Through the new mass-circulation magazines, the muckrakers addressed the public's fears over the unchecked powers of big business, and the deterioration of the quality of life in American cities and manufacturing regions. They focused on their readers' moral outrage and turned it into concerted political efforts at the polls, causing reformers to be elected and reforms and regulations to be enacted. Before long, however, the public tired of such a steady diet of exposé, and circulation for the muckraking magazines declined.

In 1906 McClure's top writers—

"*When the work [research on the oil trust for McClure's Magazine] was first announced in the fall of 1901, the Standard Oil Company, or perhaps I should say officers of the company, courteously offered to give me all the assistance in their power, an offer of which I have freely taken advantage. In accepting assistance from Standard men as from independents I distinctly stated that I wanted facts, and that I reserved the right to use them according to my own judgment of their meaning, that my object was to learn more perfectly what was actually done—not to learn what my informants thought of what had been done.*"

—from *The History of the Standard Oil Company* (1904)

Tarbell, among them—broke away to form their own magazine. Pooling their resources, they bought controlling stock in the *American Magazine*. The new magazine lacked *McClure's* muckraking spirit. "It sought to present things as they were, not as somebody thought they ought to be," Tarbell wrote. "We were journalists, not propagandists." Looking for what was good about industry and labor relations, Tarbell visited factories, and she came to admire the "Captains of Industry" and their paternalism toward the workers. She also commended the time-and-motion studies and "scientific management" theories of Frederick Taylor. This turn in Tarbell's writing surprised many of her readers, but she insisted that she was simply keeping her eye on events and reporting any developments that seemed a step ahead. Having contibuted to breaking up the "bad trusts," she felt an obligation to praise what was right about the "good trusts."

In 1915 the *American* was sold to new owners and the old staff drifted away. Tarbell bought a farmhouse in Connecticut and became interested in farming. She still wrote and gave public lectures. Having started her career writing a biography of Napoléon, she ended it by writing about modern strong men, from the "Great Engineer" Herbert Hoover to the Italian dictator Benito Mussolini, as well as flattering biographies of powerful business leaders. Looking back at the Andrew Carnegies and John D. Rockefellers of American history, Tarbell concluded: "If each of these strong men left something sinister behind, each also contributed to higher living standards and hurried on the nationalization of the country."

No matter how many articles and books she wrote, her reputation as a journalist always rested on her exposé of Standard Oil—and she remained proud of her achievement. Once, when she was an elderly woman, a young reader asked if she could rewrite "The History of the Standard Oil Company," what would she change? "Not one word, young man, not one word," she replied.

FURTHER READING

Brady, Kathleen. *Ida Tarbell: Portrait of a Muckraker.* New York: Seaview/Putnam, 1984.

Kochersberger, Robert C., Jr. *More Than a Muckraker: Ida Tarbell's Lifetime in Journalism.* Knoxville: University of Tennessee Press, 1994. [Includes selections from Tarbell's writings.]

Tarbell, Ida M. *All in the Day's Work: An Autobiography.* 1939. Reprint, Boston: G. K. Hall, 1985.

Tomkins, Mary E. *Ida M. Tarbell.* New York: Twayne, 1974.

Wilson, Harold S. *McClure's Magazine and the Muckrakers.* Princeton, N.J.: Princeton University Press, 1970.

Abraham Cahan

THE ETHNIC PRESS

The thousands of Jewish immigrants who crowded into the tenements and narrow streets of Manhattan's Lower East Side at the beginning of the 20th century struggled through a bewildering transition from Eastern Europe to America. To guide them through their assimilation into an alien culture, and for advice, inspiration, and the news, they turned to Yiddish language newspapers. The *Jewish Daily Forward*, in particular, adopted the language of the common people and treated their lives and problems intelligently and sympathetically. The paper owed its tone, style, and much of its copy to its remarkable editor, Abraham Cahan. A Russian-Jewish immigrant himself, Cahan made his people and his culture the subject of both his journalism and his literature.

As the editor of the *Jewish Daily Forward* for almost a half century, Abraham Cahan urged his reporters to write about elements of everyday life.

Written in Yiddish, the *Daily Forward* explained American politics, history, and economics and offered advice and reassurance to its immigrant readers.

The grandson of a rabbi and the son of a Hebrew teacher, Abraham Cahan was born in a small village in Lithuania and raised in Vilna, the capital, then known as the "Jerusalem of Lithuania." Lithuanian Jews spoke Yiddish (a German dialect written in Hebrew characters), but since the country was under Russian rule its secular schools taught all subjects in Russian. As a boy, Cahan rejected the traditional religious education of the yeshiva (boys' schools where lessons were taught in Hebrew) that he attended and studied Russian so that he could enter the university. Admitted to the Vilna Teachers' Institute, he found to his dismay that its teaching was almost entirely by rote. The czarist government of Russia was "not fond of young men who had independent minds," he later wrote, because their new ideas might spark revolution.

As a student, Cahan fell in with Marxist revolutionaries. In 1881, the year Cahan graduated, Czar Alexander II was assassinated. Jews became convenient scapegoats and were targeted by a wave of terror and persecution known as pogroms. Many Russian Jews fled, a large number emigrating to America. At the same time, Cahan, who had gone to teach in the village of Velizh, came under the suspicion of the local police. Realizing that he must leave, he thought first of following other Russian revolutionaries to Switzerland or of joining Jewish settlers in Palestine. Instead, he decided on America. "America! To go to America!" he thought. "To re-establish the Garden of Eden in that distant land. My spirit soared. All my other plans dissolved. I was for America!"

At 22, Cahan arrived in Philadelphia and took a train to New York City. His only knowledge of English was from a dictionary he had purchased on the way. Instead of going to adult evening school, where he doubted that the other students would be able to pronounce English correctly, he enrolled at a daytime elementary school. Cahan learned to read and speak English quickly and began teaching the new language to fellow immigrants in the rapidly growing Jewish community of the Lower East Side. He also took a job in a cigar factory, delivered lectures on socialism, and became active in the labor movement. He helped organize the first Jewish-American labor union for garment workers.

As one of the first Russian-Jewish intellectuals in America, Cahan sought to import European socialism to the New World. But he found the new political landscape vastly different. In New York he could purchase socialist newspapers openly at the news stand, unlike in Russia, where possession of such literature could lead to arrest and imprisonment. "What kind of socialism could it be without conspiracy?" he questioned. "If all is permissible and danger is absent, socialism becomes diluted and revolutionary heroism becomes impossible."

Aspiring to be a writer and journalist, Cahan submitted articles denouncing czarist Russia and

recounting tales of the Jewish community in New York to the *World* and the *New York Sun* The editor of the *Sun* accepted his material gratefully, but asked what the word "ghetto" in his title meant. It shocked Cahan that such a highly educated man could be so ignorant of a term so well known to the people of the Lower East Side, and it made him more aware of the gap between the two cultures. Cahan became one of the first journalists to address both cultures in their own languages.

In 1886 Cahan started a Yiddish-language paper, *Di Neie Tzeit* (The New Era), for which he served as editor, proofreader, bookkeeper, and advertising agent. The financially strapped paper survived only a few months. That same year he married Anna Bronstein, an immigrant from Kiev who shared his interests in literature and the arts. He devoted an increasing amount of his time to writing fiction. His first novel, *Yekl: A Tale of the New York Ghetto*, received a glowing review in the *New York World* and sold out several printings. His most renowned novel, *The Rise of David Levinsky*, published in 1917, recounted the American Jewish experience through the life of an immigrant garment manufacturer.

Torn between literature and ideology, Cahan returned to journalism in 1897 as editor of a new socialist paper, the New York *Jewish Daily Forward*. The paper was cooperatively owned and published by the Forward Association, a group drawn largely from Jewish labor unions. Internal divisions between various socialist factions split the paper's staff and affected its editorial policies. Unable to gain full editorial control, Cahan resigned. He took a job as a police reporter for

Abraham Cahan

BORN

July 7, 1860
Podberzya, Lithuania

DIED

August 31, 1951
New York, New York

EDUCATION

Teaching Certificate, Vilna Teachers' Institute, Lithuania (1881)

ACCOMPLISHMENTS

Editor, *Di Neie Tzeit* (The New Era) (1896); editor, *Arbeiter Zeitung* (Workers' Newspaper) (1891–94); police reporter, *New York Commercial Advertiser* (1897–1901); editor, *Jewish Daily Forward* (1897, 1902, 1903–51); author of *Yekl: A Tale of the New York Ghetto* (1896), *The Imported Bridegroom and Other Stories of the New York Ghetto* (1898), *The White Terror and the Red: A Novel of Revolutionary Russia* (1905), *Raphael Naarizoch (A Story)* (1907), *The Rise of David Levinsky* (1917), and *Palestine* (1934)

> *"The immigrant's arrival in his new home is like a second birth to him. . . . I conjure up the gorgeousness of the spectacle as it appeared to me on that clear June morning; the magnificent verdure of Staten Island, the tender blue of sea and sky, the dignified bustle of passing craft—above all, those floating, squatting, multitudinous windowed palaces which I subsequently learned to call ferries."*
>
> —from *The Rise of David Levinsky* (1917)

the New York *Commercial Advertiser*. Having grown so staid and conservative that it was nicknamed "Grandma," the *Commercial Advertiser* had just gained a dynamic new editor, Lincoln Steffens. He fired the professional reporters and hired a staff of enthusiastic, inexperienced writers, most of them right out of Ivy League colleges. They had complete freedom to write whatever they pleased, "as long as they wrote interestingly, sympathetically, and naturally." Steffens hired Cahan to cover the ghetto and the police courts. Said Steffens: "He brought the spirit of the East Side into our shop," arguing Marxist doctrine with other reporters and taking them on excursions to Jewish neighborhoods and the Yiddish theater.

Cahan returned to the *Jewish Daily Forward* in 1902, but resigned after another factional squabble. The following year a wave of pogroms in Russia deeply disturbed him. He went back to the *Daily Forward* with a pledge of complete editorial control, which he retained for almost a half century. As editor, Cahan abandoned long, argumentative articles on Marxist economics in favor of human-interest

stories written in an informal manner—stories that would appeal to the average reader. "If you want the public to read this paper and assimilate Socialism," he told his reporters, "you've got to write of things of everyday life, in terms of what they see and feel and find all about them."

Cahan adopted the banner headlines made popular by the "yellow press" and other devices that boosted circulation. One of the most successful features was the "Bintel Brief," meaning a bundle of letters from readers. He encouraged the people of the Lower East Side to pour out their anger, frustrations, and woes in their letters to the editor, seeking advice and reassurance. Cahan contributed editorials on everything from good manners to socialism. Writers in the *Forward* also sought to explain American politics, history, and economics. By making sense out of the strange ways of the new society, their accounts helped "Americanize" their immigrant readers.

When World War I began, Cahan went to Germany to cover the Russian Front. His hatred of czarist Russia made him sympathetic to the German cause. But when the United States entered the war, espionage laws threatened the *Forward* and required the paper to translate its war news into English for government review and possible censorship. Cahan toned down his editorials and supported the Allies' war effort. Still, he rejoiced when the Russian Revolution overthrew the czar in 1917. Although not a communist himself, Cahan defended the Bolshevik government well into the 1920s. Not until he had interviewed Russian refugees and visited the Soviet Union himself did he concede that communist rule was more rather than less repressive than the czarist regime that it had replaced.

During the 1920s, the *Forward* grew steadily less socialistic. Cahan's editorials shifted toward liberalism (that is, toward government regulation rather than government ownership of business), and during the 1930s he generally supported the New Deal programs of President Franklin D. Roosevelt. Cahan also changed his mind about the Zionist efforts to create a Jewish state in Palestine. Initially cool, he visited Palestine in 1925 and came back impressed with the "heroic fire" that burned within the Jewish settlers there.

Although the *Jewish Daily Forward* had been founded as a nonprofit paper, under Cahan's editorship it became extremely profitable. It published 12 editions in various cities with significant Jewish populations. The Forward Association distributed its profits to labor unions and social causes and made regular contributions to the Socialist party. Despite this prosperity, the paper's original base was eroding as second and third generation Jewish Americans achieved higher educations, left the trades for the professions, and

moved away from the Lower East Side. The newspaper began a slow decline, along with its aging editor. In 1946 Cahan suffered a stroke, which prevented him from going to work daily. Yet he held the title of managing editor until he died in 1951, at the age of 91. Cahan wrote his own epitaph; he wanted to be remembered as "the best foreign language editor in the United States."

FURTHER READING

Cahan, Abraham. *The Education of Abraham Cahan*. Translated by Leon Stein, Abraham P. Conan, and Lynn Davidson. Philadelphia: Jewish Publication Society of America, 1969.

Chametzky, Jules. *From the Ghetto: The Fiction of Abraham Cahan*. Amherst: University of Massachusetts Press, 1977.

Higham, John. *Send These To Me: Immigrants in Urban America*. Baltimore, Md.: Johns Hopkins University Press, 1984.

Howe, Irving. *World of Our Fathers*. New York: Harcourt Brace Jovanovich, 1976.

Rischin, Moses. *The Promised Land: New York Jews, 1870–1914*. Cambridge: Harvard University Press, 1962.

———, ed. *Grandma Never Lived in America: The New Journalism of Abraham Cahan*. Bloomington: Indiana University Press, 1985.

Sanders, Ronald. *The Downtown Jews: Portraits of an Immigrant Generation*. 1969. Reprint, New York: Dover, 1987.

Walden, Daniel, ed. *The Changing Mosaic: From Cahan to Malamud, Roth and Ozick*. Albany: State University of New York Press, 1993.

William Allen White

THE COUNTRY EDITOR

As longtime editor of the *Emporia Gazette,* William Allen White epitomized small-town life in Middle America, promoting hometown virtues and local business development.

Not until 1920 would the U.S. Census show that a majority of Americans lived in urban areas. Before then most Americans had lived in rural, farming areas and small towns, and editors of county newspapers had played a critical role in shaping their political and social thought. America's best-known small-town editor was William Allen White, who published the *Emporia Gazette* for nearly a half century. His editorials held appeal far beyond Main Street in Emporia, Kansas. He became the voice of Middle American virtues and values, at a time when the nation was growing more urban, and as national news and syndicated features were filling even small-town papers.

White was born in the town where he would spend most of his career, but he grew up in the even smaller town of Eldorado, Kansas. There his father, Allen White, was a doctor, druggist, and mayor of the town, despite being a Democrat in an overwhelmingly Republican area. White's mother, Mary Hatten White, had been a school teacher, who came to Kansas inspired by the Republican abolitionist movement. His parents' political differences, White later commented, explained some of his editorial shifts: "No wonder that I grew up full of complexes, and with a certain lack of conviction which comes from seeing both sides well presented by those you love and knowing full well there are two sides to everything, and that what seems black and white is generally gray."

White's father died in 1882, when the boy was 14. He grew close to his mother, who took in boarders to support the family. Later, when he went to the University of Kansas in Lawrence, his mother moved with him to keep house and help him with his studies. She even accompanied him on his honeymoon, when he married Sallie Lindsay in 1893, and lived next door to him until she died.

White had originally started college in Emporia but dropped out when he decided that "a big, healthy, strapping seventeen-year-old boy had no business to let his mother keep boarders to send him to college." He went to work for the *Eldorado Republican* as an apprentice printer, and his duties included sweeping out the office, running errands, and sorting and setting type. "There was a flavor in those days about the printing office," White later recalled. "Printers were supposed to graduate into editors, editors into statesmen, statesmen into leading citizens, and so rise to empyrean heights in the state and nation. This was the natural road to the White House. No printer ever had gone to the White

House, but in general all young printers expected to go there."

In 1886 he became a typesetter for the *Emporia Daily News* and filled in as a replacement for reporters on the paper. That led to a job with the *Emporia Daily Republican,* where he hired the newspaper deliverers, collected subscriptions, solicited ads, and wrote local items. Being a reporter got him free passes to ride the railroads, free meals, and treatment as a "young prince," he recalled. Covering a local murder case, he sent copies of his stories to out-of-town papers and was paid for it decently. "I was somebody, or thought I was," he later said; "probably strutted my pride!"

Even after he returned to college, White reported university doings for the *Lawrence Journal* and the *Kansas City News*. In the summer he worked as editor of the *Lawrence Evening Tribune*. It was during the Presidential election of 1888, while he was still in college, that White formally joined the Republican party. Swept up by the promise of prosperity, he concluded that things seemed good in Kansas. Just a few years later, when a major depression struck, he realized that the state had been living on borrowed money and was deeply in debt. Although White stayed a Republican in his politics and his editorials, he would swing between the conservative and progressive factions of his party.

After college, White initially wrote editorials for William Rockhill Nelson's *Kansas City Star*. As much as he admired Nelson, White longed to be independent. "I could not be happy as a hired man," he concluded, and began looking around for a small paper that he could buy. But the newspaper business was changing, requiring more capital to purchase new presses and equipment to operate a newspaper. It cost more either to set up a new newspaper or to purchase an existing one. Deciding that his talents would flour-

AMERICAN JOURNALISTS

William Allen White

BORN

February 10, 1868
Emporia, Kansas

DIED

January 29, 1944
Emporia, Kansas

EDUCATION

College of Emporia (1884–86);
University of Kansas (1886–90)

ACCOMPLISHMENTS

Reporter, *Emporia Daily Republican* (1886); editor, *Eldorado Republican* (1890–92); editorial writer, *Kansas City Star* (1892–95); editor, *Emporia Gazette* (1896–1944); author of *The Court of Boyville* (1899), *Stratagems and Spoils* (1901), *In Our Town* (1906), *A Certain Rich Man* (1909), *The Old Order Changeth: A View of American Democracy* (1910), *God's Puppets* (1916), *In The Heart of a Fool* (1919), *Politics: The Citizen's Business* (1924), *Masks in a Pageant* (1928), *Woodrow Wilson: The Man, His Times, and His Task* (1929), *A Puritan in Babylon: The Story of Calvin Coolidge* (1938), *The Changing West* (1938), and *Defense for America* (1940)

> *"What's the matter with Kansas? Nothing under the shining sun. She is losing wealth, population and standing. She has got her statesmen, and the money power is afraid of her. Kansas is all right."*
>
> —from "What's the Matter with Kansas?" editorial, *Emporia Gazette* (August 16, 1896)

ish best among readers from the "intellectually upper middle class," he wanted to acquire a paper in a college town. He tried to buy the *Lawrence Journal*, but it cost too much. Then he tried to buy the *Manhattan Mercury*, but it was not for sale. That narrowed his search to Emporia, where the 27-year-old White purchased the ailing *Emporia Gazette*. The paper had fewer than 600 subscribers, many behind in their payments. In his first editorial, published on June 3, 1895, White described himself as "a young man now, full of high purposes and high ideals." He pledged to publish "a clean, honest local paper."

The *Gazette* had originally been founded by Populists (a radical political movement of the 1890s that sought to help farmers and fight business monopolies), but White's editorials endorsed conservative Republican positions. In the 1896 Presidential election, he supported the Republican William McKinley, and dismissed as a demagogue the Democratic and Populist candidate, William Jennings Bryan. Bryan called for an inflated currency through the coinage of silver and for other federal help for rural America, but White objected both to Free Silver and to government paternalism. In America, he insisted, "it is a free for all, and in the end the keenest, most frugal, and most industrious win." His stance angered the depression-stricken farmers around Emporia. One scorchingly hot summer afternoon, a group of farmers caught the editor on the street, hooting and heckling him. After sputtering a defense of his positions, White stalked away. He returned to his newspaper office, sat down and wrote a biting, slashing, sarcastic edito-

rial called "What's the Matter with Kansas?" He ridiculed Bryan, the Populists, and their supporters for driving investments out of the state.

Other newspapers reprinted White's editorial and it eventually came to the attention of Mark Hanna, chairman of the Republican National Committee. Hanna had it distributed across the nation as a Republican campaign document. This made White's national reputation. However, just as he became a hero to conservatives, White met Theodore Roosevelt and began to shift his thinking. During their first meeting in 1897, Roosevelt overwhelmed the country editor, impressing on him "such visions, such ideals, such hopes, such a new attitude toward life and patriotism and the meaning of things, as I had never dreamed men had." Later, as President, Roosevelt would promote a new spirit of progressive reform. White joined the progressive movement, although he admitted that "All we Progressives did was catch the Populists in swimming and steal all their clothing except the frayed underdrawers of Free Silver."

Although White became a prominent Progressive, writing articles that appeared in national magazines, his *Emporia Gazette* continued to promote hometown virtues and root for business development. Like most small-town publications, the *Gazette* engaged in boosterism, to build up the local economy and to attract advertisers and subscribers. While other Progressives fought against the power of big business, White helped the railroads and other interests he considered to be vital to Kansas's growth and economic success. As the *Gazette* advertised: "For 365 days a year the *Gazette* stands up for Emporia. It stands for the town, for a decent town, for a wideawake town, for a live town."

White rejected offers to move to New York City and edit national publications. Although he remained a country editor, the country was changing. After 1903 the *Emporia Gazette* carried Associated Press stories and devoted more attention to news of the nation and the world. White sometimes worried that the paper gave too much space to sensational murder trials and other events that the AP covered. The *Gazette* tried to make national news more meaningful by tying it to local events. For instance, when U.S. troops went to the Philippines, the paper wrote about local boys fighting there. In the 1920s White's *Gazette* began carrying advertisements for national brands and for motion pictures that were being shown across the country. As the paper started to carry syndicated features, it lost some of its uniqueness. White even overcame his own long-standing objections and published cartoons as a way of attracting readers.

Although his dream was to write novels, White's talent was as an editorial writer. In 1921 he enhanced his image as the spokesman for Middle America by writing a touching editorial in memory of his daughter Mary, who had been killed when she struck a tree branch while horseback riding. He described Mary in terms that epitomized small-town virtues. The editorial appeared in countless newspapers and anthologies. If anything he wrote in his long career survived him, White mused, it would be that thousand-word tribute to his daughter. It enabled her to survive "in the hearts of her kind, high-school students and college stu-

dents" who continued to read the editorial.

By the 1920s White felt alienated from his times. He complained about the general retreat from progressivism and the spread of reactionary politics and corruption in Washington. He protested the rise of the Ku Klux Klan in Emporia and much of the Middle West. He was deeply disappointed when Herbert Hoover, whom he had supported, seemed to shrink from leadership during the Great Depression. "Go to the people, Mr. President," White exhorted in an editorial. "They are dependable. . . . Whoever is wise and honest and brave, they will follow to victory." He felt more pleased with the activism of Franklin D. Roosevelt during the 1930s, but remained suspicious of some of the big government programs of Roosevelt's New Deal.

As war spread in Europe, White in 1940 became chairman of the Committee to Defend America by Aiding the Allies. Often called the William Allen White Committee, it took the lead in fighting American isolationism and promoting aid to the European nations allied against fascism. At the time internationalism was seen to be a product of the eastern elites, and isolationism the spirit of the small towns of Middle America. It was highly significant, therefore, for the most famous country editor to call for America to accept global responsibility in the days before World War II.

When the United States entered the war, the elderly White devoted himself to writing his autobiography. Each morning a stenographer would come to his house. White would lie on a hammock on the porch of his home and dictate his reminiscences. As

usual, his writing rang true and had a deep popular appeal. He died before the publication of the *Autobiography of William Allen White*, which became a national best-seller and won a Pulitzer Prize.

FURTHER READING

Graham, Otis L. *An Encore for Reform: The Old Progressives and the New Deal*. New York: Oxford University Press, 1967.

Griffith, Sally Foreman. *Home Town News: William Allen White and the Emporia Gazette*. New York: Oxford University Press, 1989.

Jernigan, E. Jay. *William Allen White*. Boston: Twayne, 1983.

Johnson, Walter. *William Allen White's America*. 1947. Reprint, New York: Garland, 1979.

McKee, John DeWitt. *William Allen White: Maverick on Main Street*. Westport, Conn.: Greenwood, 1975.

Olsson, Karen. "The Sweet, Intimate Story of Life." *Civilization* 3, no. 4 (1996): 50-57.

White, William Allen. *The Autobiography of William Allen White*. 1946. Reprint, Lawrence: University of Kansas Press, 1990.

———. *The Editor and His People: Editorials of William Allen White*. Edited by Helen Ogden Mahin. New York: Macmillan, 1924.

———. *Forty Years on Main Street*. Edited by Russell H. Fitzgibbon. New York: Farrar & Rinehart, 1937.

———. *Selected Letters of William Allen White*. Edited by Walter Johnson. 1947. Reprint, Westport, Conn.: Greenwood, 1968.

William Monroe Trotter

DEMANDING EQUAL RIGHTS

A delegation of African-American leaders met at the White House on November 12, 1914, to protest to President Woodrow Wilson about racial segregation in the federal government. Instead of denying the charges, Wilson defended segregation as necessary for racial harmony. To Wilson's astonishment, one of the delegation argued back that black and white federal clerks had worked together agreeably since the Civil War. William Monroe Trotter, editor of the *Guardian* of Boston, had supported Wilson for President, but the anger and humiliation he felt over Wilson's racist policies worked their way into his voice.

"Your manner offends me," Wilson snapped. "In what way?" Trotter demanded. "Your tone, with its background of passion." "Mr. President, you are entirely mistaken," Trotter replied; "you misinterpret my earnestness for passion." After 45 minutes of argument, Wilson pointed the delegation to the door. The editor's encounter with the President made national headlines. A black man had argued with the President and forced him to admit that his administration promoted segregation. Many people condemned Trotter for rudeness, but others cheered him for having the courage of his convictions. No one ever made William Monroe Trotter back down in his beliefs.

All his life, Monroe Trotter (as he was called) sought to live up to the ideals of his father. James Monroe Trotter had been born the son of a slave woman and her white owner in Mississippi. In 1854 James's mother fled with her children to freedom in Cincinnati, Ohio. There he received an education and taught school. During the Civil War, James Trotter enlisted in a Boston regiment in the Union army, rising from private to second lieutenant. He led the fight for equal pay for black and white soldiers. After the war he became a clerk in the Boston post office and married Virginia Isaacs, whom he had met in Ohio. Virginia returned to her parents' home for the birth of her son William Monroe Trotter in 1872.

When Monroe was 10 years old his father quit his post office position in protest against being passed over for promotion. James Trotter then held many different jobs to support his family and also became active in politics. When Republicans abandoned Reconstruction in the South, he joined the Democratic party. The issue was not how whites treated black people, he insisted, but how blacks allowed themselves to be treated. He exhorted African Americans to pull themselves up by work and protest. In 1887 President Grover Cleveland appointed James Trotter Recorder of Deeds in Washington, D.C., a post previously held by the abolitionist journalist Frederick Douglass.

William Monroe Trotter, standing at the far right, joined W. E. B. Du Bois (seated) and other civil rights activists in the Niagara Movement.

William Monroe Trotter

BORN
April 7, 1872
Near Chillicothe, Ohio

DIED
April 7, 1934
Boston, Massachusetts

EDUCATION
A.B., Harvard College (1895)

ACCOMPLISHMENTS
Editor, *Guardian* (Boston, 1901–34)

As a child, Monroe listened to his father's stories about the abolition movement and the Civil War. He grew up determined to please his father by being better at everything than his white playmates and classmates. The only black student in his high school class, Monroe excelled in his studies and won election as class president. He was a freshman at Harvard when his father died, but his high grades earned him scholarships that paid for the rest of his education. Always near the top of his class, he became the first African American at Harvard elected to the Phi Beta Kappa honor society.

Trotter graduated from Harvard in 1895, the same year that Booker T. Washington achieved national fame for a speech in Atlanta in which he called for economic advancement for African Americans rather than social and political equality. As the president of Tuskegee Institute, a black school in Alabama, he also promoted industrial education as the best means of preparing black people to live productive lives. Washington's acceptance of racial segregation and second-class education shocked and offended Trotter. Over the next 20 years he made himself Washington's most outspoken adversary.

Trotter did not set out to crusade for equality. He wanted a career in business and went into real estate, where he prospered. He owned property all over Boston. In 1899 he married Geraldine Pindell, known as Deenie, a delicate but lively woman, and they moved into a previously all-white neighborhood. Two years later Trotter helped organize the Boston Literary and Historical Association, where educated black Bostonians met to discuss issues of the day, and where Trotter delivered stinging attacks on Booker T. Washington's subservience to whites.

Trotter was arrested while demonstrating against the motion picture *The Birth of a Nation* and its racist portrayal of the Civil War and Reconstruction.

From these meetings, Trotter and his friend George Washington Forbes conceived the idea of a new weekly newspaper, the *Guardian*, modeled after Wendell Phillips's great abolitionist newspaper, the *Liberator*. Trotter put up the initial funds, and Forbes served as coeditor, giving the paper its literary style. "With its establishment," Trotter wrote of the *Guardian*, "my decision to enter the [fight] against discrimination because of color took tangible form."

After the first issue appeared on November 9, 1901, the paper gained a circulation of 2,500 within eight months—a respectable number considering the small size of the African-American population of Boston at the time. The *Guardian* leveled a steady stream of attacks at Booker T. Washington, with the aim of unseating him as the nation's preeminent black leader. Trotter accused Washington of indifference toward racial violence, and he called on black people to protest for their rights. In 1903 Washington journeyed to Boston to speak to the National Negro Business League. From the audience Trotter tried to ask a series of pointed questions. Although Trotter denied trying to break up the meeting, a fight broke out and he was arrested for inciting the disturbance. He spent a month in jail.

His arrest caught the attention of the eminent black scholar W. E. B. Du Bois. At first Du Bois thought that Trotter had been needlessly violent, but after talking with him he came to admire Trotter's "unselfishness, pureness of heart and indomitable energy." Du Bois and Trotter became allies in the Niagara Movement, a Northern civil rights organization designed to counter Booker T. Washington's "Tuskegee Machine."

Washington's supporters retaliated by trying to drive the *Guardian* out of business with libel suits. Washington secretly helped fund other black newspapers in Boston as competition to Trotter. When these efforts failed, the plotters turned their attention to the Boston Public Library, where George Forbes was employed and drew his main salary. "Just one word from the Librarian would in my opinion shut Forbes's mouth," wrote Roscoe Conkling Bruce to Washington. "Trotter can't carry on the paper alone—& no conceivable coadjutor could equal Forbes!" Under such pressure, Forbes resigned from the *Guardian* in 1904. His departure robbed the paper of much of its literary style, but it did not deter Trotter.

During the month that he had been jailed, Trotter's wife, Deenie, helped put out the paper. Since the couple had no children, they made the *Guardian* their whole life. Trotter gave up his successful real estate business to devote himself fulltime to the paper, and Deenie worked in the office, keeping the books and editing the society pages. The *Guardian* was a weekly paper that appeared every Friday. In all his years as an editor, Trotter missed only two issues, once when he was out of the country, and once when he was bedridden with illness.

The *Guardian* was not profitable, and over time Trotter had to sell or mortgage all his property to keep publishing. While other small papers depended on political parties for subsidies, Trotter fought both parties and was at heart too independent to bind himself to patronage. His militancy frightened away many commercial advertisers, and his strong principles prevented him from accepting ads for alcohol and tobacco, or for "skin lighteners" and other bogus products aimed at African Americans. Nor was he tough enough on delinquent subscribers and others who owed him money. All that mattered to Trotter was that his paper continue to spread the word for equal rights.

Few people lived up to Trotter's expectations, and he could never see the world from others' perspectives. Trotter called Booker T. Washington a coward who lived his life "far from the field of combat." Yet unlike Trotter, who had grown up in a prosperous family in a northern city and attended the best schools, Washington had risen from slavery an coped with life in the segregated South. Trotter fought just as intensely with allies like W. E. B. Du Bois, who was closely associated with the interracial National Association for the Advancement of Colored People (NAACP). Trotter fell out with the NAACP because of his suspicions of its white leadership. Incapable of following others, Trotter founded his own organizations, such as the National Equal Rights League. But these efforts were hampered by a lack of operating funds. Instead, he promoted his ideas in the pages of the *Guardian* and in his own public protests.

A year after his celebrated confrontation with President Wilson, Trotter made headlines again when he was arrested for demonstrating against the silent picture *The Birth of a Nation*. Trotter denounced the film's racist portrayal of the Civil War and Reconstruction as "history upside down, a complete inversion of the truth." He failed to persuade Boston and other cities to ban the movie, but drew national attention to black protests against it. Meanwhile, the strain of constant work and no vacations wore Trotter down, and in 1916 his health collapsed and he was briefly hospitalized. An even greater blow occurred when Deenie Trotter died at 46 during the influenza epidemic of 1918.

> "As the American Jews and Irish have, and must save their own people in Europe, so must the northern Negro save himself by fighting the battles of the southern Negro."
>
> —from the *Guardian* (May 23, 1903)

Crushed by her death, Trotter for years afterward ran her picture on the *Guardian*'s editorial page and dedicated the paper to her memory "and the Equal Rights cause and work for which she made such noble, and total sacrifice."

He never wavered, but the times changed around him. During the 1920s, politicians of both parties had lost interest in racial justice, and the Ku Klux Klan flourished in its crusade against blacks, immigrants, Catholics, and Jews. Many African Americans abandoned the fight for integration and embraced the separatism of Marcus Garvey's "Back to Africa" movement. Black intellectuals turned from politics to the artistic and literary flourishing of the Harlem Renaissance. In the Jazz Age, Trotter's editorials against segregation seemed as out of fashion as his rumpled old suits.

After his wife's death, Trotter found it harder to publish his paper. Readers noted that his editorials seemed sloppily written and lacking their former punch. Writing in H. L. Mencken's magazine, *American Mercury*, in 1926, the black journalist Eugene Gordon dismissed the *Guardian* as "one of the most poorly-written Negro sheets in America," and declared that Trotter would "never be a newspaper man." But to keep his paper alive, Trotter had to devote more time to raising money than he did editing and writing. The search for funds became even more desperate during the Great Depression. Financial burdens caused him to lose sleep and become increasingly agitated and distraught. On the morning of his 62nd birthday, Monroe Trotter either fell or jumped to his death from the roof of his apartment house. His sister continued publishing the *Guardian* until her own death in 1957. By then a new civil rights movement had begun, and a new generation of black leaders recalled the militant spirit of the *Guardian* and its editor's willingness to resort to civil disobedience in the struggle for equal rights.

FURTHER READING

Fox, Stephen R. *The Guardian of Boston: William Monroe Trotter*. New York: Atheneum, 1970.

Harlan, Louis R. *Booker T. Washington: The Wizard of Tuskegee, 1901–1915*. New York: Oxford University Press, 1983.

Meier, August. *Negro Thought in America, 1880–1915: Racial Ideologies in the Age of Booker T. Washington*. Ann Arbor: University of Michigan Press, 1968.

Senna, Carl. *The Black Press and the Struggle for Civil Rights*. New York: Franklin Watts, 1993.

Wolseley, Roland E. *The Black Press, U.S.A.* Ames: Iowa State University Press, 1980.

H. L. Mencken

THE CAUSTIC CRITIC

P ublic school teacher John T. Scopes was arrested in Dayton, Tennessee, in 1925 for teaching the theory of evolution. Tennessee had made it a crime to teach anything other than the biblical account of human creation. Scopes's case caught the attention of newspaper columnist H. L. Mencken, who held nothing sacred. He despised the efforts by any group, whether ministers, reformers, or politicians, to force their way of thinking upon society. The *Baltimore Evening Sun* posted bail for Scopes and sent Mencken to Dayton to cover his trial. His colorful, cynical, and savagely critical columns described the hoopla surrounding the trial. "The rabble is in the saddle," he wrote, also coining the term "Bible Belt" to describe the band of fundamentalist religions that ran across the South. He especially aimed his fire at the prosecuting attorney, three-time Presidential candidate William Jennings Bryan, whom he dismissed as a bitter and bigoted old fraud. The widely

A critic of society, H. L. Mencken hoped to shock and stimulate his readers into thinking critically about issues and events.

reprinted columns shredded what was left of Bryan's reputation and established Mencken as the most famous newspaper writer of the Roaring Twenties. A man of many prejudices, H. L. Mencken was at heart a critic—of literature, music, politics, religion, and society. What inspired him as a journalist, he wrote in 1925, was his "endless interest in the stupendous farce of human existence."

Henry Louis Mencken was born into a German-American family in Baltimore, Maryland. "My grandfather made a mistake when he came to America," he once wrote of his German heritage, "and I have always lived in the wrong country." His father ran a cigar factory, enabling the Mencken family to enjoy a comfortable existence. Henry went to Baltimore Polytechnic Institute, where he was valedictorian of the class of 1896. When he graduated, he wanted to become a newspaper reporter, but his father insisted that he either go to college or work at the family cigar factory. Mencken chose the factory. When his father suffered a stroke on New Year's Eve in 1899, and died a few weeks later, Mencken felt free to follow his own desires. "I chose newspaper work without any hesitation," he later wrote, and he never had any regrets.

Rejected for a job with the Baltimore Morning Herald, the 18-year-old Mencken hung around the city room every day until the editor assigned him a story. He became the youngest reporter on the paper. Looking back on those days at the turn of the century, he later wrote: "I believe that a young journalist, turned loose in a large city, had more fun than any other man." A reporter "felt himself a part of important events, with no strings tied to him," Mencken explained. "Through his eyes thousands of people would see what was happening in this most surprising and fascinating of worlds." As a reporter, he

covered crime stories in some of the toughest neighborhoods and followed politics at City Hall.

His success won him promotion to city editor when he was just 23. A year later he was managing editor of the Herald. In 1904 a fire destroyed most of downtown Baltimore, including the Herald's headquarters. Mencken worked 72 hours straight directing coverage of the story. After that draining experience, he began to lose interest in the pressures of daily newspaper reporting and turned to commentary and criticism.

As an editor of an afternoon paper, Mencken would arrive at his desk by 8:00 A.M. and write two editorials before noon. He also read all the letters to the editor, choosing and editing those to be published. After lunch he would write a long signed article to be printed next to the editorials. "When I undertook this job it seemed easy enough, for I was bustling with ideas in those days and eager to work them off," Mencken wrote. "But in a little while I found that writing 2,000 or 3,000 words a day was really a killing chore." After the Herald closed down, Mencken switched to the Baltimore Evening Sun—a livelier and less reverent operation than its sister paper, the haughty Baltimore Morning Sun. By 1910 he was publishing a regular column, "The Free Lance," in which he took on everyone and everything with relish, hoping to shock and stimulate his readers into thinking. He never cared if people agreed with him. "I write because I like it," he insisted, "not because I want to convert anyone."

When World War I started in Europe, Mencken went abroad to cover events from Germany. His pro-German sympathies led the Sun to censor some of his dispatches in 1917. He quit in protest and went to work for the more supportive New York Evening Mail—until its editor was

H. L. Mencken

BORN
September 12, 1880
Baltimore, Maryland

DIED
January 29, 1956
Baltimore, Maryland

EDUCATION
Graduated from Baltimore Polytechnic Institute (1896)

ACCOMPLISHMENTS
Reporter, Baltimore Morning Herald (1899–1901); drama critic, Baltimore Morning Herald (1901–3); city editor, Baltimore Morning Herald (1903–4); city editor, Baltimore Evening Herald (1904–5); managing editor, Baltimore Herald (1905–6); news editor, Baltimore Evening News (1906); writer, Baltimore Sunday Sun (1906–10); book review editor, The Smart Set (1908–14); columnist, "The Free Lance," Baltimore Evening Sun (1911–15); coeditor, The Smart Set (1914–23); columnist, New York Evening Mail (1917–18); columnist, "Monday Articles," Baltimore Evening Sun (1920–38); columnist, Chicago Tribune (1924–28); editor, American Mercury (1924–33); columnist, New York American (1934–36); editor, Baltimore Evening Sun (1938); correspondent, Baltimore Evening Sun (1948); author of The American Language: A Preliminary Inquiry into the Development of English in the United States (1919–1948), The Days of H. L. Mencken: Happy Days, Newspaper Days, Heathen Days (1947), and Prejudices (1919–27)

Mencken ridiculed politicians and considered political conventions mostly shams, but he had great fun covering them from 1904 to 1948.

especially offended his sensibilities and stimulated the best of his writings. Americans in the Roaring Twenties were torn between a fascination for modern fads and a longing to return to old-time values. Mencken mocked both impulses. In 1923 the New York publisher Alfred A. Knopf invited Mencken and theater critic George Jean Nathan to coedit a new journal. The first issue of the *American Mercury* appeared in January 1924, and within three years its circulation had reached a peak of 77,000 subscribers.

Aimed at the "civilized minority" of intellectuals, the magazine blended commentary on politics, the arts, and sciences. It published such writers as Theodore Dreiser, James Weldon Johnson, and Sinclair Lewis. But the magazine was most famous for Mencken's own fiercely debunking style, which appealed to a generation made cynical by the war and the failure of the reform movements.

"This country is the home of freak economic schemes," Mencken grumbled, "as it is the happy hunting ground of the most blatant and absurd sort of charlatans in politics." Among his chief targets was the Ku Klux Klan, which he described as "a device for organizing inferiorities under a mystical superiority." He also accused the general public of being too easily misled by political hucksters: "The great majority of folk are far too stupid to see through a politician's tinsel." He warned women that winning the right to vote would only put them into economic competition with men "in a harsh and abdominal world." He condemned Prohibition as the worst excess of puritanism in America. He belittled the South as a Sahara Desert devoid of literature and art. He ridiculed the platitudes of Republican President Warren Harding, and accused the

arrested for being pro-German. Given the patriotic political climate, Mencken turned to writing books and to editing *The Smart Set,* a literary magazine. He became an influential critic of art, music, and literature. When the war ended, the *Baltimore Evening Sun* welcomed him back as a columnist, and he continued to juggle his newspaper column and magazine editing for a decade.

A German American who enjoyed his beer and Beethoven, Mencken loved liberty and hated anything puritanical. The excesses of the 1920s

Democrats of being "scarcely a party at all, but simply a loose federation of discordant minorities, chiefly devoted to civil war."

Mencken did not spare his own profession. In 1920 he charged that the average newspaper had "the intelligence of a Baptist evangelist, the courage of a rat, the fairness of a Prohibition boob-bumper, the information of a high-school janitor, the taste of a designer of celluloid valentines, and the honor of a police-station lawyer." In an essay on "Journalism in America" in 1927, he insisted that the majority of newspaper reporters "are still ignoramuses and proud of it. All the knowledge that they pack into their brains is, in every reasonable cultural sense, useless." His caustic commentary caused fellow columnist Walter Lippmann to call him "this Holy Terror from Baltimore."

Although Mencken conducted most of his editorial work in Manhattan, the nation's publishing capital, he kept his home in Baltimore. The minute the workweek was over, he hopped the train heading south. "Behind lies a place fit only for the gross business of getting money," he wrote; "ahead is a place made for enjoying it." Baltimore meant going home to the familiar. He lived in his family's row house on Hollins Street for almost all his life, except during his brief marriage. In 1930 the seemingly confirmed bachelor Mencken married Sara Haardt, a writer and English instructor at Goucher College. When Sara died in 1935, Mencken moved back with his brother in their old family home. He later confessed, "I still think of Sara every day of my life and almost every hour of the day."

The dissenting attitude that had attracted readers to Mencken during the boom years of the 1920s offended them during the awful depression of the 1930s. Although Mencken supported Franklin D. Roosevelt's campaign for the Presidency in 1932, he felt deeply suspicious of the big government programs of the New Deal—at a time when people were turning to the government for help. His irate style of criticism no longer seemed funny or productive. The circulation of the *American Mercury* declined, and in 1934 Mencken gave up the editorship. His pro-German sympathies also worked against him once again. Although he considered Adolf Hitler an "idiot," Mencken's enduring ties with all things German led some people to think that he supported the Nazis. His commentary grew so out of step with both public opinion and the *Baltimore Sun*'s editorial line that in 1938 he quit writing his weekly column. During World War II, he stopped writing for newspapers entirely. "I could not write five lines without getting beyond the bounds of the permitted," he explained.

Though retired from journalism, Mencken devoted himself to an exhaustive study of *The American Language*. He also wrote a three-volume autobiography that concentrated on the happier days of his youth and his early adventures in journalism. The well-received autobiography helped revive his national reputation. He found that what he most missed was the fun of covering the national political conventions and elections, which he had started doing back in 1904. As the election of 1948 approached, he agreed to cover the three major conventions (Republican, Democratic, and Progressive), saying: "Either they'll restore me, or they will kill me." Mencken considered political conventions great shams, but he sat through all the speeches and demonstrations

"Dayton, Tenn., July 14.—The real animus of the prosecution centers in Bryan. He is the plaintiff and prosecutor. The local lawyers are simply bottle-holders for him. He will win the case, not by academic appeals to law and precedent, but by direct and powerful appeals to the immemorial fears and superstitions of man. It is no wonder that he is hot against Scopes. Five years of Scopes and even these mountaineers would begin to laugh at Bryan. Ten years and they would ride him out of town on a rail, with one Baptist parson in front of him and another behind."

—from the *Baltimore Evening Sun* (July 14, 1925)

and worked late into the nights banging out stories on his manual typewriter. Fellow reporters watched him laughing and slapping his thigh over things he had just written. The strain, however, proved too much, and on November 23, 1948, he suffered a massive stroke. Cruelly, for the remaining eight years of his life he could no longer read or write. He died at his home on Hollins Street in 1956.

Years after his death, H. L. Mencken's reputation suffered another decline when his diaries were opened in 1981. They were filled with racial and ethnic slurs and stereotypes that reflected the prejudices of his era. Yet the bulk of Mencken's writing showed him to be a complex man who attacked everyone regardless of their race or religion. As in his writings about the Scopes trial, he often took courageous stands to defend the underdog. In the 1930s, for instance, he denounced racial lynchings on Maryland's Eastern Shore, and supported the admission of a black student to the University of Maryland law school, both unpopular stands for that time. Always a prolific writer (he guessed that he had written 5 million words

during his career), Mencken wrote what he thought, no matter who it offended. "My belief," he insisted, "is that a newspaper should tell the truth, however unpleasant."

FURTHER READING

Bode, Carl. *Mencken*. Carbondale: Southern Illinois University Press, 1969.

Fecher, Charles A. *Mencken: A Study of His Thought*. New York: Knopf, 1978.

Hobson, Fred. *Mencken: A Life*. New York: Random House, 1994.

Lippman, Theo, Jr., ed. *A Gang of Pecksniffs and Other Comments on Newspaper Publishers, Editors and Reporters by H. L. Mencken*. New Rochelle, N.Y.: Arlington House, 1975.

Manchester, William. *Disturber of the Peace: The Life of H. L. Mencken*. Amherst: University of Massachusetts Press, 1986.

Mencken, H. L. *The Diary of H. L. Mencken*. Edited by Charles A. Fecher. New York: Knopf, 1989.

————. *Happy Days, 1880–1892*. Baltimore, Md.: Johns Hopkins University Press, 1996.

————. *The Impossible H. L. Mencken: A Selection of His Best Newspaper Stories*. Edited by Marion Elizabeth Rodgers. New York: Doubleday, 1991

————. *My Life as Author and Editor*. Edited by Jonathan Yardley. New York: Knopf, 1993.

————. *Prejudices: A Selection*. Baltimore, Md.: Johns Hopkins University Press, 1996.

————. *Thirty-five Years of Newspaper Work*. Edited by Fred Hobson, Vincent Fitzpatrick, and Bradford Jacobs. Baltimore, Md.: Johns Hopkins University Press, 1994.

Williams, Harold A. *The Baltimore Sun, 1837–1987*. Baltimore, Md.: Johns Hopkins University Press, 1987.

Claude Barnett

SERVING THE BLACK PRESS

T he news business, like much of American society, was long segregated by race. Racial prejudice kept the white newspapers from hiring black reporters. Thinking back over the *New York Times*'s staff in the 1950s, it later dawned on reporter Harrison Salisbury that there were no blacks on the professional staff. "The whiteness of the *Times* was glaring," he wrote, "but I did not notice it." Blinded by this glaring whiteness, the mainstream press either ignored the African-American community or limited its coverage to crime stories. Black readers turned to the black press, which provided news about issues that the mainstream press ignored. "All civil rights," a reader once complained to a reporter for a black newspaper, "I can't even get the weather from your paper." Black reporters made civil rights their beat, and aimed their stories at publicizing the movement for racial justice and equality.

Although many black newspapers operated across the country, they were nearly all weekly papers. These papers

Claude Barnett founded the Associated Negro Press in order to supply the many small African-American newspapers with news and features.

"I believe we will build an organization so effective that it will help to transform the most potent influence in Negro life—the Negro newspaper—into an effective instrument for guiding and directing the thinking of Negroes today into channels that will not only be desirable from a national point of view, but of the greatest benefit to them individually."

—from a 1935 letter

rarely could afford to purchase news from the Associated Press and United Press International. Nor did those major wire services carry much news specifically about African Americans. As early as the 1870s, black newspapers sought to form their own press service, but none of these first efforts succeeded. Then, in 1919, Claude Barnett founded the Associated Negro Press (ANP).

Born in Florida, Claude Barnett spent most of his life in Chicago, Illinois. His father, William Barnett, worked in various hotels, traveling to different regions in different seasons, wherever the jobs were. While he moved about, his wife, Celena Anderson Barnett, made a home for their family in Chicago. William Barnett died when Claude was still a small child. To help his mother, he took a job as a houseboy in the home of Richard Warren Sears, one of the founder of Sears, Roebuck and Company. His principal job was serving breakfast to the business executive. "I admired him tremendously," Barnett later recalled, "and he not only talked quite intimately with me but used to give me tickets to the theater and concerts." His service with Sears left him deeply impressed with the possibilities of a business career.

These attitudes found reinforcement when Barnett attended Tuskegee Institute in Alabama. Founded and run by Booker T. Washington, Tuskegee emphasized economic advancement through self-discipline and cooperation between African Americans. "I virtually sat at the feet of Booker T. Washington and drank in the magic of his strength, his vision, his matchless wisdom," Barnett testified. He especially enjoyed Washington's Sunday night talks to the students in the Tuskegee chapel. As a student, Barnett worked as Washington's office assistant, and gained special notice from the school's president. Throughout his life, he sought to carry out Washington's teachings, and he served as a trustee of Tuskegee.

Although he dreamed of becoming an engineer, Barnett became convinced that an African American did not stand a chance in that field. Instead, Barnett took a post office job in Chicago. Postal work exposed him to journalism through the thousands of newspapers, magazines, and circulars going through the mail. Outside of his postal job, he began to sell advertising space for African-American publications. His principal clients were the *Chicago Defender*, one of the largest and most successful black newspapers, and *The Crisis*, a magazine published by the National Association for the Advancement of Colored People (NAACP). Always an entrepreneur, Barnett also set up a small mail order business selling portraits of famous African Americans, and founded a company that produced cosmetics specifically designed for African-American women.

While selling advertising space for newspaper publishers, Barnett discovered that many small black newspapers were starved for news and features to print. He decided to form a black news service, and took his idea to Robert Abbott, publisher of the *Chicago Defender*. Seeking Abbott's financial support, Barnett pointed out that many small black newspapers already clipped and reprinted news from the *Defender* without paying for it. But Abbott rejected the idea. Since the *Defender* published editions in other cities outside of Chicago, Abbott did not want to assist his competitors.

Undaunted, Barnett used the profits from his cosmetics company to start the Associated Negro Press on March 21, 1919. He later claimed that "Negro publishers virtually stood in line to become ANP members." More than 100 black newspapers subscribed to its services. The ANP focused exclusively on news about African Americans. Twice a week, on Friday and Monday, it mailed mimeographed news sheets. This fit the publication schedule of its papers, which initially were all weekly papers that went to press on Wednesday or Thursday. Barnett also encouraged his member papers to swap news among themselves, but because they were competing for the same readers and advertisers, the papers never embraced his reciprocal news sharing.

Wherever possible, the ANP emphasized positive news about black community, promoting self-esteem and social uplift. It tried to avoid sensationalism, although it recognized that readers often wanted news of sensational crimes. In the 1920s Barnett defined his criteria for news: "Accuracy is the first requisite ANP imposes on its staff. A constructive viewpoint is next. Human interest, racial interest, and importance to readers scattered over a wide area are other criteria. Sensationalism and scandal, unless unusual, or weighted with exceptional interest, are avoided." Because of the limited financial resources of its member papers, the ANP kept its rates low. As a result, it could not afford to hire many reporters and correspondents. Much of its news came from other sources, particularly from the *Chicago Defender*. "He's stealing my news and selling it to other papers for a profit,"

fumed Robert Abbott. There was truth in the charge: the financially strapped ANP was often little more than a "clipping service," for the same financial reasons that the *Defender* sometimes rewrote its own news from the mainstream *Chicago Tribune*.

Untrained in journalism, Barnett recognized that he was "feeling my way and shouldering this hit and miss operation alone," as he later recalled in his unfinished autobiography. He organized volunteer reporters around the country to send him news stories from their locations. Since he could often afford to pay them little more than postage, they wrote for the experience, the bylines, and the ANP press cards that got them into many events to be covered. Reporter Enoch Waters got his start in journalism while he was a student at the Hampton Institute. He sent stories about college sports to the ANP because he knew that through the news service his byline would reach many newspapers. Waters recalled that "Barnett used to write me letters from time to time congratulating me on my work . . . . That was his way of paying me." Barnett was able to pay some reporters modest amounts, which helped supplement the incomes they received from their own papers. For instance, Roy Wilkins, a reporter for the *Kansas City Call* (and later executive director of the NAACP), was an ANP correspondent.

Far-flung correspondents provided ANP with church news, local politics, women's issues, sports, and commentaries on many events pertinent to the African-American community. Langston Hughes and civil rights activist Mary Church Terrell, among many others, submitted feature pieces to the news service. In 1928 the ANP got an exclusive interview with Oscar De Priest, the first African American elected to Congress since the beginning of the century. The Great Depression of the 1930s, the election

Claude Barnett

BORN

September 16, 1890
Sanford, Florida

DIED

August 2, 1967
Chicago, Illinois

EDUCATION

Certificate, Tuskegee Institute, Alabama (1906)

ACCOMPLISHMENTS

Sold advertising space for the *Chicago Defender* and *The Crisis* magazine (1913–19); founder and director, Associated Negro Press (1919–64)

THE·BLACK·CABINET
In The
NEW DEAL

The Inside of the Outer Circle
By
EUGENE DAVIDSON
An Associated Negro Press Feature

The economic recovery programs of the New Deal made African Americans eager for Washington news. The ANP particularly reported on the activities of the highest ranking African-American federal officeholders, who were known as the Black Cabinet.

of Franklin D. Roosevelt as President, and the many New Deal programs to help the unemployed stimulated great interest among African Americans and demonstrated the need to station an ANP correspondent in the nation's capital.

With the help of a grant from the Julius Rosenwald Fund, Barnett opened a Washington bureau in 1939, to report on Washington events "as they relate to the status of Negroes in various programs of relief and recovery." But when the ANP's first Washington correspondent, Alvin White, applied for admittance to the congressional press galleries and Presidential press conferences, he found the doors firmly shut. To get a press pass, a reporter had to work for a daily newspaper. The ANP's clients were all weekly papers, except for the *Atlanta Daily World*,

which in 1932 became the nation's first and only black daily. But the *Atlanta Daily World* was unwilling to give up its advantage of being the sole daily black paper and would not acknowledge White as its correspondent.

World War II renewed Barnett's efforts to get news from Washington, but in 1942 the ANP faced unexpected competition from the newly created National Negro Publishers Association (NNPA). The publishers represented by the NNPA wanted to gain control of their own sources of news rather than remain dependent on Barnett's ANP. Barnett's style was too low-keyed and conservative for many of the younger, more activist publishers. By dividing the market, however, they prevented either news service from building a strong financial base.

Because salaries remained low, each of the men who served as Washington correspondent resigned. In 1947 Barnett reluctantly gave the job to a woman reporter, Alice Dunnigan. She applied for a press pass just as Congress was ordering that its press galleries be integrated. Although the NNPA correspondent received accreditation, Dunnigan was rejected. She then learned that Barnett had never bothered to submit an endorsement of her application. "For years we have been trying to get a man accredited to the Capitol Galleries and have not succeeded," Barnett replied. "What makes you think that you—a woman—can accomplish this feat?" To Barnett's astonishment, Alice Dunnigan won accreditation in July 1947. Then she took her congressional press pass to the White House and State Department, making her the first black reporter to hold all three coveted press passes.

During the 1950s, as the civil rights movement became a leading national story, Alice Dunnigan attended Presidential press conferences and covered news on Capitol Hill for the ANP. Civil rights organizations also sent their press releases to the ANP, as a way of reaching a wide audience of black readers. However, the white mainstream press had also begun covering the civil rights movement—and had started recruiting black journalists. As more black readers turned to the white press for national news, the black press responded by shifting its primary attention to local coverage.

The Associated Negro Press continued to provide much national news but also explored new avenues. In the 1950s Claude Barnett and his wife, Etta Moton Barnett, became increasingly concerned about the nations of Africa, which were emerging from colonial rule to independence. The Barnetts visited Africa several times and established correspondents to provide the ANP with regular sources of African news. By 1960 some 75 newspapers in Africa subscribed to the ANP, receiving their copy in either English or French.

Despite such innovations, the ANP faced mounting financial hardship. Among its members, many of the smaller papers could not pay their bills. The larger, more prosperous papers turned to the Associated Press or United Press International, which were supplying more news of specific interest to African-American readers. Integration caused the black press to lose its monopoly on news from the black community. The ANP lost business steadily until Claude Barnett offered his news service to the National Negro Publishers Association. The publishers rejected his proposal, and the Associated Negro Press went out of business in 1964, the same year that civil rights legislation outlawed segregation in the United States.

FURTHER READING

Brooks, Maxwell R. *The Negro Press Re-Examined*. Boston: Christopher Publishing House, 1959.

Dunnigan, Alice. *A Black Woman's Experience from Schoolhouse to White House*. Philadelphia: Dorrance Press, 1974.

Hogan, Lawrence D. *A Black National News Service: The Associated Press and Claude Barnett, 1919–1945*. Rutherford, N.J.: Farleigh Dickinson University Press, 1984.

Waters, Enoch P. *American Diary: A Personal History of the Black Press*. Chicago: Path Press, 1987.

Wolsely, Roland E. *The Black Press, U.S.A.* Ames: Iowa State University Press, 1980.

Dorothy Thompson

FIRST LADY OF AMERICAN JOURNALISM

In the 1942 movie *Woman of the Year*, Katharine Hepburn played an assertive woman columnist who moved within the most powerful circles, lectured to admiring audiences, and molded public opinion to her own views. Audiences instantly recognized her character as based on the life of Dorothy Thompson. During the late 1930s, Thompson's widely syndicated column, "On the Record," her monthly column in the *Ladies' Home Journal*, and her weekly radio broadcasts to the nation made her both America's most prolific woman writer and its most written-*about* writer. Called the "First Lady of American Journalism," she was judged second in prestige and influence only to First Lady Eleanor Roosevelt (who also wrote a newspaper column, "My Day"). Thompson traveled extensively, meeting presidents, prime ministers, and dictators, and reporting her findings, as well as her strong feelings on politics and international affairs. Her columns provided Americans with authoritative explanations about why the world seemed sliding toward a second world war, and advice on what to do about it.

Dorothy Thompson's weekly radio broadcasts gave her a nationwide audience for her opinionated and dramatically worded views on international affairs.

Nothing in Dorothy Thompson's childhood suggested that she would live such an unconventional life. She was born in the industrial town of Lancaster, in upstate New York, where her father, Peter Thompson, was a Methodist minister. The oldest of three children, Dorothy was a high-spirited tomboy. When she was eight, her mother, Margaret Grierson Thompson, suddenly became ill and died. For two years an aunt kept house and raised the children, until Dorothy's father married his church's stern, straightlaced organist, Eliza Abbott. When the rebellious young girl could not get along with her stepmother, Dorothy was sent to live with her aunts in Chicago. She enrolled in the Lewis Institute, a two-year junior college, where she captained the basketball team and developed her writing skills. She did well enough to continue her education at Syracuse University. During her student years, she became swept up in the woman suffrage movement and after graduation devoted herself to the successful campaign to win the right to vote for women in New York State.

Dorothy Thompson and her good friend Barbara De Porte, two thoroughly modern young women, moved to New York City in search of greater opportunities. A friend got Barbara a job on the *New York Evening Post*. Dorothy also aspired to journalism but lacked the connections to get a newspaper position. She worked instead as a publicist for a social-reform group while writing freelance articles for New York papers and magazines. Seeking greater adventures, the two women set sail for Europe in 1920. Traveling on the same ship were American delegates to a Zionist conference in London, dedicated to establishing a Jewish homeland in Palestine. Having made contacts with the delegates, Dorothy persuaded the International News Service (INS) to let her cover their

conference. The INS also published her interview with Irish independence leader Terence MacSwiney, before his death from a hunger strike against the British, and her reporting on an auto workers' strike in Rome.

For regular employment, Thompson worked for the Red Cross in France as a "manufacturer of publicity," tried writing a novel, and sent freelance articles to American papers. Still frustrated by her inability to find regular work on a newspaper, she consulted Paul Scott Mowrer, head of the Paris bureau of the *Chicago Daily News*. Mowrer suggested that she might have better luck breaking into journalism in Austria. Thompson persuaded the *Philadelphia Public Ledger* to make her an unsalaried correspondent in Vienna, and she headed there in 1921.

After learning German, Thompson fit well into the social and artistic scene of postwar Vienna. Since she had never worked in a newspaper office, she wrote more freely and less formally than other correspondents. She vividly described the sites she visited and the people and events she saw for readers back in America. In Vienna she became friends with Marcel Fodor, correspondent for a British paper, the *Manchester Guardian*. Fodor took her under his wing, covering stories with her and giving her exclusives for the *Ledger*. In one escapade, she disguised herself as a Red Cross worker to interview the deposed Austro-Hungarian king while he was plotting to restore the monarchy. The editors of the *Ledger* liked her work, put her on salary, and assigned her to cover Austria and Eastern Europe. The *Ledger*'s instructions were simple: "Get the news accurately. If possible get it first. Don't let your likes and dislikes color the facts, and remember the laws of libel and slander."

While in Vienna, Dorothy Thompson met Joseph Bard, a handsome Hungarian Jewish writer, whom

Dorothy Thompson

BORN
July 9, 1893
Lancaster, New York

DIED
January 30, 1961
Lisbon, Portugal

EDUCATION
B.A., Syracuse University (1914)

ACCOMPLISHMENTS
Foreign correspondent, *Philadelphia Public Ledger* (1921–28); Berlin bureau chief, *New York Evening Post* and *Philadelphia Public Ledger* (1925–28); syndicated columnist (1936–58); radio news commentator (1937–50s); author of *The New Russia*(1928), *I Saw Hitler!* (1932), *Refugees: Anarchy or Organization?* (1938), *Dorothy Thompson's Political Guide* (1938), *Once on Christmas* (1939), *Let the Record Speak* (1939), *Listen, Hans!* (1942), and *The Courage to Be Happy* (1957)

she fell in love with and married in 1922. She worried that her newspaper would fire her because she married, but she got a raise instead. In Vienna the newlywed couple hosted a circle of lively journalists, writers, and artists. Dorothy was a witty conversationalist who dominated group discussions. But she always put her work first. In 1925 the *Ledger* sent Thompson to head its office in Berlin, a breakthrough for a woman journalist. The assignment, however, led to a breakup in her marriage when Joseph fell in love with another woman and secured a divorce.

In 1927 the famous American novelist Sinclair Lewis fell in love with Dorothy Thompson. Lewis, the author of such popular books as *Main Street* (1920), *Babbitt* (1922), and *Elmer Gantry* (1927), was taken by her direct and unpretentious style, and proposed to her soon after they met. He pursued her across Europe to Moscow, repeating his proposals until she accepted. They married in London and honeymooned in the English countryside, while Dorothy worked on her first book, *The New Russia*. Theirs was a sophisticated and stormy marriage. A brilliant writer, "Red" Lewis won the Nobel Prize in literature in 1930, the first American author so honored. But he was also a heavy drinker with a bad temper, who could be verbally abusive and emotionally withdrawn. Dorothy and Red returned to the United States and bought a Vermont farmhouse, "Twin Farms," and an elegant apartment in Manhattan, where they entertained guests from around the world. At 36 she became a mother, but her son, Michael, grew up raised by nannies, since both his parents traveled so often.

Having given up foreign correspondence, Thompson devoted her attention to magazine articles. In November 1930 *Cosmopolitan* sent her to Germany to interview the Nazi leader Adolf Hitler, who was on the rise. Convinced that she was meeting the future dictator of Germany, she was struck almost immediately by "the startling insignificance of this man who has set the whole world agog." She dismissed him as "voluble, ill-posed, insecure," and "the very prototype of the Little Man." But her instinct in this instance turned out to be very wrong. Later, in 1934, she returned to Germany after Hitler had seized power. Ten days into her visit, German secret police ordered her to leave the country because of her critical writing about Hitler and her condemnation of his anti-Semitic ranting. Other foreign correspondents gathered at the train station to present her with roses and bid her farewell. Her expulsion from Germany made her a world-famous celebrity. Back home, a somewhat jealous Sinclair Lewis told reporters, "Dorothy has covered seven revolutions, so she ought to be able to take care of herself. She's no poor, weak, little woman who needs my help."

The front-page stories about her German experiences brought a flood of speaking invitations. One of those invitations came from a conference, run by Helen Reid, wife of the *New York Herald Tribune*'s publisher. Helen Reid offered her a regular column in the paper, pointing out that the job would pay better than her freelance writing. Thompson liked the idea, thinking that she could stay home and raise her son while she wrote her column. Just the opposite was true. The column kept her on the road, visiting foreign capitals and conducting speaking tours. Her absences also placed further strains on her marriage.

The *Herald Tribune* was a Republican newspaper that represented the eastern, moderate, international wing of the Republican party. Her column, "On the Record," appeared in the paper and its syndicate three times a week, alternating with a column by Walter Lippmann. In contrast to the austere and reserved Lippmann, Thompson wrote with flair and fury. For the most part she avoided women's issues and wrote about politics and diplomacy, so her column attracted men as well as women readers. In its first year it was carried by 130 newspapers nationwide. Written in short sentences and paragraphs punctuated by exclamation points, her columns never dodged an issue, no matter how controversial. They almost seized readers by the shoulders and shook them. Critics compared her writing style to "someone bellowing in your ear." If some complained that her columns were often strident and emotional, these qualities in fact appealed to the majority of her readers.

Dorothy Thompson's enormous success as a columnist proved too much for Sinclair Lewis, whose own career had stagnated. He resented becoming "a tail to an ascending comet." They separated in the fall of 1937 and divorced in 1942. The following year she proposed to Maxim Kopf, an Austrian-born painter and sculptor. They enjoyed a happy marriage until his death 15 years later.

With strong opinions and an imposing personal presence, Thompson developed a knack for dramatizing herself. More important, she dramatized world events that otherwise seemed remote to Americans. She wrote compellingly of the plight of European refugees and of the need for the United States to make immigration laws less strict. She denounced the popular American pilot Charles Lindbergh for his seemingly pro-Nazi leanings. In 1939 she attended a rally of the German-American Bund (American supporters of the Nazi regime) at Madison Square Garden in New York, and laughed out loud during the anti-Semitic speeches. As the audience yelled "Throw her out," she left with a police escort and made newspaper headlines for the incident.

In 1940 the *Herald Tribune* championed the internationalist Wendell Willkie for the Republican nomination for President. At first Dorothy's columns praised Willkie, but after he won the nomination she changed her mind. When she concluded that the Nazis wanted President Franklin Roosevelt out of the White House, she switched to support him, despite her past criticism of Roosevelt's New Deal. "I shall support the President because I think he has assets on his side that nobody can match," she declared. "The President knows the world." *Herald Tribune* readers were stunned by her defection, and the paper dropped one of her columns endorsing Roosevelt.

Not only did Thompson endorse Roosevelt in her columns, but she also spoke for him at political rallies and over the radio. She publicly debated the pro-Willkie writer Clare Boothe Luce. After Roosevelt won an unprecedented third term, Thompson felt "an unbridgeable hostility" toward her at the Republican-leaning *Herald Tribune*. By mutual consent she left the paper. Her column was then distributed by the Bell Syndicate and her readership increased to 8.5 million people. She kept visible in the critical New York market when her column appeared in the *New York Post*. But readers of the *Post* tended to be liberal Democrats who already agreed with her internationalist views, a factor that took some of the urgency from her writing.

Thompson made her greatest contributions to the national consciousness during the years prior to

Thompson traveled widely as a columnist for the *New York Herald Tribune*. Here she meets with members of the Czechoslovakian Brigade in 1941.

I feel as though I know that boy, for in the past five years I have met so many whose story is the same—the same except for this unique desperate act. Herschel Grynzspan was one of the hundreds of thousands of refugees whom the terror east of the Rhine has turned loose in the world. . . . Every Jew in Germany was held responsible for the boy's deed. In every city an organized and methodical mob was turned loose on the Jewish population. . . . But in Paris, a boy who had hoped to make some gesture of protest which would call attention to the wrongs done his race burst into hysterical sobs . . . he realized that half a million of his fellows had been sentenced to execution on the excuse of his deed. . . . Who is on trial in this case? I say we are all on trial. I say the Christian world is on trial. If any Jews, anywhere in the world protest at anything that is happening, further oppressive measures will be taken. . . . Therefore, we who are not Jews must speak, speak our sorrow and indignation and disgust in so many voices that they will be heard.

—from a radio broadcast on the "General Electric Hour" (November 17, 1938), referring to Herschel Grynzspan, a 17-year-old Jew whose shooting of a German diplomat set off mob violence against Jews in Germany

American entry into World War II. In recognition of her strong support for the Allies against the Nazis, British prime minister Winston Churchill wrote that "Miss Dorothy Thompson has won a famous name. She has shown what one valiant woman can do with the power of the pen. Freedom and humanity are grateful debtors." Once the United States entered the war, however, her message got lost in the general war effort. Although still considered to be one of the best-informed Americans on foreign affairs, she had a less certain grasp on the postwar world. Although Cold War conditions were indeed complex, the editor of one of her papers complained in the late 1940s, "We expect our writers to be a little more sure of themselves than our readers."

In 1945 Thompson visited Palestine and was warmly welcomed by the Zionists, whom she had long supported. But after interviewing Arab leaders, her sympathies shifted to the plight of the Palestinians. This unexpected switch alienated many Jewish readers of the New York Post, causing the paper to drop her column in 1947. This shut off her chief New York outlet. Although her writing became increasingly anti-Zionist, Thompson insisted that there was nothing anti-Semitic about her views. She decried the liberal Post's "intolerance of an opposing or differing view." She took an active role in the American Friends of the Middle East, but left that pro-Arab organization in 1957 after the Bell Syndicate threatened to drop her column.

By the 1950s Dorothy Thompson's fame and influence had declined markedly, although she continued to travel widely and lecture. When her husband, Maxim Kopf, died in 1958, she suspended her column and then retired entirely. She felt exhausted after writing her column three times a week for 21 years. In ill health, she struggled to write a memoir that she never completed. Fittingly, the world traveler and commentator died while traveling abroad to visit family members in Lisbon, Portugal.

FURTHER READING

Holtz, William, ed. Dorothy Thompson and Rose Wilder Lane: Forty Years of Friendship: Letters, 1921–1960. Columbia: University of Missouri Press, 1991.

Kurth, Peter. American Cassandra: The Life of Dorothy Thompson. Boston: Little, Brown, 1990.

Mills, Kay. A Place in the News: From the Women's Pages to the Front Pages. New York: Dodd, Mead, 1988.

Sanders, Marion K. Dorothy Thompson: A Legend in Her Time. Boston: Houghton Mifflin, 1973.

Schorer, Mark. Sinclair Lewis: An American Life. New York: McGraw-Hill, 1961.

Sheehan, Vincent. Dorothy and Red. Boston: Houghton Mifflin, 1963.

Walter Winchell

IS GOSSIP NEWS?

"Good evening, Mr. and Mrs. America, from border to border and coast to coast, and all the ships at sea. Let's go to press!" That is how Walter Winchell regularly opened his Sunday night radio broadcasts in the 1930s and 1940s. His staccato delivery made whatever he said sound urgent. Winchell had begun as a gossip columnist, but increasingly he devoted his attention to politics and foreign policy, taking a strongly anti-Nazi position. His isolationist publisher, William Randolph Hearst, protested: "You are engaged to do a Broadway gossip column," and warned Winchell against becoming too controversial. "Controversy, as you know, brings circulation," Winchell responded. "It seems like only yesterday that my critics condemned me because I mentioned that people were getting divorced or having babies. Now it is usually someone who thinks I have insulted Franco, Hitler, Mussolini, Roosevelt . . . or someone else." Despite his annoyance, Hearst did not drop Winchell's column, for fear of losing readers for his newspapers.

The inventor of the modern gossip column, Walter Winchell was the son of Russian Jewish immigrants. The family name was Weinschel, Americanized to Winchel, and

As a radio broadcaster, Walter Winchell employed a staccato delivery that made whatever he said during his weekly programs sound urgent.

"I introduce myself to you as New York's most notorious gossip, in case you have never read my drivel in the Daily Mirror *or the other papers with which I am associated. I'm the 'Peck's Blab Boy' who turns the Broadway dirt and mud into gold."*

—from a radio broadcast (May 12, 1930)

Walter later added the second "l." His father held a variety of jobs and moved the family frequently from the Lower East Side to Harlem in search of cheaper rents. Eventually, his parents separated and divorced. Desperately seeking attention, young Walter taught himself tap dancing and formed a song and dance act with two other boys. They called themselves "Little Men with Big Voices" and performed at the Imperial Theater, across the street from his apartment. After entering vaudeville, the 13-year-old Winchell dropped out of school. "From my childhood, I knew what I didn't want," he later wrote. "I didn't want to be cold. I didn't want to be hungry, homeless or anonymous."

In 1917 he and a young dancer named Rita Greene performed as "Winchell & Greene." While they were appearing in Chicago in February 1919, a blizzard hit the city. Winchell volunteered to help a friend, who reported for the *Chicago Herald-Examiner*, cover the blizzard. Despite his lack of training or experience, the *Herald-Examiner* gave him a press card and made him a traveling correspondent. Winchell married Rita Greene, and she presented him with his first typewriter.

As they traveled the vaudeville circuit, Winchell submitted news to a show-business paper, *Billboard*. His first column was called "Stage Whispers," and he signed it "The Busybody." After returning to New York, he began writing for the *Vaudeville News*, despite a warning from its editor: "Newspaper men as a class are the poorest paid professional people in the world, and very few writers ever receive an income equal to the average salary of a performer." Winchell, however, knew he was not talented enough as a performer to gain the recognition that he craved.

Spending his nights at Times Square and along Broadway, Winchell picked up tips and collected stories for his column, called "Broadway Hearsay." Fellow vaudevillians passed him news items. In 1924 he was hired by the *New York Evening Graphic*, a tabloid (a half-size newspaper for convenient reading on the subway) filled with pictures, human-interest stories, sports, and sensationalism. Its publisher wanted "sex on every front page" and was fond of printing doctored photographs. The formula attracted a large readership.

Writing a column, "Your Broadway and Mine," Winchell became well known to the top performers, politicians, and gangsters of New York's Jazz Age. It was the era of Prohibition, speakeasies, nightclubs, and bootleggers. Winchell caught the rhythm of the time and entertained his readers with Broadway's slangy prose. His vaudeville background contributed a free-spirited style that was lively, fresh, and irreverent. For many years newspapers had been publishing gossip about prominent people, especially entertainers, but fear of libel suits generally restrained the press from invading people's privacy. Winchell broke the taboo against writing about marriages, babies, divorces, and other secrets. His appeal was partly voyeurism, but he recognized that Broadway and Hollywood had created a new class of celebrities in whom the public was keenly interested. By contrast, Winchell managed to keep private most of his own life, including his divorce from Rita Greene, his marriage to dancer June Magee, his many affairs, and his troubled children.

Everyone from press agents to cab drivers gave Winchell tips for his column. He had a habit of prowling New York City late at night in his car, listening to police radio dispatches and following the action. He kept regular tables at several nightclubs, principally the Stork Club and El Morocco, making them his offices and giving them publicity that drew in patrons. His column boosted his friends and settled old scores with the stage managers, critics, and others who had humiliated him in the past. Praise in Winchell's column packed Broadway shows and made stars. Getting on his "Drop Dead" list meant being ignored or maligned, either of which could sink a performer's career.

In 1929 William Randolph Hearst's New York tabloid, the *New York Mirror,* lured Winchell away from the *Graphic.* Promoting him as the man who got "the lowdown on the high hats," Hearst distributed his column nationally through his King Features syndicate. At its peak Winchell's column appeared in 2,000 newspapers, giving him the largest readership and making him one of the wealthiest journalists of his time. Despite his success, Winchell remained fearful of failure. As another reporter noted, "He is constantly betraying a nervous, horrible fear of losing his punch, of being discarded as a vogue." This anxiety, combined with a hot temper, led Winchell into numerous feuds with other columnists and celebrities. They accused him of "keyhole journalism," "dirt-dishing," and "scandalmongering." Never careful with his facts, Winchell was once sued for libel and lost. After that he refused to write again until Hearst promised to insure him against any future charges.

Winchell became the model for the cynical, unscrupulous, fast-talking, wisecracking journalist. Hollywood promoted the image in Charles MacArthur and Ben Hecht's play and later film, *The Front Page.* Winchell once even played the lead in a radio version of *The Front Page.* He also appeared as himself in several motion pictures, and occasionally performed in musical revues. Mixing gossip, news, and humor, he was less a reporter than a journalistic entertainer. He found it easy to make the transition to radio in 1930, appearing in a popular and long-

lasting program of commentary every Sunday evening.

The stock market crash of 1929 ended the Roaring Twenties and ushered in the Great Depression. When Franklin Roosevelt was elected President in 1932, he made overtures to Winchell, inviting him to the White House and winning support in his columns and broadcasts. With many conservative newspaper columnists criticizing Roosevelt, Winchell became a cheerleader for the New Deal. He helped translate government policy into terms that average citizens could understand. This shift in focus also kept Winchell in step with the popular interests of the depression decade. Similarly, although he was not a religious man, as a Jew, Winchell hated the Nazis and repeatedly attacked Adolf Hitler in his columns.

As a gossip columnist attuned to what was "hot" and who was "in," Winchell shifted his sails with the changing winds. Having made himself the people's champion by fighting for New Deal liberalism and against the Nazis, Winchell turned reactionary during the Cold War years. In the 1950s he became close friends with the militantly anticommunist senator Joseph R. McCarthy. Critics said that the two got along so well because they were both skilled in character assassination. The Senate's censure of McCarthy for improper conduct in 1954 deflated the anticommunist movement and for the first time put Winchell out of step with public opinion. Increasingly, he appeared petty, vindictive, and self-centered, dealing in half-truths and peddling rumors. In 1954, for instance, Winchell raised unsubstantiated fears that the Salk anti-polio vaccines being given to children might be unsafe.

The advent of television further diminished him. Long a successful radio broadcaster, Winchell found himself under intense pressure to move to

Walter Winchell

BORN
April 7, 1897
New York, New York

DIED
February 20, 1972
Los Angeles, California

EDUCATION
Dropped out of public school

ACCOMPLISHMENTS
Columnist, *Billboard* (1920); columnist, the *Vaudeville News* (1920–24); columnist, *New York Evening Graphic* (1924–29); columnist, *New York Mirror* (1929–63); columnist, *New York Journal-American* (1963–66); columnist, *New York World Journal Tribune* (1966–67); syndicated columnist, King Features (1929–67); radio commentator (1930–59); television personality (1952–64); author of *Winchell Exclusive: "Things That Happened to Me—and Me to Them"* (1975)

Walter Winchell's newspaper gossip column caught the rhythm of his time and entertained his readers with Broadway's slangy prose.

television or else lose his audience. But the cameras showed him as a bald and paunchy, aging man. His hot-tempered style also seemed too impassioned for the "cool" medium of television. Ironically, he scored his greatest success as the off-camera narrator for the popular series "The Untouchables" (1959–64), a show about his heyday, the era of speakeasies and crime in the Roaring Twenties.

Winchell hung onto his column zealously, but steadily lost his audience. In 1957 he observed that the famous people who once threatened to sue him for exposing their private lives were now rattling their own skeletons by writing intimate personal accounts for prestigious magazines. His own edi-

tors often cut offending paragraphs from his columns. Readers grew more sophisticated and more suspicious of his accusations. Television was also drawing readers away from newspapers. The *Mirror* went out of business in 1963, and although Winchell shifted his column to other papers he never again enjoyed such a comfortable match.

Sinking into irrelevance, Winchell faded from the scene until his death in 1971. Rather than die with him, however, his innovations in journalism proliferated. As the columnist Leonard Lyons observed, Winchell had discovered that "people were interested in people." Not only gossip columnists but the entire newspaper business oriented itself more toward personalities. The private lives of politicians, entertainers, and the rich and famous spilled over into news stories and headlines. Winchell had helped convince the media that the public had a right to know *everything* about public figures.

FURTHER READING

Baranouw, Erik. *The Golden Web*. Vol. 2, *A History of Broadcasting in the United States*. New York: Oxford University Press, 1968.

Braudy, Leo. *The Frenzy of Renown: Fame and Its History*. New York: Oxford University Press, 1986.

Gabler, Neal. *Winchell: Gossip, Power and the Culture of Celebrity*. New York: Vintage, 1994.

Klurfeld, Herman. *Winchell: His Life and Times*. New York: Praeger, 1976.

Mosedale, John. *The Men Who Made Broadway: Daymon Runyan, Walter Winchell and Their World*. New York: Richard C. Marek, 1981.

Winchell, Walter. *Winchell Exclusive: "Things That Happened to Me—and Me to Them."* Englewood Cliffs, N.J.: Prentice-Hall, 1975.

Henry R. Luce

THE RISE OF THE NEWSMAGAZINE

hen the first issue of *Time* magazine appeared in 1923, it consisted mostly of news lifted from the *New York Times*. The snappy, opinionated "newsmagazine" primarily condensed newspaper articles for business executives too busy to wade through their daily papers. In 1925 *Time*'s publisher, Henry R. Luce, cut costs by moving the magazine's headquarters from New York City to Cleveland, Ohio, where he began reading the *Cleveland Plain Dealer*. Not until then did he realize how little national and international news reached the average newspaper reader, away from the New York dailies. Americans were not ill-informed because they received too much news to absorb, he concluded, but because they received too little. With missionary zeal, Luce set out to fill the void. His magazines would inform, educate, and lead his readers forward into "the American Century."

Born of American missionary parents, Henry Robinson Luce spent his first 14 years in various Presbyterian missionary compounds in China. This experience left the young

Publisher Henry R. Luce (right) with John Shaw Billings, the first managing editor of *Life* magazine, which successfully made photographs its central focus.

Britton Hadden, seated in the center, and Henry R. Luce, beside him on the left, with the staff of the *Yale Daily News*. They later drew the staff of *Time* magazine from Ivy League colleges.

Luce with a self-confessed romantic and idealistic view of faraway America. Although not inspired to become a missionary himself, he felt attracted to journalism because of its "possibilities of exerting influence for good." Over the years his publications would adopt a tone of missionary certainty in explaining and spreading his views. As one of his editors commented, Luce "thought the world could be understood by most people, and that once they understood it, they would want to put things straight."

When Harry Luce (as everyone called him) was 14, a rich friend of the family, Mrs. Cyrus McCormick, paid his way to the prestigious Hotchkiss preparatory school in Connecticut. To supplement his income he had to wait on tables, and he encountered snobbery from students from wealthier families. As editor of the *Hotchkiss Literary Magazine*, Luce met another school editor, Briton Hadden. Hadden was as cynical and irreverent as Luce was serious and idealistic, but they became fast

friends. They both enrolled at Yale, where they joined the staff of the *Yale Daily News* (Hadden later defeated Luce to become editor of the *News*). Luce left college to join the army during World War I, returning after the war to earn his B.A. in 1920. His patron, Mrs. McCormick, then provided funds for a year of graduate study in history at Oxford University.

But journalism, rather than history, remained his great interest. Writing to Mrs. McCormick, he explained that "the writing, the mixing in public affairs of [the] moment, the possibilities of exerting influence for good—all these appeal very strongly to me." She arranged for him to be hired as a reporter for the *Chicago Daily News*, a rather stuffy, old-fashioned newspaper. In 1921 Luce jumped at the opportunity to join his friend Hadden on the *Baltimore News*. The two began to make plans for their own weekly news magazine. In school Hadden had been greatly impressed with Homer's *Iliad*. He found its style vivid and littered with adjectives, with its sentence constructions often reversed, putting the object and verb before the subject. He planned to adopt this style for a lively and concise magazine. Hadden and Luce believed that newspapers were filled with too much detail. They would reduce this mountain of material to give their readers just the heart of the news.

Luce and Hadden contacted old schoolmates from Hotchkiss and Yale and other wealthy sources to launch *Time* magazine in 1923. Similarly, they drew from the "better schools" for editors and reporters, and aimed at an audience among the educated middle class. Editor Hadden gave *Time* its snappy, distinctive style, while Luce concentrated on managing its finances. Operating on a shoestring, the magazine could not afford to pay for original reporting at first. *Time's* early obsession with "facts," from describing the dress Queen Mary wore to counting the number of cars in Calvin Coolidge's funeral, disguised the amateurism of a staff made up mostly of rewrite editors. *Time's* writers were all anonymous. The magazine spoke with a single voice and point of view, condensing and refashioning the news to keep the stories neat and orderly, an approach that appealed to readers. In the prosperous Roaring Twenties, when President Calvin Coolidge declared that the "business of America is business," business leaders read *Time*. By 1930 a survey revealed that more American bankers read *Time* than any other magazine, and *Time* estimated that business people constituted the majority of its subscribers.

Time had reached solid financial ground when suddenly Briton Hadden took sick and died in 1929. Luce bought Hadden's stock and took control of the magazine. He was already thinking of starting another publication—an expensive, handsomely illustrated monthly magazine aimed at business executives. He called it *Fortune*. The new magazine appeared in February 1930, shortly after the stock market crash began the Great Depression. Despite this poor timing, the magazine found an audience, largely because Luce had assembled a talented staff of editors, writers, photographers, and illustrators. Luce was its driving force. When he hired photographer Margaret Bourke-White, she recorded, "His words tumbled out with such haste and emphasis that I had the feeling he was thinking ten words for every one that managed to emerge." Luce spoke in an abrupt, choppy manner, breaking off sentences and jumping from one thought to another. At

times, however, a childhood stammer would return to trip his rapid-fire delivery.

Rather than celebrate prosperity, *Fortune* set out to decipher the depression. The magazine covered unemployment and New Deal relief programs. Mostly, however, it profiled business enterprises. Identifying himself as a businessman as much as a journalist, Luce promoted a positive image of capitalism. Yet he refused to permit his publications simply to rewrite the corporate handouts that passed for articles in other business magazines. Business leaders, conditioned to controlling their images through public relations experts, were at first unprepared for Luce's independence. One board chairman wept, more in fear than in pride, when he learned that *Fortune* planned to write about his company.

In the 1930s Time, Inc., launched a weekly radio program and later a series of newsreels to be shown in motion picture theaters, both called *The March of Time*. Appearing at a time when large numbers of Americans listened to the radio nightly and went to the movies weekly, *The March of Time* newsreels were enormously successful. They drew large audiences who wanted to hear and see the events of the day. Although nominally in charge, Luce had little involvement with *The March of Time*. He never felt as comfortable with radio, newsreels, or television as he did with his publications.

Luce's next creation was a weekly pictorial magazine called *Life*, the suggestion for which emerged from his complicated personal life. Luce had been married to Lila Hotz Luce since 1923, and they had two sons. In the 1930s he fell in love with the attractive and intellectual Clare Boothe Brokaw, former editor of the stylish magazine *Vanity Fair*. Despite the

Henry R. Luce

BORN
April 3, 1898
Tengchow, China

DIED
February 28, 1967
Phoenix, Arizona

EDUCATION
B.A., Yale College (1920); graduate studies in history, Oxford University (1920–21)

ACCOMPLISHMENTS
Reporter, *Yale Daily News* (1916–18); reporter, *Chicago Daily News* (1920–21); reporter, *Baltimore News* (1921–23); editor in chief, *Time* (1923–64); editor in chief, *Fortune* (1930–64); editor in chief, *Architectural Forum* (1932–64); editor in chief, *Life* (1936–64); producer, "March of Time" radio programs (1931–45); producer, *March of Time* newsreels (1935–51); editor in chief, *Sports Illustrated* (1954–64); editorial chairman, Time, Inc. (1964–67); author of *The American Century* (1941) and *The Ideas of Henry Luce* (1969)

strong disapproval of his missionary parents, Luce divorced Lila and married Clare in 1935. It was Clare Boothe Luce who originally promoted the idea for *Life*. Luce had long recognized the value of illustrations to support the text—and had employed talented photographers such as Margaret Bourke-White and Walker Evans for *Fortune*. But *Life* would reverse the order and make photographs the central focus. The magazine would arrange photographs to form "photoessays" that told the story with captions and a brief text.

Luce expected the new magazine to sell as many as 250,000 copies a week, but within a month it was selling twice that many. Within a year the figure would pass 1 million. This unexpected success almost sabotaged the effort. Luce had set the first year's advertising rates based on a much lower pressrun, causing *Life* to lose money as more copies were printed. By 1939, with circulation up to 2 million, advertising rates had been adjusted accordingly and *Life* became an immensely profitable venture. The outbreak of World War II that year provided both global subject material and an audience hungry for photographs from the war fronts. *Life* photographers distinguished themselves as they documented the war's horrors and heroes.

The war shifted the patriotic Harry Luce's attentions from publishing to public affairs. In 1940 he threw his magazines behind Wendell Willkie, the Republican candidate for President, who advocated that the United States take a more active role in international affairs. Russell Davenport, the editor of *Fortune,* became Willkie's campaign manager. But Time, Inc.'s vast readership did not fall into step and Willkie lost to Franklin D. Roosevelt's bid for a

third term. In 1941, as the United States moved closer to war, Luce published a signed editorial in *Life* proclaiming "the American Century." Americans, he wrote, needed to recognize that they had become the most powerful and vital nation in the world. Responsibility came with great power. America could no longer afford to retreat into isolationism. If it took the lead in promoting international peace and security, then it would turn the 20th century into "the American Century."

During the war, Luce reestablished his ties to his birthplace, China. He developed such great admiration for the Chinese leader Chiang Kai-shek that he could not bring himself to believe anything critical of Chiang. Even when his favorite reporter, Theodore H. White, sent back warnings of corruption and ineptness in the Chinese government, Luce had his stories rewritten or suppressed. When the Communist Chinese overthrew Chiang in 1949, Luce's publications blamed the fall entirely on the failure of U.S. foreign policy. Although Time, Inc., took a hard anticommunist line during the Cold War, the magazines reacted scornfully toward Wisconsin senator Joseph R. McCarthy's Red-baiting tactics. When *Time* put McCarthy on its cover in 1951, the caption read: "Demagogue McCarthy."

Clare Boothe Luce won election to the U.S. House of Representatives from Connecticut in 1942 and served two terms. In 1950 Harry Luce thought about running for the Senate himself, but could never bring himself to enter politics as a candidate. Instead, the Luces promoted Dwight D. Eisenhower for President in 1952. President Eisenhower reciprocated by appointing Clare Boothe Luce ambassador to Italy.

WELCOME MR. HENRY LUCE
THE MOST FAMOUS JOURNALIST
FROM THE JOURNALISTS ASSOCIATION OF TSINGTAO

Harry Luce joined his wife to live in Rome, directing his publishing empire at long distance.

During the prosperous 1950s, *Time, Life,* and *Fortune* appealed to college-educated, suburban readers, an increasing portion of the American population. Luce suspected that this same class of readers would appreciate a higher level of sports journalism than the rest of the press offered. In 1954 Time, Inc., launched the glossy *Sports Illustrated* magazine. In addition to the major league professional sports, it also covered golf, fishing, hunting, and other sports ignored by the newspaper sport pages (although Harry Luce

himself had always been too busy for such sports).

Even as it was achieving yet another success, Luce's publishing empire faced its greatest challenge. The more popular television became, the more it drew away average readers. *Life*'s still pictures would have trouble competing with television news. The national publication of the *New York Times* would compete with *Time* and other newsmagazines. Similarly, the national distribution of the *Wall Street Journal* would undercut *Fortune.*

For years, Time, Inc., magazines spoke with a self-assured certainty on issues that reflected their publisher.

Born in China, Luce retained close ties with the Nationalist Chinese government. Here he visits journalists in Tsingtao in 1945.

"As America enters dynamically upon the world scene, we need most of all to seek and to bring forth a vision of America as a world power which is authentically American and which can inspire us to live and work and fight with vigor and enthusiasm. And as we come now to the great test, it may yet turn out that in all our trials and tribulations of spirit during the first part of this century we as a people have been painfully apprehending the meaning of time and now in this moment of testing there may come clear at last the vision which will guide us to the authentic creation of the 20th Century—our Century."

—from *The American Century* (1941)

Increasingly, the magazines took criticism for reflecting Luce's views and prejudices on politics, the arts, and other issues. Luce made no apologies. "I am a Protestant, a Republican and a free enterpriser," he proclaimed. "I am biased in favor of God, Eisenhower and the stockholders of Time, Inc.—and if anybody who objects doesn't know this by now, why the hell are they still spending 35 cents for the magazine?"

In 1958 Luce suffered a severe heart attack. He gave up smoking, began to travel more, and gradually gave up the reigns of leadership. His strong commitment to the Cold War, Nationalist China, and anticommunism led him to endorse American intervention in the Vietnam War. But the hawkish stand that made his publications popular during World War II and the Korean War began to alienate younger readers. In 1964 he stepped down as editor in chief to become "editorial chairman." He remained a major stockholder. But others were now making most of the decisions. Only after Luce's death in 1967, however, did *Time* break with President Lyndon Johnson and criticize the Vietnam War. *Life* delivered one of the most effective blows the week that it published the photographs of all 242 Americans killed in Vietnam trying to capture an obscure spot nicknamed "Hamburger Hill." These stunning photographs made Americans feel less certain about the price to be paid for "the American Century."

FURTHER READING

Baughman, James L. *Henry R. Luce and the Rise of the American News Media*. Boston: Twayne, 1987.

Griffith, Thomas. *Harry and Teddy: The Turbulent Friendship of Press Lord Henry R. Luce and His Favorite Reporter, Theodore H. White*. New York: Random House, 1995.

Halberstam, David. *The Powers That Be*. New York: Knopf, 1979.

Herzstein, Robert E. *Henry R. Luce: A Political Portrait of the Man Who Created the American Century*. New York: Scribners, 1994.

Kobler, John. *Luce: His Time, Life, and Fortune*. Garden City, N.Y.: Doubleday, 1968.

Luce, Henry. *The American Century*. New York: Farrar & Rinehart, 1941.

————. *The Ideas of Henry Luce*. New York: Atheneum, 1969.

Martin, Ralph G. *Henry and Clare: An Intimate Portrait of the Luces*. New York: Putnam, 1991.

Swanberg, W. A. *Luce and His Empire*. New York: Scribners, 1972.

Margaret Bourke-White

📷

PHOTOJOURNALIST

Nine hundred people were injured or killed when the Ohio River flooded near Louisville, Kentucky, in January 1937. The new picture magazine, *Life*, sent its top photographer, Margaret Bourke-White, to cover this terrible tragedy. Daring and fearless, Bourke-White took her cameras out on the river in rowboats that delivered relief supplies so that she could photograph the survivors. She also had an eye for the unusual and ironic. She encountered a line of black men and women and children holding baskets, shopping bags, and pails while they were waiting in line for food at a relief center. Directly behind them stood a large billboard of a prosperous, contented white family in their car, with the slogan "World's Highest Standard of Living. There's no way like the American way." The juxtaposition made a stunning photograph, which *Life* Magazine featured in its next edition. Her choice of angle and of subject reflected her feelings and point of view. Her photos told stories even without text.

She was the daughter of Joseph White and Minnie Bourke—themselves both children of immigrants living in New York City. Joseph White was Jewish and Minnie Bourke was Irish Catholic, but they had a shared interest in the Ethical Culture Society. The second of three children, Margaret White was born in her parents' home in the Bronx. When she was a child, the family moved to Bound Brook, New Jersey. Nearby her father worked as an engineer for a company that manufactured printing presses.

"It is odd that photography was never one of my childhood hobbies," Margaret later wrote, but her father had a passion for amateur photography. But in 1922 he suffered a stroke and died. Margaret was a student at Columbia University, majoring in herpetology (the study of reptiles) at the time. Soon after her father's death, she signed up for a course in photography taught by Clarence H. White. White expounded the theory that photography could be art. Photos needed to be planned carefully, he told his students: "Chance is a poor photographer."

At a summer camp, 18-year-old Margaret White taught photography to children and made her own picture postcards of the camp. When a local shop ordered some of her cards, she wrote: "I am so proud of myself now. I feel as if I could make my living anywhere." She transferred to the University of Michigan, where she began submitting photographs to the student yearbook, the *Michiganensian*. She took pictures of athletic events and climbed onto the steep roofs of the college buildings for better vistas of the campus. She decided that she wanted to be "a news photographer-

Despite the military's discomfort with having women near combat zones, Margaret Bourke-White was determined to cover World War II.

reporter and a good one." Journalism was still a male-dominated occupation, but the Jazz Age of the 1920s was rapidly opening new doors for women. Other women had succeeded as professional photographers. One of the first, Frances Benjamin Johnson, had published an article in the *Ladies' Home Journal* as early as 1897 urging women to become photographers.

Love and marriage temporarily interrupted her career plans. While still a student, Margaret married a classmate, Everett Chapman. Her husband turned out to be dominated by a mother who disapproved of his marriage and made him feel guilty. Margaret also felt afraid of marriage, because, as she confided to her diary,

"the woman so often loses her individuality." She hated being addressed as Margaret Chapman. In 1925 her husband took a job as an engineer in Cleveland and Margaret transferred to Western Reserve University. Soon after, the marriage collapsed and they divorced. To get away, Margaret moved to Ithaca, New York, to attend Cornell University, from which she graduated in 1927. She had also adopted a new name. Margaret White now hyphenated the last names of both her mother and father, giving her the more memorable, high-class-sounding name of Margaret Bourke-White.

After graduation, Bourke-White returned to Cleveland to become an architectural photographer. Local

Margaret Bourke-White

architects hired her to photograph houses they had built, and business executives employed her to photograph skyscrapers they were erecting. She also took industrial photos of Cleveland's steel mills and foundries. To get her pictures, she would go anywhere, no matter how dangerous. In 1929 the *New York Sun* ran a story headlined: "Dizzy Heights Have No Terrors For This Girl Photographer, Who Braves Numerous Perils to Film the Beauty of Iron and Steel." These photographs came to the attention of Henry R. Luce, editor in chief of *Time* magazine, who was starting a new monthly business magazine, *Fortune*. Luce wanted to produce a lavishly illustrated magazine in which pictures and words would become "conscious partners."

Margaret Bourke-White turned down a full-time job because she wanted to remain at least partly independent. Instead, she agreed to work half-time for *Fortune* while maintaining her own studio. She moved to New York City, where the magazine was headquartered, and was hired on the side to photograph construction of the new Chrysler building—often from scaffolds high above the street. Thrilled by heights, she moved her studio onto the building's 61st floor. "I feel like my own boss up there," she explained. "Nobody can reach me to give me orders." An attractive and vivacious woman who dressed stylishly, she became the subject of many stories herself. But as one of her editors noted, "She didn't boast at all, but had absolute confidence in herself."

In 1930 *Fortune* sent Bourke-White to photograph factories in the Soviet Union. She admired the Russian people for their resourcefulness, and her pictures made such good publicity for Russian trade that the government invited her back the next year. She returned again in 1932 to make motion picture travelogues and to write a book about Russia. The more she went, the less she photographed the machines. Instead, she focused on the people who operated them.

Back in the United States *Fortune* assigned her to record the hard times in the western Dust Bowl. She also photographed rural poverty in the South, from sharecroppers to chain gangs, to accompany a text written by the novelist and playwright Erskine Caldwell. Her photographs helped turn their book, *You Have Seen Their Faces*, into a great commercial success. She later married Caldwell, but that marriage, too, was short-lived and ended in divorce.

Meanwhile, Henry Luce was making plans to begin a weekly picture magazine he called *Life*. Newspapers had long carried Sunday photo sections called rotogravures (from the process of printing pictures on a rotary press), and the tabloid newspapers relied heavily on photos. Magazines also regularly published photographs, but none let pictures do the main work of telling the story. In 1936 the first issue of *Life* appeared with one of Bourke-White's photos on the cover. It showed the Fort Peck Dam, a New Deal project being constructed in Montana. Besides the turbines and other industrial photos, she submitted pictures of the workers on the dam. Not just industrial photos, she pictured them at night in bars, dancing and bowling. As *Life* explained: "What the Editors expected were construction pictures as only Bourke-White can take them. What the Editors got was a human document of American frontier life which, to them at least, was a revelation."

Working for a weekly publication increased the demands on Bourke-

BORN
June 14, 1904
New York, New York

DIED
August 27, 1971
Darien, Connecticut

EDUCATION
Columbia University (1922–23), University of Michigan (1923–25), Western Reserve University (1925–26); A.B., Cornell University (1927)

ACCOMPLISHMENTS
Photographer, *Fortune* (1929–36); photographer, *Life* (1936–57); author of *Eyes on Russia* (1931), *You Have Seen Their Faces* (1937), *Shooting the Russian War* (1942), *They Called It "Purple Heart Valley": A Combat Chronicle of the War in Italy* (1944), *"Dear Fatherland, Rest Quietly"; A Report on the Collapse of Hitler's "Thousand Years"* (1946), *Halfway to Freedom: A Report on the New India in the Words and Photographs of Margaret Bourke-White* (1949), *Portrait of Myself* (1963), and *The Photographs of Margaret Bourke-White* (1972)

"I loved the swift pace of Life assignments, the exhilaration of stepping over the threshold into a new land. Everything could be conquered. Nothing was too difficult. And if you had a stiff deadline to meet, all the better. You said yes to the challenge and shaped up the story accordingly, and found joy and a sense of accomplishment in so doing."

—from *Portrait of Myself* (1963)

White. She gave up her independent studio, but *Life* provided her with an office, a staff, and a darkroom. She objected when the first issues of *Life* credited her photos only in a small index at the back of the magazine. As a result of her prodding, Luce agreed that whenever the magazine ran four or more photos from a photographer with a story, the photographer's name would appear up front, under the title. Such credit helped make the photographers the stars of the magazine, and many of their pictures would later hang in museums. Other staff photographers had greater technical expertise, but Bourke-White's eye for content, her fearless pursuit of pictures, and her perfectionism set standards for the rest of the photographic staff to meet. Her photos helped make *Life* an instant success, far beyond Luce's greatest expectation. Male photographers, however, resented both her success and her aggressiveness. They referred to her as a prima donna, who acted as if she were royalty.

Beyond seeking to build a reputation for herself, Bourke-White was driven by many motives. She possessed enormous energy and curiosity. "Nothing attracts me like a closed door," she wrote. "I cannot let my camera rest until I have pried it open." She was also horrified by the rise of Nazism and anti-Semitism in Europe in the 1930s, and believed that democracy would prevail "as long as people really know what is going on and that the photographer has a very valuable part to do in showing what is going on." *Life* sent her back to the Soviet Union, and she was there when Germany invaded in 1941. The only foreign photographer in Moscow at the time, she took the first pictures of Stalin ever snapped by an American, and collected dramatic scenes of war-torn Russia, developing her negatives in a hotel bathtub.

Despite the military's discomfort with having women near combat zones, Bourke-White was determined to cover World War II. In 1942 she was on board the flagship of a convoy to North Africa that was torpedoed, and she was evacuated from the ship by lifeboat. Later, the army broke its rules to allow her to fly in combat missions. One pilot was startled to hear a woman's voice on his intercom asking him to roll the plane so she could shoot straight down. Her pictures appeared in *Life* with the headline: *"Life's* Bourke-White Goes Bombing." She covered the American campaigns in Italy and the Allied invasion of Germany. She was one of the first photographers to record the Nazi death camps at Buchenwald and Dachau. "Margaret came running and worked like a demon," said one *Time* correspondent. "She was a tiger. I've never seen her or any other photographer in such concentrated action in my life."

After the war, Bourke-White traveled to India to photograph the movement for independence from Britain. She grew close to the Indian leader Mahatma Gandhi, whom she admired for his self-sacrificing bravery. Her last interview with Gandhi took place only hours before his assassination. She covered his funeral while standing on the hood of a truck. She also went to South Africa, where she photographed gold miners two miles below the earth's surface. In 1952 she covered the war in Korea. One of her more memorable photographs of that war caught the reunion of a Korean mother and son who had each thought the other dead.

While lunching at the Tokyo Press Club between visits to Korea, Bourke-White had trouble walking when she rose from the table. Other distressing symptoms revealed that she had contracted the crippling Parkinson's disease. Known as "Maggie the Indestructible," she was unwilling to give in to her ailment. She exercised regularly, underwent surgery, and con-

Margaret Bourke-White took this picture of Indian independence leader Mahatma Gandhi at a spinning wheel in Poona, India, in 1946.

tinued working for as long as possible. In 1955 she won a promise from Luce that he would assign her to the first trip to the moon. But the disease drained her energy and forced her to abandon her travels. She submitted her last story to *Life* in 1957 and retired to her home in Connecticut to write her memoirs. Having wanted to go on a space shot, she lived long enough to watch the first moon landing on television. She died in 1971, just as television was putting photo magazines like *Life* out of business.

FURTHER READING

Ayer, Eleanor H. *Margaret Bourke-White: Photographing the World*. New York: Dillon, 1992.

Bourke-White, Margaret. *"Dear Fatherland, Rest Quietly"; A Report on the Collapse of Hitler's "Thousand Years."* New York: Simon & Schuster, 1946.

———. *Eyes on Russia*. 1931. Reprint, New York: AMS Press, 1971.

———. *Halfway to Freedom: A Report on the New India in the Words and Photographs of Margaret Bourke-White*. New York: Simon & Schuster, 1949.

———. *The Photographs of Margaret Bourke-White*. Greenwich, Conn.: New York Graphic Society, 1972.

———. *Portrait of Myself*. New York: Simon & Schuster, 1963.

———. *Shooting the Russian War*. New York: Simon & Schuster, 1942.

———. *They Called It "Purple Heart Valley": A Combat Chronicle of the War in Italy*. New York: Simon & Schuster, 1944.

Bourke-White, Margaret, with Erskine Caldwell. *You Have Seen Their Faces*. 1937. Reprint, Athens: University of Georgia Press, 1995.

Daffron, Carolyn. *Margaret Bourke-White*. New York: Chelsea House, 1988.

Goldberg, Vicki. *Margaret Bourke-White: A Biography*. New York: Harper & Row, 1986.

Silverman, Jonathan. *For the World to See: The Life of Margaret Bourke-White*. New York: Viking, 1983.

Ernie Pyle

WAR CORRESPONDENT

A s a teenager during World War I, Ernie Pyle wanted to quit high school and join the Navy. Many of his neighbors in Dana, Indiana, were joining, and the war seemed to offer adventure, travel, and escape from the drudgeries of farm life. Pyle's parents insisted that he graduate first, and by the time he joined the Naval Reserve the war was almost over. For years that sense of missed opportunity drove Pyle as he became a traveling newspaper correspondent. By 1940 another world war had broken out in Europe and Pyle at last fulfilled his youthful dreams—not as a soldier or sailor, but as a war correspondent. The brutal reality of the war erased any romantic illusions. He saw the war from the combat troops' perspective, capturing their attitudes and experiences in the popular columns he sent back home.

The slightly built farm boy Ernest Taylor Pyle had a restless spirit. After his short stint in the navy, he enrolled at Indiana University and studied journalism, because, as he later explained, it "offered an escape from farm life and farm animals." Not waiting to graduate, he took his first reporting job on the nearby *La Porte* (Indiana) *Herald Argus*. Soon after, the Scripps-Howard newspaper chain recruited him to move to Washington, D.C., and report for the *Washington Daily News*. That paper, a tabloid that leaned toward flashy headlines, discovered that Pyle had a flair for headline writing and moved him from reporting to the copydesk. It was the Roaring Twenties, and Pyle lived a free and easy bohemian life, playing cards at night with other reporters and consuming bootleg gin, despite Prohibition. He fell in love with another free spirit, Geraldine (Jerry) Siebolds, who had also escaped from a small town in the Midwest for a job in the capital, working as a civil service clerk. Both so enjoyed being nonconformists that when they married in 1925 they kept it secret from their friends. For years neither of them wore a wedding ring. They never had any children.

Since Ernie had an itch to travel, in the summer of 1926 they both quit their jobs, bought a car, and headed out to drive around the entire rim of the United States. They ended their 10-week, 9,000-mile trip in New York City. There Ernie joined the copydesk of the *New York Evening World*, and later the *New York Post*, and he and Jerry settled into a messy apartment in Greenwich Village. Typical of Ernie Pyle's humor was the headline he contributed at this time to a story about a motorist who was robbed of his car and left standing alongside the road: "THIEVES ROB MAN, THROW HIM AWAY."

Late in 1927 the *Washington Daily News* hired Pyle back as telegraph editor in charge of the news stories that came in over the wires from the press services. In the wake of Charles Lindbergh's daring solo flight to Paris that year, newspaper readers were keenly interested in aviation news. The *News* made Pyle their aviation reporter. Once while telephoning the paper from an airport, he witnessed a plane crash and dictated his story over the phone as the events were happening. His success in these posts led the *News* to appoint him managing editor in 1931. Pyle accepted the promotion, but hated giving up his writing and his freedom of motion as a reporter for the responsibilities of a desk job.

After contracting a severe case of the flu in 1934, Pyle was advised by his doctor to go to a warm place to recuperate. He took a leave of absence, and he and Jerry drove to Arizona and California. When they returned, he wrote a series of articles about their trip, which he published as a replacement for a vacationing columnist. The pieces were so popular that Pyle persuaded the Scripps-Howard chain to make him its roving travel correspondent. "I've had a good stroke of luck. I've finally been transferred from this man-killing job I've been on for three years," Pyle wrote to a friend. "I will go where I please and write what I please. It's just the kind of job I've always wanted."

Popular with the troops he covered, Ernie Pyle signed autographs on board a troop transport ship near Okinawa in 1945.

After reporting on World War II in Africa and Europe, Pyle was killed by a sniper on the island of Ie Shima in the Pacific. Soldiers erected this sign in his memory.

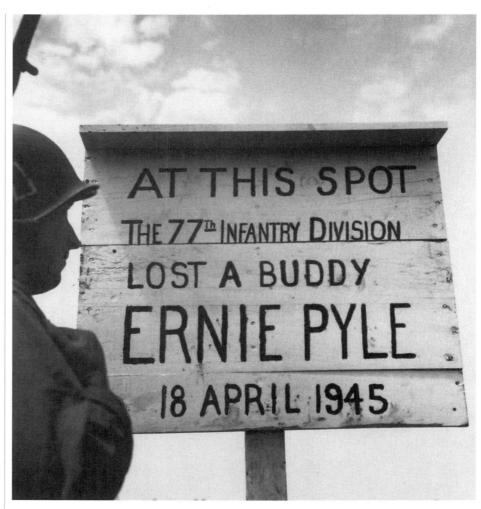

During the next five years, Ernie Pyle lived a nomadic life. He drove across the nation 35 times, also going north to Alaska, south to South America, and sailing across the Pacific to Hawaii. He traveled mostly by car, but also by train, plane, boat, and horseback. Jerry went along with him, retyping clean copies of his columns and making suggestions. She became known to his readers as "that girl who rides with me." He stopped to interview famous people and everyday folks on the street. Each week he would send six columns back to the *Washington Daily News*, which distributed them to the rest of the Scripps-Howard chain. Pyle's travel stories became enormously popular. As more cars were available and roads improved, more Americans wanted to travel. Pyle's columns gave them ideas about where they wanted to visit. But for most of his readers he traveled for them "and wrote their letters home," as he put it.

Car travel in the 1930s was not especially comfortable, and the years of wandering began to wear heavily on the couple. It was especially hard on Jerry, who grew dependent on alcohol and drugs and suffered bouts of depression. To create some stability in their lives, they built a small house in Albuquerque, New Mexico. But most of the time Ernie was on the road in search of stories.

Ernie Pyle

BORN

August 3, 1900
Near Dana, Indiana

DIED

April 18, 1945
Ie Shima, Japan

EDUCATION

Attended Indiana University
(1919–23)

ACCOMPLISHMENTS

Reporter, *La Porte* (Indiana) *Herald Argus* (1923); reporter, copy editor, *Washington Daily News* (1923–26); copy editor, *New York Evening World* and *New York Evening Post* (1926–27); rose from telegraph editor to managing editor, *Washington Daily News* (1927–35); roving columnist, Scripps-Howard Newspapers (1935–40); war correspondent, Scripps-Howard Newspapers (1940–450); author of *Ernie Pyle in England* (1941), *Here Is Your War* (1943), *Brave Men* (1944), *Last Chapter* (1946), and *Home Country* (1947)

In September 1939 war broke out in Europe, and Pyle described himself as "just about to bust I want to go over there as a war correspondent or something so bad." Jerry, a pacifist, opposed the war. "Pacifism is fine as long as there ain't no war around," Pyle wrote. "But when they start shooting I want to get close enough just a couple of times to get good and scared." In 1940 Ernie went to England to cover the German air raids on London, while Jerry stayed behind. His vivid descriptions of the Battle of Britain were widely printed in the United States and Great Britain. He returned home to find that his wife's mental health had declined markedly in his absence. Trying to force her to seek help, Ernie divorced Jerry in 1942, promising to remarry her if she made an effort to cure herself. She was committed to a sanitarium.

After the attack on Pearl Harbor in December 1941, the United States entered the war and Ernie Pyle went overseas as a war correspondent. Unlike Richard Harding Davis and other great war correspondents of the past, Pyle was not content with hobnobbing with officers and sending back reports on the battle. He wanted to see and experience the war as common foot soldiers did. Pyle boarded a transport ship carrying troops to North Africa. Despite his age and small frame (he was short and weighed only 110 pounds), he lived with the troops, ate the same food, slept in the same quarters, and got close enough to the front lines to come under attack and to view the wounded and dead.

He wrote about the soldiers' everyday experiences, making mention of their hometowns, so many of which he had visited. "War makes strange giant creatures out of the little routine men who inhabit the earth," he observed. Back home his columns gave Americans a better sense of what the war was like. He recorded the alternating monotony and terror of warfare, and the numbness that soldiers felt toward the death and devastation all around them. "They were all so young, so genuine, so enthusiastic," Pyle wrote about a group of young fliers. "And they were so casual about everything— not casual in a hard, knowing way, but they talked about their flights and killings and being killed exactly as they would discuss girls or their school lessons."

As Pyle followed the American troops into Italy, he wrote some of his most memorable dispatches. One poignant piece on the death of Captain Henry Waskow was published on the entire front page of the *Washington Daily News* and reprinted in countless other papers. His battle-front dispatches were collected and published as books, and Hollywood filmed a movie drawn from his writing, *The Story of G.I. Joe.* In 1944 Ernie Pyle won a Pulitzer Prize for his war correspondence. He wrote home to Jerry (whom he had remarried by proxy): "Of course I am very sick of the war, and would like to leave it, and yet I know I can't. I've become a part of the misery and tragedy of it for so long that I've come to feel a responsibility to it or something. I don't quite know how to put it into words, but I feel if I left it, it would be like a soldier deserting."

After Allied troops landed at Normandy in June 1944, Pyle followed them to Paris. By then he was so exhausted that he had to take a break. He returned to the United States a

At the Front Lines in Italy, January 10, 1944—In this war I have known a lot of officers who were beloved and respected by the soldiers under them. But never have I crossed the trail of any man as beloved as Capt. Henry T. Waskow of Belton, Texas.

Captain Waskow was a company commander in the 36th Division. He had led his company since before it left the States. He was very young, only in his middle twenties, but he carried in him a sincerity and gentleness that made people want to be guided by him.

"After my own father, he came next," a sergeant told me.

"He always looked after us," a soldier said. "He'd go to bat for us every time."

"I've never known him to do anything unfair," another one said.

I was at the foot of the trail the night they brought Capt. Waskow's body down. The moon was nearly full at the time, and you could see far up the trail, and even part way across the valley below. Soldiers made shadows in the moonlight as they walked.

Dead men had been coming down the mountain all evening, lashed on the backs of mules. . . . We went out into the road. Four mules stood there, in the moonlight, in the road where the trail came down off the mountain. The soldiers who led them stood there waiting. "This one is Captain Waskow," one of them said quietly.

Two men unlashed his body from the mule and lifted if off and laid it in the shadow below the stone wall. Other men took the other bodies off. Finally there were five lying end to end in a long row, alongside the road. You don't cover up dead men in the combat zone. They just lie there in the shadows until somebody else comes after them.

The unburdened mules moved off to their olive orchard. The men in the road seemed reluctant to leave. They stood around, and gradually one by one I could sense them moving close to Capt. Waskow's body. Not so much to look, I think, as to say something in finality to him, and to themselves. I stood close by and I could hear.

One soldier came and looked down, and he said out loud, "God damn it!" That's all he said, and he walked away. . . .

Another man came; I think he was an officer. It was hard to tell officers from men in the half light, for all were bearded and grimy dirty. The man looked down into his dead captain's face, and then he spoke directly to him, as though he were alive. He said, "I'm sorry, old man."

Then a soldier came and stood beside the officer, and bent over, and he too spoke to his dead captain, not in a whisper but awfully tenderly, and he said:

"I sure am sorry, sir."

Then the first man squatted down, and . . . reached up and gently straightened the points of the captain's shirt collar, and then he sort of rearranged the tattered edges of his uniform around the wound. And then he got up and walked down the road in the moonlight, all alone.

After that the rest of us went back into the cowshed, leaving the five dead men lying in a line, end to end, in the shadow of the low stone wall. We lay down on the straw in the cowshed, and pretty soon we were all asleep.

—from "Beloved Captain," *Washington Daily News* (January 10, 1944)

celebrity. First Lady Eleanor Roosevelt invited him to tea at the White House. Other reporters sought to interview him. Radio networks offered him his own program. The royalties and movie rights for his books made him a rich man.

Jerry's mental health was still precarious. An attempted suicide showed that she needed him to stay at home. There was no reason for him to go back to war correspondence. But he could not remain home for long. "The front does get into your blood," he said, "and you miss it and want to be back." Having covered the European war, he decided to see the fighting in the Pacific at firsthand. He regretted leaving his wife again. "She lives only for the day when the war is over and we can have a life together again. And that's what I live for too," he wrote. "I hope we both last through until the sun shines in the world again."

When Pyle sailed out of San Francisco, he was greeted by a thousand cheering soldiers and a 50-piece band. American military leaders believed his presence would boost servicemen's morale in the Pacific. Readers worried about his safety, and one magazine called Pyle "probably the most prayed-for man with the American troops." He traveled with the Marines from island to island, coming under heavy fire. "There's nothing romantic whatever in knowing that an hour from now you may be dead," he wrote. On April 18, 1945, Ernie Pyle was killed by a sniper's bullet on the tiny island of Ie Shima, near Okinawa. He was buried with other combat dead alongside the road (and was later removed to a military cemetery in Hawaii). In his pocket was a column he was writing about "the unnatural sight of cold dead men scattered over the hillsides and in the ditches along the high rows of hedge throughout the world. Dead men by mass production—in one country after another—month after month and year after year."

Americans reacted to Ernie Pyle's death as if he had been a member of their own family. People in his hometown wanted his body brought back home, but his wife, Jerry, stopped them. "Ernie is lying where he would wish to be, with the men he loved," she insisted. Her own health declined further, and she died in November 1945, having lost all interest in living. By then the war itself had ended. President Harry Truman, who personally announced Pyle's death to the nation, commended his contribution as America's preeminent war correspondent: "No man in this war has so well told the story of the American fighting man as American fighting men wanted it told."

FURTHER READING

Miller, Lee G. *An Ernie Pyle Album: Indiana to Ie Shima.* 1946. Reprint, Westport, Conn.: Greenwood, 1970.

———. *The Story of Ernie Pyle.* 1950. Reprint, Westport, Conn.: Greenwood, 1970.

Nichols, David, ed. *Ernie's America: The Best of Ernie Pyle's 1930s Travel Dispatches.* New York: Random House, 1989.

———, ed. *Ernie's War: The Best of Ernie Pyle's World War II Dispatches.* New York: Random House, 1986.

Painton, Frederick C. "The Hoosier Letter-Writer (Ernie Pyle)." In *More Post Biographies: Articles of Enduring Interest About Famous Journalists and Journals and Other Subjects Journalistic,* edited by John E. Drewry. Athens: University of Georgia Press, 1947.

Pyle, Ernie. *Brave Men.* New York: Holt, 1944.

———. *Ernie Pyle in England.* New York: McBride, 1941.

———. *Here Is Your War.* New York: Holt, 1943.

———. *Last Chapter.* New York: Holt, 1946.

Tobin, James. *Ernie Pyle's War: America's Eyewitness to World War II.* New York: Free Press, 1997.

Red Smith

SPORTS REPORTER

An aspiring journalist once asked Red Smith, then a sports columnist for the *Philadelphia Record,* what it took to become a sports reporter. "About the only requisites I could name for a sportswriter are those of any ordinary reporter—intelligence, common sense, and an impersonal viewpoint," Smith replied. "By the latter I mean the ability to stand a little apart, take no sides, and merely report what happens." Smith added that good sportswriters should also put "a little freshness and originality" into their accounts. "That is because in sports the important thing is the way a story is written, since the sports pages contain only a little real 'spot' news in which the facts are the all-important thing." Such were the qualities that Smith brought to sportswriting from the 1920s to the 1980s and that made his fans ask their friends: "Did you read Red Smith this morning?"

Sports of all kinds have been a daily ingredient of journalism since the 1830s, when the "penny press" began covering fights, racing, and track. By 1859 the *New York Herald* had hired a reporter to cover baseball regularly. During the 1880s, Washington correspondents supplemented their income after Congress adjourned by reporting on baseball games. Over time, the space devoted to sports increased because sports sold copies. Sports reporting also became an entryway for beginning journalists. The famed war correspondent Richard Harding Davis began his career by covering college football games, and the distinguished Washington columnist James Reston also began as a sportswriter.

During the 1920s, public enthusiasm for spectator sports made legends out of the athletes, and such gifted and colorful writers as Ring Lardner, Damon Runyon, and Grantland Rice helped to raise the standing of sports reporting. By contrast, some lesser sportswriters accepted money to write favorably about teams and players, and their columns were little more than public relations pieces. Beginning in the 1920s, newspaper writers also faced competition from radio, as they would later from television. Because games were broadcast on the radio, fans already knew the final score of the game before they read the paper. Sportswriters like Red Smith would have to find ways to make people want to read their stories.

Walter Wellesley Smith was born in Green Bay, Wisconsin, where his father operated a wholesale and retail grocery. Called "Wellesley" as a boy, he disliked the name and used a variety of nicknames until he eventually settled on "Red," after the color of his hair. As a boy, he loved fishing and baseball but was too scrawny and nearsighted to be much of a ballplayer. As Smith later wrote, he "might have been a great athlete himself except that he is small, puny, slow, inept, uncoordinated, myopic and yellow."

A friend's older brother was studying journalism, and that sounded good to Smith. Coming from a Catholic family, he enrolled at Notre Dame as a journalism student. There he ran track (unsuccessfully) for Knute Rockne, better known today as a football coach. He regularly attended Notre Dame's football games and concluded that he was a better spectator than athlete.

Smith read everything from Shakespeare to Mark Twain and Ernest Hemingway and enjoyed H. L. Mencken's reporting from the Scopes "Monkey Trial" in Dayton, Tennessee. He took journalism classes and edited the Notre Dame yearbook. After graduating in 1927, he mailed job applications to 25 newspapers. Only the *New York Times* sent a reply, and it was a rejection letter. But later that year Smith was hired as a cub reporter for the *Milwaukee Sentinel*, a Hearst paper. He covered the police beat, fires, and school board meetings. The job paid only a small salary, and when he got no raise he applied to the *St. Louis Star* as a copy editor.

In a shakeup in 1928, the *Star's* editor fired half of his sports department for taking bribes from sports promoters. "Do you know anything about sports?" the editor asked Smith. "Only what the average fan knows," he replied. When Smith promised not to take money to influence his reporting, he was made a sportswriter. In later years, Smith felt that he came to sports the right way. He advised others to become "a newspaperman first and a sportswriter next," and to serve an apprenticeship in the city room.

The *Star* sent him to cover the St. Louis Browns' spring training in 1929. That was fine with Smith, who pre-

ferred warm weather sports to winter sports "where you could freeze your toes off." He preferred baseball, football, boxing, and horse racing, and never cared much for games with a lot of movement up and down a court or field, like basketball, hockey, and soccer. At spring training, the Browns' manager, coaches, and players all taught Smith the ropes. He also spent time in the press box with sportswriters from many other papers. Never did Smith claim to be an expert or to write like one. He sought instead to describe games as a spectator, for those who were not there.

In 1933 Smith married schoolteacher Catherine (Kay) Cody and

Sportswriter Red Smith checks the latest scores from the wire service ticker tape in the *New York Herald Tribune's* sports department.

Smith in the press box on opening day at New York's Belmont Race Track in 1951. He sought to cover sporting events as a spectator for those who were not there.

looked for ways to earn more money. For a while he was a "rewrite man" at the *Star*, shaping stories that reporters called in from the scene. It was an exercise that helped him to develop his own style. He moved to Philadelphia in 1936 to write a sports column for the *Philadelphia Record*. Until then, whenever he had gotten a byline it usually read "W. W. Smith." In Philadelphia he started signing his columns "Red Smith," and the name stuck.

Those were the days, Smith later recalled, when "a daily column meant seven a week." Yet he never had a problem finding something to write about. "There was always a fight or football match or ball game or horse

race that had to be covered after the column was done," he explained. The players appreciated his style. One Philadelphia Phillie described Smith as "one of the guys," who often wrote about players' personalities or home life rather than always criticizing their playing. His columns also built Smith a popular following.

Although in his 30s and the father of two small children, Smith felt guilty about not enlisting in World War II. He took comfort, however, in knowing that the troops overseas wanted sports news. In 1944, another reporter found Smith typing early in the morning at a racetrack pressbox. Smith explained that he was writing a children's book about sports. "Why?" the other reporter asked. "Because I have to feed my kids," Smith replied, "and I can't do it on what the paper is paying me." His first book was *Terry and Bunky Play Football*.

Since New York City was both a major metropolis and the nation's media center, New York sports reporters were the highest paid in the country. When an offer finally came in 1945 to write for the *New York Herald Tribune*, Smith jumped at it. His first column appeared the day before his 40th birthday. Before long he was the *Herald Tribune*'s lead sports columnist. Smith won notice for his colorful use of quotes and dialogue. To keep the conversation flowing, he never took notes while interviewing anyone, but relied on his memory to reconstruct his subject's most picturesque expressions. Smith took his readers into the dugouts and locker rooms, whose occupants he observed with his keen eye and described with gentle humor. He wrote in a simple, straightforward manner that readers and other journalists admired. Smith said he never enjoyed writing, "but that's how I pay for this nice job."

As a paper that respected good writing, the *New York Herald Tribune* sent Smith to cover the national political conventions in the 1950s. But he turned down its invitation to become a political columnist. "I don't know where the political stories are," he protested. "But as a sportswriter needing something to write on a dull day, I know where the dugouts are."

After 20 successful years at the *Herald Tribune*, Smith was shocked when the paper closed in 1966. Although he remained a syndicated columnist, his only outlet in New York City was *Women's Wear Daily*. Also, in 1966, his wife died. Smith continued writing lighthearted columns despite his personal anguish, but his career seemed to be coming to a close. Then, in 1967 he met Phyllis Weiss, a widow with five children. They married, and Smith found himself adjusting to having teenagers in the house again.

At 66, Smith was hired to fill a vacancy as a sports columnist for the *New York Times*. Managing editor Abe Rosenthal marveled that a man of Smith's age still "embodied the spirit, vigor and youth of sports." Rosenthal did not care how old Smith was because he liked Smith's lack of pretention and his treatment of sports as entertainment and amusement. Offered a two-year contract, Smith stayed with the *Times* for the rest of his life.

Reinvigorated, Smith showed that he could change with the times. Given the turbulent nature of the 1960s and 1970s, he began commenting on social issues as they spilled over into sports, and he usually sided with the players in their labor disputes with management. "I seem to be finding this a much less pretty world than it seemed when I was younger, and I feel things should be done about it and that sports are part of this world," he wrote. The greater social awareness that crept into his columns won him a Pulitzer Prize in 1976, making him only the third sportswriter to receive that distinction.

Smith held a progressive attitude on everything except allowing women sportswriters in the men's locker rooms. "If a girl or a woman is a qualified sportswriter, an employed sportswriter, then she should have the same sources that I have," he agreed. But he also believed that athletes were entitled to some privacy. He thought women writers could do their job just as well by covering press conferences. The women sportswriters countered that Smith had always gotten his best quotes in the locker room.

Red Smith

BORN

September 25, 1905
Green Bay, Wisconsin

DIED

January 15, 1982
Stamford, Connecticut

EDUCATION

B.A., Notre Dame University (1927)

ACCOMPLISHMENTS

Editor, Notre Dame *Dome* (1925–27); reporter, *Milwaukee Sentinel* (1927–28); sports reporter, *St. Louis Star* (1928–36); sports reporter, *Philadelphia Record* (1936–45); sports columnist, *New York Herald Tribune* (1945–66); syndicated sports columnist (1966–71); sports columnist, *New York Times* (1971–82); author of *Terry and Bunky Play Football* (with Richard Mark Fishel, 1945), *The Saturday Evening Post Sports Stories* (1949), *Out of the Red* (1950), *Views of Sport* (1954), *The Best of Red Smith* (1963), *Red Smith on Fishing* (1963), *Strawberries in the Wintertime: The Sporting World of Red Smith* (1974), *Press Box: Red Smith's Favorite Sports Stories* (1976), *The Red Smith Reader* (1982), and *To Absent Friends* (1982)

"Intolerance is an ugly word, unsightly in any company and particularly so on the sports page where, happily, it does not often appear. Without laboring the point, it is fair to say that on most playing fields a man is gauged by what he can do, and neither race nor creed nor color nor previous condition of servitude is a consideration."

—from "An Ugly Word in Sports," *New York Herald Tribune* (May 10, 1947)

The *New York Times*'s sports editor from 1978 to 1980 was a woman, Le Anne Schreiber—the first woman sports editor of a major newspaper. She and Smith clashed not over gender, but politics. After the Soviet Union invaded Afghanistan, Smith wrote that the United States should boycott the 1980 Olympics in Moscow as a protest. When he devoted a second column to the subject, Schreiber refused to print it on the grounds that it contained inaccuracies and was more about foreign policy than sports. This marked the first time in 35 years that one of Smith's columns had been killed. Unfortunately for the *Times*, the column had already gone out to the syndicated papers. Its publication everywhere except the *Times* drew more attention to the column than it might otherwise have received. Much embarrassed, the *New York Times* asked Smith to write one more column on the subject, which it printed a week later. The flap gave momentum to the movement that eventually resulted in a U.S. boycott of the Moscow Olympics. Stepping away from the controversy he stirred, Smith promised that his next columns would be about "the infield fly rule."

As he grew older, Smith wrote a number of poignant obituaries for sportswriters who had been his friends and for the former athletes he had covered. His own health deteriorated and in January 1982 he announced to his readers that he was cutting back from four columns a week to three, adding: "We shall have to wait and see whether the quality improves." He died before he could write another column. In his time, Red Smith had been the most widely read sportswriter in the United States, and by all accounts the most literate. Smith himself suggested a more modest epitaph. "I respect a good reporter," he said, "and I'd like to be called that."

FURTHER READING

Berkow, Ira. *Red: A Biography of Red Smith*. New York: Times Books, 1986.

Garrison, Bruce, with Mark Sabljak. *Sports Reporting*. Ames: Iowa State University Press, 1993.

Holtzman, Jerome, ed. *No Cheering in the Press Box*. New York: Holt, Rinehart & Winston, 1974.

Kahn, Roger. *Memories of Summer: When Baseball Was an Art and Writing About It a Game*. New York: Hyperion, 1997.

Kluger, Richard. *The Paper: The Life and Death of the New York Herald Tribune*. New York: Knopf, 1986.

Rice, Grantland. *The Tumult and the Shouting: My Life in Sport*. New York: A. S. Barnes, 1954.

Smith, Red. *The Best of Red Smith*. New York: Franklin Watts, 1963.

———. *Out of the Red*. New York: Knopf, 1950.

———. *Press Box: Red Smith's Favorite Sports Stories*. New York: Norton, 1976.

———. *Red Smith on Fishing*. Garden City, N.Y.: Doubleday, 1963.

———. *The Red Smith Reader*. New York: Random House, 1982.

———. *The Saturday Evening Post Sports Stories*. New York: Pocket, 1949.

———. *Strawberries in the Wintertime: The Sporting World of Red Smith*. New York: Quadrangle, 1974.

———. *To Absent Friends*. New York: Atheneum, 1982.

———. *Views of Sport*. New York: Knopf, 1954.

Smith, Red, with Richard Mark Fishel. *Terry and Bunky Play Football*. New York: Putnam, 1945.

Woodward, Stanley, and Frank Graham, Jr. *Sportswriter*. New York: Doubleday, 1967.

Yardley, Jonathan. *Ring: A Biography of Ring Lardner*. New York: Random House, 1977.

Edward R. Murrow

THE CONSCIENCE OF BROADCASTING

I t was during the devastating German air attack on London in 1940 that Edward R. Murrow made his first impression upon American audiences. With German planes blitzing the city, Murrow conducted radio broadcasts on rooftops, describing the sights and sounds, as bombs and air-raid sirens could be heard in the background. "It's a bomber's moon out tonight," he would say, capturing the imagination of listeners thousands of miles away. He spoke in a measured, thoughtful, and wry manner that people understood and enjoyed. Wartime London forged Murrow's public image. He became the most respected American news commentator. He also acquired a refined, stylish, and impeccably tailored appearance.

Contrary to that highly cultured image, Edward R. Murrow was born Egbert Murrow in a log cabin alongside Polecat Creek, near Greensboro, North Carolina. The cabin had neither electricity nor indoor plumbing. His father, Roscoe Murrow, farmed the land, while his mother, Ethel

Edward R. Murrow, photographed here with his trademark cigarette in hand, set the standard for later broadcasters and documentary producers.

Murrow's exposure of the conditions of migrant farm workers, in the 1960 television documentary "Harvest of Shame," was regarded as his finest piece of investigative reporting.

Lamb Murrow, taught at the nearby Quaker school. In 1913, when he was five, his family moved across the country to Blanchard, Washington. There his father worked as an engineer on a train hauling lumber, and Egbert spent his summers working at logging camps. Among the robust lumberjacks, he dropped "Egbert" and began calling himself "Ed." By the time he got to college he had adopted the more formal "Edward."

Following his older brothers, Edward R. Murrow attended Washington State College in Pullman. Although he had wanted to go to the more prestigious University of Virginia, family finances could not afford it. At Washington State, however, Murrow came under the influence of a remarkable speech and drama teacher, Ida Lou Anderson. She spotted the poten-

tial of the tall, thin, darkly handsome young man with a resonant voice, and helped transform him from a lumberjack to a gentleman.

Active in campus politics, Murrow attended a meeting of the National Student Federation of America (NSFA), which propelled him to the national stage. His speech to the convention so impressed the delegates with its poised, confident, and mature manner that they elected him president of the federation. After graduation, he ran the NSFA's national office in New York City. In 1930 the NSFA sent Murrow on his first trip abroad, to an international conference of students in Belgium. The NSFA brought him into contact with the Columbia Broadcasting System (CBS), which was producing a radio program called "University of the Air." Murrow's agreement to find speakers for the program launched his impressive quarter-century career with CBS. The NSFA also introduced Ed Murrow to his bride-to-be, Janet Huntington Brewster, an NSFA delegate from Mount Holyoke College. They married in 1934.

At the time of his marriage, Murrow worried that he lacked a profession. Events in Europe intervened, however, to give him a mission. Adolf Hitler and the Nazi party were rearming Germany and pressing for territorial expansion. Britain and France at first sought to appease Hitler. While the United States remained isolationist, Americans were curious about events that might lead to a second World War.

In 1935 CBS hired Murrow to direct its educational programming. The job did not require him to be on the air himself, but to be a "director of talks," recruiting other speakers. "I don't think I could ever be a broadcaster," he told CBS news broadcaster Robert Trout, because he needed to see his listeners' faces and feel their reactions. Trout advised him not to think of the radio microphone as an amplifier to address a large crowd, but as a telephone to talk to one person. When Murrow did begin speaking on the radio, he adopted a calm, personal, and incisive style of delivery. Never having been a print journalist, he wrote his material not to be read but to be heard.

CBS sent Ed Murrow to Europe in 1937 to continue organizing radio talks, but the fast-breaking news coming from Europe put him on the air himself. He became one of the first radio foreign correspondents. When Germany annexed Austria, Murrow organized a "news roundup" of live radio transmissions from London, Paris, Vienna, and Washington, D.C., on the same program. Building on the success of this format, CBS authorized Murrow to put together a team of foreign correspondents, including William L. Shirer

in Berlin, Eric Sevareid in Paris, and a woman broadcaster, Marvin Breckinridge, in Amsterdam.

Europe went to war in September 1939, and a year later Germany launched its air attacks on London. Opening his broadcasts with a phrase suggested by his old speech teacher, Ida Lou Anderson—"THIS is London"— Murrow provided Americans with first-hand descriptions of the Battle of Britain as it happened. Janet Murrow also made broadcasts about the home-front conditions in England. Another journalist, Robert Landry, observed that Murrow had "more influence than a shipload of newspapermen. . . . 1. He beats the newspapers by hours; 2. He reaches millions who otherwise have to depend on provincial newspapers for their foreign news; 3. He writes his own headlines. His, unlike a reporter's, are not strained through . . . copy editor or headline writer . . . people begin to feel that they know him."

Murrow returned to the United States a famous correspondent. Welcomed at the White House, the Murrows dined with President Franklin D. Roosevelt on the night that Pearl Harbor was attacked. After the United States entered the war, CBS sent Murrow back to England as a war correspondent, broadening his coverage to the entire European front. He even flew on a bomber raid over Germany, and he delivered such a stirring commentary that the British Broadcasting Corporation (BBC) asked permission to rebroadcast it in England. Though that report earned Murrow prestigious awards, CBS ordered him not to risk his life by flying any more missions. Later, however, he accompanied U.S. forces as they invaded Germany and was present when the army liberated the concentration camp at Buchenwald.

After the war Murrow received offers to become a university president or a State Department spokesman.

Edward R. Murrow

BORN
April 25, 1908
Greensboro, North Carolina

DIED
April 27, 1965
Pawling, New York

EDUCATION
B.A. in speech, Washington State College (1930)

ACCOMPLISHMENTS
Radio educational director, CBS (1935–37); foreign correspondent, CBS (1937–45); director of public affairs, CBS (1945–47); "Edward R. Murrow with the News" radio broadcasts (1947–59); "Hear It Now" radio show (1947–51); "See It Now" television show (1951–58); "Person to Person" television show (1953–59); "Small World" television show (1958–60); documentary producer, "CBS Reports" (1958–60); director, U.S. Information Agency (1961–64)

"This is no time for men who oppose Senator McCarthy's methods to keep silent, or for those who approve. We can deny our heritage and our history, but we cannot escape responsibility for the result. There is no way for a citizen of a republic to abdicate his responsibilities. As a nation we have come into our full inheritance at a tender age. We proclaim ourselves—as indeed we are—the defenders of freedom, what's left of it, but we cannot defend freedom abroad by deserting it at home. The actions of the junior senator from Wisconsin have caused alarm and dismay amongst our allies abroad and given considerable comfort to our enemies, and whose fault is that? Not really his. He didn't create this situation of fear; he merely exploited it, and rather successfully. Cassius was right: 'The fault, dear Brutus, is not in our stars but in ourselves.' Good night, and good luck."

—from "See It Now" TV program (March 7, 1954)

Instead he accepted the post of news director for CBS. But his heart was not in administration, and he soon returned to the air with a nightly radio news program, "Edward R. Murrow with the News." The program mixed reporting with his own commentary on the day's events. Together with Fred W. Friendly, Murrow also produced a weekly radio documentary series, "Hear It Now." Since television was rapidly spreading across the nation, in 1951 Murrow and Friendly changed the name of the program to "See It Now." For a half hour each week it presented several stories on current issues. One of its most memorable episodes was Murrow's Christmas visit to American troops fighting in Korea.

"See It Now" broadcast during a period of great anxiety over the Cold War. An anticommunist movement in the United States blamed communist victories overseas on traitors within American society and government. This "Red Scare" spread to the media and blacklisted many radio, television, and motion picture performers, preventing them from being hired. Proof of disloyalty was not required; suspicion and accusations were enough to

destroy people's careers. Wisconsin senator Joseph R. McCarthy held Senate hearings to expose alleged communists, bullying and berating his witnesses and making reckless charges. Outraged by McCarthy's behavior and unafraid of his threats, Murrow devoted an entire episode of "See It Now" in 1954 to exposing McCarthy by his own words and actions. When McCarthy was given equal time to reply, he accused Murrow of engaging in "propaganda for communist causes." His performance only verified Murrow's warnings. McCarthy's public standing started to slip, accentuated by the public's shock in watching him on the televised Army-McCarthy hearings. By the end of the year the Senate had censured McCarthy.

"See It Now" tackled controversial issues regularly. "Why does Murrow have to save the world each week?" network officials lamented. Worried sponsors pulled out of the series, which had to compete for prime time with entertainment programs. By contrast, Murrow's celebrity interview show, "Person to Person," drew high ratings and lucrative advertising. Dismayed by these trends, Murrow delivered a scorching attack on the medium in a speech to the Radio and Television News Directors. He protested "the constant striving to reach the largest possible audience for everything." Rather than informing the nation, television was being used "to distract, delude, amuse and insulate" viewers. "This instrument can teach, it can illuminate; yes, and it can even inspire," he concluded. "But it can do so only to the extent that humans are determined to use it to those ends. Otherwise, it is merely wires and lights in a box." For serving as the conscience of the new media, Murrow won both public praise and the resentment of television executives.

CBS finally canceled "See It Now," and Murrow and Friendly made less frequent documentaries to be shown on "CBS Reports." One of these episodes in 1960 exposed the conditions of migrant workers. Called "Harvest of Shame," it was regarded as Murrow's finest piece of investigative reporting.

Murrow left broadcasting to accept President John F. Kennedy's offer to head the U.S. Information Agency—at only a tenth the salary he earned in television. Fellow journalists were upset that he would abandon journalism for propaganda, but Murrow believed it a legitimate role to promote freedom, democracy, and accurate news reporting around the world. After Kennedy's assassination, he continued briefly under President Lyndon B. Johnson, but he was uncomfortable with Johnson's crude style and troubled over the war in Vietnam. In declining health, Murrow resigned in 1964.

Murrow had been addicted to cigarettes since he was a teenager in the logging camps of the Pacific Northwest. A lit cigarette and billowing clouds of smoke around his head became his on-air trademark. Murrow smoked even during a "See It Now" episode that linked cigarettes to lung cancer. Eventually, lung cancer claimed his life in 1965, at the age of 57. His stature in television news broadcasting remains a benchmark against which later television news broadcasters and documentary producers have measured their own work. Few have met his standards.

FURTHER READING

Baranouw, Erik. *The Golden Web*. Vol. 2, *A History of Broadcasting in the United States*. New York: Oxford University Press, 1968.

Bliss, Edward, Jr., ed. *In Search of Light: The Broadcasts of Edward R. Murrow, 1938–1961*. New York: Da Capo, 1997.

Cloud, Stanley, and Lynne Olson. *The Murrow Boys: Pioneers on the Front Lines of Broadcast Journalism*. Boston: Houghton Mifflin, 1996.

Finkelstein, Norman H. *With Heroic Truth: The Life of Edward R. Murrow*. New York: Clarion, 1997.

Friendly, Fred W. *Due to Circumstances Beyond Our Control. . .* New York: Vintage, 1967.

Kendrick, Alexander. *Prime Time: The Life of Edward R. Murrow*. Boston: Little, Brown, 1967.

MacVane, William. *On the Air in World War II*. New York: Morrow, 1979.

Murrow, Edward R. *In Search of Light: The Broadcasts of Edward R. Murrow, 1938–1961*. Edited by Edward Bliss, Jr. New York: Knopf, 1967.

———. *This Is London*. Edited by Elmer Davis. New York: Simon & Schuster, 1941.

Murrow, Edward R., and Fred Friendly, eds. *See It Now*. New York: Simon & Schuster, 1955.

Persico, Joseph E. *Edward R. Murrow: An American Original*. New York: McGraw-Hill, 1988.

Sperber, A. M. *Murrow, His Life and Times*. New York: Freundlich Books, 1986.

More American Journalists to Remember

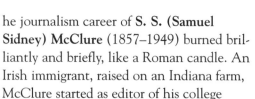

The journalism career of **S. S. (Samuel Sidney) McClure** (1857–1949) burned brilliantly and briefly, like a Roman candle. An Irish immigrant, raised on an Indiana farm, McClure started as editor of his college paper, the *Knox Student*. After graduation he launched the *Wheelman*, a magazine devoted to the craze for bicycling in the 1880s. He moved to New York City, where he formed a syndicate to sell literary works to newspapers, and he contracted with many of the best writers of his day.

In 1893 he began publishing *McClure's Magazine*, originally a literary and historical journal that by the turn of the century became the nation's leading muckraker, publishing exposés by Lincoln Steffens and Ida Tarbell. But McClure's mercurial temper led to the mass defection of his talented staff in 1906. That marked the rapid decline of *McClure's*. S. S. McClure devoted the rest of his long life to a host of idealistic and eccentric causes.

E. W. (Edward Wyllis) Scripps (1854–1926) started as an office boy at the *Detroit Evening News* and rose to found

A man of contradictions, the wealthy publisher E. W. Scripps wrote in support of the working class while living a life of luxury.

the first major newspaper chain in the United States (Scripps-McRae, later Scripps-Howard, newspapers), as well as the United Press International (UPI) wire service. A man of many contradictions, Scripps was an outspoken social critic and advocate of the working people who himself lived in luxury as a wealthy press baron. He denounced monopoly while building a string of newspapers, principally in Midwestern industrial cities. A man of courage and vision, Scripps was a great risk-taker and a rough, almost ruthless entrepreneur.

David Graham Phillips (1867–1911) tackled controversy in both his journalism and his fictional writings. Beginning as a reporter for the *Cincinnati Times-Star* and the *Cincinnati Commercial Gazette*, he was hired by the *New York Sun* in 1890 and by Joseph Pulitzer's *New York World* in 1893. A dramatic writing style and eagerness to expose corruption accounted for his recruitment, each with impressive increases in salary. Phillips left the *World* to write novels but kept up his journalism through magazine articles.

In 1906 publisher William Randolph Hearst commissioned Phillips to write a sustained attack on business control of the U.S. Senate. *Cosmopolitan* published Phillips's series, "Treason of the Senate," for nearly a year. Public reaction led to a constitutional amendment for direct election of senators, as opposed to their election by the state legislatures. Phillips was shot to death in 1911 by a man who erroneously believed that his family had been the subject of one of Phillips's novels.

When Jacob Coxey led his army of unemployed men on a march on Washington in 1894, reporter **Ray Stannard Baker** (1870–1946) accompanied the procession, sending back dispatches to the *Chicago News-Record*. At first skeptical, Baker grew sympathetic to their plight and more aware of America's social and economic problems. He carried his social consciousness with him to the staff of *McClure's Magazine* in 1898, where he joined Lincoln Steffens and Ida Tarbell as the nation's leading muckrakers. Called "America's Number 1 Reporter," he wrote about employer-labor relations, federal regulation of business, and race relations. Once close to Theodore Roosevelt, Baker switched his allegiance to Woodrow Wilson and handled Wilson's press relations during negotiations for the Treaty of Versailles. He devoted his last years to writing Wilson's official biography.

The great chronicler of Americana **Mark Sullivan** (1874–1952) began reporting as a student for the West Chester, Pennsylvania, *Village Record*. After attending Harvard Law School, he returned to journalism as the author of muckraking articles about political corruption and patent medicine scandals for the *Atlantic Monthly*, *McClure's*, and *Collier's Weekly*. During the Progressive Era, Sullivan wrote a regular column, "Comment on Congress," for *Collier's* that attacked conservatives and supported President Theodore Roosevelt. Briefly editor of *Collier's*, he left to report on World War I and the peace talks that followed. From the 1920s until his death, Sullivan wrote a syndicated column for the *New York Herald Tribune*. Increasingly alienated

Called "America's Number 1 Reporter," Ray Stannard Baker had access to the nation's leaders from both parties. Here he interviews Virginia senator Claude Swanson.

Heywood Broun crusaded for the underdog in his newspaper columns and organized a labor union for journalists—the American Newspaper Guild.

from his times, the once progressive muckraker ended his career nostalgically cataloging American politics, customs, literature, and music in a six-volume history of the years from 1900 to 1925.

Born of former slave parents in Georgia, just after the Civil War, **Robert S. Abbott** (1868–1940) was educated at Hampton Institute and received a law degree from the Kent College of Law in Chicago. Having trained at his stepfather's print shop, he determined to establish a newspaper. In 1905 he launched the *Chicago Defender,* which became one of the largest and most successful African-American weekly papers. Beyond its Chicago edition, the *Defender* published editions in several other cities with substantial black populations, giving it a national audience and making Abbott a wealthy man. Although he was solemn and deliberate, Abbott produced a lively and energetic paper that campaigned unfailingly for racial integration and civil rights.

The daughter of the editor and publisher of the *Springfield* (Illinois) *Republican,* **Nellie McAleney Revell** (1872–1958) started on a rival newspaper until she had proved herself as a reporter and was hired by her father's paper. She reported for papers in Chicago, Denver, Seattle, and San Francisco before joining the *New York World.* The *World* assigned her to cover everything from the coronation of the czar of Russia to prizefights. But when the *World* tried to put her columns on the women's page, she quit. After the same thing happened at the *New York Evening Mail,* she resigned to become a Broadway press agent. Sidelined for years by severe back problems, she published three books about her struggle to recover. In 1930 the National

Broadcasting Company (NBC) hired Revell to conduct radio interviews with prominent actors, athletes, and politicians, and to do a program called "Neighbor Nell."

A Harvard dropout, **Heywood Broun** (1888–1939) joined the *New York Morning Telegraph* in 1908 as a sports reporter and later became its drama critic and literary editor. Switching to the *New York World* in 1921, he wrote one of the first signed opinion columns, "It Seems to Me." Although his column often dealt with humorous subjects, Broun also tackled such serious issues as the pending execution of the anarchists Nicola Sacco and Bartolomeo Vanzetti. He became so impassioned about the Sacco and Vanzetti case that the *World* suspended his column until he changed the subject. When he criticized the paper for its timidity, he was fired. He returned to the *Telegraph* (which later merged into the *World-Telegraph*). Broun joined the Socialist party in 1930 and ran unsuccessfully for Congress. In 1933 he organized a labor union for journalists, the American Newspaper Guild, becoming its first president.

Born in Mankato, Minnesota, **Marvel Jackson Cooke** (1903–) graduated from the University of Minnesota and headed to New York City's Harlem in 1926, at the height of the Harlem Renaissance. She joined the staff of the *Amsterdam News,* the city's leading African-American newspaper, first as secretary to the society editor and later as the paper's first woman reporter. Cooke specialized in stories dealing with the arts. When she organized the first newspaper guild at a black newspaper, the owner fired the entire editorial staff. The ousted staff picketed for 10 weeks until the paper was sold and the new owners hired them back. Cooke's labor interests drew her into membership in the Communist party. In 1942 she switched to the *People's Voice*, becoming its assistant managing editor. In 1950 she was hired on the otherwise white male staff of the *New York Daily Compass*. The first black woman to report for a white newspaper, she left journalism when that paper closed in 1952.

Colonel **Robert R. McCormick** (1880–1955) published the *Chicago Tribune* in an almost baronial manner. Although he acquired his education and style of dress in England, McCormick developed a passionate patriotism for America and made his newspaper a leading voice of isolationism. The *Tribune* opposed American entry into World War I, the Versailles Treaty, the World Court, and any effort to aid the Allies before World War II. In 1942 McCormick's *Chicago Tribune* published a story revealing that the United States had broken Japan's secret military codes. This recklessness reflected his belief in the absolute right of the press to criticize its government whether in war or peace.

McCormick's cousin, **Eleanor M. "Cissy" Patterson** (1881–1948), made the *Washington Times-Herald* a lively, colorful, and successful paper. Cissy Patterson's prominent newspaper family never encouraged her own journalistic ambitions. She dabbled as a newspaper and magazine writer and novelist before persuading publisher William Randolph Hearst to let her take over his failing *Washington Herald*. Few gave her much chance of success. But Patterson merged the paper with the *Washington Times*, hired an energetic staff—including a large number of women reporters—and introduced flashy headlines, spicy news, and large

doses of society gossip. All this boosted the paper's circulation significantly. Yet its fortunes depended heavily on its publisher, and the paper could not survive long without her. After her death the *Times-Herald* was absorbed into the *Washington Post*.

Dashing and fearless, **Floyd Gibbons** (1887–1939) was severely wounded and lost an eye while covering the fighting during World War I. Afterward, he made a white eye patch his trademark. His reporting career started in Minneapolis in 1907. He moved to the *Chicago Tribune* and was sent to cover Pancho Villa's raids across the Mexican border and then to Europe during the World War. Gaining a national reputation as a war correspondent, he became director of foreign news for the *New York Tribune*. Gibbons shifted to radio in the 1920s with a program called "The Headline Hunter." There he pioneered live coverage of events with a portable shortwave transmitter, and entertained audiences with his machinegun rapid speech and irreverent attitude toward the news.

Fulton Lewis, Jr. (1903–66), began his career on the staff of the *Washington Herald*, a Hearst paper, as a reporter, editor, and columnist. In 1937 Lewis started a news commentary program, "The Top of the News," on a local Washington radio station that was later broadcast nationally on the Mutual Broadcasting System. Angered that the congressional press galleries admitted only newspaper correspondents, he lobbied Congress for the creation of a radio gallery (later the radio and television gallery) in 1939. Conservative in his thinking, Lewis was a persistent critic of Franklin Roosevelt's New Deal and Harry Truman's Fair Deal. In the 1950s Lewis

The flamboyant publisher Eleanor "Cissy" Patterson made the *Washington Times-Herald* a lively and colorful paper.

allied himself so closely with Senator Joseph McCarthy's anticommunist crusade that his stature and audience declined along with the senator's.

Lowell Thomas (1892–1981) grew up in the mining camps of Cripple Creek, Colorado, where he heard the miners' stories of their adventures in exotic, far-off places. While attending law school in Chicago, he took a job reporting for the *Chicago Journal* to help pay his expenses. He found the law boring and got more enjoyment out of covering Chicago's raucous local news. Thomas went to Europe to cover World War I and spent the next decade as a foreign correspondent for the *New York Globe*. He reported on the adventures of T. E. Lawrence in Arabia, climbed the Himalayas, and went through the Malay jungle on an elephant.

In 1930 the sales director for the Columbia Broadcasting System (CBS) heard Thomas lecture and hired him as a radio news commentator to replace Floyd Gibbons. Thomas's rich baritone and confident knowledge of the world won him an audience. He continued broadcasting the news, from all over the world, for the next 45 years.

Pollster **Elmo Roper, Jr.** (1900–71) left a sales career in 1933 to begin market research that pioneered in the sampling of small cross sections of the population that reflected general public sentiments. In 1935 *Fortune* magazine hired Roper to publish regular surveys of public opinion. In contrast to the *Literary Digest*, whose poll predicted the election of Alfred

Landon in 1936, Roper's polls correctly indicated that Franklin D. Roosevelt would win a landslide reelection. After the election the *Literary Digest* went out of business and Roper launched his own polling firm, later known as Roper Research Associates. In 1940 the Columbia Broadcasting System hired Roper to analyze voting trends on election evening. Throughout the rest of his career he regularly conducted polls and presented the results in newspaper columns, magazine articles, and radio broadcasts.

The first woman to win a Pulitzer Prize in journalism, **Anne O'Hare McCormack** (1882–1954) began her career with a weekly religious magazine, the *Catholic Universe Bulletin* in Cleveland, Ohio. Because her husband's business as an importer frequently took them to Europe, she began sending occasional articles to the *New York Times* in 1920. Her reporting led to a full-time position in 1922, and eventually to a three-times-a-week column, "Abroad." She covered everything from the rise of fascism in Europe to the advent of the New Deal at home, interviewing Hitler, Mussolini, Stalin, Churchill, and Franklin D. Roosevelt. Her growing stature within the *New York Times* led to her appointment as the first woman member of that prestigious paper's editorial board.

Serious to the point of being stodgy, **Arthur Krock** (1886–1974) for 30 years wrote a politically influential newspaper column, "In the Nation," for the *New York Times*. Born in

Kentucky, he started as a reporter on the *Louisville Herald* and became managing editor of the *Louisville Courier-Journal*. After feuding with its owner, he left to become an editorial writer for the *New York World*. Krock next joined the editorial staff of the *New York Times*. In 1932 the *Times* sent him to head its Washington bureau—temporarily, he thought. He held that post until 1953, writing the lead stories out of Washington and a column that appeared four times a week on the editorial page of the *Times*. As bureau chief, he obtained exclusive interviews with Washington's highest sources, which made him a frequent winner of Pulitzer Prizes.

A voice of Southern liberalism before the civil rights movement began, **Ralph McGill** (1898–1969) started writing for the *Nashville Banner* while still a student at Vanderbilt. In the 1920s he did both news and sports reporting and wrote a humorous syndicated column, "I'm the Gink." He joined the *Atlanta Constitution* in 1929 as a sports editor, rising to become editor in chief by 1942. As editor, he carried on the tradition of an earlier Atlanta editor, Henry Grady, promoting the "New South" through modernization of industry and agriculture and moderation in race relations. McGill's editorials called for an end to segregation and defended sit-ins, freedom rides, and other civil rights activities. In 1959 he won the Pulitzer Prize for his editorial on the bombing of an Atlanta synagogue.

The "Washington Merry-Go-Round" column written by **Drew Pearson** (1897–1969) won fame for exposing the behavior and misdoings of Washington officials. Pearson was the diplomatic correspondent of the *Baltimore Sun* when he and another reporter, Robert S. Allen, anonymously published *Washington Merry-Go-Round*, a highly critical, gossip-filled book that became a national best-seller. The book cost them their jobs but won them a widely syndicated column. After Allen left to go in the army during World War II, Pearson continued to write the muckraking column (later with Jack Anderson) until his death. He was never hesitant to take on powerful political figures. One of his last exposés led to the censure of Senator Thomas Dodd for financial misconduct.

A thoughtful critic of the press, **A. J. (Abbott Joseph) Liebling** (1904–63) began as a sportswriter for the *New York Times* and later became a feature writer for the *Providence Journal* and the *New York World-Telegram*. His career shifted in 1935 when the *New Yorker* magazine hired him to write on any subject—from sports to religion and politics. Following his war correspondence from Europe during World War II, Liebling took over the *New Yorker*'s regular column called "The Wayward Press." For the next two decades he looked over the shoulders of reporters, editors, and publishers, followed trends in the industry, and pointed out its defects. His best articles were published as books: the *Wayward Pressman* (1947) and the *Press* (1961).

President John F. Kennedy opened Presidential press conferences to live television coverage. Here Kennedy meets with the press on November 20, 1962, after the Cuban Missile Crisis.

4 The Modern Journalist (1945–present)

The Cold War of the late 20th century elevated both the stakes of journalism and the status of journalists. As the nation worried that any international incident might trigger nuclear war, the opinions of authoritative columnists seemed to carry more weight than did those of the politicians they wrote about. Television news broadcasters gained even greater visibility and clout, eventually causing Vice President Spiro Agnew to lash out at television news broadcasting. "No medium has a more profound influence over public opinion," Agnew charged, and yet there seemed to be no checks on its vast power. Nor, he insisted, did the views of these journalists represent the views of the American people. Agnew's efforts to intimidate the media failed, and yet political leaders of all parties have continued to try their best to manipulate the media for their own advantage.

The media saw its role as society's watchdog. Especially as younger reporters, women, and minorities entered into the mainstream press, they sought to force society to confront the most difficult issues: racial discrimination, environmental pollution, poverty at home, and military interventions abroad. Investigative reporters exposed corporate abuses, caught the government telling lies, and caused a powerful President of the United States to resign under fire. The courts, in several key cases, protected the press against libel suits and government attempts to suppress information. These actions reasserted the public's ultimate right to know.

The public sometimes complained that the media emphasized the most negative aspects of society, and yet what the public bought and watched seemed to send the opposite message. "The public, as measured by its reading habits, does not so much object to 'bad' news as it wants a balanced diet, with more 'good' news," *New York Times* editor Max Frankel assessed. "And the public, as measured by television ratings favors trashy gossip about the rich and famous, 'magazine' exposés of skulduggery and hourly updates about a certain murder trial."

Satellites, computers, and fax machines turned the media into global empires that reported the news instantly from around the world at any time of the day or night. "Television news is a picture of the news," a handbook for CBS broadcasters explained; "it is a factual, concise presentation of news which, in one way or another, has an effect upon the people who turn to your program for a picture of what is happening to their world." Television allowed viewers to see and hear the news, often as it was happening. Not only did the assassination of President John F. Kennedy dominate the airwaves, but viewers witnessed the shooting of his assassin.

Competition from television caused newspapers and magazines to change. The national daily paper USA Today pioneered in adopting a televisionlike format of colorful maps and graphics and snippets of news stories. Whatever the medium, reporters, editors, and broadcasters all searched for a balance of news that was both important and interesting. News remained both a business and a public service that sought to tell the public not only what it wanted to know, but what it ought to know. The news would always be more than "just the facts." Deciding whom to interview and what to report shapes the agenda and molds public opinion. Journalists, those who report, package, and distribute the news, whether by newsletter, newspaper, magazine, radio, television, or computer, define what news is.

Walter Lippmann

POWERFUL PUNDIT

As Cold War tensions between the United States and the Soviet Union mounted perilously in 1961, Soviet premier Nikita Khrushchev granted an interview to the American newspaper columnist Walter Lippmann. Before he left Washington, the journalist lunched at the White House with President John F. Kennedy to discuss U.S.-Soviet relations. As he boarded a plane to Rome—his first stop before going to Moscow—he was handed a note from Khrushchev asking to postpone the meeting for a week. "Impossible," Lippmann replied. By the time the plane landed in Rome, word came that the Soviet premier had rearranged his own plans in order to meet with him. Such was the influence of Walter Lippmann.

The man whom presidents, premiers, kings, and dictators accommodated was America's most prestigious columnist and public philosopher. The author of many thoughtful books, Lippmann might have made his career teaching at a university, but he aimed for a larger audience of newspaper readers. His columns were read religiously at the State Department, the White House, and the Senate Foreign Relations Committee and influenced the course of

Walter Lippmann (left) worked together with Franklin D. Roosevelt (center) during the First World War when Roosevelt was assistant secretary of the Navy. Together with William Blackmen (right), they constituted the Arsenal and Navy Yard Wage Commission. Later, however, during Roosevelt's Presidency, Lippmann opposed many of the President's policies.

Although primarily a newspaper columnist, Walter Lippmann also addressed issues through radio and television commentary.

became president of Harvard's Socialist Club and wrote radical-leaning articles for the *Harvard Illustrated* and the *Harvard Monthly*. After graduation he worked as a cub reporter for the *Boston Common*, a reform-minded weekly paper, and then spent a year as a research assistant for the famed muckraking magazine writer Lincoln Steffens, helping him with articles for *Everybody's* magazine.

Stepping beyond writing into politics, Lippmann next took a job with the newly elected Socialist mayor of Schenectady, New York, but he was already beginning to move away from radicalism. Lippmann never completely trusted the masses and believed in progressive leadership by an educated elite. Democracy, he wrote, was "not so much a way of expressing the wisdom people have, as it is a way of enabling them to get wisdom." He pursued these themes in his first book, *A Preface to Politics*, which was published to considerable acclaim in 1913. Among those who were impressed by the book was Herbert Croly. About to launch a reform journal, *The New Republic*, Croly spotted Lippmann's potential as a political journalist and invited him to join the magazine's staff.

Although it intended to emphasize domestic reform, *The New Republic* became preoccupied with the war that began in Europe in 1914. Previously, Lippmann had given little thought to foreign affairs and wished that money spent on military weapons could be diverted to improving society. His radical friends viewed the war as a fight between European nations over colonies, and they wanted the United States to stay neutral. But as the war progressed, Lippmann warned of the danger of the U.S. disarming in "an armed world." He called for America to abandon its isolationism and play a more active role in world politics. President Woodrow Wilson was mov-

American policy. They also influenced other journalists. The columnist James Reston observed of Lippmann: "He has given my generation of newspapermen a wider vision of our duty. He has shown us how to put the event of the day in its proper relationship to the history of yesterday and the dream of tomorrow."

Lippmann came from a well-to-do family. An only child, he grew up in Manhattan, attended prestigious private schools, and traveled annually to Europe with his parents. At Harvard University he excelled in his studies but found many of the social clubs closed to him because he was a Jew. Instead of joining the social clubs, he

ing in that same direction, and in 1916 Lippmann met with Wilson and his chief foreign policy adviser, Colonel Edward House.

When the United States entered World War I in April 1917, Lippmann volunteered to help the war effort. Secretary of War Newton D. Baker appointed him as his assistant. Colonel House then borrowed Lippmann to help prepare the United States's war aims—known as Wilson's Fourteen Points. In 1918 Lippmann joined the army's military intelligence branch as a captain. He was in Europe, writing propaganda pieces to sway German public opinion, when the war ended. Lippmann hoped to play a role in the drafting of the peace treaty, but was excluded when President Wilson came to Paris to lead the negotiations himself.

Disillusioned with the Allies' vindictiveness toward Germany, Lippmann returned to the United States, rejoined *The New Republic*, and gave assistance to the senators who eventually defeated the Treaty of Versailles and the League of Nations. Later, Lippmann regretted this decision: whatever the flaws of the League of Nations, he decided, the United States had been wrong to retreat into isolationism after the war.

Lippmann's experience writing propaganda made him rethink the role of the press and public opinion in a democracy. Did the press give the public the information necessary to make intelligent decisions? In 1922 he dealt with these issues in his book, *Public Opinion*. People's cultures make them reduce other people and events to stereotypes, Lippmann wrote. What they believe are "facts" are really opinions that keep them from seeing the truth. Society asked people to make judgments on great issues of war and peace that were beyond their everyday experiences. The press might cast a spotlight on specific issues, but it could not hope to keep the public informed

about everything. Lippmann concluded that society should allow well-informed experts to make its critical decisions.

Yet at the very time that Lippmann extolled the virtues of a "specialized class" of intellectuals and experts, he was widening his own audience. Lippmann surprised everyone by quitting *The New Republic* and becoming editorial page director of a daily newspaper, the *New York World*. Then the nation's leading liberal newspaper, the *World* had a largely blue-collar readership. During the 1920s, Lippmann helped keep the *World* a beacon of liberalism, whose editorial lead many other papers followed. But the *World* began slipping financially and in 1931 the Pulitzer family sold the paper. The *New York Herald Tribune* then invited Lippmann to publish a column four times each week. "Today and Tomorrow," or "T&T," as it was known among journalists, ran from 1931 until 1967. By contrast to the liberal, Democratic *World*, the *Herald Tribune* was a staunchly Republican paper, giving Lippmann a wealthier, managerial class of readers. In syndication his column reached as many as 200 other papers in the United States and abroad. (In 1962 Lippmann switched the column from the *Herald Tribune* to the *Washington Post.*)

Lippmann wrote his columns in a study surrounded by reference books, newspapers, a globe, and a shortwave radio. It was a serious column that avoided anything that seemed trivial and personal. Rather than being entertaining, it focused on educating readers on national and international issues of the day. Lippmann's columns were fairly difficult to read, and he clearly aimed for a well-educated, thoughtful audience.

In contrast to the restrained, contemplative tone of his columns, Walter Lippmann's personal life underwent turmoil and disruption. In 1917 Lippmann had married Faye Albertson,

Walter Lippmann

BORN

September 23, 1889
New York, New York

DIED

December 14, 1974
New York, New York

EDUCATION

A.B., Harvard University (1910)

ACCOMPLISHMENTS

Reporter, *Boston Common* (1910–11); research assistant to Lincoln Steffens (1911–12); editorial assistant, *Everybody's* magazine (1912); editor, *The New Republic* (1914–17, 1919–22); columnist, *Vanity Fair* (1920–34); editorial page director, *New York World* (1922–31); syndicated columnist, *New York Herald Tribune* (1931–62), *Washington Post* (1962–67); columnist, *Newsweek* (1963–71); author of numerous books, including *A Preface to Politics* (1913), *Liberty and the News* (1920), *Public Opinion* (1922), *American Inquisitors* (1928), *A Preface to Morals* (1929), *The Method of Freedom* (1934), *The Good Society* (1937), *U.S. Foreign Policy: Shield of the Republic* (1943), *The Cold War* (1947), *Essays in the Public Philosophy* (1955), *The Communist World and Ours* (1959), and *Western Unity and the Common Market* (1962)

It seems to me clear that the Democratic Party today is unable to offer the country the genuine prospect of a coherent government. . . . This leaves us with Nixon as the one and only candidate who can be elected and shows promise, like it or not, of being able to put together an administration to run the government. . . . I do not shrink from the prospect of Nixon as president. He is a very much better man today than he was ten years ago, and I have lived too long to think that men are what they are forever and ever . . . Such confidence as I have in Nixon's foreign policies rests on the belief that his greatest ambition will be to be elected for two terms, and that he knows as well as anyone else that if he is bogged down in Vietnam, he will become as unpopular as [Lyndon] Johnson and [Hubert] Humphrey are today. He must find a solution to Vietnam in order to be more than a one-term President.

I think Nixon's whole future will be staked on getting a cease-fire and a self-respecting withdrawal of our land forces. That is the best I am able to hope for. But I see nothing better in Humphrey.

All in all, we cannot deny that the near future will be difficult, and I have come to think that on the central issue of an organized government to deal with, Nixon is the only one who may be able to produce a government that can govern.

—from "Nixon's the Only One," *Washington Post* (October 6, 1968)

whom he had known since his student days at Harvard. A high-spirited, attractive woman who loved to dance, she seemed the opposite of the serious-minded Lippmann. By the 1930s Lippmann's unhappiness with his marriage led him to an affair with Helen Byrne Armstrong, the wife of his friend Hamilton Fish Armstrong, who edited the journal *Foreign Affairs*. When Armstrong discovered some letters that Lippmann had written to his wife, he confronted Lippmann. Walter and Helen decided to divorce their spouses and marry each other. The scandal made it uncomfortable for them to remain in New York City, so they moved to Washington, D.C. Lippmann rationalized the move by asserting that the center of news had shifted away from New York to Washington in the 1930s.

His political views, which had shifted from radical to progressive to liberal, grew more conservative during the New Deal. Lippmann supported Franklin Roosevelt for President but his preference for order and logic caused him to be dismayed over the messy and experimental nature of many of Roosevelt's reforms. He opposed Roosevelt's reelection and attacked plans to increase the size of the Supreme Court, a move designed to "pack" the Court with pro-New Deal justices. However, as events in Europe and Asia became more troubling, with the rise of fascist dictatorships and the threat of another world war, Lippmann became more supportive of Roosevelt and his internationalist policies.

An internationalist himself, Lippmann remained suspicious of any efforts to make the United States the policeman of the world. When President Harry Truman pledged to "contain" international communism, Lippmann warned that such a policy inevitably would require sending American troops to fight in the remotest parts of the world, and would ally the United States with corrupt and tyrannical governments simply because they were anticommunist. He published his columns in a book called *The Cold War*, which gave a name to the era, even though American policymakers declined to follow his advice.

Lippmann's worst fears were confirmed in the 1960s when the United States went to war in South Vietnam, turning a nationalistic civil war into an international struggle to contain communism. Although Lippmann admired President Lyndon B. Johnson, he did not consider the war to be in the best interests of the nation. Some columnists grow out of touch with the public mood as they grow older, but Lippmann's writings against the war found an appreciative younger audience in the student antiwar movement. At the same time, CBS Television began an annual series of television interviews with Lippmann. These popular programs helped him reach an even wider audience. He received the Pulitzer Prize and the Presidential Medal of Freedom. Convinced that Lippmann shaped American foreign policy, many foreign leaders made themselves available for interviews whenever he traveled overseas. Readers turned to Lippmann's columns to make sense out of perplexing world problems. He remained influential until he retired from his newspaper column in 1967 and from his *Newsweek* magazine column in 1971.

As a columnist, Lippmann tended to be a lecturer. Critics noted that his writing often adopted a superior tone. He was not always correct in his assessments, nor even consistent, having moved from the political left to the right. But he remained open-minded and unbound by ideologies. As Lippmann explained in one of his books, *The Good Society:* "For more than twenty years I have found myself writing about critical events with no better guide to their meaning than the hastily improvised generalizations of a rather bewildered man. Many a time I have wanted to stop talking and find out what I really believed. For I should have liked to achieve again the untroubled certainty and assured consistency which are vouchsafed to those who can wholeheartedly commit themselves to one of the many schools of doctrine. But I am not able to find in any of the schools a working philosophy in which I could confidently come to rest."

FURTHER READING

Adams, Larry L. *Walter Lippmann*. Boston: Twayne, 1977.

Childs, Marquis, and James Reston, eds. *Walter Lippmann and His Times*. New York: Harcourt, Brace, 1959.

Dam, Hari N. *Intellectual Odyssey of Walter Lippmann*. New York: Gordon Press, 1973.

Forcey, Charles. *Crossroads of Liberalism: Croly, Weyl, Lippmann and the Progressive Era, 1900–1925*. New York: Oxford University Pres, 1961.

Lippmann, Walter. *The Cold War* Boston: Little, Brown, 1955.

———. *The Communist World and Ours*. Boston: Little, Brown, 1959.

———. *Conversations with Walter Lippmann*. Boston: Little, Brown, 1965.

———. *The Essential Lippmann*. Edited by Clinton Rossiter and James Lare. New York: Random House, 1963.

———. *Public Philosopher: Selected Letters of Walter Lippmann*. Edited by John Morton Blum. New York: Ticknor and Fields, 1985.

———. *Western Unity and the Common Market*. Boston: Little, Brown, 1962.

Luskin, James. *Lippmann, Liberty and the Press*. Birmingham: University of Alabama Press, 1972.

Ricco, Barry D. *Walter Lippmann—Odyssey of a Liberal*. New Brunswick, N.J.: Transaction Publishers, 1994.

Rivers, William L. *The Opinionmakers*. Boston: Beacon, 1967.

Steel, Ronald. *Walter Lippmann and the American Century*. Boston: Little, Brown, 1980.

Weinganst, David Elliott. *Walter Lippmann: A Study in Personal Journalism*. New Brunswick, N.J.: Rutgers University Press, 1949.

I. F. Stone

THE
NONCONFORMIST'S
NEWSLETTER

During the Vietnam War, Carl Marcy, chief of staff of the Senate Foreign Relations Committee, noticed an odd thing about the press. Many reporters covered the committee's hearings, but they rarely returned to look at the transcripts that were produced after the hearings. The exception, he observed, was the independent journalist I. F. "Izzy" Stone, who seldom came to the hearings. "But he invariably came to the committee offices the day after a hearing meticulously to read the transcript. So he got his stories in depth and with nuances." Because of severe hearing problems, Stone tended to rely on his careful reading of official, written documentation, and he often found what others missed.

In 1953, after 20 years as an editorial writer and reporter, Stone started his own weekly newsletter, *I. F. Stone's Weekly.* It was literally a one-man shop, written, edited, and published by Stone, with the assistance of his wife, Esther. Beginning with only 5,000 subscribers, it eventually reached some 73,000, including the White House and some 40 members of Congress. Influenced by the writings of both Thomas Jefferson and Karl Marx, Stone was radical without being dogmatic. His newsletter drew on his knowledge of history, literature, philosophy, and current events and on his skills as an investigative reporter.

He was born Isidor Feinstein, the first child of Russian-Jewish immigrant parents. He grew up over his parents' general store in Haddonfield, New Jersey, not far from Philadelphia. As a boy, Izzy Feinstein read everything from philosophy to the daily newspapers. When he was 14, he produced his own journal, *The Progress,* for three issues until his parents made him stop because it was distracting him from schoolwork. He hated working in his father's store, but there one day he waited on the wife of newspaper publisher J. David Stern and told her about his aspirations. At his wife's urging, Stern came by the store and offered Izzy a job as the Haddonfield correspondent for his *Camden Courier-Post.* Later, as a student at the University of Pennsylvania, he also copyedited for the *Philadelphia Inquirer.* But as a Jew he was barred from the staff of his campus paper, the *Daily Pennsylvanian.*

Bored with his classes and preferring to read on his own, he dropped out of the university in favor of the newsroom. He showed a talent for writing, but not for getting along with editors. After young Feinstein feuded with his city editor in Camden, publisher Stern transferred him to the *Philadelphia Record.* There Izzy Feinstein became the nation's youngest editorial writer.

Special Issue for Draftees

What Every Young Man Should Find Out About His Mother

I. F. Stone's Weekly

VOL. III, NO. 31   AUGUST 15, 1955   101   WASHINGTON, D. C.   15 CENTS

A Startling Report Most of the Nation's Press Ignored Shows the Landy Case Far from Exceptional

How The Army Controls The Minds of Our Youth

Politically, Feinstein was shifting to the left. In 1924 he supported Robert La Follette, the Progressive candidate for President. By 1928 he worked for the Socialist Norman Thomas. Then after the stock market crash of 1929 triggered a depression, he moved toward the Communists. Later, however, his dismay over Stalin's authoritarian regime in the Soviet Union caused him to sever his Communist ties. Instead, his publisher saw Franklin D. Roosevelt's New Deal as the solution to America's economic catastrophe. In 1933 J. David Stern bought the *New York Post*, which he turned into a pro-New Deal paper. He sent his young editorial writer there to take charge of the *Post*'s editorial page.

In the 1930s the American Left was deeply troubled over the rise of Adolf Hitler's anti-Semitic Nazi party in Germany. Communists who sought to protect the Soviet Union from Germany promoted a "Popular Front," which united the otherwise warring factions on the left. This came as a relief to Feinstein, who believed that the sectarian squabbles among New York radicals had undermined their ability to reform society. The spread of anti-Semitism prompted him to change his name in 1937. Publisher Stern wanted the *Post* to seem "less Jewish," and Feinstein concluded that his own articles might be more effective in fighting fascism if their byline

was not so "obviously Jewish." He became "I. F. Stone."

In addition to his editorial work for the *Post*, Stone frequently published articles in *The New Republic* and *The Nation*. When the *Post* changed owners, he shifted full time to *The Nation*, which sent him to Washington as its correspondent. He arrived there at a time when Roosevelt's New Deal and the coming of World War II had made Washington the nation's news capital. He also reported for a new pro-New Deal, anti-isolationist newspaper called *PM*. Reporting for both a magazine and a newspaper set a hectic pace for him. Stone recalled that once when he missed his Thursday night deadline, he flew to New York and went to *The Nation*'s office, where he wrote a 1,500-word column, went to a Turkish bath to relax, and then rushed to *PM* to write a story that made page one before catching the train back to Washington.

During World War II, when the United States and the Soviet Union were allies against Germany, Stone's Washington reporting gained him attention and respectability. But after the war, when relations between the United States and the Soviet Union deteriorated into a Cold War, any criticism of U.S. policy was looked upon as subversive. When Stone appeared as a panelist on the television news program "Meet the Press," some of the

Radical in viewpoint but conservative in format, *I. F. Stone's Weekly* drew on its editor's knowledge of history, literature, and philosophy and on his skills as an investigative reporter.

I. F. Stone thrived in his role as a lone gadfly against the establishment.

guests did not like his questioning and accused him of being a "Red." A succession of left-leaning newspapers for which Stone wrote went out of business, and in 1952 he found himself unemployed. The rise of the anti-communist movement (known as "McCarthyism" after Senator Joseph McCarthy's crusade to root out suspected subversives) made it a difficult time for a radical journalist to get a job. But he vowed to keep on fighting even if he had to "crank out a paper on a mimeograph machine in the cellar." With $3,500 severance pay from his

last newspaper job and a loan from a friend, he started *I. F. Stone's Weekly*.

Stone dedicated his *Weekly* to justice and civil liberties, and promised "to do as sober, accurate, and principled a job of reporting" as he could. The newsletter carried no advertisements and relied entirely on subscriptions for revenue. He wrote a page a day, edited and laid out the material, and personally carried the copy to the printer. "My idea was to make the *Weekly* radical in viewpoint but conservative in format," he later explained. Having to cover the government without assistance, and with very poor hearing, he began reading the voluminous publications of government agencies to catch what other reporters were missing. "A good way to read a government document is backwards," he once advised. "They're very long, and you get the clues in the last pages. . . . that's where you find the body buried."

After years of working for others, Stone found writing a newsletter a liberating experience, since being able "to spit in their eye, and do what you think is right, and report the news, and have enough readers to make some impact, is such a pleasure." *I. F. Stone's Weekly* became a leading dissenter against the Cold War and was skeptical of official government pronouncements. The FBI kept him under surveillance and many government officials would not talk to him. Some members of Congress denounced him as a communist sympathizer. Other Washington correspondents treated him coldly. Yet he thrived on his role as a lone gadfly against the establishment. His readers appreciated his nonconformity and his uncovering of facts that government agencies tried to hide or that the mainstream press overlooked.

For years *I. F. Stone's Weekly* followed American policies in Vietnam. He believed that the Cold War blinded the United States to nationalist aspirations of former colonial people in places like Southeast Asia. He warned against backing dictators solely because they were anticommunist. Although American foreign policymakers seemed confident that they could enforce their will in Asia, Stone compared the region to "a vast marsh where swarming gnats can devour a giant." He sus-

pected that government officials were falsifying the record to win public approval. When President Lyndon Johnson sent to Congress the Gulf of Tonkin Resolution, which authorized the President to use whatever force necessary to prevent communist aggression in South Vietnam, Stone devoted the entire August 24, 1964, issue of his *Weekly* to dissecting the resolution and raising doubt about it.

Stone was among the first journalists to question whether President Johnson was telling the truth. The *New York Times* correspondent Tom Wicker later noted that "before any of us had the courage to think for ourselves, rather than take what the President said, he was doing it." His skepticism, shrewd assessments, and persistent opposition to the Vietnam War allied him with the antiwar movement, and he served as a link between the Old Left of the 1930s and the New Left of the 1960s. Ironically, growing opposition to the war in Vietnam helped integrate the independent gadfly Stone into the mainstream. It brought him closer to such eminent journalists as Walter Lippmann, who now shared his suspicion of what the government was saying.

The turmoil of the 1960s took its toll on Stone's health and caused him to curtail his activities. In 1967 the *Weekly* became a *Bi-Weekly,* and it closed entirely at the end of 1971. Stone devoted himself to writing for the intellectual *New York Review of Books,* but resigned in opposition to some of its publication policies. He spent his retirement learning Greek in order to write a history of the trial of Socrates. In his book he sought to understand why the Athenian democracy put a great philosopher to death,

I. F. Stone

BORN

December 24, 1907
Philadelphia, Pennsylvania

DIED

June 18, 1989
Boston, Massachusetts

EDUCATION

Attended University of Pennsylvania (1924–27), received B.A. in 1975

ACCOMPLISHMENTS

Editor, *The Progress* (1922); reporter *Haddonfield* (N.J.) *Press* (1922–23); reporter, *Camden* (N.J.) *Courier-Post* (1923–24, 1927–31); copy editor, *Philadelphia Inquirer* (1927); editorial writer and reporter, *Philadelphia Record* (1931–33); editorial writer, *New York Post* (1933–39, 1949); associate editor, *The Nation* (1938–1940); Washington editor, *The Nation* (1940–46); reporter, columnist, editorial writer, *PM* (1942–48); reporter, columnist, editorial writer, *New York Star* (1948–49); reporter, columnist, editorial writer, *New York Daily Compass* (1949–52); editor, *I. F. Stone's Weekly* (1953–67); editor, *I. F. Stone's Bi-Weekly* (1967–71); contributing editor, *New York Review of Books* (1964–76); author of numerous books

Within two years you may see a flaming ball rocket up from the earth's surface and swing into position in an orbit around it. Do not regard the spectacle with complacency. These satellites will grow larger and more numerous; men will go up in them. Voyages to the moon will follow. After that the distant realm of planet and star will lie open to Man.

Beware in time. This is a breed which has changed little in thousands of years. The cave dweller who wielded a stone club and the man who will soon wield an interstellar missile are terribly alike. Earth's creatures feed upon each other, but this is the only one that kills on a large scale, for pleasure, adventure, and even—so perverse is the species—for supposed reasons of morality.

Should you start a secret mission of inquiry, you will find that the sacred books on which the young of the various tribes have been brought up for thousands of years glorify bloodshed. Whether one looks in Homer, or the Sagas, or the Bible, or the Koran, the hero is a warrior. Someone is always killing someone else for what is called the greater glory of God.

This is not a creature to be trusted with the free run of the universe. At the moment the human race seems to be temporarily sobered by the possession of weapons which could destroy all life on earth except perhaps the mosses and the fungi. The current rival tribes, the Russians and the Americans, fear the other may use the new device against them. They may soon be transferring to outer space the hates that in every generation have brought suffering to the earth. It might be wise to stop them now, on the very threshold of the open and as yet unpolluted skies.

—from "Note to the Rest of the Universe," *I. F. Stone's Weekly* (August 8, 1955)

analyzing the distant past with the same precision as he did current politics. His other writings were also reissued in a set of books collectively titled "A Nonconformist History of Our Times." Reflecting on his long career, Stone maintained that independence was essential for keeping an open mind and not automatically embracing the established way of thinking. "These big establishment figures—not that I'm against them, but I think my stuff is going to last longer than they can."

FURTHER READING

Cottrell, Robert C. *Izzy: A Biography of I. F. Stone*. New Brunswick, N.J.: Rutgers University Press, 1992.

Lader, Lawrence. *Power on the Left: American Radical Movements Since 1946*. New York: Norton, 1979.

O'Neill, William L. *A Better World: The Great Schism: Stalinism and the American Intellectuals*. New York: Simon and Schuster, 1982.

Pater, Andrew. *I. F. Stone: A Portrait*. New York: Pantheon, 1988.

Protess, David L., et al. *The Journalism of Outrage: Investigative Reporting and Agenda Building in America*. New York: Guilford Press, 1991.

Stern, J. David. *Memoirs of a Maverick Publisher*. New York: Simon and Schuster, 1962.

Stone, I. F. *The Best of I. F. Stone's Weekly: Pages from a Radical Newspaper*. New York: Penguin, 1973.

———. *The Hidden History of the Korean War*. 1952. Reprint, Boston: Little, Brown, 1988.

———. *The Trial of Socrates*. Boston: Little, Brown, 1988

———. *Underground to Palestine*. 1946. Reprint, New York: Pantheon, 1978.

James Reston

INFLUENCE AND RESPONSIBILITY

or nearly a half century James "Scotty" Reston operated a pipeline to the most powerful officials in Washington as the representative of the nation's most influential newspaper, the *New York Times*. Fellow columnist Joseph Kraft once observed that on some big matters the State Department informed Reston "almost automatically, as it would the representative of a major power." Although he was seen as the ultimate insider, who generally went easy on the establishment, Reston repeatedly scooped the rest of the press corps with stories based on leaks that angered and embarrassed government officials. He never hesitated to criticize those in power and frequently managed to get under the skins of Presidents. Dwight D. Eisenhower once exploded: "Who does Scotty Reston think he is, telling me how to run the country!"

A short, ruddy-faced man, described by another reporter as having "a way of looking straight into your eyes with

Editors—and readers—of the *New York Times* appreciated James Reston's ability to distill complex issues into a few sentences of straightforward prose. Here on election night in 1954, Reston (right) works with Bill Lawrence (left) and Bill Blair to prepare the lead story.

"President Johnson has started his campaign for re-election. He has been out on the stump three times in the last few days, testing the gullibility of the electorate, and judging by his opening themes, we are in for 17 months of bull-roaring exaggeration."

—from "Washington: My Fellow Americans," *New York Times* (June 30, 1967)

grave attentiveness that was flattering and reassuring," Scotty Reston took his nickname from his birthplace. He was born into a working-class family near Glasgow, Scotland. His parents were strict Presbyterians who preached lifting oneself up through hard work. "It's no sin to be poor," his mother instructed, "but it is one to stay poor." When he was 11, in 1920, his family moved to the United States and settled in Dayton, Ohio, where his father worked as a mechanic for Delco, a subsidiary of General Motors.

As a boy, Scotty Reston caddied at a local golf course to earn extra money. Among the golfers he caddied for was former Ohio governor James Cox, publisher of the local newspaper and defeated Democratic candidate for President in 1920. After graduation from high school, Reston spent a year editing the factory paper, *Delco Doings*, before going to the University of Illinois School of Journalism. At Illinois, Reston earned letters in golf and soccer and reported on campus sports for the school paper. In his senior year the bank on which his tuition check had been written failed and the university asked that he leave. Reston rushed back to Dayton, where Governor Cox provided him with a $100 loan and promised him a job after he graduated. In 1932 he joined the staff of Cox's *Dayton Daily News* as a sportswriter. His interest in sports led to jobs as a publicity agent for the sports department of Ohio State University and for the Cincinnati Reds baseball team.

While accompanying the Reds to New York City, Reston interviewed with the Associated Press and was hired as a sportswriter. He also wrote a weekly column, "A New Yorker at Large." In 1935 he married his college sweetheart, Sally Fulton, who had also gotten a job in New York, editing the *Junior League* magazine. They raised a family of three sons.

The Associated Press transferred Reston to London in 1937 to cover major sporting events in Europe. War with Germany was the big story of the day, but Reston enjoyed covering sports. Unlike foreign policy, where everything was usually hidden, sports were played out in the open, and the players spoke candidly about their feelings. Between sporting events, the AP assigned him to cover the British Foreign Office. Without any special access to the men at the top, he cultivated the friendship of the younger foreign service officers. They provided him with useful information about the crisis over Czechoslovakia and Britain's attempts to appease Hitler. Events spiraled at such a pace that the *New York Times* correspondent in London needed help, and he persuaded the *Times* to hire Reston as his assistant. The sportswriter became a full-fledged diplomatic correspondent.

As Reston reported on the German blitz of London, he worried over the quality of his writing. The chief correspondent advised him to "think about it as if you were writing a letter to a friend back home." He took the advice to heart, and in later years as a columnist he described his effort as trying "merely to pass on some informative footnotes to the news of the day, as if in a letter to a thoughtful friend." Editors at the *Times* came to appreciate Reston's ability to distill complex issues into a few sentences of straightforward prose.

Illness sent Reston back to the United States in 1941 and he was assigned to the Washington bureau of the *New York Times*. Washington, Reston later recalled, seemed "so orderly and sanitary after the rubble and stench of bombed-out London." Unlike the British, who were united behind the war effort, Americans were bitterly divided between isolationists and those who sought to aid the Allies. Reston's first book, *Prelude to Victory*, fiercely denounced isolationism. Pleased with his writing in the book, *Times* editors encouraged him to tackle more analytical pieces. Reston also grew close to his Washington neighbor, Michigan Republican senator Arthur Vandenberg. Long a leader of the isolationist forces, Vandenberg was jolted by the Japanese attack on Pearl Harbor into the realization that America could no longer stand alone. Reston privately helped draft a "speech heard round the world" in which Vandenberg switched from isolationism to internationalism. Reston then reported positively about the speech in the *New York Times*.

During the war, Reston covered the negotiations that took place in Washington toward creating a new international peace-keeping organization, the United Nations. Diplomatic talks take place in secret, behind closed doors. When the State Department would not answer reporters' questions, Reston reasoned that the delegation most unhappy with the direction of the talks would cooperate with the press. His reasoning proved to be correct when the Chinese delegation secretly leaked to him the main position papers of the negotiations. Reston's scoop won him his first Pulitzer Prize and a reputation as a top Washington insider.

For many years the Washington bureau of the *New York Times* was run by the crusty, domineering Arthur Krock. Krock did not appreciate the attention lavished on his young staff member, but admitted that Reston was "the best telephone man in the business." That is, whenever necessary he could phone contacts in high places to provide information or confirm suspicions. In 1953, when the *Washington Post* offered to make Reston its managing editor, Krock voluntarily stepped down as chief of the Washington bureau in Reston's favor so that Reston would "stay with the *Times* for life."

As bureau chief, Reston revitalized the *Times*'s Washington coverage. He scouted for reporters who were well educated, serious, and able to explain complex issues for readers. The staff of correspondents he put together included Russell Baker, Tom Wicker, Neil Sheehan, and Anthony Lewis, known collectively as "Scotty's boys" or "Reston's Rangers." The mostly male team reflected Reston's traditional attitude toward women. When reporter Mary McGrory applied for a job with the *Times*'s Washington bureau, Reston would hire her only if she agreed to work part-time on the bureau's switchboard. She refused. Reporter Nan Robertson recalled that Reston invited only the men on the staff to councils in his office, or to lunch at his club (which did not admit women).

Always competitive, Reston admitted that as head of the *Times*'s Washington bureau he had definite advantages over other reporters. The *Times* was read by the people who made the news: government officials, diplomats, and business leaders. Those newsmakers, Reston commented, "also know that we handle the news with care." He always combined his great influence with an equally high sense of responsibility. Operating in the tense days of the Cold War between the democracies of the West and the communist regimes of the East, Reston believed that the press should not publish every secret, but should sometimes restrain itself to protect the national security.

That attitude was put to a test in 1961, when *New York Times* reporter Tad Szulc uncovered evidence that an anti-Castro brigade of Cuban refugees planned to launch a U.S.-sponsored invasion of Cuba. Reston advised that the story be toned down, and shortly afterward the ill-fated Bay of Pigs invasion took place. Critics charged that Reston and the *Times* went too easy on the political establishment, but after

James Reston

BORN

November 3, 1909
Clydebank, Scotland

DIED

December 6, 1995
Washington, D.C.

EDUCATION

B.S., University of Illinois School of Journalism (1932)

ACCOMPLISHMENTS

Editor, *Delco Doings* (1927–28); sportswriter, *Dayton* (Ohio) *Daily News* (1932–33); reporter, Associated Press (1934–39); foreign correspondent, *New York Times* London bureau (1939–41); Washington correspondent, *New York Times* (1941–89); chief of Washington bureau, *New York Times* (1953–64); columnist, *New York Times* (1960–89); executive editor, *New York Times* (1968–72); publisher, the *Vineyard Gazette* (1968–95); author of *Prelude to Victory* (1942), *Sketches in the Sand* (1967), *The Artillery of the Press: Its Influence on American Foreign Policy* (1969), *Washington* (1986), and *Deadline: A Memoir* (1991)

the Bay of Pigs, Reston talked more about the need for press skepticism of government policies.

As the United States moved deeper into the Vietnam War, both Presidents John F. Kennedy and Lyndon B. Johnson complained about the American newspaper reporters in Saigon that kept contradicting official reports. Feeling there was no way to judge the conflicting sides from Washington, Reston went to Vietnam in 1965. He returned disturbed about the brutality and futility of the war. Slowly he changed from supporting the war to skepticism. An indignant President Johnson later complained that reporters were "like a bunch of sheep in their own profession and they will always follow the bellwether sheep, the leaders of their profession, [Walter] Lippmann and Reston. As long as those two stayed with me, I was okay. But once they left me . . . everyone else left me."

In 1971 the *New York Times* obtained copies of the Pentagon Papers, a top-secret government analysis of how the United States had gotten into the Vietnam War. President Richard Nixon demanded that the *Times* suppress the material to protect national security, but Reston urged its publication, saying that if the *Times* did not publish it, then the *Vineyard Gazette* (the little weekly paper that his family published on Martha's Vineyard) would. The *New York Times* went ahead with the Pentagon Papers, and the Supreme Court rejected the government's effort to ban its publication.

Reston stepped down as Washington bureau chief in 1964 to devote full attention to his three-times-a-week column "Washington," nationally syndicated to hundreds of newspapers. A shake-up at the *Times* in 1968 moved Reston to New York as the paper's executive editor. He instituted a number of creative reforms but did not enjoy management. Each week he commuted back to Washington for a few days to write his column and maintain his high-placed sources. Finally, Reston extracted himself from editing to return full-time to Washington and his column, which he continued until his retirement.

Looking back, Scotty Reston concluded that newspaper reporting was both meaningful and self-satisfying. "It not only involves a man in the struggles of his time, thus keeping him from going to sleep," he asserted, "but gives him the opportunity unmatched by the university or the law, to write on the big issues when people are paying attention."

FURTHER READING

Cose, Ellis. *The Press*. New York: William Morrow, 1989.

Halberstam, David. *The Powers That Be*. New York: Alfred A. Knopf, 1979.

Reston, James. *The Artillery of the Press: Its Influence on American Foreign Policy*. New York: Harper & Row, 1969.

———. *Deadline: A Memoir*. New York: Random House, 1991.

———. *Sketches in the Sand*. New York: Knopf, 1967.

———. *Washington*. New York: Macmillan, 1986.

Rivers, William L. *The Opinionmakers*. Boston: Beacon Press, 1967.

Robertson, Nan. *The Girls in the Balcony: Women, Men, and the New York Times*. New York: Random House, 1992.

Salisbury, Harrison E. *Without Fear or Favor: An Uncompromising History of the New York Times*. New York: Times Books, 1980.

Talese, Gay. *The Kingdom and the Power*. New York: World Publishing Company, 1969.

Joseph Alsop

COLD WAR COLUMNIST

S oon after he became a Washington correspondent in 1936, Joseph Alsop covered a Senate investigation into how the United States entered the World War I. The investigation convinced Alsop, along with many other Americans, that arms manufacturers (or "merchants of death" as the press called them) had provoked the United States into entering the war. As a result, Alsop supported neutrality laws that were designed to keep the United States out of World War II. But then events in Europe profoundly shook Alsop's assumptions. He came to see that Hitler's aggression had to be stopped and that neutrality laws would never protect America. Alsop became an advocate of United States leadership in world affairs. Throughout his many years as a syndicated columnist, he never wavered from that conviction. During the Cold War, Alsop's columns

Joseph Alsop (left) and his brother Stewart often aimed their syndicated newspaper column at policymakers rather than at the average American reader.

As a columnist, Alsop pressed the U.S. government to take a more vigorous stand against international communism.

warned Americans of the menace of international communism and advocated a military response to communism around the world. By the time of the Vietnam War in the 1960s, he had become the leading "hawk" in the American press.

Joseph Wright Alsop V was born into a proud old New England family. His grandmother was a sister of Theodore Roosevelt. While growing up on his family's farm in Connecticut, Alsop was so overweight that he had difficulty playing sports or making many friends. He grew especially close to his brothers, Stewart and John, and his sister, Corinne. Young Joe Alsop devoted much of his childhood to reading the books in his father's library and developing a passion for literature and art. Then he was sent off to attend the exclusive Groton School, with the sons of the best families. At Harvard University, he majored in English literature, reading everything he thought necessary to become an "educated gentleman." Later in life, he said the very idea of an "educated gentleman" made

him realize "how callow I was and how snobbish was the little world I came from."

When he graduated from Harvard, Alsop considered going to law school, but a council of his relatives presided over by his indomitable grandmother ruled that out. Too many other relatives who became lawyers had also become alcoholics, the family decided. Since Joseph Alsop had demonstrated a talent for writing, they found him a job through their friends Ogden and Helen Reid, who owned the *New York Herald Tribune*. Alsop moved to Manhattan in 1932 and began reporting for the *Herald Tribune*. One day the paper would send him to interview people living in the shacks in Central Park known as "Hoovervilles" (after President Herbert Hoover), and the next day he might interview a movie star at a fashionable hotel. In 1935 a trial was held in New Jersey of the man accused of kidnapping and murdering the infant son of the famous aviator Charles Lindbergh. Alsop's lively coverage of the Lindbergh kidnapping trial attracted much attention and earned him promotion to Washington correspondent. The editors of the Republican *Herald Tribune* observed that Alsop "was reeking with Roosevelt blood," by which they meant he "had that Harvard manner, that peculiar self-assurance, or brashness, which characterizes all Roosevelts," including President Franklin D. Roosevelt and his wife, Eleanor. Such Roosevelt connections would give Alsop special access to the most powerful sources in the government.

To Joe Alsop, covering Washington meant dining out nightly with the city's elite, which only added to his corpulent frame. When he developed an irregular heartbeat, he was warned by his doctor that unless he lost weight he would be dead within a year. Combining a rigorous diet with exercise, Alsop lost 65 pounds. Able to move about and breathe more easily, he declared that his "newfound youth of spirit coincided with the beginning my real adult life as a professional newspaperman."

In 1937 Alsop joined with Robert Kintner to write a syndicated column, "Capital Parade," an inside look at politics, government, economics, and foreign policy. The column was successful, but as war spread around the world neither man wanted to sit out events as a commentator, and in 1940 they gave up the column. Kintner joined the army, while Alsop became a naval intelligence officer. He was sent to Bombay, India, but found it too far removed from the real action. He developed a friendship with Claire Chennault, a former air corps officer who recruited 100 pilots (known as the "Flying Tigers") to run supplies to China during its war with Japan. With Chennault's help, Alsop was transferred to China as administrator of the Lend-Lease program that provided U.S. supplies to China and other wartime allies. Alsop also became the unofficial publicist for Chennault.

Alsop was attending a meeting in the Philippines when the Japanese bombed Pearl Harbor. He flew to Hong Kong, which very soon after was captured by the Japanese. Alsop became a prisoner of war and used his months of captivity to study Chinese language, art, and culture. Eventually released, he made his way back to China, where he spent the rest of the war. A man of strong opinions, Alsop frequently voiced disagreement with the top American general in China, Joseph "Vinegar Joe" Stilwell, who sourly described him as "Alslop."

After the war, Joe Alsop returned home and proposed to the *New York Herald Tribune* that he and his younger brother Stewart jointly write a column. Their column, called "Matter of Fact," ran three times a week. In syndication it reached 200 newspapers in the United States and Western Europe. Stewart had never worked for a newspaper, but he was a thoughtful, even-tempered writer who balanced his more passionate and often melancholy brother Joe. The Alsops determined not simply to present opinion, but to report something new in each column. That often meant traveling to the world's trouble spots to see things for themselves. They cultivated friends in the White House, the State Department, the Central Intelligence Agency, and other sources of valuable information. Quite often they aimed their columns at the President, the Pentagon, and other policymakers rather than at average readers.

Joe Alsop entertained the nation's movers and shakers at his home in Washington's fashionable Georgetown neighborhood. He possessed an almost theatrical personality, famous for its eccentricities and mannerisms and his loud after-dinner arguments. He dressed in English tailor-made suits and Italian silk shirts. He never learned to drive and refused to own a television set. The journalist Neil Sheehan found Alsop a man of strange contrasts. In his personal life he could be "a man of kindness, loyalty and consideration to his friends and relatives." But in his professional life he could be ferocious. "He did not see those who disagreed with him as merely incorrect and misguided. He depicted them as stupid men who acted from petty or selfish motives."

After World War II, the Alsops raised concern over the Soviet Union's

Joseph Alsop

BORN
October 11, 1910
Avon, Connecticut

DIED
August 29, 1989
Washington, D.C.

EDUCATION
A.B., Harvard University (1932)

ACCOMPLISHMENTS
Reporter, *New York Herald Tribune* (1932–36); Washington correspondent, *New York Herald Tribune* (1936–37); syndicated columnist (1937–40, 1945–74; with Stewart Alsop, 1945–58); author of *The 168 Days* (with Turner Catledge, 1938), *Men Around the President* (1939), *We Accuse* (with Stewart Alsop, 1954), *The Reporter's Trade* (with Stewart Alsop, 1958), *FDR: A Centenary Remembrance* (1982), and *"I've Seen the Best of It": Memoirs* (with Adam Platt, 1992)

"Being a newspaper columnist is a little like being a Greek chorus. You report, you analyze, you comment and you describe the parts of the drama that do not take place on the open stage. Since irony is a principal ingredient of the political drama, anyone who spends much time in the chorus is bound to remember a good many ironical episodes. . . .

The ironies of the business underline the cardinal rule that a newspaper man's feet are a lot more important than his head. But there is another rule as well. A newspaper man must never forget that the drama in which he is one of the chorus is a . . . real-life drama of national and human destiny."

—from "Hail and Farewell," *New York Herald Tribune* (March 12, 1958)

aggressive tendencies. "Must America Save the World?" was the title of one of their magazine articles in 1948, to which they answered yes. Their columns pressed the Truman administration to take a more vigorous stand against international communism. They decried cuts in defense spending and warned Americans that their liberties were in danger. Their constant and sometimes exaggerated assessments of the Soviet menace most likely contributed to American anxiety during the Cold War and to the anticommunist hysteria at home. Having helped unleash the demon, the Alsops were appalled at government loyalty programs and over Senator Joseph McCarthy's congressional witchhunting. They used their columns to defend those government officials they believed were falsely accused of communist sympathies. Most notably, they rallied behind J. Robert Oppenheimer, the scientist who had led the Manhattan Project to build the first atomic bomb, and they were outraged when Oppenheimer lost his security clearance because of allegations of disloyalty.

During the 1950s, Joe Alsop tried hard to persuade the U.S. government to rescue the French at Dien Bien Phu, a besieged outpost in Southeast Asia. When the French finally withdrew, the independent states of Laos, Cambodia, and North and South Vietnam were created. Alsop became a steadfast defender of the anticommunist government in South Vietnam. He coined the expression "domino theory," warning that if Vietnam fell to the communists, all of Asia would fall after it like a row of dominoes. Alsop further disagreed with President Dwight Eisenhower's efforts to reduce America's military budget, and he warned his readers of a "missile gap," in which the Soviet Union was producing more long-range missiles than the United States. This information turned out to be wrong, but it strongly influenced Massachusetts senator John F. Kennedy, who made it a theme of his campaign for President in 1960. After Kennedy was elected, he discovered that the "missile gap" had never existed.

In 1958 the Alsop brothers ended their joint column and began to write separate columns. For years they had worked out of a basement office in Joe's house in Georgetown. Joe was alarmist, while Stewart was cautious. Joe accused Stewart of writing bland columns, and Stewart called Joe's writing shrill. Quarrels over expenses and Joe's abrasive personality finally broke up the partnership.

On his own, Joe Alsop reached the height of his influence during the Kennedy administration. On the night of Kennedy's inauguration, the new President paid a surprise visit to a party at Alsop's Georgetown house. Alsop gained access to the highest levels of the Kennedy administration. He devoted much of his column to the need to stand up against the Soviet Union in Berlin, Cuba, and Vietnam. He visited South Vietnam many times and pressed the administrations of John Kennedy and Lyndon Johnson to send American troops to Vietnam. President Johnson sought his advice on Vietnam policy and referred to him as "General Alsop." His travels to Vietnam resembled those of an army general rather than a journalist. The military provided him with special planes and arranged briefings with commanders in Saigon or on the field. More skeptical journalists felt that such special treatment blinded Alsop to the realities of the war. Antiwar demonstrators ridiculed Alsop's hawkish columns and his "my-country-right-or-wrong" school of journalism. When the war became stalemated and no victory was in sight, *New York Times* columnist Arthur Krock sneered that if a war-crimes tribunal was ever held, then Joseph Alsop should be tried for talking Kennedy and Johnson into going to war.

Increasingly, during the 1960s, Joe Alsop grew out of touch with his times. His defense of the unpopular war led him to complain that he had become "a kind of dinosaur surviving on a forgotten past, when people didn't always talk guff and quite often weighed the vital interests of the United States." He could not understand the "defeatist" mood that had overtaken American public opinion. "I became perhaps too passionately involved with the events I was seeking to cover," Alsop later reflected. "I admit this now, although I do not apologize for it, for in Vietnam, as everywhere, I continued to do my best to follow the rule I had set long ago in China: to go and see for myself the weather in the streets."

During one of his visits to South Vietnam in 1968, Alsop was shocked to hear that Lyndon Johnson had withdrawn from the 1968 Presidential race, concluding that the President had lost

his nerve. Alsop was not happy over the election of Richard Nixon, whom he had opposed in the past, but he came to admire Nixon's foreign policies. The Watergate scandal, which drove Nixon from office and tarnished the Presidency, greatly depressed him. When other journalists crowed over Nixon's fall, Alsop felt "isolated and suddenly out of fashion."

During these years, Alsop also led a troubled personal life. When he visited Moscow in 1957, Soviet secret police photographed Alsop in a homosexual encounter. After attempts at blackmail failed, the Soviets made a clumsy attempt to discredit Alsop by sending copies of the photograph to leading American journalists. Not one printed a word about the story. In 1961 Alsop married the widow of an old friend, and he and his wife, Susan Mary, were socially close to the Kennedy family. Joe Alsop was devastated by Kennedy's assassination in 1963. "Now nothing seems worth doing," he wrote Jacqueline Kennedy. In 1973 Alsop and his wife separated and soon after divorced. His brother Stewart died from leukemia in 1974. That same year, 63-year-old Joe Alsop chose to retire from writing his own column. He lived his last years in Georgetown, surrounded by his library and art treasures that he had collected around the world, writing a book on *The Rare Art Traditions*, and arguing with his dinner guests over politics and foreign affairs.

Joe Alsop brought to his columns a remarkable breadth of knowledge. Fellow columnist Edwin Yoder marveled that Alsop was able to hang a column on an otherwise ordinary subject like farm subsidies "upon a passage from the Roman historian Livy or Edward Gibbon's speculations on the decline and fall of the Roman Empire as upon the headline story of the day before." Nor did he separate himself from the events he was writing about.

When he felt angry, morose, or amused by a subject, he conveyed those feelings to his readers. At bottom, he described himself as a "reporter-columnist," interpreting what happened today for tomorrow's newspapers. "Facts alone in the long run possess influence," Alsop insisted. "If a member of my trade forgets this important truth, and begins to think his readers will be guided by his personal opinion, it is time for him to think about retiring."

FURTHER READING

Almquist, Leann Grabavoy. *Joseph Alsop and American Foreign Policy: The Journalist as Advocate*. Lanham, Md.: University Press of America, 1993.

Alsop, Joseph. *FDR: A Centenary Remembrance*. New York: Viking, 1982.

Alsop, Joseph, with Adam Platt. *"I've Seen the Best of It": Memoirs*. New York: Norton, 1992.

Alsop, Joseph, and Stewart Alsop. *We Accuse*. New York: Simon & Schuster, 1954.

Aronson, James. *The Press and the Cold War*. Boston: Beacon Press, 1973.

Bayley, Edwin R. *Joe McCarthy and the Press*. New York: Pantheon, 1981.

Cohen, Bernard C. *The Press and Foreign Policy*. Princeton, N.J.: Princeton University Press, 1963.

Merry, Robert W. *Taking on the World: Joseph and Stewart Alsop—Guardians of the American Century*. New York: Viking, 1996.

Yoder, Edwin M., Jr. "Gentleman Journalist." *Civilization* 2(2): 34–41.

———. *Joe Alsop's Cold War: A Study of Journalistic Influence and Intrigue*. Chapel Hill, N.C.: University of North Carolina Press, 1995.

Ethel L. Payne

RAISING QUESTIONS THAT NEEDED TO BE RAISED

At one of President Dwight D. Eisenhower's press conferences in 1954, the Washington correspondent for the African-American *Chicago Defender*, Ethel Payne, rose to ask when the President planned to ban racial segregation in interstate travel. Clearly annoyed, Eisenhower replied that he would do what was fair but would not support any special interests. Other reporters were surprised at the angry tone of the President's response. Eisenhower preferred to avoid such thorny problems as civil rights, but Payne believed that by asking questions he did not want to hear she was helping to move civil rights to the front pages. Afterward, Payne encountered Presidential retaliation. President Eisenhower ignored her at his press conferences, no matter how she waved to get his attention. Although he

Ethel Payne fought all her life to bring about social change and to correct injustices, using her incisive and uncompromising journalism to promote her causes.

had called on her seven times in the first two years of his Presidency, Eisenhower recognized her only twice more during the next six years. When President John F. Kennedy entered the White House in 1961, he called on Ethel Payne at his first press conference, symbolizing a changed attitude toward civil rights.

Ethel Payne's father was a Pullman car porter who died when she was 12 years old. Her widowed mother raised six children by taking in boarders, doing house cleaning, and teaching in high school. Each night she read aloud from favorite books by such authors as Louisa May Alcott and Paul Laurence Dunbar, and encouraged her children to pursue their educations. Ethel wanted to become a lawyer, but found it extremely difficult then for a young black woman to enter law school. Later in life, she observed that as a lawyer she would have focused on civil rights and civil liberties, but that journalism, "particularly where you could be independent and voice your own views," served the same purpose.

She attended two local colleges and then worked in the Chicago Public Library. A young man who worked in the post office proposed marriage, but Payne wanted a more adventurous and challenging life. "I just didn't want to be caught in the humdrum routine," she later reflected. "I wanted to do something." She accepted a job as a hostess for the Army Special Services Club in Tokyo, Japan. For three years she planned recreational activities for African-American troops. All the while she kept a diary of what she saw and heard about relations between African Americans and Japanese and about life in the still largely segregated U.S. military forces. When the Korean War started in 1950, the *Chicago Defender* sent reporter Alex Wilson to report on the conditions of black troops in combat. When he stopped in Japan, he met

Payne and read her diary. Impressed, he sent the diary back to the *Defender,* which published lengthy excerpts. The newspaper articles got Payne into trouble with the military, which objected that her critical commentaries would have a negative affect on morale. But the articles also got her a job as a reporter for the *Chicago Defender.*

Payne was amazed at the public reaction to her articles. "The newspapers were just jumping off the stands," she recalled. "Circulation just boomed." She returned to Chicago as a reporter in 1951, and took night courses at the school of journalism at Northwestern University. Hired as a feature writer, Payne made it clear that she wanted to be on the front pages, not back in the women's pages. "I had no taste for society news, none whatsoever," she said. "I don't go for what I consider the fluff." She preferred writing about serious social and political issues. One of her earliest stories dealing with problems surrounding the adoption of African-American babies won an award from the Illinois Press Association for the best news story in 1952. That recognition gave her the opportunity to cover anything she wanted, and led her to write a series of exposés about social conditions in Chicago. She also received an attractive job offer from another newspaper. To keep Payne with the *Chicago Defender,* her editors sent her to Washington, D.C., as their one-person news bureau at the capital. She arrived in 1953, at the beginning of both the Eisenhower administration and the modern civil rights movement.

In the 1950s very few of the major metropolitan daily newspapers hired black reporters. Although many white journalists were liberals who viewed civil rights issues sympathetically, racial integration was not necessarily their top priority. It fell to Ethel Payne and the small number of other

Ethel L. Payne

BORN
August 14, 1911
Chicago, Illinois

DIED
May 28, 1991
Washington, D.C.

EDUCATION
Attended Crane Junior College and Medill School of Journalism in Chicago, and Garrett Institution, Evanston, Illinois, in the 1940s

ACCOMPLISHMENTS
Staff writer, *Chicago Defender* (1951–53); Washington bureau chief, *Chicago Defender* (1953–73); associate editor, *Chicago Defender* (1973–78); commentator, "Spectrum," CBS Radio and Television (1972–78); commentator, "Matters of Opinion," WBBM-CBS Radio, Chicago (1978–82); syndicated columnist for African-American newspapers (1978–91)

"I was a one-person operation. I had no staff. So the best I could do was build up sources. And fortunately I was able to do that—at the Pentagon, the State Department, the White House. I was unable to cover everything at one time, but when people saw I was serious, they began sending me stories and tips.

And of course, there was the whole civil rights struggle, and what was behind the continuing racism in the armed forces. I examined the State Department and its attitude, which was very biased at the time. Blacks had no positions of influence, nothing at the policy level. This was a pervasive pattern throughout the federal government, and I felt it was not only very unfair to blacks, it was unfair to poor people, period."

—from the *Chicago Tribune* (July 31, 1988)

African-American reporters in the capital to ask the questions that other reporters often neglected to raise, and to write about national issues from a black perspective. Not all the key national events were confined to Washington. When a seamstress named Rosa Parks was arrested in Montgomery, Alabama, in 1956, for refusing to give up her seat to a white passenger on a crowded bus, the incident touched off a bus boycott led by the young Baptist minister Martin Luther King, Jr. Payne called her editors in Chicago and asked to go to Montgomery to cover the boycott. Her stories, filed from Alabama, appeared on the front pages of the *Defender* for the next three months. "Mrs. Parks' act of rebellion touched off one of the most amazing reactions in the turbulent history of racial relations in the South," read one of her stories. "For this is not only a fight for courteous and equitable treatment, this is the first organized and disciplined revolt against a cruel and inhuman custom."

As a reporter, Payne rarely wrote about herself, but her newspaper often put her name into the headlines. When she traveled throughout the Deep South, writing of race relations there, the *Chicago Defender* promoted the series with her photograph and the headline: "ETHEL PAYNE TO TELL OF SOUTH." In 1955 the *Defender* sent her to Indonesia to cover the first major Asian-African conference, which was dedicated to ending colonialism and fighting racial discrimination. After the conference, Payne returned via nine different Asian and European cities. Her front-page stories appeared under such headlines as "BOMBAY TO ETHEL IS HEAT, PEOPLE AND KINDLY DOCTOR," and "ETHEL PAYNE BACK AND GLAD OF IT." By these headlines, her editors acknowledged that Payne's stories sold newspapers.

Her confrontations with President Eisenhower brought Payne national notoriety, and some complaints—even from her own mother—that she was needlessly upsetting the President. People said that she was privileged to attend Presidential press conferences, and should keep quiet and not stir things up. Payne did not see that as her purpose. "If you have lived through the black experience in this country, you feel that every day you're assaulted by the system," she responded. "You are either acquiescent, which I think is wrong, or else you just rebel, and you kick against it. I wanted to constantly, constantly, constantly hammer away, raise the questions that needed to be raised."

An angered Presidential press secretary, James C. Haggerty, once called

Payne to his office and accused her of violating the White House Correspondents Association's rules. She had written some articles for a magazine published by a labor organization, the Congress of Industrial Organizations (CIO). Haggerty said that broke the rule against White House correspondents engaging in political activities. Payne pointed out that she met all the Correspondents Association's requirements of being a full-time newspaper reporter, that she had written only occasionally for the CIO to supplement her income, and that she was no longer writing for that organization. When newspaper columnist Drew Pearson learned of the incident, he wrote a column that accused Haggerty of harassing Payne, and the White House dropped the complaint.

In the 1960s Payne covered events in Washington and in the South, including the Selma to Montgomery March, the Birmingham demonstrations, and the March on Washington. She spent three months in South Vietnam in 1966 reporting on African-American troops in that war. "I recognized the danger of it, the risk of it," she said, "but it was a gamble and adventure and it appealed to me." In 1972 she began recording her commentary three times a week for a CBS radio feature called "Spectrum," which advertised that it presented "Varying shades of personal opinion on current issues." For years she did radio and television appearances along with her regular newspaper reporting, and later had her own news commentary program on a Chicago radio station.

By 1973 the *Defender* had brought Ethel Payne back to Chicago as associate editor of the paper, but editing made her feel "like a fish out of water." She had long since outgrown local news and wanted to get back to Washington and to do more overseas reporting. So she left the *Chicago Defender* in 1978 to become a lecturer and freelance writer. She also taught

for a year at Fisk University in Nashville, Tennessee, which established the Ethel L. Payne Chair in Journalism. Well into her 70s, she continued to write a syndicated column for black newspapers scattered across the country. "I saw myself as an advocate as much as being a newspaper person," Payne explained in an interview near the end of her life. She hoped that people would remember her not as a passive observer of events but as an agent for change. "I fought all of my life to bring about change, to correct the injustices and the inequities in the system." When Payne died in 1991, the *Washington Post* commented that "her voice was low, but her questions were piercing. . . . The proof of her professionalism—fairness, straightforward accounts of all sides and independence of views—was in her writings."

FURTHER READING

Mills, Kay. *A Place in the News: From the Women's Pages to the Front Pages*. New York: Dodd, Mead, 1988.

Payne, Ethel. "Loneliness in the Capital: The Black National Correspondent," in *Perspectives of the Black Press: 1974*, edited by Henry G. LaBrie III. Kennebunkport, Maine: Mercer, 1974.

————. Oral history interviews recorded by Kathleen Currie for the Washington Press Club Foundation, Archives of the National Press Club, Washington, D.C.

Pinckney, Darryl. "Professionals." *New York Review of Books* 34 (April 20, 1995): 43–49.

Senna, Carl. *The Black Press and the Struggle for Civil Rights*. New York: Franklin Watts, 1993.

Streitmatter, Rodger. "No Taste for Fluff: Ethel L. Payne, African-American Journalist." *Journalism Quarterly* 68 (Fall 1991): 528–540.

————. *Raising Her Voice: African-American Women Journalists Who Changed History*. Lexington: University Press of Kentucky, 1994.

Wolseley, Roland E. *The Black Press, U.S.A.* Ames: Iowa State University Press, 1990.

Walter Cronkite

AMERICA'S "MOST TRUSTED MAN"

After the Vietcong's surprise Tet offensive against South Vietnam in January 1968, CBS anchorman Walter Cronkite broadcast a special report from South Vietnam. Breaking his usual policy of reporting the news without commentary, Cronkite declared that the American people had too often been deceived by the false optimism of their leaders. "To say that we are closer to victory today is to believe in the face of the evidence, the optimists who have been wrong in the past," he declared. "To say that we are mired in stalemate seems the only realistic, yet unsatisfactory conclusion." The United States needed to negotiate a peace, "not as victors, but as an honorable people who lived up to their pledge to defend democracy, and did the best they could." Watching the broadcast at the White House, President Lyndon B. Johnson turned to his aides and sighed, "It's all over." If he had lost Walter Cronkite, Johnson knew that he had lost Middle America.

At its peak, the "CBS Evening News with Walter Cronkite" appeared on more than 200 stations each night. Twenty-six million Americans watched the program. President Johnson (whose own family owned a CBS television station in Texas) knew that public opinion polls ranked Cronkite the "most trusted man in America." A "credibility gap" had developed that caused people to question their government. Americans found Cronkite's assessment of the war more believable than anything the President of the United States might say.

Although he made his reputation in broadcasting, Walter Cronkite had roots in print journalism. Born in Saint Joseph, Missouri, he was raised in Kansas City and then Houston, Texas. A short story about a reporter in *American Boy* magazine inspired his youthful ambitions. While a student at the University of Texas, Cronkite worked part-time covering state politics in Austin for the *Houston Press*. He dropped out of college to join that paper's staff in Houston, at a salary of $15 a week. He wrote obituaries, reported on Sunday sermons, and reviewed a few movies. But riding the bus to work, he observed that "watching others reading my story or stories of the day was one of life's great pleasures."

While visiting his grandparents in Kansas City, Cronkite read about the start of a new radio station, KCMO. He applied for a job and was hired as a news and sports announcer. The station asked him to broadcast as "Walter Wilcox." That way the station owned the name, to prevent him from taking listeners with him if he moved to another station. One day the station manager ordered

Seen here on "The Morning Show" in 1954, Walter Cronkite hosted a variety of programs before becoming CBS News anchorman.

Cronkite to broadcast news of a spectacular fire at city hall. Cronkite refused until he had checked its accuracy. As he suspected, the fire story turned out to be greatly exaggerated, but he was fired for failing to follow orders. "The KCMO experience cooled any thought I had that radio might be an interesting medium in which to practice journalism," he concluded. After working briefly as a football play-by-play announcer, he returned to print with a job at United Press, a wire service that provided news to papers across the country.

The UP's busy Kansas City bureau taught Cronkite to sort through wire stories from around the world and decide which ones to relay to local papers—and how to trim those stories to size. Constant deadlines caused lots of pressure, but Cronkite really enjoyed the work. "Here I was, just a kid, shaping the front pages of the small client newspapers in that part of the Midwest." In 1940 he married Elizabeth (Betsy) Maxwell, a columnist and women's editor for the *Kansas City Journal*.

United Press sent Cronkite to London to cover World War II. There he came to the attention of the famous CBS correspondent Edward R. Murrow, who offered to hire him as a radio news broadcaster. Cronkite's previous experience had led him to dismiss radio as a news medium, yet he knew that Murrow had lifted radio's stature. The job offer would also more than double Cronkite's salary. He accepted, but when the UP raised his salary and assured him a promotion, he told Murrow that he had changed his mind. Murrow was astonished that anyone would choose the drudge work of wire service reporting over the glamour of broadcasting. "Ed didn't take it too kindly," Cronkite recalled. "After that incident, I always felt that Murrow had a question mark in his mind concerning me."

After covering the war from the Battle of the Atlantic to D-Day and the Battle of the Bulge, Cronkite went

"From Dallas, Texas, the flash—apparently official. President Kennedy died at 1 p.m. Central Standard Time—a half hour ago. Vice President Johnson has left the hospital in Dallas, but we do not know where he has proceeded. Presumably, he will be taking the oath of office shortly, and become the thirty-sixth President of the United States."

—from a CBS broadcast (November 22, 1963)

to Moscow for the United Press. That cold and dismal assignment, and the birth of his first child, made him reassess his career. Reporters tended to start with wire services and then move to other jobs that were less demanding and paid better. Concluding that he had gone as far as he could with United Press, Cronkite went back to radio in 1948 as Washington correspondent for a group of Midwestern radio stations. He thought he might eventually return to Kansas City as manager of a station, until the outbreak of the Korean War in 1950 changed everything.

Ed Murrow called to offer Cronkite a CBS assignment in Korea. This time he accepted. Just before Cronkite was due to go overseas, CBS asked him to set up a news department for its new television station in Washington, D.C. Since this was years before satellite linkage existed, Cronkite had almost no film to show on the program. Instead he used charts and a blackboard to explain to viewers the daily reports from Korea. His years as a wire service editor, sifting through masses of material and culling out the key issues, helped him make sense out of the Korean story for television viewers. "I had a gut feeling that television news delivery ought to be as informal as possible," he later explained. He succeeded so well that CBS decided against sending him to Korea.

So impressed was CBS News that it featured Cronkite on its Sunday morning public affairs programs and made him the anchor for its broadcasts of the Republican and Democratic National Conventions in 1952. Operating out of the CBS Convention Booth, Cronkite performed magnificently, whether reading from a prepared script or ad libbing as events developed. He helped CBS outscore the other networks. When friends advised him to get an agent to negotiate a higher salary, Cronkite began to

wonder if television news was just "show business." During the 1950s he served as narrator of a program called "You Are There," which dramatically re-created historical events. He also hosted "Air Power," "The Twentieth Century," "The Morning Show," and "Eyewitness to History."

In 1962, Walter Cronkite became anchor for the CBS nightly national news program. At the time, national news broadcasts were only 15 minutes long, giving affiliated stations the other 15 minutes for local news. This short format made news programs little more than a series of headlines, with practically no analysis. Then in 1963 the networks expanded the national news to half an hour. With more time to fill, newer cameras that could be more easily transported to the scene of events, and satellite technology to retrieve and broadcast that film quickly—even live—the networks had to build up their news operations.

Other veteran correspondents at CBS had trained under Ed Murrow and shared his belief that broadcasters should not suppress their personal convictions, but should speak out against injustices. Never having been closely associated with Murrow, Cronkite held a newspaper reporter's belief in presenting the news without taking sides. "My job was to try as hard as I could to remove every trace of opinion from the broadcast," he insisted. He generally declined to offer any personal commentaries on the evening news. Cronkite also lacked Murrow's intense appearance. He seemed more relaxed and reassuring, unafraid to smile at human foibles or to show enthusiasm for space flight. He ended his nightly broadcasts with a folksy: "And that's the way it is. . . ." Before long, viewers were calling him "Uncle Walter."

On the first half-hour news program, in September 1963, Cronkite interviewed President John F. Kennedy at his home in Hyannisport,

Massachusetts. Much of their talk dealt with the deteriorating situation in Vietnam. In November, Kennedy was assassinated in Dallas, and Cronkite, in his shirtsleeves, made the first television announcement of the President's death. He stayed on the air with the agonizing story for hours. Despite this magnificent performance, Cronkite and the CBS News ran second in the ratings to NBC's popular Huntley-Brinkley Report (featuring Chet Huntley and David Brinkley). CBS managers grew so nervous over the ratings that in 1964 they replaced Cronkite with their own two-person team of correspondents to cover the conventions. The replacement team did not work well, and for future conventions CBS returned to Cronkite, who gave what people called not gavel-to-gavel but "Walter to Walter" coverage. During the late 1960s, Cronkite's news program moved to the top of the ratings, and it stayed there until he retired in 1981.

Cronkite's efforts to keep his own views out of the news broadcasts caused some Democrats to suspect him of being a Republican, while many Republicans were convinced he was a Democrat (he was registered to vote as an independent). President Lyndon Johnson worked hard to win Cronkite's support, especially for the Vietnam War. Cronkite reported from Vietnam several times, even wearing a military flight suit. Only after Cronkite concluded that Johnson had deceived him did he make his famous declaration that the war had become a stalemate.

No politician distrusted the media more intensely than Richard Nixon. When Nixon became President in 1969 he sought to neutralize criticism from television commentators by accusing them of having a liberal bias against him. Nixon's Vice President, Spiro Agnew, charged that "a small group of men, numbering perhaps no more than a dozen 'anchormen,' com-

mentators, and executive producers" decided what was news and how to present it. Agnew asserted that the views of this fraternity did not represent the views of the average person, and he accused television news of presenting a "narrow and distorted picture of America." Cronkite considered this charge "an implied threat to freedom of speech in our country." He publicly called on print journalists to stand with television news broadcasters "in understanding that a threat against one newsman is an attack against us all." Opinion polls showed that Cronkite retained a higher degree of public confidence than did either Nixon or Agnew.

Unintimidated, Cronkite devoted large parts of his evening news broadcasts in 1972 to evidence that linked the Watergate burglary to a campaign of political sabotage by the Nixon administration. Although Nixon won a landslide reelection that year, the charges would not go away. The media relentlessly pursued the Watergate story, a Senate committee investigated, and a special prosecutor brought formal charges. In 1973 Agnew resigned as Vice President over charges of bribery and income tax evasion. In 1974 Nixon resigned the Presidency to avoid impeachment. Despite his role in exposing the Nixon administration, Cronkite still rejected an advocacy role for television news. "The basic function of the press has to be the presentation of all the facts on which the story is based," he insisted. The people need the facts to make up their own minds, he believed, not a newscaster to tell them how to think.

When he reached age 65, Walter Cronkite retired, at the height of his popularity. His viewers had come to expect the "CBS Evening News" to be "the *New York Times* of television." But after he retired, he thought the program had turned into a tabloid. Faced with competition from 24-hour-

Walter Cronkite

BORN
November 4, 1916
Saint Joseph, Missouri

EDUCATION
Attended University of Texas, Austin (1933–35)

ACCOMPLISHMENTS
Reporter, *Houston Press* (1936–37); news and sports reporter, KCMO radio, Kansas City, Missouri (1937); football announcer, WKY radio, Oklahoma City (1938); correspondent, United Press International (1939–48); Washington correspondent for Midwestern radio stations (1948–50); correspondent, CBS radio and television (1950–62); narrator and host of such television programs as "You Are There," "Air Power," "The Twentieth Century," "The Morning Show," and "Eyewitness to History"; anchorman, "CBS Evening News With Walter Cronkite" (1962-81); author of *Eye on the World* (1970), *The Challenges of Change* (1971), and *A Reporter's Life* (1996)

Cronkite reported personally on the war in Vietnam, making several trips there in the 1960s. His conclusion that the war was mired in stalemate helped change American public opinion.

and thoughtful news documentaries of the past. The networks seemed increasingly less interested in reporting the news than in building up their ratings. Cronkite did not envy the generation of news broadcasters who followed him.

a-day cable news programs, network news managers sought to attract viewers by reducing serious news coverage of foreign and national events in favor of human interest stories with a lighter touch. Calling this "trivializing" the news, Cronkite lamented the general decline in standards of television news.

After Cronkite retired as an anchorman, CBS never asked him back as an occasional commentator on the evening news broadcasts. His old colleagues in the newsroom seemed uncomfortable with his presence. But while devoting much of his retirement to sailing and other hobbies, he also served on CBS's board of trustees. There he protested when the network's business managers put "trashy syndicated 'news' shows" on prime time in place of the more serious

FURTHER READING

Braestrap, Peter. *Big Story: How the American Press and Television Reported and Interpreted the Crisis of Tet 1968 in Vietnam and Washington*. Boulder, Colo.: Westview, 1977.

Cronkite, Walter. *The Challenges of Change*. Washington, D.C.: Public Affairs Press, 1971.

————. *Eye on the World*. New York: Cowles Books, 1971.

————. *A Reporter's Life*. New York: Knopf, 1996.

Gans, Herbert J. *Deciding What's News: A Study of CBS Evening News, NBC Nightly News, Newsweek, and Time*. New York: Random House, 1979.

Gates, Gary Paul. *Air Time: The Inside Story of CBS News*. New York: Harper & Row, 1978.

Halberstam, David. *The Powers That Be*. New York: Knopf, 1979.

Hallin, Daniel C. *The "Uncensored War": The Media and Vietnam*. New York: Oxford University Press, 1986.

Hammond, William M. *The Military and the Media, 1962–1968*. Washington, D.C.: U.S. Army Center for Military History, 1988.

Metz, Robert. *CBS: Reflections in a Bloodshot Eye*. New York: Signet, 1976.

Marguerite Higgins

"TROUBLE IS NEWS"

arguerite Higgins felt disappointed when her paper, the *New York Herald Tribune*, assigned her to head its Tokyo bureau in April 1950. She had been covering the dramatic events in Cold War Berlin, and she feared that Tokyo would be a quieter assignment, making it harder to get her stories on page one. But two months after she arrived in Japan, war broke out in nearby Korea. Higgins immediately boarded a plane for the war zone, ignoring the danger. She reached Seoul during the North Korean invasion of the city and joined the mass evacuation of South Koreans. Typing her stories on the hood of a jeep, she discovered there was no way to send them back to her paper other than for her to fly them back to Japan. When she returned again to Korea, however, a military officer stopped her. "You can't stay here," he warned. "There may be trouble." "I wouldn't be here if there was no trouble," Higgins replied. "Trouble is news and gathering news is my job."

After convincing her publisher that a woman could do the same job as a man, Marguerite Higgins covered World War II, the Korean War, and the Vietnam War.

Higgins and fellow correspondent Homer Bigart battled each other for front-page space in the *Herald Tribune* during the Korean War.

In an omen of Marguerite Higgins's pioneering career as a woman war correspondent, her parents first met in a bomb shelter in Paris during World War I. Lawrence Higgins was then an American pilot in the army air corps, and Marguerite de Godard was a young Frenchwoman. They married soon thereafter and moved to Hong Kong, where he was a freight manager for the Pacific Mail Steamship Company, and where their daughter, Marguerite, was born. At the age of six months, she contracted malaria and her parents took her to recover at a mountain resort in a part of Indochina that later became Vietnam—a country

that would deeply affect her life. When Marguerite was five, her father's company transferred him to Oakland, California, and she grew up there. The stock market crash of 1929 cost her father his job and made her think about her own future. "I began to worry about how I would earn a living when I grew up," she later recalled.

Maggie Higgins's father found another job, and her mother taught French at the prestigious Anna Head School in return for a scholarship for her daughter. An excellent student, Higgins enrolled at the University of California at Berkeley. During her freshman year, she joined the student newspaper, the *Daily Californian*, whose youthful radical and pacifist leanings she shared. In 1940 she spoke at a campus protest meeting against British imperialism. An attractive, vivacious young woman, she rejected a marriage proposal at graduation in order to attend the Columbia School of Journalism in New York City.

Moving into a grimy apartment in Greenwich Village and living a bohemian life-style, Maggie Higgins also led her class at Columbia. When she applied to report on campus activities for the *New York Herald Tribune*, she told the city editor: "I know you said you didn't want to hire a woman reporter. But I had to try. I know I could do a good job for you." She pointed out that with so many men going off to war, the paper would be smart to hire women. She got the job. When the wife of Chinese leader Chiang Kai-shek was a patient in a New York hospital, Higgins evaded restrictions against the press by carrying supplies behind a nurse into the hospital room. That scoop impressed the *Herald Tribune* enough to hire her as a regular staff reporter. For the rest of her career, Higgins took pride in interviewing people who never talked to the press, and she earned a reputation as a highly aggressive reporter.

In 1942 she married a radical philosophy professor, Stanley Moore, who had joined the army air corps and was leaving for London. Higgins herself wanted to be a war correspondent. She convinced her publisher, Helen Reid, that as a woman she could do the same job as any man. After getting the assignment, Higgins donned an army uniform and helmet and sailed for Europe. In London she rejoined her husband, who was both surprised and threatened by her self-assurance,

resilience, and determination. Their reunion made them realize that their marriage had been a mistake, and they soon divorced. Higgins's fluency in French got her transferred to liberated Paris. From there she provided her paper with a rush of war-related stories.

Anxious to see combat, Higgins accompanied American troops into Germany, filing her bylines: "With the 7th Army." She wrote graphic accounts of the Nazi death camp at Buchenwald, and at Dachau, SS officers attempted to surrender to her as the first American they had encountered. An American army officer tried to drag her from the concentration camp, saying, "Don't you realize the place is raging with typhus? Get out of there!" Higgins shouted back, "I've had my typhus shot! Lay off me! I'm doing my job!"

Success as a war correspondent led to Higgins's appointment to head the *Herald Tribune*'s Berlin bureau, when she was only 26. The end of World War II saw a breakdown of relations between the United States and the Soviet Union. Divided Berlin became a center of high-level diplomatic negotiations and also a military confrontation point. In 1948 the Russians blockaded Berlin, but the United States and its European allies overcame the blockade through a sustained airlift of supplies. Higgins's coverage repeatedly made the front pages. Fiercely competitive, she carried on famous feuds with other correspondents. The *Herald Tribune* decided to give her a rest at a quieter location and shifted her to Japan in 1950—just before North Korea invaded South Korea.

Traveling with little more than her typewriter and a toothbrush, Higgins sent back dramatic exclusives from Korea. Her first headline read:

Marguerite Higgins

BORN
September 3, 1920
Hong Kong

DIED
January 3, 1966
Washington, D.C.

EDUCATION
B.A., University of California at Berkeley (1941); M.S., School of Journalism, Columbia University (1942)

ACCOMPLISHMENTS
Reporter, University of California at Berkeley *Daily Californian* (1937–41); reporter, *Vallejo (California) Times-Herald* (1941); war, foreign, and diplomatic correspondent, *New York Herald Tribune* (1942–63); columnist, *Washington Evening Star* (1963–66); columnist, Long Island, New York, *Newsday* (1963–66); author of *War in Korea—Report of a Woman Combat Correspondent* (1951), *News Is a Singular Thing* (1955), *Red Plush and Black Bread* (1955), *Jessie Benton Fremont* (1962), *Overtime in Heaven: Adventures in the Foreign Service* (with Peter Lisagor, 1964), and *Our Vietnam Nightmare* (1965)

"With the United States Marines at Inchon, Korea—Heavily laden United States Marines, in one of the most technically difficult amphibious landings in history, stormed at sunset today over a ten-foot seawall in the heart of the port of Inchon and within an hour had taken three commanding hills in the city.

"I was in the fifth wave that hit 'Red Beach,' which in reality was a rough vertical pile of stones over which the first assault troops had to scramble with the aid of improvised landing ladders topped with steel hooks."

—from *New York Herald Tribune* (September 18, 1950)

"SEOUL'S FALL BY A REPORTER WHO ESCAPED." But since newspapers considered war to be a man's business, the *Herald Tribune* dispatched to Korea its senior foreign correspondent, Homer Bigart. Korea was too small for the two of them, Bigart told Higgins, advising her to leave or be fired. She refused, choosing to risk both her life and her job. Relishing a spirited competition between its star reporters, the *Herald Tribune* would not order Higgins back to Japan. She traveled with the troops, describing the hazardous conditions they faced, and how ill-equipped and unprepared they were for the brutality of war. One wounded soldier asked her, "How come you're here if you don't have to be?" "I'm a war correspondent," she explained. "People back home want to know what's going on here."

Lieutenant General Walton W. Walker, commander of the American forces in Korea, ordered Higgins out. "This is just not the type of war where a woman ought to be running around the front lines," he fumed. She went over his head and appealed to General Douglas MacArthur, who ordered her readmitted. Her competition infuriated Homer Bigart, who complained that Higgins's "I-was-there" style of reporting dealt too much with herself and that she treated General MacArthur and military leaders far too respectfully. Bigart resented Higgins's recklessness because she was forcing him to take hazardous chances to get his own stories. "I wanted her out of there in the worst way but couldn't get her transferred," Bigart later said. Higgins simply would go anywhere and do anything to get her story, even making the dangerous landing at Inchon with the Marines. The Higgins-Bigart contest produced such outstanding reporting that they jointly won the Pulitzer Prize for war correspondence.

Maggie Higgins returned to the United States a celebrity. Her book, *War in Korea*, became a best-seller and she was much in demand as a lecturer. In 1952 she married Air Force General William Hall. They had three children, one of whom died in infancy. But marriage and a family did not stop Higgins from her worldwide foreign correspondence. During the 1950s she traveled around the world, making several stops in Vietnam, a potential troublespot in Southeast Asia. When her husband went to the Pentagon, Higgins shifted her base from New York to Washington, D.C., and began covering the State Department.

Never willing to play by the rules—since the rules so often excluded her as a woman—Higgins created another stir in the 1950s when she endorsed such commercial products as typewriters, toothpaste, and cigarettes. The Standing Committee of Correspondents at the congressional press galleries reminded her that its rules forbade holders of the congressional press pass from any "paid publicity or promotion work." She responded by resigning from the press gallery. She did not need to be part of the pack, she retorted, because she wanted only exclusive stories. In 1963 she ended her long association with the *New York Herald Tribune* to become a columnist for the *Washington Star* and the Long Island, New York, newspaper *Newsday*. "A reporter writes what other reporters write and all he can do is try to write it better," Higgins observed. "A columnist can . . . draw some conclusions."

Her last major dispute involved Vietnam. During her many visits there, Higgins had come to admire South Vietnamese president Ngo Dinh Diem. While the American press corps stationed in Saigon was critical of Diem, she argued that the situation would worsen without him. The correspondent for the *New York Times* in Vietnam, David Halberstam, accused Higgins of not being skeptical enough of what high-ranking military officers were telling her. She replied: "When a correspondent who's fought in World War II or Korea interviews a military man, he has some understanding of his problems. They may not agree at all, but they speak the same language." The trouble with the younger generation of reporters, she concluded, was that they had never served in combat.

Later, when President Diem was overthrown and assassinated, Higgins laid the blame on the United States government and warned that Vietnam was becoming an American nightmare. While writing a book on the subject in 1965, she made her 10th trip to Vietnam, where she acquired a rare tropical disease. Back in Washington, Higgins was hospitalized. She died a few months later at the age of 45. Her funeral drew the nation's leading politicians and military brass, and she was buried at Arlington National Cemetery. Her colleagues in the press corps, who had so long bristled over her aggressiveness, credited her success in journalism to her great personal courage and to the risks she would take to get a story.

FURTHER READING

Higgins, Marguerite. *Jessie Benton Fremont*. Boston: Houghton Mifflin, 1962.

———. *News Is a Singular Thing*. Garden City, N.Y.: Doubleday, 1955.

———. *Our Vietnam Nightmare*. New York: Harper & Row, 1965.

———. *Red Plush and Black Bread*. Garden City, N.Y.: Doubleday, 1955.

———. *War in Korea—Report of a Woman Combat Correspondent*. Garden City, N.Y.: Doubleday, 1951.

Higgins, Marguerite, with Peter Lisagor. *Overtime in Heaven: Adventures in the Foreign Service*. Garden City, N.Y.: Doubleday, 1964.

Kluger, Richard. *The Paper: The Life and Death of the New York Herald Tribune*. New York: Knopf, 1986.

Knightley, Phillip. *The First Casualty: From Crimea to Vietnam: The War Correspondent as Hero, Propagandist, and Myth Maker*. New York: Harcourt Brace Jovanovich, 1975.

Marzlof, Marion. *Up from the Footnote: A History of Women Journalists*. New York: Hastings House, 1977.

May, Antoninette. *Witness to War: A Biography of Marguerite Higgins*. New York: Penguin, 1985.

Mills, Kay. *A Place in the News: From the Women's Pages to the Front Pages*. New York: Dodd, Mead, 1988.

Allen Neuharth

REINVENTING THE NEWSPAPER

The pressures of modern life force print and broadcast media to compete for people's limited time. As patterns of life, work, and commuting changed in the 1950s and 1960s, people abandoned afternoon newspapers and turned to television for their news. A new generation grew up watching TV, without seeming to need newspapers. More than 300 newspapers across the country went out of business.

Many people blamed unions and the rising cost of newsprint for these failures, but Allen Neuharth of the Gannett Company newspaper chain thought that the real culprit was mismanagement. He argued: "Newspapers could not only survive but thrive, if they figured out how to appeal to the television generation, how to modernize their equip-

Learning from his earlier mistakes, Allen Neuharth built Gannett into one of the most profitable newspaper chains by creating papers that appealed to the television generation.

ment to produced higher-quality newspapers at lower costs, and how to reach out for new audiences in mushrooming growth areas." Neuharth hired pollsters to conduct surveys to find out what people wanted. Armed with the results of those surveys, in 1982 he bucked the trend by creating a new newspaper, *USA Today*, that would reach the entire nation. His willingness to break with tradition in a dramatic way—and to prove the experts wrong—was the result of his own disastrous start in journalism.

Neuharth overcame a hard childhood in South Dakota. His father, a farmer, had been injured while plowing and died when Al was less than two years old. His mother washed dishes at a cafe during the day and took in laundry at home at night to support her two sons. Al felt resentful that his mother had to work so much harder than some of the "shiftless men" in their little farm town—something that made him keenly aware of economic discrimination against women. When his mother could not afford to buy him the new bicycle he wanted, he delivered newspapers to pay for a secondhand bike. After a knee injury benched him in sports, he joined the high school newspaper. He became editor of the paper and began to dream of someday publishing his own newspaper.

After serving in the army during World War II, Neuharth returned to marry his high school sweetheart and enroll at the University of South Dakota. The GI Bill paid his college tuition. During the summers, he reported for various newspapers in South Dakota, and after he graduated he joined the Associated Press. But Neuharth was an ambitious young man in a hurry. He and a college friend decided to create a weekly journal covering all sports in South Dakota. Raising capital by selling $50,000 in stocks, they launched *SoDak Sports* in

1952. Neuharth served as editor and publisher and wrote many of the stories. Readers enjoyed the sports journal but advertisers remained suspicious. After two years, *SoDak Sports* shut down.

Having lost all the money his stockholders had invested, Neuharth said he "wound up broke, in debt, and bloodied, but not bowed." Determined to climb back, he insisted, "The bigger you fail, the bigger you're likely to succeed later." Needing to get away from South Dakota to start anew, he took a job as a reporter with the *Miami Herald*. He started out scared that he might not measure up to the more seasoned reporters on the staff. But it did not take long for Neuharth to realize that he had worked much harder on *SoDak Sports* than was required for a daily paper. After many of his stories appeared on page one, he told his wife, Loretta, "I'm smarter and have more potential than anyone in the *Herald* newsroom. I don't think there is anything that can stop me." He declined an offer to become Washington bureau chief and instead became city editor—because that post offered a more direct route to the top management. In short order he was assistant managing editor.

In 1960, the Knight-Ridder newspaper chain, which owned the *Miami Herald*, transferred Neuharth to a leadership position at its flagship paper, the *Detroit Free Press*. As he was soaring at Knight, he received a job offer from the Gannett newspapers, a much smaller regional chain that was based in upstate New York. "I did a coldly calculating analysis of whether Neuharth, then age thirty-eight, would be better off in ten or twenty years in an organization like Knight or Gannett," he recalled, and decided that he had a better shot at becoming boss at Gannett. Although more prestigious, Knight-Ridder was a family operation with several members of the

Allen Neuharth

BORN
March 22, 1924
Eureka, South Dakota

EDUCATION
B.A., School of Journalism, University of South Dakota (1950)

ACCOMPLISHMENTS
Reporter, *Rapid City* (South Dakota) *Journal* (1948); sportswriter, *Mitchell* (South Dakota) *Daily Republic* (1949); staff writer, Associated Press (1950–52); editor and publisher, *SoDak Sports* (1952–54); rose from reporter to assistant managing editor, *Miami Herald* (1954–60); assistant executive editor, *Detroit Free Press* (1960–63); general manager, *Rochester Democrat and Chronicle* and *Times Union* (1963–66); executive vice president of Gannett (1966–70); president of Gannett (1970–79); chairman and chief executive officer of Gannett (1979–89); columnist, *USA Today* (1982–); chairman, Gannett Foundation and Freedom Forum (1989–); author of *Confessions of an S.O.B.* (1989)

With *USA Today*, Neuharth sought to win back the audience that newspapers had lost to television. This is the first issue, published in 1982, with a welcome notice to readers in the bottom right-hand corner.

Miller, former chief of the Washington bureau of the Associated Press. No one stood directly in line to succeed him. Neuharth went to Gannett determined to build it into a rival to Knight and other newspaper chains.

Paul Miller made Neuharth general manager of Gannett's two leading newspapers in Rochester, New York, and later executive vice president of the chain. Miller was anxious to expand beyond a regional chain of papers and to move into television as well. In order to finance its planned expansion, Gannett offered 500,000 shares of stock in 1967. This new stock offering, which followed a long newspaper strike that had put several major papers out of business in New York, received little enthusiasm on Wall Street. As Miller noted, very few stockbrokers knew much about the newspaper business "and fewer still knew or cared much about Gannett." Miller and Neuharth began a promotional campaign to explain to financial analysts that despite the failures of newspapers in New York City, they were a booming business in smaller cities across the country. "Paul Miller and I did a lot of preaching," said Neuharth.

In 1970 the *New York Daily News* tried to lure Neuharth away from Gannett, but he used that job offer to pressure Miller into stepping aside and making him president of Gannett. By 1979 Neuharth replaced Miller as chief executive officer. Gannett's revenues rose dramatically. Neuharth also moved the company from Rochester, New York, to a more nationally visible location in Arlington, Virginia, across the Potomac River from Washington, D.C. Gannett grew into a media empire of 85 papers and 26 radio and television stations.

"Personally I had the world by the tail in 1979," Neuharth assessed. "I was

Knight family standing ahead of him in the line of succession. By contrast, no members of the Gannett family ran that company. After the founder, Frank Gannett, died in 1947, presidency of the chain had been assumed by Paul

fifty-five, CEO of the USA's largest newspaper company, making more than a million dollars a year." Flown about in company jets and chauffeured in limousines, he had homes and offices in New York City, Washington, D.C., Cocoa Beach, Florida, and Lake Tahoe, Nevada. Among his acquaintances, he counted presidents, prime ministers, entertainers, and athletes, and could obtain the best seats at the Super Bowl or the World Series. But he felt that Gannett was still "a big company of mostly smaller operations," and he still had something to prove personally.

Neuharth had partially compensated for his failure at *SoDak Sports* by creating a successful new paper in Cocoa Beach, Florida, close to the Kennedy Space Center, called *Today* and billed as "Florida's Space Age Newspaper." In 1982 he went further and launched a new national newspaper, *USA Today*. The *Wall Street Journal* and the *New York Times* also aimed for national audiences, but both reached more elite, specialized readerships. Neuharth aimed at the mass market for average readers, especially those who were not regular newspaper readers. Surveys targeted potential readers who were under 35, single people, African Americans, and Hispanics. Newspapers were too drab and filled with murky black-and-white pictures, few graphs, and stories that meandered for page after page. They were losing the competition with television news broadcasts that reduced stories to sound bites and colorful videos. Neuharth supervised the creation of a more eye-catching paper that would have color pictures, graphs, and weather maps, that would confine stories to one page, often to just a few paragraphs or a box, and that would give greater attention to celebrities, sports, and other popular subjects. He wanted it short and snappy enough to win back the television generation.

Drawing on reporters who wrote for the Gannett chain as a whole, Neuharth devised a system whereby the first few paragraphs from any of their stories would be a summary of the entire story. The summary could appear in *USA Today*, while other papers in the chain were free to publish all or large parts of the rest of the copy. Critics grumbled about this practice, comparing *USA Today* to fast-food chains and labeling it "McPaper." Rather than take offense, Neuharth turned the fast-food analogy around as a compliment: "I saw it as a shorthand way to communicate to the public what we were trying to do: Lots of news, in interesting bits and pieces. Tastes good and makes you feel good. In a colorful, smooth, slick package with ink that doesn't dirty your hands the way many gray newspapers do."

The experts predicted that *USA Today* would flop. One Wall Street media analyst declared, "A national daily newspaper seems like a way to lose a lot of money in a hurry." In the planning stages, Gannett had called it Project NN for "National Newspaper," but some said it stood for "Neuharth's Nonsense." Neuharth had to persuade Gannett's board of directors to take a gamble, and he had to convince other Gannett papers that *USA Today* would not draw away their readers. Despite its anticipated failure, *USA Today* flourished—although not until its circulation passed 5 million did advertisers fully recognize its potential. Meanwhile, other newspapers copied its flashier elements, such as color pictures, weather maps, and graphics.

At first *USA Today* tried to do

> *"Many of you have a love/hate relationship with your newspaper. But even when you criticize it, you call it 'my newspaper.' Even though most of you spend more time watching television than reading, you still consider your newspaper an indispensable part of your daily lifestyle."*
>
> —from *Confessions of an S.O.B.* (1989)

everything differently. It sought to emphasize the good news rather than the bad. One early headline focused on the survivors of an airline crash rather than on those who had died. Another headline proclaimed: "MEN AND WOMEN ARE DIFFERENT." Much of the front page was devoted to Hollywood stars and professional athletes. The paper had no foreign correspondents and almost no foreign news. Critics complained that it might be sleek but it lacked substance. Reporters complained that without the color and graphics the stories read like wire-service reports, with almost no individual style or voice. Over time, however, the paper began to cover more "hard news," so that its front pages began to resemble those of other papers in the types of stories they featured.

"I became a much-discussed and cussed medial mogul," Neuharth claimed proudly. Among his accomplishments, Neuharth made *USA Today* a model for hiring, training, and promoting women and minorities for its staff and management. He also devoted much attention to promoting the newspaper business in the public arena, devoting many of his columns in *USA Today* to some of the abuses of journalism that needed correcting, such as his opposition to the reliance on anonymous sources. He won admirers for reinventing the American newspaper and helping it survive against the broadcast media—although his critics said that the price was lowering standards for the entire industry. To Neuharth, however, the best measure of success was the expansion of Gannett into one of the world's largest and most profitable newspaper chains, and the creation of a new national newspaper that almost everyone else had thought impossible. Once and for all that got the "*SoDak Sports* monkey" off his back.

FURTHER READING

Brandt, J. Donald. *A History of Gannett, 1906–1993*. Arlington, Va.: Gannett, 1993.

Cose, Ellis. *The Press*. New York: Morrow, 1989.

Hartman, John K. *The USA Today Way: A Candid Look at the National Newspaper's First Decade (1982–1992)*. Mount Pleasant: Central Michigan University, 1992.

Kurtz, Howard. *Media Circus: The Trouble with America's Newspapers*. New York: Random House, 1993.

Neuharth, Allen. *Confessions of an S.O.B.* New York: Doubleday, 1989.

Prichard, Peter. *The Making of McPaper*. New York: Andrews, McMeel & Parker, 1987.

Rupert Murdoch

GLOBAL MEDIA BARON

Television has had a devastating impact on newspapers and magazines since the 1960s. Readers increasingly got news and entertainment from electronic broadcasting as satellites beamed words and pictures instantly around the world. In a notable book published in 1964, *Understanding Media,* the Canadian communications scholar Marshall McLuhan proclaimed: "Time has ceased, space has vanished. We now live in a global village, a simultaneous happening." Among the first media moguls to comprehend the new potentials was Rupert Murdoch. Literally a man of the world, Murdoch was born in Australia, educated in Great Britain, and became an American citizen. In each of those countries he directed a vast media enterprise. By the 1990s his News Corporation employed more than 30,000 people, published newspapers and magazines around the world, and broadcast into millions of homes, producing billions of dollars in revenue.

Although he owned newspapers on several continents, Rupert Murdoch saw television and satellite communications as the future of journalism, and he built a vast media empire.

After taking over the *New York Post*, Murdoch gave it his brand of snappy headlines and sensational stories and shifted its editorial leaning from liberal to conservative.

When asked about his global empire, Murdoch insisted that what interested him most was gaining influence, not money. "It goes back to my father, to my background," he said, "having been brought up to believe that there was an opportunity to have influence and to do something with that influence." His father, Keith Murdoch, had been a legendary newspaper publisher in Australia. As a reporter in 1915, he had exposed the British bungling of the invasion of Gallipoli during World War I. Thousands of Australian and New Zealand troops were killed or wounded there, leading the British to call off that ill-fated campaign. He returned to Melbourne to take control of a chain of newspapers, magazines, and radio stations. Tall, handsome, outgoing, and politically conservative, the publisher was knighted by Queen Elizabeth as Sir Keith.

In many ways Sir Keith's son Rupert differed greatly from his father. At school Rupert disliked organized sports and had few close friends.

Guarded, shy, and restless, he always felt himself more of an outsider than part of the establishment. His politics leaned far to the left. As a student at Oxford, he kept a bust of the communist leader Lenin on his mantle. In 1952, when Sir Keith died of cancer, his 21-year-old son wanted to keep his father's newspapers. But in fact his father had been manager rather than owner of the chain. Sir Keith did own two newspapers, but his widow sold one of them, the *Brisbane Courier-Mail*, to pay taxes.

After gaining a little bit of experience on Fleet Street (the hub of newspaper publishing in London), Rupert Murdoch returned to Australia to take over his father's only remaining paper, the *Adelaide News*, and its Sunday edition, the *Adelaide Sunday Mail*. He fought a spirited battle for circulation against the larger, more established paper, the *Adelaide Advertiser*. Young Murdoch impressed everyone with his energy and zest. "He was always up and going," said one of his staff. People wondered if "the Boy Publisher" aimed to beat his father by building an even bigger, more powerful empire.

Blending flashy headlines, bizarre stories, and sex to attract readers, he began acquiring control of other newspapers and magazines across Australia. An ardent Australian nationalist, in 1964 he created the first Australia-wide newspaper, *The Australian*, which sought to overcome rivalries between the country's seven states. A more serious paper than his others, *The Australian* covered national issues in greater depth and gave more emphasis to foreign news. Also in the mid-1960s, Murdoch fell in love with Anna Torv, a newspaper reporter. He divorced his first wife and married Anna in 1967. A Catholic and a con-

Rupert Murdoch

servative, she exerted an influence on his changing political views.

While he expanded his empire in Australia, Murdoch's ambitions brought him back to Britain. He bought a London Sunday tabloid, *News of the World,* from the Carr family, who had controlled it for 80 years. In a spirited bidding war with other potential buyers, Murdoch had gotten the paper by promising to run it in partnership with the Carrs. Once he took over, however, Murdoch concluded that the paper was a total wreck and needed to be drastically overhauled as he saw fit. The Carr family felt betrayed and the incident forged an impression of Murdoch as ruthless and devious. Next Murdoch bought the *London Sun,* a working-class tabloid, which he enlivened with photos of bare-breasted women ("Sunbirds") and rumors about the British royal family. He also reversed the paper's traditional support for the Labour party into an endorsement of the Conservatives. In addition to his racy tabloids, Murdoch purchased the prestigious *Times* of London and the *Sunday Times.* All of his papers strongly supported Prime Minister Margaret Thatcher and her free-market programs.

Murdoch explained his shift from socialist to capitalist as a result of his confrontations with Britain's powerful labor unions, which fostered "featherbedding"—using more workers than needed for a job. In the 1980s he made an audacious move to cut his labor costs in Britain by building a new headquarters at Wapping, near London. There, computer-operated printing presses were secretly installed. When negotiations with the unions failed, Murdoch moved his operations to Wapping and hired nonunion workers. A barbed-wire fence—and a large

police force sent by the Conservative government—kept union pickets at a distance from "Fortress Wapping."

Anxious to spread his media empire to United States markets, Murdoch began by purchasing newspapers in San Antonio, Texas. He also founded a new supermarket tabloid, the *National Star.* To make the *Star* a no-holds-barred gossip and scandal sheet, he imported its staff from Australia and Great Britain. Eager to break into the big New York City media market, Murdoch made overtures to Dorothy Schiff, the publisher of the *New York Post.* Beset with labor troubles and competition from larger papers, she was ready to sell. Murdoch gave the *Post* his brand of snappy headlines and sensationalist stories, and shifted its editorial policies from liberal to conservative.

Reporters on the *Post* complained about the abrupt shift away from the paper's liberal, reformist politics, to which Murdoch replied that they should resign if they disagreed with him. He also distanced himself from other New York publishers. When a newspaper strike occurred in New York in 1978, the publishers sought to present a united front to reduce featherbedding. Murdoch broke with the others so that the union would keep the *Post* publishing, with the agreement that they would give his paper the same terms that the other papers negotiated. Such self-centered attitudes made Murdoch extremely unpopular among other journalists. They described him as a pirate and a predator and referred to his papers as sleazy products that pandered to the worst public cravings. The editor of the *New York Times,* Abraham Rosenthal, called him "a bad element, practicing mean, ugly, violent journalism." *Fortune* mag-

BORN
March 11, 1931
Melbourne, Australia

EDUCATION
M.A., Worcester College, Oxford University (1953)

ACCOMPLISHMENTS
Subeditor, *London Daily Express* (1953); publisher, in Australia: *Adelaide News, The Australian, Melbourne Herald, Brisbane Sun,* and *TV Week;* publisher, in New Zealand: *Wellington Dominion;* publisher, in Great Britain: *News of the World, Sun, Times, Sunday Times, London Post, Today;* publisher, in the United States: *San Antonio Express, San Antonio News, Village Voice* (New York), *New York Post, Boston Herald, Chicago Sun-Times, New York Magazine, National Star, TV Guide, Weekly Standard,* HarperCollins and Zondervan Publishing; publisher, in Hong Kong: *South China Morning Post;* chairman and chief executive officer, News Corporation Limited, Southern Television Corporation (Australia), London Weekend Television and Sky Television (Great Britain), Fox Television Network; chairman, Twentieth Century Fox Productions; chairman, Delphi, on-line access to the Internet

"[Newspapers can bring to television] the habit of topicality, the ability to gauge and lead public opinion, the capacity to understand public needs and tastes and provide for them, the courage to try new ideas even in the face of skepticism, the constant striving to develop standards of the community, and the general closeness to the community which is essential to a newspaper."

—upon applying for a license to operate a commercial television station in Sydney, Australia (1961)

azine wrote: "Murdoch's tabloids luridly depict a world in which fiendish criminals prey on women and children, evil immigrants menace the natives, and most government affairs are too tedious to note." Murdoch's supporters responded that he enlivened his papers, entertained his readers, and employed a lot of journalists.

As much as Murdoch loved newspapers, he recognized that television, satellite communication, and computers were the wave of the future. He owned television networks in Australia and Great Britain and in the United States his News Corporation purchased a controlling interest in the Fox Network. Challenging the major networks, Fox specialized in such programs as "The Simpsons" and "Melrose Place," professional football, and a Murdoch-style tabloid news program, "A Current Affair."

Entering American television, however, meant dealing with a federal law that prohibited foreigners from controlling U.S. television stations. Murdoch solved this dilemma by becoming a naturalized American citizen in 1987. Other networks complained that his operating funds still came from his Australian holdings. But Murdoch's endorsement of conservative political candidates and financial contributions to their campaigns earned him much sympathy in Washington. The Federal Communications Commission eventually ruled in Murdoch's behalf, despite its finding that the foreign ownership of Fox exceeded the federal limit.

Too often, Murdoch's editorial policies seemed designed to promote his commercial interests. His political support for Margaret Thatcher in Britain and Ronald Reagan in the United States had helped his business ventures win favorable rulings from their governments. Similarly, despite his preaching of freedom through free enterprise and international telecom-

munications, Murdoch capitulated to the communist government of China in order to enter its vast markets. In return for permission to broadcast in the People's Republic of China, Murdoch's Star Network dropped its broadcasts from the British Broadcasting Corporation (BBC), whose news programs had offended Chinese communist leaders.

A creative, risk-taking media entrepreneur, Rupert Murdoch came close to losing his empire to bankruptcy more than once, but always managed to recover. Murdoch was clearly willing to do whatever was necessary to promote his empire, whether that meant changing his nationality, his politics, or his principles. He told interviewers that he gained pleasure both from building his worldwide enterprises and from getting involved with a day-to-day campaign on one of his newspapers. "I was an Australian nationalist when I was younger," Murdoch reflected. "Today I would describe myself as being totally internationalist, free market, believing that most people will benefit most and the world will be a better place from having free markets. In ideas as well as goods."

FURTHER READING

Auletta, Ken. "The Pirate." *New Yorker* 71 (13 November 1995): 80–94.

Kiernan, Thomas. *Citizen Murdoch*. New York: Dodd, Mead, 1986.

Leapman, Michael, *Arrogant Aussie: The Rupert Murdoch Story*. Secaucus, N.J.: Lyle Stuart, 1985.

Munster, George. *Rupert Murdoch: A Paper Prince*. New York: Viking, 1985.

Shawcross, William. *Rupert Murdoch: Ringmaster of the Information Circus*. New York: Simon & Schuster, 1993.

Tuccille, Jerome. *Rupert Murdoch*. New York: Donald I. Fine, 1990.

Georgie Anne Geyer

A "LOVE AFFAIR WITH THE WORLD"

ow does one make contact with an underground guerrilla movement in a country where every security force is searching for them—and more than eager to kill to find them?" wrote Georgie Anne Geyer about her experiences as a foreign correspondent in Guatemala in 1966. "By looking around. I mean *really* looking around. One must psych out the society and judge where are the weak points, the soft spots, the places where one can probe and possibly make a breakthrough." Risking her life by going into the mountains, Geyer not only found the Guatemalan guerrillas but interviewed their leader. Her articles were reprinted in newspapers around the world and established her reputation. She had achieved an ambition that almost none of her colleagues back at the *Chicago Daily News* had thought possible.

As a child growing up on the South Side of Chicago, Georgie Anne Geyer wanted to know everything about the world, and she read her way through the local library. Her father, Robert Geyer, ran a dairy that provided milk for a hamburger chain and made the family prosperous. Her

Georgie Anne Geyer first made her reputation as a foreign correspondent by interviewing underground guerrilla rebels in Guatemala in the early 1960s.

Geyer interviews Palestinian leader Yasir Arafat. She believed she had an advantage as a woman in gaining interviews, because revolutionaries often saw male reporters as part of the establishment.

mother, after whom she was named, was a housewife who complained so much about her work at home that young Georgie developed a deep distaste for the traditional "women's role." Although her family believed that women should marry early and raise large families, Geyer wanted to be free to explore the world and understand it, and she concluded that she could never attain such freedom in marriage. She enrolled in the journalism school at Northwestern University. There she hated courses in reporting, copyediting and typesetting, preferring to read history, political science, and literature.

What she called her "love affair with the world" began when she received a Fulbright scholarship to study in Vienna, where she learned to speak German. She was living in Austria when the Soviet Union suppressed a revolution in neighboring Hungary. Although she returned home with a serious case of hepatitis, she was more concerned with world news.

In 1959 Geyer joined the staff of the *Chicago Daily News* as a society

reporter, expected to write for the "women's pages." Within a year she shifted to covering city news. One of her first assignments had her pose as a waitress at a Mafia wedding. The *Daily News* ran a front-page picture of Geyer in her waitress uniform, accompanied by her account of the event. But Geyer wanted to get beyond local reporting and become a foreign correspondent. The men at the paper considered this ambition a laughing matter. She was a woman in her twenties, while their foreign correspondents were all men over fifty. When her paper would not send her abroad, she applied for and received a private grant to underwrite six months in Latin America. The *Daily News* agreed to let her report from there during her stay.

Foreign correspondents were few in number and had an elite status among journalists. As Geyer's colleague Mike Royko observed, they had to be "outstanding reporters, exceptional writers, self-motivators, imaginative, determined, adventurous, able to cover a war or a fast-breaking revolution." Royko recalled how the men in the newsroom chuckled when the persistent young woman managed to get assigned to South America, but they stopped laughing when she read her stories. Geyer developed a knack for interviewing seemingly inaccessible sources. She believed it was an advantage being a woman, since people on the fringes of society, like revolutionaries, saw male reporters as part of the establishment. When she returned to Chicago able to speak Spanish, she received further assignments in Latin America. The *Daily News* sent her to cover the revolution in the Dominican Republic in 1965. The following year she visited Cuba and interviewed Fidel Castro.

Geyer had an ability to guess where the next big story would break and get there before anyone else, no matter how remote the location. Despite her daring adventures in Guatemala and elsewhere, however, she had trouble escaping from an image she described as "a wholesome, blond, smiling girl next door." Her *Chicago Daily News* editor, Roy Fisher, wrote in his column, "Hollywood couldn't imagine a foreign correspondent like Georgie Anne Geyer. . . . She would be better cast as a pretty school teacher than as a cool, nerveless foreign correspondent who thrives on hazardous assignments."

Ready for a change, Geyer left Latin America in 1967 to cover the Soviet Union. She discovered that it was difficult to report on a society where she could not ask direct questions because people could not talk freely. "You find yourself sifting every grain of talk and truth, trying to find out what is real." Although people in the West thought that all Russians were hard-line communists, Geyer detected a generational shift of "new Russians" who would cause major changes within totalitarian Russia. Her journalism took her to the Middle

East, where she was the first Western correspondent to interview Iraq's dictator Saddam Hussein, and where she conducted long talks with Palestinian leader Yasir Arafat, Libyan ruler Muammar Qaddafi, and Iran's Ayatollah Khomeini (whom she described as "a huge black moth of a man"). She also spent years researching and writing a biography of Fidel Castro, work that caused the Cuban government to bar her from returning to that country. She observed that other correspondents hedged their criticism of Castro in order to maintain their access. "That's the way dictators and totalitarian crowds have controlled the crowds," Geyer steamed. "None of us should do it."

After a decade of constant travel, Geyer felt the need to settle down in one place. In 1975 she established a base in Washington, D.C., where she began a syndicated column that appeared three times each week, and also appeared a television news analyst. Being a columnist did not stop her from reporting. Her column gave her a chance to express her opinions, but she always considered herself "more of a reporter than a theoretician." Her knowledge of the world, her ability to interview international leaders, and her regular trips to the world's hot spots, gave substance to her columns. In 1976, while reporting from Angola, she was arrested and interrogated by the Marxist government for hours to find the names of those she had spoken to, and then deported when she refused to identify her sources. The incident brought home the danger of her work. Back when she reported from the mountains of Guatemala, she had never thought she could die. "My body was so strong I would just take it for granted, and I was developing my brain," she said. "But now it's the other way around, and my brain is supporting my body." She felt she could make her contribution to the news by asking

Georgie Anne Geyer

BORN
April 2, 1935
Chicago, Illinois

EDUCATION
B.S., Northwestern University, 1956

JOURNALISM
Feature writer, *Chicago Daily News* (1959–1964); foreign correspondent, *Chicago Daily News* (1964–1974); columnist, Los Angeles Times Syndicate (1975–1980); columnist, Universal Press Syndicate (1981–); news commentator, PBS's "Washington Week in Review"; author of *The New Latins: Fateful Change in South and Central America* (1970), *The New 100 Years War* (1972), *The Young Russians* (1975), *Buying the Night Flight: The Autobiography of a Woman Foreign Correspondent* (1983), *Guerrilla Prince: The Untold Story of Fidel Castro* (1991), *Waiting for Winter to End: An Extraordinary Journey Through Soviet Central Asia* (1994), and *Americans No More* (1996)

"Alma Ata, Kazakhstan. In the elegant conference room of the presidency, the man unquestionably the star of the Kazakh show is President Nursultan Nazarbayev, who is holding court with the visiting French foreign minister's delegation. He is handsome and slick, with his blunt nose, carefully combed hair and wily eyes. But his face is nearly expressionless, and I find myself uneasily searching for some remote resemblance.

Then it hits me: the late Mayor Richard J. Daley of my hometown of Chicago! Just another oddity of beguiling Kazakhstan."

—from "Kazakh Leaders Grapple with Change" (syndicated column, March 4, 1992)

deeper questions and putting complex issues together.

Always ready to grab her suitcase and head for the airport, Geyer continued to find travel intellectually invigorating, even if it grew more tiring physically. It was not in her nature to stop. She insisted that she needed "a lot of intellectual, psychological, and emotional input." Armed with a battery-operated electric typewriter, Geyer traveled the world. On one trip alone she visited Germany, Poland, Yugoslavia, Greece, Israel, Jordan, Kuwait, and India. She always did a great deal of research in advance and then immersed herself in the culture on the scene. As a correspondent and columnist, she felt her greatest need was to understand other cultures and explain them to her American readers. "People in other cultures are different," she insisted. "That's what's so interesting—to see their perceptions."

Through all her travel and her years of writing, Geyer took pride in remaining unpredictable. She resisted being labeled a conservative or liberal, terms she considered outworn and unhelpful. Instead she insisted that she was independent of any party or ideology, aiming only to be reasonable and rational. "That sounds dull, but it isn't," she said. "I don't want my column to be one where people say I know what Georgie Anne's going to say today."

FURTHER READING

Braden, Maria. *She Said What? Interviews with Women Newspaper Columnists.* Lexington: University Press of Kentucky, 1993.

Edwards, Julia. *Women of the World: The Great Foreign Correspondents.* Boston: Houghton Mifflin, 1988.

Geyer, Georgie Anne. *Americans No More.* New York: Atlantic Monthly Press, 1996.

———. *Buying the Night Flight: The Autobiography of a Woman Foreign Correspondent.* New York: Delacorte, 1983.

———. *Guerrilla Prince: The Untold Story of Fidel Castro.* Boston: Little, Brown, 1991.

———. *The New Latins: Fateful Change in South and Central America.* Garden City, N.Y.: Doubleday, 1970.

———. *The New 100 Years War.* Garden City, N.Y.: Doubleday, 1972.

———. *Waiting for Winter to End: An Extraordinary Journey Through Soviet Central Asia.* Washington, D.C.: Brassey's, 1994.

———. *The Young Russians.* Homewood, Ill.: ETC Publications, 1975.

Hess, Stephen. *International News and Foreign Correspondents.* Washington, D.C.: Brookings Institution, 1996.

Hohenberg, John. *Foreign Correspondence: The Great Reporters and their Times.* Syracuse, N.Y.: Syracuse University Press, 1995.

Mills, Kay. *A Place in the News: From the Women's Pages to the Front Page.* New York: Dodd, Mead, 1988.

Bob Woodward and Carl Bernstein

INVESTIGATIVE
REPORTERS

Early on Saturday morning, June 17, 1972, the general counsel of the Democratic National Committee called the managing editor of the *Washington Post* to report that five men had been arrested while breaking into the Democrats' headquarters at the Watergate building in Washington, D.C. Seeing it as a local crime story, the managing editor called the paper's Metro editor, who in turn called a few of his reporters. One call went to Bob Woodward, a novice with only nine months on the staff. When he got to the newsroom, Woodward noticed that Carl Bernstein, a brash and aggressive local reporter, was also working on the burglary. "Oh God, not Bernstein," he groaned. That afternoon, Woodward went to the courthouse, where a routine bond hearing was being held for the suspects. Evidence indicated that the men had been installing electronic eavesdropping devices. One of the defendants, James McCord, identified himself as a security consultant recently retired from the government. "Where in the government?" the judge asked. "CIA," replied McCord. Woodward suddenly knew he had a story. It appeared on the front page of the next day's *Washington Post* under the headline: "5 HELD IN PLOT TO BUG DEMOCRATS' OFFICE HERE."

Carl Bernstein (left) and Bob Woodward had different personalities and temperaments, but together they formed an effective reporting team.

Bob Woodward

BORN

March 26, 1943
Geneva, Illinois

EDUCATION

B.A., Yale University (1965)

ACCOMPLISHMENTS

Reporter, *Sentinel* (Montgomery County, Maryland, 1970–71); reporter, *Washington Post* (1971–78); Metro editor, *Washington Post* (1979–81); assistant managing editor, *Washington Post* (1981–); author of *All The President's Men* (with Carl Bernstein, 1974), *The Final Days* (with Carl Bernstein, 1976), *The Brethren: Inside the Supreme Court* (1979), *Wired: The Short Life and Fast Times of John Belushi* (1984), *Veil: The Secret Wars of the CIA* (1987), *The Commanders* (1991), *The Man Who Would Be President: Dan Quayle* (with David Broder, 1992), *The Agenda: Inside the Clinton White House* (1994), and *The Choice* (1996)

The *New York Times,* by contrast, buried the story on page 30. In retrospect, the *Post* had a natural advantage in covering Watergate because everyone mistook it for a local story. Senior national reporters for the *New York Times* and the *Washington Post* initially discounted the incident. They accepted the White House's disclaimer that it had nothing to do with this "third-rate burglary." They saw President Richard Nixon as too smart—and too far ahead in the polls—to stoop to such petty political tricks. Woodward and Bernstein would never have gotten the story otherwise.

Before Watergate, Woodward and Bernstein had never worked together, but they soon became so linked that people called them "Woodstein." Their backgrounds, temperaments, and personalities seemed entirely different, and yet they shared a single-minded determination to uncover good stories. Both young and single, they were willing to work late nights and weekends. They were ambitious to get out of the Metro section and onto the front page. Watergate would make them the nation's most famous investigative journalists.

Bob Woodward grew up in an affluent suburb of Chicago. A good student, voted "most likely to succeed," he was conservative in his dress, manners, and politics (he voted for Nixon in 1968). Woodward joined the Navy Reserve Officers Training Corps (ROTC) that helped pay his way through Yale University in exchange for later service in the Navy. In college he wrote for the student yearbook, the *Yale Banner.* After graduation he spent five years in the navy as a communications officer. He married his high school sweetheart, but they were apart during his long cruises. When he was transferred to the Pentagon in Washington, his wife, a student in California, decided against moving back with him and the marriage ended. Following the path of his father, an attorney, Woodward entered Harvard Law School. But at 27 he was older than the rest of his classmates and had a sense that time was passing him by. He dropped out of law school and applied for a job reporting for the *Washington Post.* The editors advised him to get some experience first and referred him to a suburban weekly paper, the Montgomery County, Maryland, *Sentinel.*

Desperate to prove himself, Woodward not only handled the stories assigned to him but developed many more himself. He moved beyond tree plantings and civic meetings to cover government corruption and political reform. Taking his clippings back to the *Post,* he pestered the paper into hiring him for the metropolitan staff. The *Post* made him a police reporter, but he continued developing his own ideas for a wide variety of stories. Driven by insecurity and a compulsive desire to succeed, he produced more front page bylines than any other local reporter.

Carl Bernstein took an entirely different path to the *Post'*s Metro section. Unlike the clean-cut, Ivy League Woodward, who showed respect toward his editors, Bernstein was a long-haired counterculture type who argued about everything. Bernstein had a difficult childhood. His parents, as suspected members of the Communist party, had been hounded during the anticommunist movement of the 1950s. His father, a labor organizer, wound up running a laundromat. The

FBI regularly kept track of the family. Carl grew up less radical than rebellious, getting himself into trouble and showing little interest in school. He barely graduated from high school and dropped out of the University of Maryland. Instead, at 16 he became a copyboy for the *Washington Star*. Bernstein loved the newsroom and showed it. The *Star* promoted him to telephone dictationist, a post in which he took down reporters' stories over the phone for publication. One summer he temporarily worked as a reporter but was sent back to dictationist when the regular reporters returned from vacation.

Rather than accept the demotion, Bernstein at 19 became a reporter for the *Elizabeth* (New Jersey) *Daily Journal*. The small paper gave him wide leeway to write about local affairs, for which he won a number of awards. His drive and his awards earned him a job reporting for the *Washington Post*, even though his appearance and personality often grated on its editors. He kept erratic hours and was sloppy in appearance and lax about money—his own and the paper's. He was difficult to work with and to live with (his marriage to another *Post* reporter had quickly ended in divorce). He fought with editors over his assignments and any changes they made to his copy. But Bernstein possessed two valuable qualities: he was an excellent writer, and he could get people to tell him what he wanted to know. "I can get along with a cop or a Cabinet officer," Bernstein claimed. Although only 28 in 1972, Bernstein had already been writing for the *Post* for six years when the Watergate break-in occurred.

For the first Watergate account, Woodward and police reporter Al Lewis wrote the main story, while Bernstein wrote a "sidebar" (a short piece to run alongside the main story) about the burglars. By July 3 Woodward and Bernstein's first joint byline appeared. The two reporters followed a notation in one of the burglars' address book for E. Howard Hunt at the "W. House." They found that Hunt had worked at the Nixon White House and for the Committee for the Re-Election of the President. Bernstein went to Florida, where he traced a check cashed by one of the burglars to a Nixon-for-President campaign contribution. Both became convinced that the trail of the Watergate burglary would lead eventually to the President of the United States.

Since high-level government officials were fiercely protective of the President, Woodward and Bernstein worked from the bottom up. They interviewed secretaries and lower-level aides, often at night at their homes. Not everyone would talk to them, but some wanted to unburden themselves of troublesome facts. The reporters sought to "triangulate information" by collecting several different versions of each aspect of the story to reconcile any discrepancies and decide where the truth lay. They also rewrote each other's drafts. Bernstein, the better writer, polished Woodward's stilted prose, while the more cautious Woodward toned down Bernstein's accusations. Their managing editor, Benjamin Bradlee, considered their best asset to be their willingness to work spectacularly hard. "They would ask fifty people the same question, or they would ask one person the same question fifty times, if they had reason to believe some information was being withheld."

AMERICAN JOURNALISTS

Carl Bernstein

BORN
February 14, 1944
Washington, D.C.

EDUCATION
Attended the University of Maryland (1961–64)

ACCOMPLISHMENTS
Copyboy and dictationist, *Washington Star* (1960–63); reporter, *Washington Star* (1963–65); reporter, *Elizabeth* (New Jersey) *Daily Journal* (1965–66); reporter, *Washington Post* (1966–76); ABC Washington bureau chief (1979–81); ABC News correspondent (1981–84); contributing correspondent, *Time* magazine (1990–91); visiting professor, New York University (1992–); author of *All The President's Men* (with Bob Woodward, 1974), *The Final Days* (with Bob Woodward, 1976), *Loyalties: A Son's Memoir* (1989), and *His Holiness: John Paul II and the Hidden History of Our Time* (with Marco Politi, 1996)

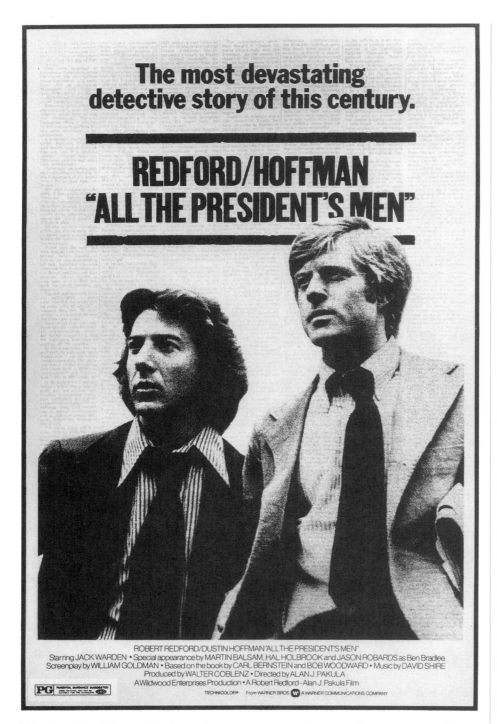

The most devastating
detective story of this century.

**REDFORD/HOFFMAN
"ALL THE PRESIDENT'S MEN"**

ROBERT REDFORD/DUSTIN HOFFMAN "ALL THE PRESIDENT'S MEN"
Starring JACK WARDEN • Special appearance by MARTIN BALSAM, HAL HOLBROOK and JASON ROBARDS as Ben Bradlee
Screenplay by WILLIAM GOLDMAN • Based on the book by CARL BERNSTEIN and BOB WOODWARD • Music by DAVID SHIRE
Produced by WALTER COBLENZ • Directed by ALAN J. PAKULA
A Wildwood Enterprises Production • A Robert Redford - Alan J. Pakula Film
PG PARENTAL GUIDANCE SUGGESTED   TECHNICOLOR®   From WARNER BROS W A WARNER COMMUNICATIONS COMPANY

Woodward and Bernstein's dramatic account of how they got the Watergate story became a best-selling book and a hit motion picture, both titled *All the President's Men.*

As their revelations appeared in print, the Nixon administration started threatening the *Post*. There were hints that the government might not renew the broadcast licenses for the *Post*'s radio and television stations, or that

the Internal Revenue Service would audit their tax returns. Editors and reporters suspected that their phones were being tapped and that they were being followed. Veteran editors and reporters protested that two green-horns were jeopardizing the newspaper's future. The *Post*'s publisher, Katharine Graham, worried that being so far out in front on the story left the paper in an exposed position. "No matter how careful we were," she said, "there was always the nagging possibility that we were wrong, being set up, being misled." Ironically, the intense pressure that the Nixon administration put on the paper convinced Graham and managing editor Bradlee that the story must be true. However, they insisted that any information that Woodward and Bernstein attributed to an unnamed source had to be verified by at least one other source, that nothing from another newspaper could be reprinted until confirmed for accuracy, and that senior editors read everything before it was published.

Nixon's supporters accused the *Post* of "innuendo, third-person hearsay, [and] unsubstantiated charges." This made the use of anonymous sources particularly tricky. Some people could not talk for the record for fear of losing their jobs. But were they telling the truth, or did they have a personal or political ax to grind? Woodward claimed to have a high-level source inside the executive branch who would only talk to him on "deep background" (for information only, not to be quoted or identified). He did not identify the source, known as "Deep Throat," to his editors or publisher. Deep Throat steered Woodward's investigations, confirmed his findings, and warned him of dangers. Critics later charged that there was no Deep Throat, or that he was just a composite of several different sources. Woodward, however, always insisted that Deep Throat was a real person.

Richard Nixon's reelection in 1972 seemed to kill the Watergate story. Weeks went by after the election without a Woodward and Bernstein story in the *Post,* leading some people to speculate that the story had been politically motivated. But a month later the *Post* published a Woodward and Bernstein byline that further tied the White House to the Watergate burglars, and then more stories followed. By then other newspapers, magazines, and news broadcasters were in hot pursuit, turning up new evidence. The Senate had created a special investigative committee, and President Nixon, still proclaiming his own innocence, had approved the appointment of a special prosecutor.

As the spotlight shifted, Woodward and Bernstein signed a lucrative contract to publish a book on their experiences. *All the President's Men* appeared on the first anniversary of the Watergate break-in and became a huge national best-seller, and later a Hollywood movie. The *Post* also received a Pulitzer Prize in public service for their reporting. By August 1974, the accumulated evidence made it clear that the President had ordered a coverup not just of the Watergate burglary but of a long list of other illegal activities. Facing impeachment, President Nixon resigned. Having played a major role in the unmaking of the President, Woodward and Bernstein wrote another book on *The Final Days* of the Nixon administration.

Two obscure local reporters became national celebrities. Their fame inspired countless young people to attend journalism school and pursue careers as investigative reporters. Their books and movie contract had made them wealthy, but also complicated their lives. Second marriages for both men failed (Woodward later married for a third time), and the future seemed anticlimactic. They had taken leaves of absence from the *Post* to write their books. Bernstein returned to the paper in 1976 but soon resigned. He wrote an investigative piece, "The CIA and the Media," for *Rolling Stone* magazine and later spent four years as Washington bureau chief and television correspondent for ABC News. Bernstein devoted much of his time to writing a book about his parents' ordeal and his own childhood in the 1950s As a freelance writer he seemed to have exhausted his ambitions as a journalist.

By contrast, Woodward reestablished himself at the *Washington Post,* where he became editor of the paper's Metro section. Then, in 1981, a young African-American woman reporter on his staff, Janet Cooke, won the Pulitzer Prize for her story of an eight-year-old drug addict, "Jimmy's World." The article relied on pseudonyms to protect its subject and sources, but it was soon revealed that Jimmy had been entirely fictional. Greatly embarrassed, the *Post* accepted Cooke's resignation and returned the Pulitzer. Cooke blamed the incident on the competitiveness at the *Post* that had pressured her to succeed at any cost. Soon afterward, Woodward left his editorial post to head a small team of investigative reporters for the *Post.* He continued

FBI agents have established that the Watergate bugging incident stemmed from a massive campaign of political spying and sabotage conducted on behalf of President Nixon's re-election and directed by officials of the White House and the Committee for the Re-Election of the President.

The activities, according to information in FBI and Justice Department files, were aimed at all the major Democratic presidential candidates and—since 1971—represented a basic strategy of the re-election effort.

During the Watergate investigation federal agents established that hundreds of thousands of dollars in Nixon campaign contributions had been set aside to pay for an extensive undercover campaign aimed at discrediting individual Democratic presidential candidates and disrupting their campaigns.

"Intelligence work" is normal during a campaign and is said to be carried out by both political parties. But federal investigators said what they uncovered being done by the Nixon forces is unprecedented in scope and intensity.

Following members of Democratic candidates' families; assembling dossiers of their personal lives; forging letters and distributing them under the candidates' letterheads; leaking false and manufactured items to the press; throwing campaign schedules into disarray; seizing confidential campaign files and investigating the lives of dozens of campaign workers.

—from the *Washington Post* (October 10, 1972)

to produce exposés, but devoted more of his time to writing a string of best-selling books, which demonstrated his many high-level sources inside the federal government. Yet even there his persistent use of anonymous sources left lingering question marks about his credibility. That was the burden that went with the glory of "Woodstein's" style of investigative reporting.

FURTHER READING

Bernstein, Carl, and Bob Woodward. *All The President's Men.* New York: Simon & Schuster, 1974.

———. *The Final Days.* New York: Simon & Schuster, 1976.

Bradley, Benjamin C. *A Good Life: Newspapering and Other Adventures.* New York: Simon & Schuster, 1995.

Downie, Leonard, Jr. *The New Muckrakers.* Washington: New Republic Book Company, 1976.

Emery, Fred. *Watergate: The Corruption of American Politics and the Fall of Richard Nixon.* New York: Random House, 1994.

Havill, Adrian. *Deep Truth: The Lives of Bob Woodward and Carl Bernstein.* Secaucus, N.J.: Carol, 1993.

Kutler, Stanley I. *The Wars of Watergate: The Last Crisis of Richard Nixon.* New York: Viking, 1996.

Roberts, Chalmers M. *In the Shadow of Power: The Story of the Washington Post.* Cabin John, Md.: Seven Locks Press, 1989.

Schudson, Michael. *Watergate in American Memory: How We Remember, Forget, and Reconstruct the Past.* New York: Basic Books, 1992.

Bernard Shaw

WORLD NEWS LIVE

Several months after Iraq invaded Kuwait in August 1990, the Cable News Network (CNN) sent its Washington anchorman, Bernard Shaw, to Baghdad to interview Iraqi leader Saddam Hussein. With the United States on the brink of war with Iraq, U.S. President George Bush warned CNN: "I certainly hope you get Bernie in and out of there soon." Just before Bush launched Operation Desert Storm in January 1991, the White House alerted the media that its correspondents in Iraq would be in danger. But CNN owner Ted Turner replied: "We have a global job to do and we should do it. Those who want to come out can come out." Shaw and CNN correspondents Peter Arnett and John Holliman elected to stay. When allied bombs began falling on Baghdad, they viewed the scene from their hotel room.

Rather than limit himself to an anchor desk, Bernard Shaw traveled from Iraq to China, braving dangerous situations to broadcast live reports for CNN.

"The skies over Baghdad have been illuminated," Shaw reported. "We're seeing bright flashes going off all over the sky." For the next 16½ hours they kept up their exclusive commentary. Although some critics accused CNN of giving publicity to Iraq, the network insisted that its mission was to present news of the world, not just news from a U.S. perspective. Even President Bush admitted that he learned much by watching CNN's reports from Iraq.

By reporting live during the bombing of Baghdad, Bernard Shaw followed his childhood hero, Edward R. Murrow, who had broadcast during the German bombing of London in World War II. Shaw grew up in Chicago, the son of a housepainter and a housekeeper. His father, an avid newspaper reader, brought home stacks of newspapers and magazines. Young Bernie was more excited by television news. "When I was about eleven years old, I discovered Edward R. Murrow on CBS," he recalled. "I watched him all the time. By age thirteen I decided that I wanted to do what Edward R. Murrow did." The lack of African-American news reporters on television at the time did not discourage him. "I didn't see [Murrow] as white," he said. "I saw him as a journalist."

In high school, Shaw did morning radio programs over the public address system, announced at sporting events, and wrote for the school newspaper. His teachers and classmates expected him to go on to college, but Shaw's family could not afford the tuition. Instead, he joined the U.S. Marine Corps, the branch of the military he considered to be the toughest and most disciplined. While serving in Hawaii in 1961, Shaw learned that CBS news broadcaster Walter Cronkite was visiting the islands. He called Cronkite's hotel repeatedly trying to meet him,

and finally encountered him in the lobby. "He was the most persistent guy I've ever met in my life," Cronkite chuckled. "I was going to give him five begrudging minutes and ended up talking to him for a half-hour. He was just determined to be a journalist." Impressed with the young marine, Cronkite predicted that someday they would be colleagues at the same network.

Honorably discharged from the Marines in 1963, Shaw enrolled at the Chicago campus of the University of Illinois. In addition to his classes, he volunteered to work for free in the newsroom of a local radio station. The following year the station switched from music to an all-news format. When Martin Luther King, Jr., came to Chicago to stage a civil rights rally, Shaw asked to cover the event. The management agreed to pay him $50 a day as its reporter on the scene. Shaw worked hard and slept little over the next several days, later describing it as "a typical instance of a young novice getting an opportunity and going berserk in the process of doing the job. But I did so well they put me on staff."

He juggled college and radio reporting until 1968. His station sent him to Memphis to report on Dr. King's assassination, and then brought him back to Chicago to cover the riots that followed. His professional skill and demeanor caught the attention of the Westinghouse Broadcasting Company, which owned the radio station where he worked. Westinghouse offered Shaw the prestigious assignment of White House correspondent. Although it meant that he could not finish his last year of college, Shaw realized that the job offer was too good to decline.

He reported over the radio on Washington until 1971, when CBS

Bernard Shaw

News hired him for its prestigious Washington bureau. The first night that one of his pieces aired on the "CBS Evening News with Walter Cronkite," he noticed that "there was this visible smile on Walter Cronkite's face when he said, 'And Bernard Shaw reporting.'" Shaw felt emotionally and professionally gratified to work for CBS—Edward R. Murrow's old network. As a general assignment correspondent, Shaw covered all of Washington, from the State Department to the Supreme Court. After a few years, however, he sought an assignment overseas. "I don't think you can really understand the importance of some of the things that happen in Washington and other capitals unless you've been a foreign correspondent," he reasoned. Shaw asked CBS News to let him cover Latin America. When CBS declined, he switched to ABC News.

Although based in Florida, Shaw spent 85 percent of his time out of the country, as his wife, Linda, observed unhappily, leaving her to raise their two children. He reported on the Panama Canal treaties, the revolution in Nicaragua, and the economic crisis in Chile. In 1978 he was one of the first correspondents to reach Jonestown, Guyana, after 900 American followers of a crazed cult leader committed mass suicide there. Finally, after one of his ABC colleagues was killed in Nicaragua, Shaw concluded that it was time to return to the United States. He became ABC News senior correspondent on Capitol Hill. He had higher ambitions, however. "I thought the crowning part of my long march would be the role of anchorman," bringing together his experiences overseas, in Washington, and in local news reporting. "It's vitally important that an anchor know how to write, that he's been in the trenches,

that he understands the story." But Shaw recognized that there were many talented people ahead of him at ABC News.

In 1980 Shaw received an offer to anchor the news for an entirely new network: Ted Turner's 24-hour-a-day cable news service, CNN. Shaw knew he was taking a terrific gamble, leaving one of the three major networks to take a job with "a network that didn't exist." But recalling how his hero, Murrow, had pioneered in television news during the 1950s, Shaw chose the new route. CNN started with a slap-dash quality that caused some to call it the "Chaos News Network." Shaw worked out of a small office in Washington, linked by satellite to the network's headquarters in a ramshackle wood frame house in Atlanta. During an early broadcast, a cleaning woman walked between him and the camera and emptied his wastebasket while he was on the air. Cable television came slowly to larger cities like Washington, D.C., so initially Shaw as an anchor was more familiar to viewers overseas than in much of the United States. But as the network grew steadily, it added new bureaus and viewers and moved into modern headquarters in Washington and Atlanta.

Being on the air 24 hours a day gave CNN an advantage over the other network news bureaus, with their regular morning and evening programs, especially when it came to reporting late-breaking news. Shaw was the first television anchorman to report that a gunman had shot and wounded President Ronald Reagan in 1981. He found such unscripted episodes the "maximum challenge" and the most rewarding moments of his work as a journalist. "When it's a breaking story, and uncertain events and factors are tumbling in on you, and you've got to

BORN

May 22, 1940
Chicago, Illinois

EDUCATION

Attended University of Illinois, Chicago (1963–68)

ACCOMPLISHMENTS

Reporter, WNUS-radio, Chicago (1964–66); newswriter, WFLD-TV, Chicago (1965–66); reporter and White House correspondent, Group W, Westinghouse Broadcasting Company (1966–71); Washington correspondent, CBS News (1971–77); Latin American bureau chief, ABC News (1977–79); Capitol Hill correspondent, ABC News (1979–80); Washington news anchor, CNN (1980–)

"If you're wondering how CNN has been able to bring you this extraordinary story . . . we brought in our own flyaway gear, about eighteen oversized suitcases with our satellite gear. . . . we unpacked our transmission equipment and our dish. So whatever you've seen in the way of pictures and, indeed, in the way of words, came from our microwave units at Tiananmen Square bounced right here to the hotel, through our control room on one of the upper floors—I won't mention the floor for protective reasons—back down through cables, up on the CNN satellite dish, up on the satellite, and to you across the world."

—from Tiananmen Square, Beijing, China (May 20, 1989)

separate the certain from the uncertain and report those facts and new developments calmly, put them all in perspective . . . ," he explained. "That's what I love most about anchoring."

Shaw and his network grew in prestige. In October 1987 President Reagan invited "all four networks" to interview him in the Oval Office. Shaw joined CBS's Dan Rather, NBC's Tom Brokaw, and ABC's Peter Jennings, extremely pleased that he had achieved equality. "I believe in cutthroat competition," he said. "I will try to beat Dan, Tom or Peter every time I can."

During the 1988 Presidential elections, Shaw drew notice for his sharp questioning of the candidates. He infuriated the Republican Vice Presidential candidate, Dan Quayle, by asking whether he had joined the National Guard in the 1960s because he was afraid of getting killed in Vietnam. During a televised debate, Shaw asked Democratic Presidential candidate Michael Dukakis if he would persist in opposing the death penalty if his wife were brutally raped and murdered. Dukakis's dispassionate reply helped defeat his candidacy.

Rather than limit himself to reading the news from an anchor desk, Shaw traveled the world for CNN. He reported live from Tiananmen Square in Beijing in 1989, when Chinese troops suppressed prodemocracy demonstrators. He broadcast from Los Angeles just minutes after a devastating earthquake hit the city. But his coverage of Baghdad during the first day of allied bombing of the city was Shaw's most remarkable achievement. Not one to risk his life foolhardily, Shaw had been preparing to leave Baghdad when the bombing started. But he stayed at "the center of hell," as he called it, to report to CNN via telephone after the other American networks had been cut off and the other Western reporters had fled to safety. When affiliates of the other networks broadcast CNN's exclusive reports from Iraq, they demonstrated that the Cable News Network had achieved the respect that it had long desired.

FURTHER READING

Allen, Thomas B. *War in the Gulf.* Atlanta: Turner Publications, 1991.

Benjaminson, Peter. "Bernard Shaw," in *Contemporary Authors*, vol. 119. Detroit: Gale Research Company, 1987.

Goldberg, Robert, and Gerald Jay Goldberg. *Citizen Turner: The Wild Rise of an American Tycoon.* New York: Harcourt Brace, 1995.

Kurtz, Howard. "Bernard Shaw, Under Siege." *Washington Post*, January 22, 1991.

Smith, Perry M. *How CNN Fought the War.* New York: Carol, 1991.

Whittemore, Hank. *CNN: The Inside Story.* Boston: Little, Brown, 1990.

Cokie Roberts

"POLITICS IS OUR FAMILY BUSINESS"

O nce, when *New York Times* correspondent Steve Roberts called on Senator Bob Dole, the senator told him: "I'd rather be talking to your wife." Then he laughed and added, "But then, I guess you'd rather be talking to mine." By that double-edged jest, Senator Dole meant that despite the *Times*'s enormous prestige, a senator would rather be interviewed by a prominent radio and television correspondent like Cokie Roberts than by a newspaper reporter, even for such a major national paper. And he also recognized that reporters valued an interview with a cabinet secretary, like Secretary of Transportation Elizabeth Dole, more than with a leading member of Congress. Senator Dole was indicating that women had made considerable gains in both politics and journalism—two areas in which Cokie Roberts felt quite at home.

Mary Martha Corinne Morrison Claiborne Boggs was born the third child of Hale and Corinne "Lindy" Boggs, in New Orleans, Louisiana. Hale Boggs had served one term in

Cokie Roberts (center), with her mother, brother, father, and sister-in-law, attended the Democratic National Convention in 1972.

From her childhood on, Cokie Roberts knew her way around Congress, had met its leadership, understood its operations, and could explain its legislative maneuvering.

Although called "little Corinne" after her mother, her brother, Tommy, had trouble saying "Corinne" and called her "Cokie" instead. The nickname stuck. As a child, she spent many an afternoon exploring the halls of the United States Capitol, where her father worked. She sat on the knee of "Mr. Sam" Rayburn, the powerful Speaker of the House, and got to know other members of Congress and their staffs. Senators Lyndon B. Johnson and John F. Kennedy were among the eminent dinner guests at the Boggs family's home. These childhood contacts provided her with a familiarity that would breed confidence and sources when she returned as an adult to report on Congress.

"I suppose I expected my life to be like my mother's," Cokie Roberts once reflected. Lindy Boggs was her husband's closest confidante and partner in his political pursuits, but she organized her own life around his career. Cokie Roberts majored in political science at Wellesley College. After graduating in 1964, she worked for Altman Productions, a television production company run by the mother of one of her Wellesley classmates. At age 22 she hosted a regular Sunday afternoon public affairs program on local Washington television. In 1966 she married Steven Roberts, whom she had met in college. President Lyndon Johnson and members of the cabinet and the Congress attended the wedding. Since Steve was reporting for the *New York Times*, she quit her job in Washington and moved to New York City. "For eight months I job-hunted at various New York magazines and television stations," she recalled, "and wherever I went I was asked how many words I could type." In 1969 the *Times* sent Steve Roberts to head its bureau in Los Angeles, where Cokie produced

the House of Representatives, lost his bid for renomination in 1942, and then enlisted in the navy during World War II. When he returned from the service, he ran again for Congress and won back his old seat. Reelected to the next 13 Congresses, Hale Boggs rose to whip and then Democratic majority leader of the House of Representatives, just one step away from becoming Speaker. His career required his children to spend half the year in New Orleans and the other half in Washington, D.C. Fortunately, Cokie attended Catholic schools, whose curricula were nearly the same in both cities.

a children's television program, "Serendipity."

Tragedy struck in October 1972, when Hale Boggs, then majority leader of the House, flew to Alaska to campaign for the reelection of Democratic representative Nick Begich. Somewhere between Anchorage and Juneau, their small plane vanished. A massive 39-day search failed to discover any wreckage and the men were never found. Persuaded by friends and political allies, Lindy Boggs filed to run for her husband's seat. She won the election and spent the next 20 years in Congress.

From Los Angeles the *New York Times* sent Steve Roberts to Athens, Greece, in 1974. In addition to raising her two children, Cokie worked as a stringer, reporting occasionally for CBS radio and television. The family enjoyed living abroad and expected to be transferred next to Bangkok, Thailand. Instead, the *Times* called Steve Roberts back to its Washington bureau. They arrived just as Lindy Boggs was putting the family's large home in Bethesda, Maryland, up for sale so that she could move to an apartment. "It's a good thing we came home," said Cokie. "You were about to sell my house out from under me." They bought her childhood home and settled back into Washington politics and society. Once again, Cokie went out looking for work.

Reporter Nina Totenberg heard that Cokie Roberts was job hunting and urged her to apply at National Public Radio (NPR). The public radio network produced "Morning Edition" and an evening news program, "All Things Considered." NPR had a good record for hiring women reporters—some said because it paid salaries too low to attract many men. Roberts's first big assignment after she was hired as a

news correspondent in 1977 was to cover the first American visit of Pope John Paul II. As a Catholic, her knowledge of Church history and liturgy helped her produce thoughtful reports that impressed the NPR management. Yet NPR president Frank Mankiewicz had one problem: he said that "Cokie" was a cute nickname, but asked why she did not use her formal name on the air. "Would you believe Mary Martha Corinne Morrison Claiborne Boggs Roberts?" she replied—and remained Cokie thereafter.

Recognizing her intimacy with Capitol Hill, NPR sent Cokie Roberts to cover Congress. Fellow NPR correspondent Linda Wertheimer, who had spent years at the Capitol trying to understand the legislative lingo and how Congress really worked, was amazed when Cokie adapted so effortlessly. "I had the feeling that she was born to understand Congress," Wertheimer commented. Roberts knew her way around. She had already met most of the leadership, understood the way the institution operated, and could explain complex legislative maneuvers in a simple, straightforward, and wry manner. Other reporters might ridicule Congress and try to tear it down, but Roberts insisted, "I just love the institution. I want it to be better."

Family connections provided a clear asset. Speaker Tip O'Neill, who years earlier had replaced Hale Boggs as majority leader, liked to say, "I give you girls from NPR first shot at everything." Her brother, Tommy Boggs, a prominent Washington lobbyist, also passed her useful tips about what was happening. But her mother, a member of the House, never slipped her information. "They always had a completely professional and ethical relationship with me when I was in Congress,"

Cokie Roberts

BORN
December 27, 1943
New Orleans, Louisiana

EDUCATION
B.A., Wellesley College (1964)

ACCOMPLISHMENTS
Associate producer and television host, Altman Productions, Washington, D.C. (1965–66); reporter, editor, Cowles Communications (1967); producer, WNEW-TV, New York City (1968); producer, children's television program, "Serendipity," KNBC-TV, Los Angeles (1972–74); reporter, CBS Radio and Television, Athens (1974–77); correspondent, National Public Radio (1977–); correspondent, "The McNeil-Lehrer NewsHour," Public Broadcasting Service (1984–88); cohost, "The Lawmakers," Public Broadcasting Service (1981–84); correspondent, ABC News (1988–)

"The network [National Public Radio] has become a major news source for a lot of influential people in this country. I walk into the U.S. Capitol every single day Congress is in session and of the 535 congressmen and senators, 250 just heard me fifteen minutes before on the radio. Now that's very nice, and for a reporter it means that access is total."

—from a 1990 interview

Lindy Boggs said of her daughter and son-in-law: "I didn't give them any scoops, and they didn't ask me any prying questions." When the House debated a controversial pay raise for itself, one of her NPR editors considered removing Cokie Roberts from the story because her mother stood to benefit from the raise. But the rest of the management disagreed. None questioned her objectivity as a journalist.

At the time Roberts began reporting from Capitol Hill, the cable TV network C-SPAN started broadcasting gavel-to-gavel coverage of the House and Senate. C-SPAN generated much interest and gained loyal viewers, yet most Americans lacked the time or the tolerance to watch the entire proceedings. People still needed reporters to condense the daily legislative business and explain what it all meant. With 535 members of Congress to quote, some broadcasters showed a weakness for featuring politicians who were outrageous and would say anything, rather than those who worked quietly but effectively to pass legislation. Roberts tried to avoid that trap, but she admitted that "when presented with a funny, smart person who actually has some standing inside the institution, the temptation to use him or her repeatedly is almost irresistible." She sometimes feared that the articulate conservative Republican representative Henry J. Hyde and liberal Democratic representative Barney Frank were going to be permanent debaters in her stories.

Roberts, Totenberg, and Wertheimer provided thoughtful and stimulating news coverage that drew faithful listeners to NPR (which in place of advertisements existed largely on the annual financial contributions of its listeners). They also started a

union at NPR. Describing their strategies, Totenberg described herself as the Screamer, called Linda the Rational One, and said that Tactful Cokie usually closed the deal. Roberts won notice for maintaining her composure under the most trying circumstances, but once at a staff meeting she snapped: "We're tired of being this underpaid, we're tired of working in a filthy, dirty, disgusting building . . . and we don't see how we can continue doing it." NPR subsequently moved to new headquarters.

Public approval of her congressional reporting brought an invitation to do commentary on the Public Broadcasting System television program "The McNeil-Lehrer NewsHour." Roberts also hosted her own PBS program on Congress, "The Lawmakers." When PBS covered the explosive Iran-Contra hearings in 1987, the network made Judy Woodruff its anchor, had Elizabeth Drew of the *New Yorker* magazine provide analysis, and had Cokie Roberts interview members of Congress. They were the first all-woman news team on television, and viewer response was highly favorable.

Roberts also observed that newer members of Congress felt more comfortable with television. "These are politicians who grew up with television sets in their homes, entered politics as Americans watched a war and an impeachment in their living rooms, and elected the candidates who came on during commercial breaks." They were her generation, and they were eager to get their faces and political messages on television, further elevating the stature of television broadcasters on Capitol Hill. Able to look and sound cool and collected, and having an attractive appearance on camera, Roberts easily made the transition to television. In 1988 ABC News hired her (at many times her NPR salary) to report for its evening news program, "World News Tonight with Peter Jennings," to occasionally host the late-night "Nightline," and to offer commentary on its Sunday morning discussion program, "This Week with David Brinkley." National television exposure made Roberts an easily recognized celebrity and brought lucrative speaking engagements. Yet she continued to work as a senior news analyst for NPR. She juggled two jobs, she explained, "because the medium of radio is just different. Your writing is much more a part of the story. What you are aiming for in radio is for people to *imagine* the pictures."

Former newscaster Linda Ellerbee denounced the bulk of television newscasters as "Twinkies." "You've seen them on television," she wrote in her book *And So It Goes,* "acting the news, modeling and fracturing the news while you wonder whether they've read the news—or if they've blow-dried their brain too." No one called Cokie Roberts a "Twinkie." She came to television in middle age, as a result of years of experience and recognition as a knowledgeable reporter of national politics. She impressed people with her versatility, as she shifted easily from radio to television and from reporting to commentary. Despite her family's political involvement, people regarded her reporting as fair, evenhanded, and "centrist"—leaning to no party or ideology. Politicians of all hues appreciated her informative style of reporting, although they knew she could be a tough questioner. Once, after she grilled the independent Presidential candidate Ross Perot, he complained that he had nothing against reporters, except for women reporters, because

they were "all trying to prove their manhood."

Meanwhile, her husband, Steve Roberts, chaffed under the *New York Times's* restrictions against its reporters appearing on television. In 1986 he quit the *Times* to write for *U.S. News & World Report* and later as a newspaper columnist. This allowed him to appear on such television news programs as PBS's "Washington Week in Review." Proud of his wife's accomplishments, he coped well with her fame. "Look, I was attracted to her because she was such a strong and confident woman," he told one interviewer. "It's no surprise to me what's happened to her."

FURTHER READING

Boggs, Lindy. *Washington Through a Purple Veil: Memoirs of a Southern Woman.* New York: Harcourt Brace, 1994.

Collins, Mary. *National Public Radio: The Cast of Characters.* Washington, D.C.: Seven Locks Press, 1993.

Dreifus, Claudia. "Cokie Roberts, Nina Totenberg and Linda Wertheimer." *New York Times Book Review,* January 2, 1994.

Hendrickson, Paul. "Roberts Rules." *Washington Post Magazine,* June 20, 1993.

Roberts, Cokie. "Leadership and the Media in the 101st Congress" In *Leading Congress: New Styles, New Strategies,* edited by John J. Kornaki. Washington, D.C.: Congressional Quarterly Press, 1990.

Sanders, Marlene and Marcia Rock. *Waiting for Prime Time: The Women of Television News.* Urbana: University of Illinois Press, 1988.

Manuel
de Dios
Unanue

MARTYR FOR THE
FIRST AMENDMENT

he investigative reporter Manuel de Dios Unanue spent his last evening, on March 11, 1992, talking Presidential politics at his favorite restaurant in the New York City borough of Queens. Shortly after 9:00 P.M., as de Dios was paying his bill, a hooded young man stepped up behind him, fired two shots into the back of his head, and then fled. The journalist died instantly. His execution-style slaying seemed terribly similar to the many drug-related crimes that he had written about as a reporter and editor for New York's Spanish-language newspaper *El Diario-La Prensa.* "As editor in chief, he made a lot of enemies," said the paper's city editor. De Dios wrote about political corruption and international drug traffickers, exposés that brought him many death threats. "On the day that I'm taken out," de Dios correctly predicted, "they're going to sell a lot of papers."

International turmoil shaped Manuel de Dios's life. His parents, José and María Dolores de Dios Unanue, had left Spain after General Francisco Franco seized control there. They settled in Cuba, where his father opened a restaurant and his mother taught business education in a high school. The third of their five children was Manuel de Dios Unanue (his formal name combined both his parents' surnames, but he went by de Dios). He entered a Jesuit seminary when he was 14, intending to become a priest. Eager to share their strong feelings about social and political justice, the seminary student and his friends published their own small newspaper, which denounced the increasingly repressive regime of Cuban dictator Fulgencio Batista. When the Catholic Church opposed Fidel Castro's revolution against Batista, de Dios quit the seminary. Later he felt disappointed when the Cuban revolution turned the country into a communist dictatorship. "As a young man, he was very idealistic," his sister recalled. "He was always fighting for his ideals."

After living briefly in Spain and in Miami, Florida, de Dios enrolled at the University of Puerto Rico. He worked his way through school by cleaning offices and restaurants. Eventually, he earned a master's degree in criminology, writing his thesis on the Cuban judicial system under Castro. He taught for two years in Puerto Rico and then in 1973 moved to New York City, where he took charge of press relations for the Migration Division of the Puerto Rican Department of Labor. In that capacity he listened to many Puerto Rican migrant farm laborers, and then visited farms to investigate their complaints and try to improve their working conditions. He also worked with the Hispanic Criminal Justice Task Force. But what he really wanted was to become a journalist.

A year after coming to New York City, de Dios met and married an airline flight attendant, María Félix, and they moved to an apartment in Queens. With his wife's savings, de Dios started a small Spanish-language weekly paper, *El Hispano*. That paper lasted only four months. He tried publishing a soccer magazine, and when that failed he worked as a private investigator. When he was 34, de Dios received a call from the New York daily newspaper *El Diario-La Prensa,* offering him a job as a police reporter. He jumped at the opportunity and quickly established himself as an aggressive investigator. De Dios took on two terrorist organizations: the left-wing FALN, which sought independence for Puerto Rico, and the right-wing Omega Seven, an anti-Castro Cuban group. Omega Seven was believed responsible for bombing the lobby of *El Diario*'s headquarters in retaliation for de Dios's reporting. Despite threats against his life, he refused to stop. "No one can tell me what I can't write," he insisted.

De Dios shifted to cover New York's City Hall when Edward I. Koch became mayor in 1978. At first de Dios admired Koch, but as the mayor moved away from the reform groups that had put him into office, the reporter lost faith in him. By 1984, when de Dios became editor of *El Diario,* he had broken entirely with Koch, whom he considered to be hostile to New York's Hispanic community. As editor, de Dios hired young and energetic men and women as reporters, and he drove them hard. Impatient and demanding, he sometimes ordered reporters away from their desks and finished writing their stories himself. Although at times they called him "the dictator," the staff admired him for generating the fire that drove the paper to greater heights. When one of his reporters observed that as an editor he dressed neatly in three-piece suits and trimmed off his long hair, de Dios replied that since he caused so much controversy with his ideas, he did not

want to distract people by his appearance.

At the time of his editorship in the 1980s, the Hispanic population of the United States grew rapidly, with the largest share of the growth coming by migration. Many of the new arrivals could not read English. English-language newspapers like the *Miami Herald* started Spanish editions, and Spanish-language newspapers expanded to meet the fast-growing new market. These papers paid special attention to the problems of Hispanic neighborhoods.

Assessing these problems, de Dios put illegal drugs at the top of the list. Ever since his student years he had kept his own filing system, which included a growing number of stories about the shipment of illegal drugs from South America to the United

An aggressive investigator, Manuel de Dios Unanue ignored threats against his life. "No one," he said, "can tell me what I can't write."

> El Cartel no se ha rendido. Ni se rendirá. Cuando caigan Escobar o los integrantes del clan de los Ochoa, si es que algún día caen, otros ocuparán sus puestos. El consumo de cocaína es cada día mayor en los Estados Unidos, y mientras no se desarrolle una campaña efectiva para erradicar el mal en las entrañas del monstruo, la oferta nunca disminuirá. Es una guerra que nadie sabe adonde va a llevar. Una guerra sucia en la que no habrá vencidos ni vencedores, sólo víctimas.
>
> The [Medellín] Cartel has not surrendered. Nor will it surrender. When Escobar or the members of the Ochoa clan fall, if someday they do fall, others will take their places. The consumption of cocaine is greater every day in the United States, and as long as an effective campaign is not developed to eradicate this disease, the supply will never diminish. No one knows where this war will lead. This dirty war in which there will be neither winners nor losers, only victims.
>
> —from *Los Secretos del Cartel de Medellín* (The Secrets of the Medellín Cartel; 1988)

States. In 1986, although still married, he fell in love with a Colombian-born photographer, Vicky Sánchez. Through her connections he learned more about the Colombian drug cartels.

The two biggest cartels were the Medellín and Cali, named for the Colombian cities where they were located. They controlled most of the cocaine sold in the United States. The larger Medellín cartel operated mostly in California, Florida, and Europe, leaving the New York City markets to the Cali cartel. The cartel smuggled drugs into New York and divided them among some 50 top distributors, who then sold smaller qualities to thousands of street-level dealers. In 1986, when an oversupply of cocaine began forcing prices down, the Medellín cartel moved into the New York City market, and a violent struggle between the two cartels followed. At the same time the U.S. Drug Enforcement Agency (DEA) expanded its New York-based task force and uncovered much of the cartel's distribution system, seizing tons of cocaine and millions of dollars in drug profits. The DEA brought people to trial on drug charges and the evidence they put into the public court record provided more leads for an investigative reporter like Manuel de Dios to follow.

In 1988 de Dios published a book exposing the Medellín cartel, which included photographs of Queens business people who cooperated with the drug dealers by laundering money for them. DEA agents used de Dios's book as a guide for further investigations.

After leaving *El Diario* in a dispute with its publishers, de Dios started his own weekly (later monthly) paper called *Cambio XXI* (Change in the 21st Century). Working out of his apartment and writing most of the copy himself, de Dios used the paper to warn New York's Hispanic community about the corrupting influences of the cartels. He also began writing a new book on the Cali cartel. De Dios especially embarrassed the Cali organization by showing how many small businesses had cooperated by laundering drug money, and by publishing pictures of the cartel leaders along with organizational charts.

In Colombia the cartels eliminated journalists who dared to expose their operations—a practice they now exported to the United States. In late 1991 the Cali cartel commissioned one of its contract killers, John Howard Mena, to arrange for someone to kill Manuel de Dios. Mena wondered why, since other newspapers like the *New York Times* had also run stories on cartel operations. He was told that "whoever tangled with the Cali would lose." Mena later testified: "That was why he was being murdered, because of the book." Through intermediaries, Mena hired a 17-year-old illegal immigrant from Colombia, Wilson Alejandro Mejía Vélez, to kill the journalist.

New York City police investigated numerous leads. In de Dios's long career, he had made numerous enemies. "There must have been at least a hundred threats on his life," said Fernando Moreno, who had worked with him at *El Diario*. "It's incredible when you analyze where the threats came from—Dominicans here, Cubans there, organized crime, Colombians." Police investigated de Dios's personal life, political activities, and the subjects of his exposés. At the time of his death de Dios had gone deeply into debt to publish *Cambio XXI*, and had just started a new magazine, *Crimen* (Crime). But the police discounted any connection between his finances and his death. In the last issue of *Cambio XXI*, de Dios had written that despite his money problems he would not be blackmailed by the drug traffickers. Police and prosecutors determined that the murder had aimed at silencing the journalist.

Two years after de Dios's death, Wilson Alejandro Mejía Vélez was convicted of his murder. Testimony at the trial revealed that the assailant was simply carrying out a job and did not even know who de Dios was when he shot him. Five others pleaded guilty to conspiring to arrange the murder. In sentencing Mejía to life in prison, the judge noted that de Dios had died for "exercising his constitutional rights that are guaranteed to him under the First Amendment." The U.S. government persuaded Colombia to renew its pressure on the drug cartels. Colombia raided the Cali's headquarters and offered rewards for the capture of its leaders. In July 1995 police in Bogotá arrested the head of the Cali cartel, José Santacruz Londoño, who was believed to have ordered de Dios's death. He was indicted in New York on charges of shipping cocaine and laundering a fortune in drug money. The arrests were the result of Manuel de Dios's unrelenting efforts to expose drug corruption. "In the end, he died the way many of us expected him to," said Albor Ruiz, who had worked for de Dios at *El Diario-La Prensa*. "He was always looking for the truth. . . . It never crossed his mind to compromise."

FURTHER READING

Berkeley, Bill. "Dead Right." *Columbia Journalism Review* 32 (March/April 1993): 39–45.

Cooper, Mary H. *The Business of Drugs*. Washington, D.C.: Congressional Quarterly, 1990.

Curry, George E. "Investigators Try to Solve Puzzle of Latino Journalist's Slaying." *Chicago Tribune*, April 5, 1992.

Dao, James. "Death of a Crusader with Enemies." *New York Times*, June 8, 1992.

Fried, Joseph P. "Youth Guilty in the Slaying of an Editor." *New York Times*, March 10, 1994.

McGee, Jim. "Violent Streak Raises Cali Cartel's U.S. Profile." *Washington Post*, March 27, 1995.

Moses, Paul, and Mitch Gelman. "His Murder a Matter of 'When' Not of 'If.'" *Newsday*, February 2, 1993.

Manuel de Dios Unanue

BORN

January 4, 1943
Camagüey, Cuba

DIED

March 11, 1992
Elmhurst, New York

EDUCATION

M.S. in criminology, University of Puerto Rico (1971)

ACCOMPLISHMENTS

Editor and publisher, *El Hispano* (1975); reporter, New York *El Diario-La Prensa* (1977–84); editor, *El Diario-La Prensa* (1984–89); editor, *Cambio XXI* (Change in the 21st Century) (1988–92); talk-show host, "What Others Silence," Radio America (1989–90); columnist, *Impacto* (1990–91); editor, *Crimen* (Crime) (1992); author of *El Caso Galíndez: Los Vascos en Servicios de Inteligencia de EE.UU.* (The Galíndez Case: Basques in the U.S. Intelligence Services) (1982), and *Los Secretos del Cartel de Medellín* (The Secrets of the Medellín Cartel) (1988)

More American Journalists to Remember

The son of a Baptist preacher, **Palmer Hoyt** (1897–1979) grew up in churches across the country before attending a Baptist college in Oregon. Starting as a copy reader at the *Portland Oregonian* in 1926, Hoyt worked his way up to night city editor and then to managing editor and publisher. During World War II, he volunteered for the Office of War Information in Washington. After the war, Hoyt took over as editor and publisher of the *Denver Post* (1946–70), a sagging paper known for its sensationalism. Hoyt reinvigorated the paper by expanding its national and international coverage, opening its editorial pages to minorities, and making it a policy to keep editorial comment out of its news pages. Although Hoyt and his paper leaned toward the Republicans, his editorials were highly skeptical of Senator Joseph McCarthy's anticommunist crusade, and accused the senator of making irresponsible accusations. Hoyt's fearlessness and insistence on objectivity helped make the *Denver Post* an influential and respected newspaper.

A path-breaking Washington correspondent for African-American newspapers, **Louis Lautier** (1897–1962) was born in Louisiana and attended Howard Law School in Washington, D.C. He worked as a legal stenographer for the Justice Department during the New Deal while also reporting on Washington for several African-American newspapers. When the United States entered World War II, Lautier lobbied to try to end segregation in the armed services. He became Washington correspondent for the National Negro Publishers Association (1946–61), covering Presidential press conferences at the White House. Recognizing his stenographic skills, other White House reporters regularly checked with Lautier on the accuracy of their quotes. In 1947 the Senate Rules Committee ordered the Standing Committee of Correspondents to admit Lautier to the congressional press galleries—making him the first African American to sit in the press galleries since Frederick Douglass. Similarly, in 1955 Lautier became the first African-American member of the National Press Club. A quiet man who was never a crusader, he nevertheless wrote about the outrages of segregation and spoke out for school integration, especially in Virginia, where he lived.

As a reporter, **Harrison E. Salisbury** (1908–93) considered himself to be a "disturber of the peace." Born in Minnesota, he lost his editorship of the University of Minnesota student newspaper after criticizing the school's administration. He started as a United Press (UP) reporter in Chicago, and during World War II went to Europe, the

Middle East, and Russia as a UP correspondent. In 1949 Salisbury joined the *New York Times*, where he remained for the rest of his career. His reporting from Moscow won him a Pulitzer Prize and the anger of Soviet premier Josef Stalin. After 1959 Salisbury shifted his focus to Asia, and particularly to the People's Republic of China. During the Vietnam War, he won praise and government condemnation for his reporting both from the Pentagon and from behind enemy lines in Hanoi. Such controversial assignments reflected his belief in the necessity "of reporting the unpopular event at the most . . . difficult touchy moment."

Under the pen name "Herblock," **Herbert L. Block** (1909–) started drawing editorial cartoons for a hometown paper, the *Chicago Daily News*, in 1929. He became a nationally syndicated cartoonist before going into the army, where he edited a feature service for army newspapers during World War II. After the war, in 1945, he joined the *Washington Post,* and his cartoons appeared on its editorial page for the next 50 years. During the 1952 Presidential election, the *Post* endorsed the Republican candidate, Dwight Eisenhower, while Herblock favored the Democrat, Adlai Stevenson. When the *Post* dropped his cartoons, many readers protested. Thereafter, Herblock grew even more independent, often taking more liberal stands than his paper's editorials. Herblock's pen particularly skewered Richard Nixon, from his first year in the House of Representatives in 1947 until his resignation as President during the Watergate scandal in 1974.

Born in Boston, **Theodore H. White** (1915–86) graduated from Harvard as a history major. He became a foreign correspondent for *Time* magazine and headed its China bureau during World War II. Contrary to the leanings of his publisher, Henry R. Luce, White's reporting from China

revealed the weaknesses in the Nationalist government that would lead to a Communist revolution. Breaking with Luce, he returned to the United States, where he briefly served as editor of the *New Republic*. He left editing to cover European affairs for the *Reporter* and American politics for many different magazines. His account of the Kennedy-Nixon campaign, *The Making of the President, 1960,* won a Pulitzer Prize. With his emphasis on color, personality, and behind-the-scenes maneuvering, he greatly influenced the future reporting of Presidential politics.

For more than 50 years, Herblock skewered politicians—especially Richard Nixon—in his editorial cartoons for the *Washington Post.*

Daniel Schorr, here broadcasting from Hungary, became a foreign correspondent for CBS News before returning to the United States to cover American politics.

Reporting was a frame of mind, **Daniel Schorr** (1916–) insisted, that required him to remain an outside observer while others argued and advocated causes. Yet as an investigative reporter, he managed to rile the tempers of many of those he reported on. During World War II, Schorr reported from Europe as a stringer for different newspapers and radio stations, in search of a regular job. In 1953 Edward R. Murrow heard Shorr's radio reports on a flood in Holland and hired him as a CBS radio and television correspondent. CBS sent Schorr to cover Latin America, Europe, and the Soviet Union, then brought him back to the United States in 1966 to cover American politics. His reporting on the Nixon administration, especially his persistent investigations into the Watergate scandal, won him a place on President Nixon's "enemies list" and eventually contributed to the pressure that led Nixon to resign in 1974. Two

years later, Schorr himself had to resign from CBS when it was revealed that he had leaked to a newspaper a secret report on the investigation of the CIA by Congress—a report that his network had not allowed him to air. Exiled from television, the veteran Schorr returned to radio as a commentator on national and international affairs for National Public Radio.

The daughter of Lebanese immigrants, **Helen Thomas** (1920–) was raised in Detroit. After graduating from Wayne State University, she went to Washington as a copy girl for the *Washington Daily News*. During World War II, when men were drafted or were going overseas as war correspondents, she was hired by the United Press to cover Washington city news and write local radio news stories. During the 1950s, she reported on the Justice Department. Shifting to the White House to cover the First Lady, she got a break when Jacqueline Kennedy's popularity put Thomas's stories on the front page across the country. Thomas later became United Press International's White House bureau chief, the first woman to hold that post. She also protested against the exclusion of women from the National Press Club and the prestigious Gridiron Club, whose journalist members entertained the president and members of Congress at the annual Gridiron Club dinners. She later became the Gridiron's first woman member—and its president.

David Brinkley (1920–) started reporting in high school for the Wilmington, North Carolina, *Star-News* (1938–41) and later went to Washington during World War II as a radio broadcaster for the National Broadcasting Company (NBC). He moved into television news in 1947. NBC teamed Brinkley with the veteran newsman Chet Huntley to host the "Huntley-Brinkley Report" (1956–70). The coupling of the dour Huntley and the wry, younger Brinkley caught favor, and they became the most popular news team on television. In 1963 their nightly news program was expanded from 15 to 30 minutes. After Huntley retired, Brinkley hosted "NBC Magazine." In 1983 he shifted to the American Broadcasting Company (ABC), which offered him a Sunday morning program of news analysis, "This Week with David Brinkley." Brinkley's gift for irony, as well as a tone of voice and facial expressions that expressed skepticism without specific comment, helped lighten the often somber news that he reported.

The investigative columnist **Jack Anderson** (1922–) started reporting for the *Salt Lake Tribune* while he was a freshman at the University of Utah. His exposé of the remnants of polygamy embarrassed Mormon elders, who suggested that he drop out of college to fulfill his missionary obligations to his church. While in Asia during his military service in World War II, he reported for the *Desert News* and the army newspaper *Stars and Stripes*. In 1947 he became an assistant to the muckraking columnist Drew Pearson. By 1966 Anderson shared the column's byline, and when Pearson died in 1969 he took it over. Exposing waste and corruption in government, Anderson won a Pulitzer Prize for uncovering scandals in the Nixon administration. With a staff of 20 full-time and freelance writers digging up information, Anderson produces 365 columns a year that are syndicated to more than 1,000 newspapers.

After graduating from Paine College in Georgia, **Louis Lomax** (1922–70) earned master's degrees from American University and Yale University. While a philosophy professor at Georgia State University, he began reporting for the *Afro-American*. He then became a feature writer for the *Chicago American* (1947–58), where he covered the beginnings of the modern civil rights movement. WNTA-TV in New York City made Lomax the first African-American television news broadcaster in 1958. He served as a news analyst for KTTV in Los Angeles and later hosted his own television program, "Louis Lomax." To these accomplishments he added a syndicated newspaper column. In the 1960s Lomax identified with the more

The combination of dour Chet Huntley (right) and witty David Brinkley found favor with television viewers and made them a popular news team.

Editor and columnist William F. Buckley (left) shakes hands with Senator Robert F. Kennedy, whose liberal politics the conservative Buckley lambasted.

militant civil rights organizations, but he debated the Black Muslim leader Malcolm X, arguing against racial separation. Lomax turned from journalism to history, writing such books as *The Negro Revolt* (1962) and *To Kill a Black Man* (1968), on Malcolm X's assassination, and eventually returned to teaching at Hofstra University.

William F. Buckley (1925–) started as a conservative critic of the liberal order and over the years saw the political establishment shift toward his way of thinking. After graduating from Yale University, he first made his name with a book, *God and Man at Yale* (1951), which accused Yale of trying to turn its students into "atheistic socialists." In 1955 he founded the *National Review,* a weekly journal that provided an outlet for conservative writers. Although the *National Review* regularly operated in the red, Buckley supported it

through his own independent wealth and his annual fund-raising drives. In 1962 Buckley began a syndicated newspaper column to promote his conservative views. This led to a weekly television program, "Firing Line," on the Public Broadcasting Service (PBS). His sardonic humor and extensive vocabulary drew attention to the ideas he espoused. Beyond writing, he founded the Young Americans for Freedom and ran for mayor of New York City as the Conservative party candidate.

Writing from the outlook of blue-collar, ethnic New York City, **Jimmy Breslin** (1929–) has identified himself and his writing almost entirely with the Big Apple. He began on the *Long Island Press* and reported for the *New York World-Telegram* and the *New York Journal-American.* The success of his first book—*Can't Anybody Here Play This Game?* about the New York Mets—won him a job as a sports columnist for the *New York Herald Tribune.* He adopted the colorful, personal "new journalism" that the *Herald Tribune's* staff was creating, and expanded his column beyond sports to all matters of life and death. In 1976 Breslin won national attention when a serial killer who called himself the "Son of Sam" began a correspondence with him that Breslin published in his *New York Daily News* column. Critics charged that he was exploiting the news rather than reporting it. But Breslin as a columnist continued to interject himself, his opinions, and his politics into his stories in a way that went far beyond the limits set for the average reporter.

After graduating from the University of Chicago at 18 and getting a master's degree in political science, **David Broder** (1929–) began his journalism career at the *Bloomington* (Illinois) *Pantagraph* (1953–55). He later went to Washington to join the staff of the *Congressional Quarterly*, which tracked legislative and political processes on Capitol Hill. Fascinated by American elections, he became a political reporter for the *Washington Star* (1960–65) during the Kennedy-Nixon campaign in 1960. Broder then gained the seemingly ideal job of senior political correspondent for the *New York Times* but quit because he felt the editors distorted his stories and put more emphasis on prominent people than on substantive analysis. He then joined the *Washington Post* as a reporter and columnist. Writing a column allowed him to interpret events and keep his opinions out of his news reporting. A scrupulously honest reporter, Broder tried to avoid close friendships with the politicians he covered or any semblance of taking sides. He also made a practice of writing an annual column that reported whatever he had gotten wrong during the past year.

When he joined the *Los Angeles Times*, **Ruben Salazar** (1928–70) refused to call himself a Mexican-American reporter and said he was simply a reporter doing his job. He had come to the United States from Mexico as a child and was naturalized in 1949. A series of reports he wrote for the *Times* on Mexican Americans in California, examining problems of unemployment, poor housing, and the lack of political power, won a number of awards. His next assignments took him away to cover American military intervention in the Dominican Republic and the war in Vietnam. But then his experience heading the *Times*'s Mexico City bureau reinforced his personal concerns about the plight of Mexican Americans. He returned to California to become news director of the Spanish-language television station KMEX and to write weekly opinion columns for the *Los Angeles Times*. On television and in his column, he exposed Los Angeles police brutality in the Mexican-American community and became an advocate of Chicano support for the anti–Vietnam War movement. While Salazar was covering an antiwar rally with his TV crew, police attacked the crowd, and he was shot and killed by a police officer. In life and death, Salazar became a symbol of rising self-awareness within the barrio, or Hispanic community.

Although her mother had given up a career in journalism when she married, **Gloria Steinem** (1934–) sought to follow her abandoned career. After graduating from Smith College, she worked as a freelance writer, publishing articles on the beginnings of the women's movement. Steinem even posed as a waitress at the Playboy Club to write the article "I Was a Playboy Bunny." In 1968 she became a columnist for *New York Magazine*, devoting her attention to liberal politics and causes. At that time Steinem's concerns about a woman's right to an abortion drew her into the feminist movement. In 1971 she became the founding editor of *Ms.*, a feminist magazine that was strikingly different from the average "woman's magazine" of its time in everything from the controversial subjects it tackled to the advertisements it chose to run. *Ms.* operated as a tax-exempt foundation until it was sold to a publishing conglomerate in 1987. By then a national spokesperson for feminist issues, Steinem remained as a consultant to the magazine she launched, but devoted more of her time to writing and lecturing.

A Harvard graduate, **David Halberstam** (1934–) broke into journalism on the West Point, Mississippi, *Daily Times Leader* and spent four years on the Nashville *Tennessean* before joining the *New York Times*. As a foreign correspondent, he reported from Africa, Eastern Europe, and Southeast Asia, making his mark with his reporting from Vietnam in 1962 and 1963. His skepticism about the official pronouncements of American military advisers, his criticism of South Vietnamese president Ngo Dinh Diem as incompetent, and his assessment of America's Vietnam policy as a "quagmire" angered President John F. Kennedy, who urged the *Times* to remove Halberstam from Saigon. However, Halberstam's reports strongly influenced those who came to oppose the Vietnam War, and won him a Pulitzer Prize. In 1967 he became a contributing editor of *Harper's* magazine, holding that post until 1972 when he launched a successful career writing numerous books on contemporary history.

Seymour Hersh (1937–) went to Washington from Chicago in 1965 as a reporter for the Associated Press. While covering the Pentagon during the Vietnam War, he avoided the formal, high-level press briefings and instead rooted out stories through lower-level bureaucrats, who revealed what the top brass tried to hide. In October 1967 he joined a peace demonstration at the Pentagon, and in 1968 served as press secretary for the peace Presidential candidate Eugene McCarthy. As a freelance writer he uncovered the American massacre of Vietnamese civilians at My Lai. This led to his appointment to the Washington bureau of the *New York Times* as an investigative reporter. His stubborn questioning of authority and dogged pursuit of scandal led to his

exposés of the Nixon administration's secret bombing of Cambodia, incidents connected with the Watergate scandal, and the Central Intelligence Agency's role in overthrowing the government of Chile.

Ellen Goodman (1941–) set off originally on a conventional path that took her from school to marriage to raising a family. In 1961 she became a researcher for *Newsweek*, in what she called "one of those underpaid, semi-slave jobs they used to give overeducated women." When her husband's work took the family to Detroit, Goodman started writing feature stories about women's issues for the *Detroit Free Press* (1965–67). Then the family moved to Boston, where she wrote for the "women's section" of the *Boston Globe* (1967–74). When the women's rights movement propelled the issues she was writing about to the front pages and the editorial pages, Goodman became a columnist. At first she took a combative approach, quick to invoke her own "sense of certainty." Over time, however, Goodman adopted a calmer, more conversational, even humorous, approach to the everyday issues that confront people, although retaining her feminist perspective.

The son of two teachers, **George F. Will** (1941–) brought an intellectual approach to journalism. Will studied philosophy at Oxford University and earned a Ph.D. in political science from Princeton. After teaching for a few years, he went to Capitol Hill as an aide to Republican senator Gordon Allott of Colorado. When Allott lost his bid for reelection, William F. Buckley's *National Review* hired Will as an editor. However, he fell out of favor with the magazine by arguing that President Nixon deserved impeachment for his involvement in Watergate. Will became a regular columnist

for the *Washington Post* and *Newsweek* as well as a television news analyst, at a time when news organizations, accused of having a liberal bent, were seeking conservative perspectives. As a columnist, Will expressed opinions that could be quite unpredictable. He applied his intellect to a range of interests that stretched from national security to baseball, provoking and appealing to readers across the political spectrum.

Constance Yu-Hwa Chung, known to television viewers as **Connie Chung** (1946–), graduated from the University of Maryland and got her first job as a news copyperson, writer, and reporter for WTTG-TV, a television station in Washington, D.C. The Columbia Broadcasting System (CBS) television affiliate in Washington hired her as a general reporter in 1971, and she covered the Presidential election and the Watergate scandal before heading to

California as news anchor for KNXT in Los Angeles (1976–83). Personable and talented as an interviewer, Chung was recruited by the rival National Broadcasting Corporation (NBC), where she anchored a variety of programs, including "News at Sunrise," the Saturday "NBC Nightly News" (1983–89), and several news documentaries—although some critics called her programs "popumentaries," for lowering journalistic standards to attract audiences. CBS enticed her back to host her own programs, "Saturday Night with Connie Chung," "Face to Face," "Eye to Eye," along with the Sunday "CBS Evening News." In 1993 CBS made her the first woman coanchor of its nightly news broadcast. Chung and coanchor Dan Rather made an uncomfortable team, however, and the program's decline in ratings led to her termination as anchor in 1995.

Gloria Steinem (center, with long hair) meets with the staff of *Ms.* magazine. Her concern for women's rights led her to found the magazine and made her a national spokesperson for feminist issues.

Museums and Historic Sites Relating to American Journalism

Newspapers such as the *New York Times* (http://www.nytimes.com) and *Washington Post* (http://www.washingtonpost.com), television stations, and other media centers in larger cities often offer public tours. Call or write to newspapers or stations that you are interested in seeing to find out whether tours are available, when they are scheduled, and whether there are any fees. You can also visit many of the sites across the country that have been important in the lives and careers of American journalists, as well as museums that show how news was and is reported. The following are some places of interest associated with the journalists in this book.

General Interest

CNN Center
1 CNN Center at International Boulevard and Marietta Street
Box 105366
Atlanta, GA 30348-5366
Telephone: (404) 827-2300
http://www.cnn.com/StudioTour

The headquarters of the Cable News Network provides a 45-minute tour of its various studios and operations. Starting with an eight-story escalator ride, the tour includes exhibits, observations of newsrooms and live news broadcasting, and demonstrations of how weather maps and other television graphics work.

Eureka Sentinel Museum
Intersection of Bateman and Monroe Roads
Box 82
Eureka, NV 89316
Telephone: (702) 237-5010

During the gold and silver mining boom of the 1870s, newspapers such as the *Eureka Sentinel* sprang up in many frontier mining towns, and ended just as quickly when the boom collapsed. Located in an 1879 brick building, the Sentinel Museum features the paper's original printing presses and other equipment, as well as newspapers and posters from the 1870s and 1880s.

Museum of Television and Radio
1 East 53rd Street
New York, NY 10022
Telephone: (212) 752-4690
http://www.mtr.org/tour/nymsm.htm
465 North Beverly Drive
Beverly Hills, CA 90210
Telephone: (310) 786-1000
http://www.mtr.org/tour/camsm.htm

Created in 1975 by William Paley, founder and president of the CBS network, the Museum of Television and Radio houses thousands of radio and television tapes and scripts from the 1920s to the present. Visitors can listen to early radio programs or view classic television. The museum offers exhibits, seminars, lectures, and courses on a wide range of topics relating to the broadcast media.

In 1996 the Museum of Television and Radio opened a West Coast facility Beverly Hills. Visitors can view television programs, listen to radio broadcasts, and attend seminars with broadcast journalists, writers, performers, directors, and producers on a wide range of subjects relating to the media.

National Museum of American History (Smithsonian Institution)

Constitution Avenue between 13th
   and 14th Streets, NW
Washington, DC 20560
Telephone: (202) 357-2700
http://www.si.edu/organiza/museums/
   nmah/nmah.htm

Among the Smithsonian's diverse exhibits are displays of the history of communication and information, from printing presses and print shops to the impact of the telegraph, telephone, radio, television, and computer networks.

Newseum

1101 Wilson Boulevard
Arlington, VA 22206
Telephone: (888) NEWSEUM
http://www.newseum.org

The first museum devoted entirely to how and why news is made opened in 1997. Funded by the Freedom Forum, a nonpartisan foundation dedicated to free press, free speech, and free spirit, the Newseum includes a news history gallery featuring great newspaper and magazine stories of all time, together with news broadcasts. An interactive newsroom gives visitors a chance to be a TV anchor, a radio sportscaster, a newspaper reporter, or a front-page editor. Adjoining the museum is

Freedom Park, which salutes pioneers in the news media and honors journalists from around the world who died while trying to report the news.

Park Row

Lower Manhattan, across from City
   Hall Park
New York, NY

The 19th-century center of New York City's fiercely competitive newspaper business was Park Row, a street facing City Hall, where much of the city's news was generated. Most of the buildings that once housed the *Tribune*, the *World*, and other papers have been demolished. But the building in which the *New York Times* operated from 1858 to 1904 (before its move to Times Square) still stands at 41 Park Row. As a reminder of Park Row's past, a statue of a rumpled-looking Horace Greeley stands in City Hall Park.

Printers Row Printing Museum

715 South Dearborn
Chicago, IL 60605
Telephone: (312) 987-1059

This industrial museum is housed in a late-19th-century building in Chicago's old Printers Row District. Its collections include old printing presses, posters, playbills, and other items of that era.

Sites Related to Specific Journalists

Ernie Pyle State Historic Site

North of Route 36
Dana, IN 47847
Telephone: (317) 665-3633

This relocated and restored farmhouse was the birthplace of Ernie Pyle, who became the nation's favorite war correspondent, and who was killed while covering World War II. The house contains family furnishings and photographs, as well as Pyle's books and newspaper columns. World War II Quonset huts serve as the visitor center

Franklin Court

Between Chestnut and Market and 3rd
   and 4th Streets
Philadelphia, PA 19106
Telephone: (215) 597-8974
http://www.libertynet.org/~inhp/
   franklin-court.html

From 1722 until his death in 1790, Benjamin Franklin owned, lived in, and operated his print shop in the area known today as Franklin Court, near Philadelphia's Independence Hall. Although Franklin's house no longer stands, the storefront that once housed the *Aurora* newspaper has been preserved and displays a 1780s printing press and bindery operation. The complex also includes an underground theater, museum, archaeological exhibit, and post office.

Frederick Douglass National Historic Site (Cedar Hill)

1411 W Street, SE
Washington, DC 20020
Telephone: (202) 426-5961

A slave who fled to freedom and became an abolitionist speaker, newspaper editor, and statesman, Frederick Douglass spent his last years, from 1877 to 1895, at Cedar Hill, a 19th-century Victorian house on a hillside across the Anacostia River from Washington, D.C. Maintained and operated by the National Park Service, Cedar Hill includes a visitor center with a film and exhibits on Douglass's life. The house, with its magnificent library, looks just as it did when he lived there.

Hearst Castle

Off SR 1
San Simeon, CA
Telephone: (805) 927-2020
http://www.hearstcastle.org

Wealthy newspaper publisher William Randolph Hearst, owner of a chain of newspapers and radio stations, collected art and architecture from around the world. In 1919 he began construction of his "castle," to incorporate and display this fabulous collection. The 127-acre estate, located in California on a 1,600-foot mountain overlooking the Pacific Ocean, contains a 115-room main house, three guesthouses, and elaborate pools, fountains, and statuary. A visitor center, guided tours, and films tell the story of Hearst, his castle, and the many celebrities he once entertained.

Mark Twain Boyhood Home and Museum

208 Hill Street
Hannibal, MO 63401
Telephone: (573) 221-9010

Samuel Clemens's father built this house in 1843, and the author who became known as Mark Twain lived there between the ages of seven and eighteen. The house has been restored to that era, and is next to a museum containing many of Twain's original manuscripts, books, and photographs.

Mark Twain House

351 Farmington Avenue
Hartford, CT 06105
Telephone: (860) 247-0998
http://www.hartfordct.com/mthone.
 html
http://www.connecticut.com/tours/
 MarkTwain

Made rich and famous by his writings, Mark Twain built this large Victorian house between 1873 and 1874 and lived there for 17 years. Twain hired Louis Comfort Tiffany to decorate the elaborate house.

Mark Twain Museum

C Street between Union and Taylor
 Streets
P.O. Box 392
Virginia City, NV 89440
Telephone: (702) 847-0525

When young Mark Twain went west in the 1860s, he worked as a reporter for the Nevada *Territorial Enterprise*. The building that housed the paper now exhibits its printing presses, newspaper office furniture, and other Twain-era memorabilia.

Noah Webster's House, Greenfield Village

20900 Oakwood Boulevard
Dearborn, MI 48124
Telephone: (313) 271-1620

Automobile manufacturer Henry Ford had the house where Noah Webster worked on the first American dictionary, in New Haven, Connecticut, moved to this historical park in Michigan.

War Correspondents' Arch

Gathland State Park, at South
 Mountain
1 mile west of Burkittsville,
 off MD Route 17
Washington and Frederick Counties,
 MD
Telephone: (301) 791-4767
http://www.gacc.com/dnr/All/Western/
 Gathland.html

Civil War correspondent George Alfred Townsend (who wrote under the pseudonym of GATH) dedicated a large stone arch in 1896 as a memorial to his fellow war correspondents and artists and to those who covered other wars around the world. Their names are inscribed on the arch, along with such famous journalistic remarks as Henry Stanley's "Dr. Livingston, I presume." Now maintained by the National Park Service, the arch stands alone in a country park, not far from Harpers Ferry and the Antietam battlefield.

Further Reading

Each of the major entries in *American Journalists* includes a list of readings related to individual people profiled in the book; refer to the index for page references. The following reading list is divided into sections for general works and books on print and broadcast journalism, and supplements the individual entries. Although the sources listed vary in level of difficulty, most are written for a general audience.

General Histories

Altschull, J. Herbert. *Agents of Change: The Role of the News Media in Human Affairs*. New York: Longman, 1984.

Bagdikian, Ben H. *The Media Monopoly*. Boston: Beacon, 1990.

Baughman, James L. *The Republic of Mass Communication: Journalism, Filmmaking, and Broadcasting in America Since 1941*. Baltimore: Johns Hopkins University Press, 1992.

Cater, Douglas. *The Fourth Branch of Government*. New York: Vintage, 1965.

Chancellor, John, and Walter R. Mears. *The News Business*. New York: Harper & Row, 1983.

Clurman, Richard M. *Beyond Malice: The Media's Years of Reckoning*. New York: New American Library, 1990.

Hallin, Daniel C. *The "Uncensored War": The Media and Vietnam*. New York: Oxford University Press, 1986.

Herman, Edward S., and Noam Chomsky. *Manufacturing Consent: The Political Economy of the Mass Media*. New York: Pantheon, 1988.

Hess, Stephen. *International News and Foreign Correspondence*. Washington, D.C.: Brookings Institution, 1996.

———. *News and Newsmaking*. Washington, D.C.: Brookings Institution, 1995.

———. *The Washington Reporters*. Washington, D.C.: Brookings Institution, 1981.

Lang, Gladys Engel, and Kurt Lang. *The Battle for Public Opinion: The President, the Press, and the Polls during Watergate*. New York: Columbia University Press, 1983.

Leonard, Thomas C. *The Power of the Press: The Birth of American Political Reporting*. New York: Oxford University Press, 1986.

Lichter, S. Robert, Stanley Rothman, and Linda S. Lichter. *The Media Elite*. Bethesda, Md.: Adler & Adler, 1986.

McLuhan, Marshall. *Understanding Media: The Extensions of Man*. 1964. Reprint, Cambridge: MIT Press, 1994.

Owen, Bruce M. *Economics and Freedom of Expression: Media Structure and the First Amendment*. Cambridge, Mass.: Ballinger, 1975.

Ritchie, Donald A. *Press Gallery: Congress and the Washington Correspondents*. Cambridge: Harvard University Press, 1991.

Rivers, William L. *The Adversaries: Politics and the Press*. Boston: Beacon, 1970.

Roshco, Bernard. *Newsmaking*. Chicago: University of Chicago Press, 1975.

Rubin, Bernard, ed. *Small Voices and Great Triumphs: Minorities and the Media*. New York: Praeger, 1980.

Sabato, Larry J. *Feeding Frenzy: How Attack Journalism Has Transformed American Politics*. New York: Free Press, 1991.

Schilpp, Dadelon Golden, and Sharon M. Murphy. *Great Women of the Press*. Carbondale: Southern Illinois University Press, 1983.

Schudson, Michael. *The Power of News*. Cambridge: Harvard University Press, 1995.

Schwarzlose, Richard A. *The Nation's Newsbrokers*. 2 vols. Evanston, Ill.: Northwestern University Press, 1989–90.

Servan-Schreiber, Jean-Louis. *The Power to Inform: Media: The Information Business*. New York: McGraw-Hill, 1974.

Stephens, Mitchell. *A History of News: From the Drum to the Satellite*. New York: Penguin, 1988.

Tebbel, John. *The Media in America*. New York: Thomas Y. Crowell, 1974.

Thomas, Dana L. *The Media Moguls: From Joseph Pulitzer to William S. Paley: Their Lives and Boisterous Times*. New York: Putnam, 1981.

Weaver, David H., and G. Cleveland Wilhoit. *The American Journalist: A Portrait of U.S. News People and Their Work*. Bloomington: Indiana University Press, 1986.

Wolfson, Lewis W. *The Untapped Power of the Press: Explaining Government to the People*. New York: Praeger, 1985.

Print Journalism

Andrews, J. Cutler. *The North Reports the Civil War*. 1955. Reprint, Pittsburgh: University of Pittsburgh Press, 1985.

———. *The South Reports the Civil War*. 1970. Reprint, Pittsburgh: University of Pittsburgh Press, 1985.

Aronson, James. *The Press and the Cold War*. 1973. Reprint, New York: Monthly Review Press, 1990.

Bagdikian, Ben H. *The Effete Conspiracy and Other Crimes by the Press*. New York: Harper & Row, 1972.

———. *The Information Machines: Their Impact on Men and the Media*. New York: Harper & Row, 1971.

Bailyn, Bernard, and John B. Hench, eds. *The Press and the American Revolution*. Worcester, Mass.: American Antiquarian Society, 1980.

Baldasty, Gerald L. *The Commercialization of News in the Nineteenth Century*. Madison: University of Wisconsin Press, 1992.

Beasley, Maurine, and Katherine T. Theus. *The New Majority: A Look at What the Preponderance of Women in Journalism Education Means to the Schools and to the Profession*. Lanham, Md.: University Press of America, 1988.

Beasley, Maurine, and Sheila Gibbons. *Taking Their Place: A Documentary History of Women in Journalism*. Washington, D.C.: American University Press, 1993.

Benjaminson, Peter. *Death in the Afternoon: America's Newspaper Giants Struggle for Survival*. Kansas City: Andrews, McMeel & Parker, 1984.

Bennett, W. Lance. *News: The Politics of Illusion*. New York: Longman, 1988.

Biagi, Shirley. *NewsTalk I: State-of-the-Art Conversations with Today's Print Journalists*. Belmont, Calif.: Wadsworth, 1987.

Blondheim, Menahem. *News Over the Wires: The Telegraph and the Flow of Public Information in America, 1844–1897*. Cambridge: Harvard University Press, 1994.

Bogart, Leo. *Press and Public: Who Reads What, When, Where, and Why in American Newspapers*. Hillsdale, N.J.: Lawrence Erlbaum, 1989.

Braden, Maria. *She Said What? Interviews with Women Newspaper Columnists*. Lexington: University Press of Kentucky, 1993.

Braestrup, Peter. *The Big Story*. New Haven: Yale University Press, 1983.

Broder, David. *Behind the Front Page: A Candid Look at How the News is Made*. New York: Simon & Schuster, 1987.

Clark, Charles E. *The Public Prints: The Newspaper in Anglo-American Culture, 1665–1740*. New York: Oxford University Press, 1994.

Cohen, Bernard. *The Press and Foreign Policy*. Princeton, N.J.: Princeton University Press, 1963.

Collins, Jean E. *She Was There: Stories of Pioneering Women Journalists*. New York: Julian Messner, 1980.

Cose, Ellis. *The Press*. New York: William Morrow, 1989.

Crouse, Timothy. *The Boys on the Bus*. New York: Ballantine, 1973.

Czitrom, Daniel J. *Media and the American Mind, From Morse to McLuhan*. Chapel Hill: University of North Carolina Press, 1982.

Daniels, Jonathan. *They Will Be Heard: America's Crusading Newspaper Editors*. New York: McGraw-Hill, 1965.

Dates, Jannett L., and William Barlow, eds. *Split Image: African Americans in the Mass Media*. Washington, D.C.: Howard University Press, 1990.

Dicken-Garcia, Hazel. *Journalistic Standards in Nineteenth-Century America*. Madison: University of Wisconsin Press, 1989.

Downie, Leonard, Jr. *The New Muckrakers*. Washington, D.C.: New Republic Books, 1976.

Edwards, Julia. *Women of the World: The Great Foreign Correspondents*. Boston: Houghton Mifflin, 1988.

Elwood-Akers, Virginia. *Women War Correspondents in the Vietnam War, 1961–1975*. Metuchen, N.J.: Scarecrow Press, 1988.

Epstein, Edward Jay. *Between Fact and Fiction: The Problem of Journalism*. New York: Vintage, 1975.

Gans, Herbert J. *Deciding What's News: A Study of CBS Evening News, NBC Evening News, Newsweek and Time*. New York: Vintage, 1980.

Glessing, Robert J. *The Underground Press in America*. 1970. Reprint, Westport, Conn.: Greenwood, 1984.

Goldstein, Tom. *The News at Any Cost: How Journalists Compromise Their Ethics to Shape the News*. New York: Simon & Schuster, 1985.

Goldstein, Tom, ed. *Killing the Messenger: 100 Years of Media Criticism*. New York: Columbia University Press, 1989.

Good, Howard. *The Journalist as Autobiographer*. Metuchen, N.J.: Scarecrow Press, 1993.

Grauer, Neil A. *Wits & Sages*. Baltimore: Johns Hopkins University Press, 1984.

Grossman, Michael Baruch, and Martha Joynt Kumar. *Portraying the President: The White House and the News Media*. Baltimore: Johns Hopkins University Press, 1981.

Halberstam, David. *The Powers That Be*. New York: Knopf, 1979.

Hamilton, John Maxwell, and George A. Krimsky. *Hold the Press: The Inside Story on Newspapers*. Baton Rouge: Louisiana State University Press, 1996.

Hess, Stephen. *The Ungentlemanly Art: A History of Political Cartoons*. New York: Macmillan, 1975.

Hilderbrand, Robert C. *Power and the People: Executive Management of Public Opinion in Foreign Affairs, 1897–1921*. Chapel Hill: University of North Carolina Press, 1981.

Johnstone, John W. C., Edward J. Slawski, and William W. Bowman. *The News People: A Sociological Portrait of American Journalists and their Work*. Chicago: University of Illinois Press, 1976.

Juergens, George. *News from the White House: The Presidential-Press Relationship in the Progressive Era*. Chicago: University of Chicago Press, 1981.

Kielbowicz, Richard B. *News in the Mail: The Press, Post Office, and Public Information, 1700–1860s*. Westport, Conn.: Greenwood, 1989.

Knight, Oliver. *Following the Indian Wars: The Story of Newspaper Correspondents Among the Indian Campaigners*. Norman: University of Oklahoma Press, 1993.

Kobre, Sidney. *The Yellow Press and Gilded Age Journalism*. Tallahassee: Florida State University, 1964.

Kurtz, Howard. *Media Circus: The Trouble With America's Newspapers*. New York: Times Books, 1994.

Lawson, Linda. *Truth in Publishing: Federal Regulation of the Press's Business Practices, 1880–1920*. Carbondale: Southern Illinois University Press, 1993.

Leonard, Thomas C. *News for All: America's Coming of Age with the Press*. New York: Oxford University Press, 1995.

Levy, Leonard W. *Emergence of a Free Press*. New York: Oxford University Press, 1985.

Lewis, Anthony. *Make No Law: The Sullivan Case and the First Amendment*. New York: Random House, 1991.

Liebling, A. J. *The Press*. 1961. Reprint, New York: Ballantine Books, 1975.

Linley, William R. *20th Century American Newspapers: In Content and Production*. Manhattan, Kans.: Sunflower University Press, 1993.

Linsky, Martin. *Impact: How the Press Affects Federal Policymaking*. New York: W.W. Norton, 1986.

MacArthur, John R. *Second Front: Censorship and Propaganda in the Gulf War*. New York: Hill and Wang, 1992.

MacNeil, Neil. *Without Fear or Fervor*. New York: Harcourt Brace, 1940.

Miller, Sally M. *The Ethnic Press in the United States: A Historical Analysis and Handbook*. Westport, Conn.: Greenwood, 1987.

Mills, Kay. *A Place in the News: From the Women's Pages to the Front Pages*. New York: Dodd, Mead, 1988.

Milton, Joyce. *The Yellow Kids: Foreign Correspondents in the Heyday of Yellow Journalism*. New York: Harper & Row, 1989.

Mott, Frank Luther. *A History of American Magazines*. 5 vols. Cambridge: Harvard University Press, 1930–1968.

———. *The News in America*. Cambridge: Harvard University Press, 1962.

Nerone, John C. *The Culture of the Press in the Early Republic—Cincinnati, 1793–1848*. New York: Garland, 1989.

Ricchiardi, Sherry, and Virginia Young. *Women on Deadline: A Collection of America's Best*. Ames: Iowa State University Press, 1991.

Robertson, Nan. *The Girls in the Balcony: Women, Men and the New York Times*. New York: Random House, 1992.

Roeder, George H. *The Censored War: American Visual Experience During World War Two*. New Haven: Yale University Press, 1993.

Ross, Ishbel. *Ladies of the Press*. 1936. Reprint, New York: Arno Press, 1974.

Rutland, Robert A. *The Newsmongers: Journalism in the Life of the Nation, 1690–1972*. New York: Dial Press, 1973.

Schlesinger, Arthur M. *Prelude to Independence: The Newspaper War on Britain, 1764–1776*. New York: Knopf, 1957.

Schudson, Michael. *Discovering the News: A Social History of American Newspapers*. New York: Basic Books, 1978.

Siegal, Leon V. *Reporters and Officials: The Organization and Politics of Newsmaking*. Lexington, Mass.: D.C. Heath, 1973.

Smith, Culver H. *The Press, Politics, and Patronage: The American Government's Use of Newspapers, 1789–1875*. Athens: University of Georgia Press, 1977.

Smith, James Morton. *Freedom's Fetters: The Alien and Sedition Laws and American Civil Liberties*. Ithaca, N.Y.: Cornell University Press, 1956.

Smith, Jeffrey A. *Printers and Press Freedom: The Ideology of Early American Journalism*. New York: Oxford University Press, 1987.

Starr, Louis M. *Bohemian Brigade: Civil War Newsmen in Action*. 1954. Reprint, Madison: University of Wisconsin Press, 1987.

Stewart, Donald H. *The Opposition Press of the Federalist Period*. Albany: State University of New York Press, 1969.

Streitmatter, Rodger. *Raising Her Voice: African-American Women Journalists Who Changed History*. Lexington: University Press of Kentucky, 1994.

Summers, Mark Wahlgren. *The Press Gang: Newspapers and Politics, 1865–1878*. Chapel Hill: University of North Carolina Press, 1994.

Thorn, William J. *Newspaper Circulation: Marketing the News*. New York: Longman, 1987.

Tucher, Andie. *Froth & Scum: Truth, Beauty, Goodness, and the Ax Murder in America's First Mass Medium*. Chapel Hill: University of North Carolina Press, 1994.

Weisberger, Bernard A. *The American Newspaperman*. Chicago: University of Chicago Press, 1961.

Wicker, Tom. *On Press*. New York: Viking, 1978.

Wolfe, Tom, and E. W. Johnson, eds. *The New Journalism*. New York: Harper & Row, 1970.

Wolseley, Roland E. *The Black Press, U.S.A.* Ames: Iowa State University Press, 1971.

Broadcast Journalism

Adler, Renata. *Reckless Disregard: Westmoreland v. CBS et al, Sharon v. Time*. New York: Knopf, 1986.

Auletta, Ken. *Three Blind Mice: How the TV Networks Lost Their Way*. New York: Random House, 1991.

Barnouw, Erik. *History of Broadcasting in the United States*. 3 vols. New York: Oxford University Press, 1966–70.

————. *The Sponsor: Notes on a Modern Potentate*. New York: Oxford University Press, 1978.

————. *Tube of Plenty: The Evolution of American Television*. New York: Oxford University Press, 1978.

Baughman, James L. *The Republic of Mass Communication: Journalism, Filmmaking, and Broadcasting in America Since 1941*. Baltimore: Johns Hopkins University Press, 1992.

Biagi, Shirley. *NewsTalk II: State-of-the-Art Conversations with Today's Broadcast Journalists*. Belmont, Calif.: Wadsworth Publishing, 1987.

Charnley, Mitchell V. *News by Radio*. New York: Macmillan, 1948.

Combs, James. *Nightly Horrors: Crisis Coverage in Television Network News*. Knoxville: University of Tennessee Press, 1985.

Culbert, David Holbrook. *News for Everyman: Radio and Foreign Affairs in Thirties America*. Westport, Conn.: Greenwood, 1976.

Epstein, Edward Jay. *News from Nowhere: Television and the News*. New York: Random House, 1973.

Fallows, James. *Breaking the News: How the Media Undermine American Democracy*. New York: Pantheon, 1996.

Folkerts, Jean, and Dwight L. Teeter. *Voices of a Nation*. New York: Macmillan, 1989.

Frank, Reuven. *Out of Thin Air: The Brief Wonderful Life of Network News*. New York: Simon & Schuster, 1991.

Gans, Herbert J. *Deciding What's News: A Study of CBS Evening News, NBC Evening News, Newsweek and Time*. New York: Vintage Books, 1980.

Gelfman, Judith. *Women in Television News*. New York: Columbia University Press, 1976.

Halberstam, David. *The Powers That Be*. New York: Knopf, 1979.

Hess, Stephen. *Live from Capitol Hill! Studies of Congress and the Media*. Washington, D.C.: Brookings Institution, 1991.

Hirsch, Alan. *Talking Heads: Political Talk Shows and Their Star Pundits*. New York: St. Martin's Press, 1991.

Iyengar, Shato, and Donald R. Kinder. *News That Matters: Television and American Opinion*. Chicago: University of Chicago Press, 1987.

Lasher, Marilyn A. *The Chilling Effect in TV News: Intimidation by the Nixon White House*. New York: Praeger, 1984.

MacNeil, Robert. *The People Machine: The Influence of Television on American Politics*. New York: Harper & Row, 1968.

Matusow, Barbara. *The Evening Stars: The Making of Network News Anchors*. Boston: Houghton Mifflin, 1983.

O'Connor, John E., ed. *American History/American Television*. New York: Unger, 1983.

Oslin, George P. *The Story of Telecommunications*. Macon, Ga.: Mercer University Press, 1992.

Robinson, John P., and Mark R. Levy. *The Main Source: Learning from Television News*. Beverly Hills, Calif.: Sage, 1986.

————. *Poor Reception: Misunderstanding and Forgetting Broadcast News*. Hillsdale, N.J.: Lawrence Erlbaum, 1987.

Sanders, Marlene, and Marcia Rock. *Waiting for Prime Time: The Women of Television News*. New York: Harper & Row, 1988.

Small, William. *To Kill a Messenger: Television News and the Real World*. New York: Hastings House, 1970.

Sterling, Christopher H., and Timothy R. Haight, eds. *The Mass Media: Aspen Guide to Communication Industry Trends*. New York: Praeger, 1977.

Trotta, Liz. *Fighting for Air: In the Trenches with Television News*. New York: Simon & Schuster, 1991.

Waller, Judith S. *Radio: The Fifth Estate*. Boston: Houghton Mifflin, 1950.

White, Paul. *News on the Air*. New York: Harcourt, Brace, 1947.

Biographical Directories and Bibliographies

Ashley, Perry J., ed. *American Newspaper Journalists, 1690–1872*. Detroit: Gale, 1985.

———. *American Newspaper Journalists, 1873–1900*. Detroit: Gale, 1983.

———. *American Newspaper Journalists, 1901–1925*. Detroit: Gale, 1984.

———. *American Newspaper Journalists, 1926–1950*. Detroit: Gale, 1984.

———. *American Newspaper Journalists, 1951–1990*. Detroit: Gale, 1993.

Bedford, Barbara. *Brilliant Bylines: A Biographical Anthology of Notable Newspaperwomen in America*. New York: Columbia University Press, 1986.

Contemporary Authors. Detroit: Gale. Published annually since 1962.

Current Biography. New York: H. H. Wilson. Published annually since 1940.

Dictionary of American Biography. New York: Scribners. Published annually since 1928.

Downs, Robert B., and Jane B. Downs. *Journalists of the United States: Biographical Sketches of Print and Broadcast News Shapers from the Late 17th Century to the Present*. Jefferson, N.C.: McFarland, 1991.

James, Edward T., et al. *Notable American Women*. 4 vols. Cambridge, Mass.: Belknap Press, 1971–80.

McKerns, Joseph P. *Biographical Directory of American Journalism*. Westport, Conn.: Greenwood, 1989.

———. *News Media and Public Policy: An Annotated Bibliography*. New York: Garland, 1985.

Riley, Sam G. *Biographical Directory of American Newspaper Columnists*. Westport, Conn.: Greenwood, 1995.

Riley, Sam G., ed. *American Magazine Journalists, 1741–1850*. Detroit: Gale, 1988.

———. *American Magazine Journalists, 1850–1900*. Detroit: Gale, 1989.

———. *American Magazine Journalists, 1900–1960*. Detroit: Gale, 1994.

Taft, William H. *Encyclopedia of Twentieth-Century Journalists*. New York: Garland, 1986.

Who's Who and Who Was Who. New Providence, N.J.: Marquis. Published annually since 1899.

Periodicals

The American Editor: Bulletin of the American Society of Newspaper Editors

American Journalism Review (formerly *Washington Journalism Review*)

Columbia Journalism Review (published by the Graduate School of Journalism, Columbia University)

Editor & Publisher

Forbes MediaCritic

Journal of Mass Media Ethics (published by the Department of Communications, Brigham Young University)

Journalism History (published by the Department of Journalism, California State University, Northridge)

Journalism and Mass Communications Quarterly (formerly *Journalism Quarterly*, published by the Association for Education in Journalism and Mass Communications)

Journalism Monographs (published by the Association for Education in Journalism)

Media Studies Journal (formerly *Gannett Center Journal*, published by the Freedom Forum Media Studies Center, Columbia University)

Nieman Reports (published by the Nieman Foundation at Harvard University)

Television Quarterly (published by the National Academy of Television Arts and Science)

Index

References to main biographical entries are indicated by **bold** page numbers; references to illustrations are indicated by *italics*.

Acknowledgments

Several people read portions of the text and made helpful suggestions. My thanks go to James L. Baughman, Anne G. Ritchie, Marion Elizabeth Rodgers, and James A. Sayler, and to Nancy Toff, Tara Deal, and Anna Eberhard Friedlander of Oxford University Press for their always availing editorial guidance.

Picture Credits

American Museum of Natural History (Dept. of Library Services): 48 (# 124781); AP Wide World Photos: 203; Architect of the Capitol: 32; Art Resource (National Portrait Gallery, Smithsonian Institution): 78; from *The Art and Politics of Thomas Nast*, by Morton Keller (Oxford University Press, 1968): 117, 118, 120; The Boston Athenaeum: 67, 68, 90; Boston Public Library: 130, 246; Chicago Historical Society: 195 (ICHI-22294), 198 (ICHI-16314); courtesy CNN: 297; courtesy Cokie Roberts: 302; Corbis–Bettmann: 208, 259, 264, 284; courtesy *El Diario:* 307; courtesy Emily Rauh Pulitzer (private collection): 133 (photo by David Gulick); courtesy Fox Television: 283; courtesy Gannett Co., Inc.: 278; Georgia Department of Natural Resources: 47; courtesy Georgie Anne Geyer: 287 (photo by Henry Herr Gill), 288; courtesy Harvard University Portrait Collection (Bequest of Dr. John Collins Warren, 1856): 16; from *The Innocents Abroad*, by Mark Twain (1869): 107; John F. Kennedy Library: 242 (# AR 75950); Library of Congress: cover (top left and right insets), 8, 11, 13, 21, 22, 27, 31, 35, 38, 42, 51, 54, 57, 58, 64, 78, 79 (left and right), 85, 89, 95, 102, 105, 108, 114, 123, 136, 138, 143, 144, 147, 149, 150, 154, 156, 157, 160, 167, 170, 172, 174, 177, 178, 182, 188, 205, 227, 228, 237, 238, 239, 245, 269, 273, 274, 312, 313, 314; courtesy Manoogian Foundation: 8; courtesy Margaret Bourke-White Estate: cover (bottom inset), 216, 219; Martin Luther King Library: 221, 231, 232, 252, 260, 290; from *Memoirs of an Editor*, by Edward P. Mitchell (Scribners, 1924): 127, 128; Minnesota Historical Society: 71; Missouri Historical Society, St. Louis: 99; *Ms.* magazine: 317 (photo by Michael Alexander, 1979); Museum of Fine Arts, Boston: 153, 221 (M.&M. Karolik Collection), 23 (M.&M. Karolik Collection), 252 (M.&M. Karolik Collection), 260 (M.&M. Karolik Collection), 291 (M.&M. Karolik Collection); Museum of Modern Art: 294; Reprinted with permission from the July 6, 1865, issue of *The Nation*: 112; National Archives: 61, 213, 222, 272, 311; *New York Times:* 255 (from *New York Herald Tribune*, 7/2/50; ©1950, New York Herald Tribune, Inc. All rights reserved. Reproduced by permission); Collection of the New-York Historical Society: 110; New York Public Library, General Research Division, Astor, Lenox, and Tilden Foundations: 15, 28 (print collection Miriam and Ira D. Wallach Division of Art), 140, 141; New York University, Tamiment Institute Library: 251; Pratt Free Library, Baltimore: 190, 192; Schomburg Center for Research in Black Culture, New York Public Library: 93, 163; Smithsonian Institution: 19 (#17539B), 62 (#73-5136), 80 (#62640-5), 82 (78-14200), 86 (14225), 96 (#56002), 159 (#71-1125), 236 (#71-895); courtesy of South Caroliniana Library, University of South Carolina, Columbia: 209; Syracuse University Library: 200; Tennessee Historical Society: 119; University of Chicago Library: 164; U. S. Senate Historical Office: cover (background), 2; U.S. House of Representatives, Office of Photography (photo by Dev O Neill): 301; *USA Today:* 280; Virginia State Library and Archives: 72; W. E. B. Du Bois Library (Special Collections and Archives), University of Massachusetts, Amherst: 187; Yale University (Manuscripts and Archives): 210.

Donald A. Ritchie is associate historian of the U.S. Senate. He is the author of *Press Gallery: Congress and the Washington Correspondents* (which won the Richard Leopold Prize of the Organization of American Historians), *Doing Oral History, The Senate, The U.S. Constitution,* and *James M. Landis: Dean of the Regulators.* He is coauthor of a high school textbook, *History of a Free Nation,* and a curriculum package entitled *American History and National Security.* Dr. Ritchie has contributed articles to many reference works on the Congress and in 1990 he won the James Madison Prize for the best article on the history of the federal government, presented by the Society for History in the Federal Government. Dr. Ritchie has served on the editorial boards of *The Public Historian* and the National Council on Public History, was editor of *The Maryland Historian,* and is series editor of the Twayne oral history series. A member of the council of the Organization of American Historians and a former president of the Oral History Association, he also teaches in the Cornell in Washington program.

GEORGE HAIL FREE LIBRARY

3 2297 00046 5009

920
R

Ritchie, Donald A.

American journalists

$35.00

DATE			

002089   9648317